CHINA IN A POLYCENTRIC WORLD

CONTRIBUTORS

HELEN H. CHEN

EUGENE CHEN EOYANG

MARK E. FRANCIS

ANN-MARIE HSIUNG

FENG-YING MING

GRETA AI-YU NIU

DAVID PALUMBO-LIU

MICHELLE YEH

ZHANG LONGXI

YINGJIN ZHANG

JOHN YU ZOU

CHINA IN A POLYCENTRIC WORLD

Essays in Chinese Comparative Literature

Edited by YINGJIN ZHANG

STANFORD UNIVERSITY PRESS
Stanford, California

Stanford University Press
Stanford, California
© 1998 by the Board of Trustees of the
Leland Stanford Junior University
Printed in the United States of America
CIP data appear at the end of the book

For Su, Mimi, and Alex

ACKNOWLEDGMENTS

This volume of essays is based on an international conference entitled "Literature, History, Culture: Re-envisioning Chinese and Comparative Literature" held at Princeton University on June 24–26, 1994, which I organized as president of the American Association of Chinese Comparative Literature (AACCL) for 1993–94. More than fifty scholars from the United States, China, Taiwan, and Europe attended the conference. Andrew Plaks of Princeton University offered some opening remarks, and Zhang Longxi of UC-Riverside, Qian Zhongwen of the Chinese Academy of Social Sciences (Beijing), and Eugene Eoyang of Indiana University delivered feature presentations at the plenary sessions. Given space limitations, the present volume represents only a small portion of the papers delivered at the conference.

I would like to acknowledge the support of the conference advisory committee (Eugene Eoyang, Leo Ou-fan Lee, Perry Link, and Andrew Plaks) and its program committee (Gloria Shen and Yaohua Shi). The conference received funding from the Pacific Cultural Foundation in Taiwan and, in the United States, from the China and Inner Asia Council of the Association for Asian Studies. The Department of East Asian Languages and Cultures and the East Asian Studies Center of Indiana University as well as Conference Services of Princeton University provided timely assistance. Specifically, I would like to thank Benita Brown, Cindy Horr, Yoshio Iwamoto, Richard Rubinger, Sue Tuohy, and George M. Wilson.

To better represent the current field of Chinese comparative literature and cultural studies, I have solicited a few essays not included in the conference. The essays by David Palumbo-Liu, Michelle Yeh, and myself appeared earlier in *CLEAR* (1992), *Journal of Asian Studies* (1996), and *Modern Chinese Literature* (1995), respectively; I thank these journals for permission to reprint the essays here. I also appreciate the patience, understanding, and cooperation of all the contributors during the editing process. The Introduction was written while I was on a summer faculty fellowship at the Research and Graduate School of Indiana University, and I completed the bulk of the editing as a postdoctoral research fellow at the Center for Chinese Studies, University of

Michigan. I would like to express my gratitude to those institutions in addition to my home department for providing research assistance in the final preparation of the manuscript, to Helen Chen, Stephanie DeBoer, and Paola Voci for their help with the Character List and the Index, and to Julian Stringer for converting the references in two chapters.

My sincere thanks go also to Eugene Eoyang, Yi-Tsi Mei Feuerwerker, David Palumbo-Liu, David Rolston, Xiaobing Tang, Zhang Longxi, John Ziemer, and two anonymous Stanford University Press reviewers for reading earlier drafts of the Introduction and my essay; to Dudley Andrew, Ted Foss, William Lyell, Maureen Robertson, Steven Unger, and Jing Wang for their invitations and their comments on my lectures at their institutions; to Cao Shunqing, John J. Deeney, and Yue Daiyun for providing relevant materials; to my colleagues at Indiana and Michigan, in particular Matei Calinescu, Robert Eno, Sumie Jones, Gregory Kasza, Shuen-fu Lin, Stuart McDougal, and Michael Robinson; to John Ziemer for his continuous encouragement of this and other projects of mine; to Helen Tartar for her supervision of the final production; to Andrew Lewis and Nathan MacBrien for their meticulous editing; and, last but not least, to my wife Su and my daughter Mimi for supporting me on nearly all occasions, including tedious moments of stuffing envelopes and attaching address labels for AACCL mass mailings, and to my son Alex for creating cheerful moments in our family life.

Y.Z.

CONTENTS

Contributors   XI
A Note on Romanization   XIII

Introduction:
Engaging Chinese Comparative Literature and Cultural Studies
YINGJIN ZHANG   1

PART ONE: DISCIPLINE, DISCOURSE, CANON

1. The Challenge of East-West Comparative Literature
   ZHANG LONGXI   21

2. The Utopias of Discourse:
   On the Impossibility of Chinese Comparative Literature
   DAVID PALUMBO-LIU   36

3. Canon Formation in Traditional Chinese Poetry:
   Chinese Canons, Sacred and Profane
   MARK E. FRANCIS   50

PART TWO: GENDER, SEXUALITY, BODY

4. A Feminist Re-Vision of Xu Wei's *Ci Mulan* and *Nü zhuangyuan*
   ANN-MARIE HSIUNG   73

5. Gender, Subjectivity, Sexuality: Defining a Subversive Discourse
   in Wang Anyi's Four Tales of Sexual Transgression
   HELEN H. CHEN   90

6. Consuming Asian Women:
   The Fluid Body of Josie Packard in *Twin Peaks*
   GRETA AI-YU NIU   110

PART THREE: SCIENCE, MODERNITY, AESTHETICS

7. Travel and Translation:
   An Aspect of China's Cultural Modernity, 1862–1926
   JOHN YU ZOU — 133

8. Baoyu in Wonderland: Technological Utopia
   in the Early Modern Chinese Science Fiction Novel
   FENG-YING MING — 152

9. The Texture of the Metropolis:
   Modernist Inscriptions of Shanghai in the 1930s
   YINGJIN ZHANG — 173

10. The Cult of Poetry in Contemporary China
    MICHELLE YEH — 188

11. Tianya, the Ends of the World or the Edge of Heaven:
    Comparative Literature at the Fin de Siècle
    EUGENE CHEN EOYANG — 218

REFERENCE MATTER

Notes — 235
Character List — 283
Index — 301

CONTRIBUTORS

Helen H. Chen completed her Ph.D. in comparative literature at the University of Texas, Austin, and has taught at Indiana University and Swarthmore College. Her dissertation is titled "Rehistoricizing Desire and Communist Idealism: Contemporary Chinese Fiction since the Mid-1980s."

Eugene Chen Eoyang is Professor of Comparative Literature and East Asian Languages and Cultures at Indiana University. He is the author of *The Transparent Eye: Translation, Chinese Literature, and Comparative Poetics* (1993) and *The Coat of Many Colors: Reflections on Diversity by a Minority of One* (1995); the editor of *Selected Poems of Ai Qing* (1982); and the coeditor (with Lin Yao-fu) of *Translating Chinese Literature* (1995). He served as president of the American Comparative Literature Association (1995–97) and is one of the cofounders and coeditors of *CLEAR*.

Mark E. Francis completed his Ph.D. in Chinese literature at Stanford University and is Assistant Professor of Asian Languages and Literatures at the University of Auckland in New Zealand. His dissertation is titled "Standards of Excess: Literary Histories, Canons, and the Reception of Late Tang Poetry."

Ann-Marie Hsiung completed her Ph.D. in East Asian languages and literatures at the University of Hawaii, Manoa, and currently teaches at Nanyang Technological University in Singapore. Her dissertation is titled "Seeking Women in Pre-modern Chinese Texts: A Feminist Re-Vision of Ming Drama (1368–1644)."

Feng-ying Ming completed her Ph.D. in comparative literature at UCLA and has taught at Middlebury College and Whittier College. Her dissertation is titled "Romance, Detective Novel, and Science Fiction: The Late Qing Polygeneric Novels."

Greta Ai-Yu Niu is a Ph.D. candidate in English at Duke University. She is writing a dissertation titled "People of the Pagus: Orientalized Bodies and Migration in an Asian Pacific Rim."

David Palumbo-Liu received his Ph.D. in comparative literature from the University of California, Berkeley, and is Associate Professor of Comparative

Literature at Stanford University. He is the author of *Poetics of Appropriation: The Literary Theory and Practice of Huang Tingjian* (1993) and *The Narrating of Asian America* (forthcoming); the editor of *The Ethnic Canon: Histories, Institutions, and Interventions* (1995); and the coeditor (with Hans Ulrich Gumbrecht) of *Streams of Cultural Capital: Transnational Cultural Studies* (1997).

Michelle Yeh received her Ph.D. in comparative literature from the University of Southern California and is Professor of Chinese at the University of California, Davis. She is the author of *Modern Chinese Poetry: Theory and Practice Since 1917* (1991); and the editor and translator of *Anthology of Modern Chinese Poetry* (1992).

Zhang Longxi received his Ph.D. in comparative literature from Harvard University and is Professor and Director of Comparative Literature at the University of California, Riverside. He is the author of *Ershi shiji xifang wenlun shuping* (A critical introduction to twentieth-century Western theories of literature, 1986), *The Tao and the Logos: Literary Hermeneutics, East and West* (1992), which won honorable mention for the 1994 AAS Joseph Levenson prize, and *Mighty Opposites: From Dichotomies to Differences in the Comparative Study of China* (forthcoming).

Yingjin Zhang received his Ph.D. in comparative literature from Stanford University and is Associate Professor of Chinese, Comparative Literature, and Film Studies at Indiana University. He is the author of *The City in Modern Chinese Literature and Film: Configurations of Space, Time, and Gender* (1996); the coauthor (with Zhiwei Xiao) of *Encyclopedia of Chinese Film* (1998); and the editor of *Romance, Sexuality, Identity: Cinema and Urban Culture in Shanghai, 1910s–1940s* (forthcoming).

John Yu Zou is a Ph.D. candidate in comparative literature at the University of California, Berkeley. He recently held a Mellon fellowship and is writing a dissertation titled "Tilted Charisma: Male Feminist Theater in Modern China."

A NOTE ON ROMANIZATION

The *pinyin* system is used throughout the book. For the sake of clarity and consistency, most other forms of romanization used in quoted passages have been converted into *pinyin*, except for personal names and bibliographical data.

CHINA IN A POLYCENTRIC WORLD

Introduction

Engaging Chinese Comparative Literature and Cultural Studies

YINGJIN ZHANG

This volume of essays on Chinese comparative literature and cultural studies aims to bring together several lines of scholarly inquiry. Like a few previous publications that ventured into the academically marginal space of Chinese comparative literature and which appeared in a geopolitically marginal place like Hong Kong,[1] the present volume must assume a set of interrelated responsibilities: it must reflect on the status of Chinese comparative literature, reconfigure the boundaries of literature and other disciplines, refashion certain methodologies and theories, and reread selected canonical as well as marginal writers and texts from new perspectives. In the current academic climate, where the time-honored systems of literary scholarship are frequently being disrupted if not altogether dismantled, and where any paradigm shifts, methodological innovations, and institutional changes are likely to meet with enthusiastic endorsement as well as trenchant criticism,[2] a project like the present volume finds itself situated in a site of academic production marked by profound ironies.

The first irony a project of Chinese comparative literature and cultural studies has to confront arises from the different ways in which literary scholars in the United States and in China have responded to comparative literature in recent years. A general skepticism of the conventional generic categories (e.g., studies of influence, of genre, of theme, and of literary movement and periodization) has prevailed in the United States to such an extent that leading scholars of comparative literature often bypass the standard taxonomies and that the once preeminent "French school" and the "American school" have now been reduced to merely the "French hour" and the "American hour" in the history of the discipline.³ In mainland China, on the contrary, it is precisely these same taxonomies that have been neatly charted and widely disseminated in college textbooks and scholarly publications, while the decade-long discussion of the "Chinese school" (*Zhongguo xuepai*) has made comparative literature one of the fastest growing and most visible disciplines in the humanities.⁴ However, in an extremely ironic way, a recent announcement in China that the "Chinese school" is presented with a "historical mission" to carry international comparative literature to new heights has run counter to an equally recent declaration in the United States of the "impossibility"—at least in theoretical terms—of Chinese comparative literature as a discourse of "transparency" (a utopian construct that I shall discuss more fully later).⁵ What is more, the irony in question is compounded by the persistence of "mutual parochialism" as exemplified in the impatience of Western theorists in their dealings with Chinese texts and in the hostility of hardcore sinologists in their dealings with comparative literature.⁶

The second irony confronted by scholars of Chinese comparative literature and cultural studies arises from the putatively irreconcilable difference between "Western theory" and the "Chinese text." On the one hand, Western theory may be privileged as not just instrumental but virtually indispensable by a "subaltern" who wants to speak in the West, and may therefore be inscribed in such a love-hate relation: " 'Western theory' is there, beyond my control; yet in order to speak, I must come to terms with it."⁷ On the other hand, training in or exposure to Western theory may be deemed so detrimental that scholars of Chinese comparative literature are constantly reminded, sometimes by Western critics, of the dangers of a "wholesale application of Western theories and methods to Chinese literature."⁸ For some scholars, what may be more alarming than an "encroachment" of theory into literary studies is that nowadays "it has become possible to publish articles in the literature field that make few or even no references to stories, plays, or poems."⁹ In one extreme case, not only is theory judged to be a "potentially dominant institution" in itself; it is actually imagined to have "the express purpose of driving literature (as we have known it) out of business."¹⁰ At stake here, obviously, are the traditional notions of what constitutes literature and what counts as literary studies. Nevertheless, occasional alarms aside, traditional scholarship and theoretical innovations are being pursued simultaneously, as what falls under the "Chinese school" (with its consistent emphasis on traditional Chinese literary criticism) can testify; for some scholars, it is a dialectic between these two lines of inquiry that will "move Comparative Literature along."[11]

The ironies in which scholars of Chinese comparative literature and cultural studies find themselves implicated, in spite of themselves, indicate clearly that there is no easy way out of the intellectual dilemma, and that neither an outright rejection of "contaminating" Western theory nor a total disregard of the "naive" Chinese text will carry us anywhere. Instead, critical engagements in both theoretical or methodological issues and literary or cultural texts will prove a more fruitful undertaking.

The Notions of the "Chinese School" of Comparative Literature

Despite occasional disputes, the term "Chinese school" of comparative literature is generally attributed to Gu Tianhong (Ku Tim-hung) and Chen Pengxiang (*alias* Chen Huihua), two Taiwanese scholars who edited in 1976 a pioneering work, *Bijiao wenxue de kentuo zai Taiwan* (Breaking ground for comparative literature in Taiwan).[12] In the preface they offer this definition: "The Chinese school of comparative literature is a type of study which has recourse to Western literary theory and methodology in such a way as to contest and modify them and to apply them to Chinese literature."[13] The "Chinese school," in other words, is distinguished from Western comparative literature in that it studies Chinese literature with recourse to Western theory but without recourse to comparison with Western literature. In this inception stage, therefore, the "Chinese school" was already closely linked to Western theory.

A year later, John Deeney (or Li Dasan as he is called in Chinese) published an article explicitly titled "Bijiao wenxue Zhongguo xuepai" (The Chinese school of comparative literature) in an influential Taiwanese literary journal, *Zhongwai wenxue*. Construed as a "manifesto to the future," Deeney's article enumerates five goals for the Chinese school: (1) to identify and promote the "national characteristics" (*minzuxing*) of Chinese literature; (2) to expand the horizon of comparative literature to include literary movements in the non-Western areas; (3) to be a spokesperson for non-Western countries, especially for the "Third World" countries; (4) to strive for a truly "globalized" (*shijiehua*) comparative literature by supplementing Western with non-Western literary experience; and (5) to eradicate the ignorance and arrogance of many scholars East and West.[14] It is evident that at least on their rhetorical surface, Deeney's vision of the "Chinese school" differs from that of Gu and Chen's: whereas Deeney primarily aims to enrich international comparative literature by promoting Chinese literature, Gu and Chen aim to enrich Chinese literary studies by way of Western theory.

In the subsequent years, John Deeney traveled frequently between Taiwan and Hong Kong and assumed the role of spokesman for the Chinese school. His vision and ambition were further endorsed by some senior mainland scholars after comparative literature was formally reinstituted there in the early 1980s.[15] By 1987 Deeney was confident enough to declare: "The existence of the 'Chinese School' of comparative literature is already well established, as so many learned organizations and abundant publications exploring all issues of the discipline from a Chinese perspective amply testify."[16] What Deeney saw as the best evidence for his claim was the rapid development of comparative literature in mainland China since the late 1970s, which had extended the term "comparative literature" to include not only other Eastern literatures but also the literature of China's "ethnic minorities" (*shaoshu minzu*) and that of overseas Chinese (*haiwai huaren*). While advocating "a *composite* approach to fostering the building up of the 'Chinese School,'" Deeney felt an urgent need for "an articulation of [its] underlying theory and methodology."[17]

Works on Chinese comparative literature appeared in increasing numbers, and discussions of the Chinese school were undertaken in a more sophisticated manner from the late 1980s on. To give a recent example, Cao Shunqing, a mainland scholar, came up in early 1995 with an ambitious study of the "essential features" of the theory and methodology of the Chinese school. After contending that the major contribution of the French school consists in its crossing of the borders of nations (hence its international character) and that of the American school in its crossing of the borders of disciplines (hence its interdisciplinary character), Cao predicts that the Chinese school will contribute to the newest development in comparative literature by crossing the borders of cultures (hence its intercultural character). "Intercultural" studies (*kua wenhua yanjiu*), therefore, has become an essential feature and to a great extent has influenced a number of methodologies adopted in the Chinese school, such as the "elucidation method" (*chanfa fa*), the "search for roots through cultural models" (*wenhua mozi xungen fa*), and the "dialogic study" (*duihua yanjiu*).[18] Obviously, there are many points of overlap among the methodologies Cao enumerates, and none of them dominates the practice of Chinese comparative literature at present.

From the perspective of the current theoretical developments in the West, however, Cao's schematic—and admittedly rather reductionist—characterization of the three "schools" of comparative literature is, to say the least, far from accurate. In the United States, for instance, studies of influences and parallels are no longer the dominant methodologies in comparative literature; nor are the French and the American schools—if such schools ever formally existed—considered to be major concerns by comparatists in their teaching and research. In the context of "an unprecedented international boom" of cultural studies over the past decade,[19] "intercultural studies" may characterize comparative studies in the West as much as it does in China. One ready example is Charles Bernheimer's recent collection of three reports by the American Comparative Literature Association (issued in 1965, 1975, and 1993), for which he deliberately chose the term "multiculturalism" to highlight the controversy generated by the new multicultural orientations in the United States.[20] It would be virtually impossible, therefore, for a Chinese comparatist to overlook the "intercultural" aspects of many recent developments in Western literary theory (e.g., Third World literature and postcolonial discourse), especially when one claims an intercultural perspective to be the most salient feature of the Chinese school. In other words, intercultural studies cannot be parochially defined as a national characteristic unique to the Chinese school, nor can one practice Chinese comparative literature without a serious intercultural mediation with the rest of the world.

Re-envisioning Chinese Comparative Literature and Cultural Studies

The brief delineation in the preceding section is not intended as a promotion or a dismissal of the Chinese school. Instead, it aims to provide a historical and intellectual context from which we can re-envision Chinese comparative literature and cultural studies as a category broad enough to embrace multiple approaches currently adopted in the field. To begin with, Chinese comparative literature and cultural studies differs from the Chinese school of comparative literature in that the former is conceived as an open intellectual space dissociated from any nationalistic or political implication the latter may have contained.[21] Furthermore, "Chinese comparative literature and cultural studies" is a more flexible term which may refer not only to Chinese-Western or East-West comparative literature but also to a type of critical study of Chinese texts characterized more by its theoretical concerns than by its comparative orientation. Finally, "Chinese comparative literature and cultural studies" acknowledges the increasing importance of culture in comparative literature studies, with "culture" here covering both elite (literary) culture and mass or popular culture.

The term "Chinese comparative literature and cultural studies" thus favors "Chineseness" as a *cultural* rather than ethnic, national, or political reference point. The qualifying word "Chinese" here does not imply any essentialist or exclusionist concept of "China" as a self-enclosed entity squarely seated at the center of the world (*Zhongguo*); rather, it merely specifies a branch of comparative literature and cultural studies that focuses on Chinese texts that has been successfully practiced by Chinese and non-Chinese scholars for decades. Although in demographic terms the majority of contributors to this volume are ethnically Chinese, originally from mainland China (four), Taiwan (three), and the United States (three), this fact alone does not automatically constitute a political statement, simply because the volume is based on the fourth conference of the American Association of Chinese Comparative Literature (AACCL), an organization with a large percentage of Chinese and Chinese-Americans. As much as I wanted a balanced representation, I was constrained by the specific circumstance under which the present volume took shape.

Historically, the AACCL was founded in 1987 by a group of Chinese students in the United States to promote a marginal line of critical inquiry within the Eurocentric discipline of comparative literature. It is interesting to note that for many years the office of the AACCL was located in Indiana University, a former stronghold of the "American school" of comparative literature,[22] and this enclave of Chinese comparatists in the United States had expanded its membership internationally and increased its visibility to such an extent that by March 1993 the AACCL was able to convene its third conference in conjunction with the annual meeting of the American Comparative Literature Association (ACLA) at Indiana University. As Eugene Chen Eoyang points out, the "contextual anomaly" of the AACCL has conferred on its members a certain unique point of view: "It is neither parochially Chinese or nationalistic, nor is it personally unattached to China. We may say, on the one hand, it is a Chinese point of view liberated from the nationalism of mainland scholars; and it is also an American point of view, enhanced by a personal engagement (in most cases, a native engagement) with Chinese culture."[23]

Ostensibly, what we witness here is the emergence of a type of "Chinese culturalism" that transcends geopolitical borders and conflicts. As Chinese comparatists on both sides of the Taiwan Strait come to meet in the United States on a regular basis, it becomes apparent that such critical engagements in Chinese comparative literature and cultural studies have made possible certain topics and certain strategies of discourse. Pauline Yu acknowledged at the second conference of the AACCL, held at UCLA in March 1992: "There is clearly a new generation of scholars who, rather than wallowing in the endless rounds of agonized and inconclusive soul-searching or hysterical name-calling that have consumed those of us in the forty- and fifty-something generation, have simply cut through the morass and forged ahead."[24] Nevertheless, this forging ahead does not mean that the new generation is no longer interested in such questions as institutional changes, paradigmatic shifts, or other critical debates, for these questions were repeatedly addressed by the AACCL conferences and by its members' recent publications.[25] What better distinguishes the new generation from the old one is that the new generation no longer make an "either/or" choice between Western theory and Chinese literature: we can never return to a pristine state of Chinese literature, uncontaminated by any critical language, nor can we aspire to be anything but cross-cultural, comparative critics as we approach the next millennium.

The strategic preference of "both/and" (i.e., engaging both Chinese literature and Western theory) over "either/or" (in the form of many presumed binary oppositions, sinology versus theory being only one of them) necessarily entails a great deal of border-crossing in recent Chinese comparative literature studies.[26] However, recognizing the fluidity of boundaries does not amount to collapsing or erasing all differences and distinctions. For this reason, Pauline Yu insists on the necessity of "engaging in a double critique" to secure a self-reflexive position for Chinese comparatists, and Eugene Eoyang recommends a "co-oppositional discourse"—"a program that would require the *cooperation* of seemingly opposing view-points, and at the same time *co-opt* seemingly contrasting vantage points."[27] One immediate result of such "double critiques" or "co-oppositional" moves is the convergence of multiple critical views in Chinese comparative literature and cultural studies, which precludes any monolithic character for the new generation, ideological or otherwise.

The awareness of the fluid boundaries explains a number of differences—in both its coverage and its approaches—by which this volume is marked off from earlier efforts. To begin with, this volume does not abide by conventional taxonomies in comparative literature, which, in Claudio Guillién's recent account, includes these five classes of investigation: genres, formal proceedings, themes, literary relations, and historical configurations.[28] To a considerable extent, these standard categories were reflected in the selections of the previous volumes published in Hong Kong. For instance, generic study was exemplified by Andrew Plaks's comparison of full-length *xiaoshuo* and the Western novel, thematic study by C. H. Wang's reading of the bird as messenger of love in allegorical poetry, formal proceedings by Han-liang Chang's structural analysis of Tang *chuanqi*, literary relations by Marián Gálik's study of the genesis of modern Chinese literary criticism, and historical configurations by Tak-wai Wong's discussion of period style and periodization in literary historiography.[29]

Furthermore, the present volume shifts the emphasis from Chinese-Western comparativism to critical (that is, theoretically engaged) readings of Chinese texts. Although cases of Chinese-Western influences and parallels may be observed in passing (e.g., in Michelle Yeh and Yingjin Zhang), the focus of most essays in this volume is the Chinese experience as inscribed in a variety of texts and practices in literature and culture. Grouped around general topics of discipline and discourse (Part I), gender and sexuality (Part II), and science and modernity (Part III), these essays study different shades of the "Chinese experience" by critically examining numerous literary themes: displacement (in Eugene Eoyang), technological utopia (in Feng-ying Ming), urban imagination (in Yingjin Zhang), sexual transgression (in Helen Chen), transvestism (in Ann-Marie Hsiung), and suicide (in Michelle Yeh). In spite of their focus on Chinese texts, however, all contributors to this volume place their examples of Chinese experience in comparative perspective by engaging, in varying degrees, current Western theories and methodologies (e.g., feminism, gender theory, and postcolonial discourse). Subject to such a critical reading, the "Chineseness" of these texts is historicized and becomes relational to the outside world. This is particularly true in the cases of cultural modernity (in John Zou), urban experience (in Yingjin Zhang), and the cult of poetry (in Michelle Yeh), where the experiential realm of the Chineseness has already been infiltrated by Western cultural elements (e.g., colonial discourse, bourgeois lifestyle, and consumer culture). In cases like these, the constructed nature of Chinese experience comes to the fore under critical scrutiny from the perspective of comparative literature and cultural studies.

Needless to say, the methodological changes I have delineated here, especially the emphases on theoretical investigation and border-crossing, are by no means an isolated phenomenon in Chinese comparative literature and cultural studies. As a matter of fact, since the 1970s, "comparative literature—by virtue of its identification with literary theory—seemed to be in the vanguard of literary study."[30] Many national literatures, English and French in particular, quickly followed in the new theoretical direction and the result was, in Gerald Graff's words, a "theory explosion" in the late 1980s.[31] With the rise of culturally oriented fields of analysis, such as film studies, cultural studies, and postcolonial studies, border-crossing has become frequent in academic research, and its effect has been both profound and far reaching. From the 1980s on, even social scientists began to adopt a self-reflexive stance and to question, within their disciplinary frameworks, how meaning is constituted and how knowledge of cultures is textually produced.[32]

The fact is, however, that Chinese comparative literature remained marginal in academia, even though it has developed closely with the rest of literary studies in the United States and even though China has gained increasing importance in the geopolitical world order over the past decades. The alleged lack of public interest alone does not account for this marginality, because "what seems to fascinate, at this point, the majority of our students is the Herculean effort to become familiar with, to describe, and to make part of our active experience those cultures and literatures that had been kept in the background under the traditional hegemony of Eurocentric (and probably also male) values and paradigms."[33] A more direct cause for the marginality in question has been attributed to the sheer indifference of many leading Western theorists, who have never ceased to astound China scholars with their undisguised Eurocentrism, which is manifest in the form of either "a rather patronizing tolerance [or] an all-too-visible impatience."[34] The resulting unequal distribution of power and knowledge between China and the West has emerged as a pressing problem for Chinese comparatists, not the least because they are often forced to dilute their cultural codes and learning in order to engage in theoretical dialogue with the West (or otherwise to run the risk of being unheeded or even unheard). On the other hand, very few Western theorists would care to spend time researching Chinese literature and culture, for it is academically not worth their time; even if they occasionally do, their theorizing might immediately encounter suspicion, if not resistance, and would potentially do more harm than good to their academic reputations.[35]

To be distinguished from a shrinking group of the most hard-core philologists and sinologists who resolutely refuse comparative work and are "content to remain within the safe confines of a single dynasty, genre, or botanical species,"[36] the committed Chinese comparatists are now faced with at least the following three options in dealing with their marginality in the West. The first option is to launch a sustained critique of "the hegemonic status of Western theoretical thinking" in exclusively Western theoretical terms.[37] Ironically, this initially "oppositional" discourse often turns out to be a cooperative force because the end result of such a critique is invariably a correction, and therefore enhancement if not perfection, of Western theory and its hegemonic status. What is more, such a critique usually prioritizes Western issues over Chinese concerns and is consequently easier to institutionalize within Western academia.[38] The second option is to study comparative poetics and to introduce Chinese aesthetics to the Western world. This constructive, theory-oriented method has so far produced the most remarkable scholarship in Chinese-Western comparative literature and is still widely pursued.[39] The third option, which is adopted by the majority of essays in the present volume, is to practice a critical, theoretically informed reading of Chinese literature and culture. In contrast to the other two options, this last one does not make it its goal to test the validity or to contest the limit of Western theory;[40] instead, it is interested primarily in excavating the concealed sites of knowledge production and in uncovering the hidden meanings in Chinese literature and culture.

In this third option, therefore, literary and cultural texts constitute the ground for serious "archaeological" projects. This explains why the *text* assumes more significance in the present volume than either the author or the style (as reflected in conventional approaches, like biographic criticism and the study of artistic features). In many cases, noncanonical, unofficial, or historically insignificant texts (e.g., Xu Wei's plays, Guo Songtao's journals, Hei Ying's urban story, and post-Menglong poetry) are brought forth from the forgotten shelves of literary archives or the margins of literary production and are subjected to critical scrutiny in order to reveal their crucial links to larger issues in Chinese history and culture, such as canon formation, gender construction, urban experience, colonial situation, postcolonial migration, and the impact of consumer culture.

The essays in this volume cover a wide selection of genres and periods in Chinese literature and culture, ranging from traditional poetics and drama to contemporary fiction and poetry. Only one essay, Greta Niu's study of a recent American television drama, falls outside these categories, but it deals specifically with the fetishization of the screen image of a Chinese-American actress in North America. With the exceptions of Eugene Eoyang, a pioneer of Chinese-Western comparative literature, and David Palumbo-Liu, Michelle Yeh, and Zhang Longxi, three well-known scholars in comparative literature and cultural studies, all contributors to this volume belong to a new generation who received their doctoral training in the United States from the mid-1980s to the mid-1990s. The significance of this new generation and their impact on academic institutions have been increasingly felt and publicly acknowledged by senior members in both Chinese and comparative literature in the United States.[41]

Engaging Texts

At the present stage of academic development we need truly "engaged" scholars—those who are dedicated to both Chinese and Western texts—as much as we need "engaging texts"—writings that will appeal to the readers and will in turn engage them in the advancement of Chinese comparative literature and cultural studies. The first kind of engagement is best exemplified in Zhang Longxi's and David Palumbo-Liu's essays. Leading the discussion in Part I, "Discipline, Discourse, Canon," which tackles the issues of institutional history and critical strategy in Chinese and comparative literature, Zhang unambiguously declares in "The Challenge of East-West Comparative Literature" that literary theory provides the ground for comparison in East-West studies. After a survey of recent Western reflections on the disciplinary changes within comparative literature, he points out an issue more serious than a mere neglect of East-West comparative literature, namely, a dismissal of Chinese comparative literature as purely "utopian." He reveals the dangers characteristic of a totalitarian anti-utopia, and promotes the idea—utopian as it might be—of cross-cultural understanding through comparative studies. For this purpose, he argues that the establishment of a Chinese school of comparative literature is a less urgent issue than the solidity of scholarship to be achieved by Chinese comparatists, and further locates the major problem not in the application of Western theory to Chinese texts, but in the unequal relationship between the two. Taking parallelism as an appropriate metaphor for comparative literature itself, he finally envisions a kind of study based on the model of mediation rather than confrontation or juxtaposition, a study of theoretical issues that are common to and shared by Chinese and Western traditions in different but comparable manifestations.

While concurring with Zhang Longxi on the importance of mediation between Chinese and Western texts, David Palumbo-Liu addresses the historical and institutional assumptions and practices that have complicated such a vision as Zhang's of cross-cultural studies. First published in 1992 as a response to Jonathan Chaves's polemical criticism of Stephen Owen's role in spreading a Western theoretical "virus" across Chinese literary studies, Palumbo-Liu's "Utopias of Discourse: On the Impossibility of Chinese Comparative Literature" argues that the enterprise of Chinese comparative literary criticism will remain one without a "legitimate" discourse (it will be, as he puts it, "u-topic") if it insists upon absolutely transparent, "ideology-free" discourse. In his view, a sinologist's project to return to the text in its "pre-critical," "pristine" linguistic state is purely utopian in that the quest for a nonideological discourse only serves to mask its presumed "cultural authority." On the other hand, a similarly utopian move may result in a comparatist's blind faith in "scientific objectivity" (as represented by an inventory of categories, including genre, form, mode, style, rhetoric, prototype, plot, symbol, motif, and allusion)—"blind" because it evades certain fundamental questions regarding the relationships of ideology to aesthetics and theory. Palumbo-Liu suggests that we engage instead in a critical awareness of the way Chinese comparative studies necessarily suppresses but does not erase ideology, and that rather than simply say that "everything is ideological," it is crucial to note more precisely the nature of the various ideologies that inform critical studies and what they allow and disallow, as they are embedded in specific institutional, national, and material histories.

In a sense, Palumbo-Liu has envisioned a number of critical issues that are addressed by several other contributors to this volume. Ann-Marie Hsiung, for example, analyzes the kinds of "speaking positions" that were available to an eccentric Ming dramatist, and Helen Chen investigates how gender experience was invalidated and revalidated by contending cultural ideologies in contemporary China. More pertinent to premodern Chinese literature, Mark Francis's "Canon Formation in Traditional Chinese Poetry: Chinese Canons, Sacred and Profane" revisits the constitution of literature by surveying the canonization process in traditional Chinese poetry. He first defines the concept of canon and then distinguishes the Chinese canon from the Western. While addressing the double function of the *Shijing* as a canonical text (*jing* as part of the normative warp on the loom of civilization) and a literary classic (the *Shijing* as the origin and the model of the *shi* genre), he draws our attention to the presence of "margins" within the center—noncanonical elements such as erotic themes or emotional excess within the canon—and to the various ways the later commentators responded to these negative examples. He proceeds further to describe the *Chuci* as the "other" canon, which represents an alternative, "Southern" tradition in Chinese poetry, but which did not attain the normative power of the *Shijing*. Finally, he discusses the development of the anthology as a canonizing institution in Chinese literary culture and traces the pluralistic if not binary legacy of the *Shijing* and the *Chuci* in subsequent literary anthologies.

The remaining essays in the volume illustrate the second kind of engagement mentioned above, namely, engagement with primary literary or cultural texts. All three contributors to Part II, "Gender, Sexuality, Body," have adopted a feminist approach in their study of instances of subversion and containment in Chinese and Western cultures. In "A Feminist Re-Vision of Xu Wei's *Ci Mulan* and *Nü zhuangyuan*," Ann-Marie Hsiung concentrates on a marginal author in traditional Chinese literature. The Ming dramatist Xu Wei has been considered an eccentric figure mainly because he rejected the Confucian norm and presented in his plays a number of strong women characters who challenged the patriarchal value system. Upon closer scrutiny, however, Hsiung discovers that in spite of his display of the superiority of women over men in terms of both military skills and intellectual capacity, Xu Wei ultimately subjugated women to patriarchy and through such subjugation symbolically contained their previous subversiveness as revealed in their transgressive acts of assuming male roles. By contextualizing Xu's plays in his life experience and in Ming cultural history, Hsiung further demonstrates that the "masculine" women in Xu's plays might be an effective—albeit unconventional—vehicle through which Xu vented disillusionment and frustration at his repeated failures in civil examinations. Xu's strong women, therefore, served multiple, often ambivalent functions. Despite their final containment of woman's subversion, Xu's texts inevitably called into question gender ideology and the gendered structure of power in traditional China.

Helen Chen's "Gender, Subjectivity, Sexuality: Defining a Subversive Discourse in Wang Anyi's Four Tales of Sexual Transgression" continues the feminist reading of subversion but takes us to contemporary Chinese fiction. She starts by noting that feminism had been inscribed in the grand narrative of nation-building since the early twentieth century and that gender difference had been erased by the communist discourse of class and revolution. In the post-Mao era, a number of writers began to challenge the taboo of sexuality in the name of humanism, but they still viewed *qing* (passion and sentiment) as superior to *yu* (sexual desire). In Wang Anyi's four tales of sexual transgression, however, "spiritual love" is replaced by sexual desire. Wang gives sexual desire a transformative power, which not only helps her female character regain subjectivity but also makes her male character a better man, transformed, for instance, from a brutal abuser to a worshiper of feminine beauty. In Wang's writings, female consciousness is often achieved through transgressive sexual acts (e.g., premarital sex and adultery), which prove subversive of both traditional Confucian values and repressive communist ideology.

Greta Niu's "Consuming Asian Women: The Fluid Body of Josie Packard in *Twin Peaks*" brings us to the emerging field of media studies in a transnational setting. The essay focuses on the image of the character Josie Packard, a mysterious young Oriental woman played by the former Chinese, now Chinese-American, film star Joan Chen in *Twin Peaks*, a popular television series directed by David Lynch. In her analysis, Niu reveals the intricate, at times unconscious, ways the representation of this "other" woman is implicated in many larger sociopolitical issues, such as regional anxiety, colonialist mentality, Orientalist discourse, sexual fantasy, and undisguised misogyny. In her readings of the "white triangle," the trope of passing, the mail-order catalogs, and the constructions of Asian consumers as feminine and of Asian women as fetish, Niu argues that the visual consumption of *Twin Peaks* itself is offered as one form of Orientalism, that all sociocultural problems unresolved in the television series are located in the fluid body of Joan Chen, and that the fluidity in question may be symbolically circumscribed by the culturally imposed, colonialist boundaries.

Part III, "Science, Modernity, Aesthetics," is centered around modernity and its multifaceted manifestations in modern China. John Zou's "Travel and Translation: An Aspect of China's Cultural Modernity, 1862–1926" claims that travel and translation are two cultural behaviors that informed virtually all modernizing schemes in China since the 1860s. Historically positioned against the overwhelming shadow of Western imperialist hegemony, travels in the West and the translation of Western works were sponsored by the Qing court and originally meant to remedy deficiencies in China. However, these two types of "cultural trafficking" subsequently engendered a dilemma for the people involved, making them at once the powerless witnesses to Western wonders whose responsibility was simply to record and reproduce a textual West and the powerful subjects whose Western knowledge enabled them to participate in Chinese political reforms. Selecting a prominent figure from each of the three stages in China's modernization in the late Qing and early Republican periods, Zou traces in Guo Songtao's travelogues to the West, Wang Guowei's commentary on translation, and Lu Xun's abandonment of medicine for literature a gradual move toward the uncoupling of the complementarity between Western power and Chinese deficits.

Feng-ying Ming's "Baoyu in Wonderland: Technological Utopia in the Early Modern Chinese Science Fiction Novel" continues to explore the issue of modernity but focuses on science fiction as an example of what she terms the "polygeneric novels" in late Qing China. She first delineates a number of ways in which Chinese intellectuals responded to modern Western civilization. Then, reading through Wu Woyao's *New Story of the Stone* (1905), she discovers the twofold function that science fiction performed at the time: it served both as an instrument to introduce Western wonders and as an exercise to project the literati's utopian fantasy. What she finds of great interest in Wu's novel is that rather than admire everything Western, the new Baoyu assumes a composite image of the Chinese knight errant, the Confucian scholar, the Taoist alchemist, and the ancient military hero. This image, she contends, demonstrates that humanistic concerns outweighed scientific interests in Chinese science fiction of the time. After a brief discussion of *The World Underneath the Ground* (1903), Lu Xun's rewriting of Verne's fiction, Ming finally concludes that late Qing science fiction constituted a locus for the integration of old and new, native and foreign.

Yingjin Zhang's "Texture of the Metropolis: Modernist Inscriptions of Shanghai in the 1930s" deals with the attempt in early twentieth-century China to make sense through imaginative writing of a different experience of modernity—though perhaps no less technological in nature—that new phenomenal reality called the city. He starts with a survey of four modes of city narrative and moves to a close reading of a little-known modernist story by Hei Ying, which appeared in the popular Shanghai pictorial *Liangyou* (The young companion) in 1934. Zhang shows how Hei Ying imagined and articulated the modern city through a variety of perceptions (e.g., voyeurism) and conceptions (e.g., the city as enigmatic woman) and what these perceptions and conceptions reveal about the nature of the urban experience in modern China. In the concluding section, he further discusses "artistic modernity" as represented by Shanghai modernist writers of the 1930s and the historical contribution they made to the development of modern Chinese literature.

Michelle Yeh's "Cult of Poetry in Contemporary China" brings us to a contemporary scene in Chinese poetry. Concentrating on the "post-Menglongshi" period since the mid-1980s, she studies a unique recent phenomenon—"the cult of poetry"—as manifest in four major aspects: the elevation and deification of poetry, the sense of crisis, images of the poet, and the construction of a genealogy of poets. She gathers ample textual evidence from contemporary, often unofficial publications and takes note of a particularly significant but extreme act—suicide—committed by a number of young Chinese poets. She traces the influence on such acts of heroism and martyrdom to a dozen foreign poets. Although the recurring religious motifs, the profound personal crises, and the sacrificial images of the poet in contemporary Chinese poetry clearly arose as a response to a mundane world marked by a repressive political system and a rampant consumerism, Yeh points out that the Chinese avant-garde poets may in fact be complicit with the Maoist discourse in their deification of poetry and that the "cult phenomenon"—an exclusive male practice—has already generated "anti-cult" reactions in recent years.

Michelle Yeh's reflections on the "cult of poetry" and its dissipation in contemporary China bring us up to the mid-1990s, a new fin de siècle that poses new challenges to comparative literature as a discipline. In his "Tianya, the Ends of the World or the Edge of Heaven: Comparative Literature at the Fin de Siècle," Eugene Eoyang entertains a "decentered" view of the world and encourages us to take up the new challenges. Concurring with Zhang Longxi that East-West comparative literature has long been marginalized, Eoyang nevertheless takes a different strategic position and reviews the field of comparative literature by attending to specific "localities" and their constantly shifting borders. Moving from the image of "the end of the world" implied in the Chinese term *tianya* to the recurrent theme of exile in world literature, he claims that being displaced is exactly where one attains a true vision of the world. He distinguishes four sets of displacements—the physical (exile), the psychological (alienation), the linguistic (translation), and the epistemological (marginalization)—and reconfigures the frontier and the center by asserting that we are now "centered" at the edge of the world. Moreover, he reexamines the notion of margin and points out that it is precisely the areas characterized as "marginal" which yield new insights and new knowledge. Referring to three disproportionate maps of the United States as examples of localized knowledge production, he concludes that our discoveries must be made at the frontier, and that an entire atlas of "disproportionate" maps may actually enable us to perceive the whole without any false objectivity.

The adaptation of a new "decentered" view of the world, nevertheless, does not automatically translate into a resolution of epistemological or ideological problems we are now facing in the new fin de siècle. As pointed out at the beginning of this introduction, Chinese comparatists often find themselves in a site of academic production marked by profound ironies. To take the cultural scene of mainland China in the 1990s for example, it has been variously described as "the downfall of elite culture" (*jingying wenhua de shiluo*) and "the crisis of the humanist spirit" (*renwen jingsheng de weiji*).[42] The confrontation between "elite" literature and mass or popular culture (*dazhong wenhua*) on an unprecedented scale since the mid-1980s has occasioned a heated debate in Chinese intellectual circles.[43] With its emphasis on the "intracultural" issues, this new debate apparently differs from the old one, which centered on the Chinese school of comparative literature, but the two are actually related in several ways. For instance, both debates involve the question of Western theory. The frequent evocation of up-to-date Western critical terminology, most noticeable in all sorts of "post's"—poststructuralist, postmodernist, postcolonialist, postindustrial, post–Cold War, postcommunist, posthistoricist, postindividualist, postrevolutionary, and post–New Era—in the current debate points clearly to the persistence of profound ironies in comparative studies mentioned at the beginning of this introduction.[44] Moreover, a recent return to the "national characteristic"—this time in the name of Chinese "national studies" (*guoxue*)—is itself a marked comment on a certain type of mentality or propensity in Chinese intellectuals: to retreat into the age-old tradition as a space sealed off from foreign influences, be they the influences of Western theoretical discourse or of Chinese consumer culture.

To end this introduction with a brief reference to a new debate in contemporary China is not just to add one more item to our research agenda, but to highlight a number of recurring themes in our ongoing engagements in Chinese comparative literature and cultural studies. Many essays collected in this volume, for instance, investigate what Lydia Liu identifies as key issues in a study of translingual practice in modern China—"the rhetorical strategies,

Introduction 17

translations, discursive formations, naming practices, legitimizing processes, tropes, and narrative modes that bear upon the historical conditions of the Chinese experience of the modern."[45] This volume, however, has extended the scope of critical investigation to include traditional Chinese literature, and it has demonstrated the usefulness of comparative perspectives in studying a number of periods, genres, themes, and media. It is our belief that, regardless of its relatively marginal status in both Chinese and Western academia, Chinese comparative literature and cultural studies will continue to develop into the next millennium. Indeed, as China struggles to redefine itself in a polycentric world, scholars are faced with new challenges and new possibilities, and research projects on the cross-cultural, interlingual, and transnational aspects of Chinese literature and culture thus possess global relevance, historical urgency, and local significance all at once.[46]

Part One

Discipline, Discourse, Canon

Chapter 1

The Challenge of East-West Comparative Literature

ZHANG LONGXI

It may well be purely coincidental that two books were published in English in 1993 that tried to take stock of the conceptualization, methodology, history, and recent development of comparative literature with a view to pointing out some new directions for further exploration: Susan Bassnett's *Comparative Literature: A Critical Introduction*, and Claudio Guillén's *Challenge of Comparative Literature*, which originally appeared in Spanish in 1985 as *Entre lo uno et lo diverso: Introducción a la literatura comparada*. One year earlier, the March/June 1992 issue of the *Canadian Review of Comparative Literature / Revue Canadienne de Littérature Comparée* put out a number of articles that surveyed the field for changing configurations and new formations, and more recently, the American Comparative Literature Association commissioned a report on the state of the discipline, which was published with a number of responses in 1995 by the Johns Hopkins University Press as *Comparative Literature in the Age of Multiculturalism*, a significant title that clearly indicates the need for a fresh look at the discipline. There may still be others that have escaped my attention and limited knowledge, but the books and journal articles I have mentioned seem sufficient to indicate a tendency in the field of comparative literature toward self-examination. New development in two particular areas has called for such a self-examination: the predominant influence of literary theory and, closely related to it, the increasing interest in non-Western literatures and cultures. There is every indication that the present seems to be a propitious time for East-West comparative literature to grow and prosper; in reality, however, great challenges still await us.

Bassnett argues that the new comparative literature is moving away from traditional Eurocentric concerns and questioning the Western canon of great European masters, and that this tendency is precipitated especially by feminism and postmodernist theories. "The time has come," she declares, "to recognize that we now have a post-European model of comparative literature, one that reconsiders key questions of cultural identity, literary canons, the political implications of cultural influence, periodization and literary history and firmly rejects," she adds, "the ahistoricity of the American school and of the formalist approach."[1] Bassnett's terms "the American school" and "the formalist approach" refer to the study of literature for purely aesthetic values without consideration of its national character and its socioeconomic or political context, and to the belief that great works of literature exemplify some universal truths and have an ennobling and humanizing effect. To see these as characteristic of a so-called American school, however, tends to obfuscate the issue because formalism is not a national attribute and is surely not limited to the works of American comparatists. There is also a Russian formalism, for example, and its contribution to contemporary literary theory is well known. According to Bassnett, comparative literature in the formalist sense, or what she calls "the Literature-as-universal-civilizing-force approach," is now dead, but it lives on in some alternative forms and is "revitalized and politicized" in gender studies, cultural studies, and translation studies.[2] Although she has pronounced traditional comparative literature dead in the West, she seems to believe that the new and politicized comparative literature "is expanding and developing in many parts of the world where it is explicitly linked to questions of national culture and identity."[3] Laying special emphasis on the connection of comparative literature with national consciousness, Bassnett turns to questions of national identity, Orientalism, and postcolonial theory and advocates examining the relationship of England and Ireland as colonizer and the colonized by comparing the literatures of the British Isles. For an introduction to comparative literature, which one would expect to call for the expansion of critical horizon rather than its contraction, the argument for comparing English, Irish, Welsh, and Scottish literatures as "the proper business of British comparatists" seems a rather unusual move and an unfortunate narrowing of vision.[4] Of course, Bassnett mentions comparative literature in India and also discusses some Latin American writers for raising the question of national and cultural identities in the postcolonial world, but in her conceptualization of comparative literature beyond the frontiers of Europe, there is very little mention of China or East Asia. For a consideration of East-West or Chinese-Western comparative literature, therefore, Bassnett's book turns out to be less helpful than one might have hoped.

Bassnett's vision of the future of what she calls the "new comparative literature" as explicitly linked with the fate of nationalism does not look particularly encouraging either, because the use of comparative literature to boost national pride and indigenous cultural heritage, a practice typical of the early days of European comparative literature, is not as progressive an alternative, politically and otherwise, as she seems to imply. National consciousness and cultural identities are indeed highly contested issues in the debate about postcolonialism and subaltern studies, but it is questionable, as some critics have suggested, whether postcolonial theory can offer a productive paradigm for generating a cultural critique that is hitherto unavailable in the social and political context of China and the other East Asian countries.[5] In China, nationalism in cultural terms can easily form an alliance with political conservatism and traditionalism in their effort to suppress any change and reform in political and economic structure as well as in language and forms of literary expression, and the East-West dichotomy implicit in the nationalist argument can hardly offer a constructive paradigm in literary and cultural studies. Reading Bassnett's book, which speaks of the crisis and death of comparative literature in the West, of nationalism and the anxiety of cultural identity in a postcolonial world in the East, and which is pervaded by an urgent sense of strife and confrontation, one almost forgets that many people come to literature and literary study in the first place for another, altogether different reason, a perhaps simpler but more joyful reason, for what Roland Barthes once called "le plaisir du texte." In her vision of a "politicized" comparative literature that has discarded aesthetic values along with formalism, there is little room for such a pleasure. But are we supposed to appreciate a work of literature only as a social document, a profession of ideological commitment, a political manifesto, a manifestation of cultural identity, or an expression of nationalist sentiment? Are we to consider the "purely aesthetic" as always completely opposed to the "purely" political? For the Chinese and the student of Chinese literature, the message that literature and politics are connected is not news, and the implications of insisting that this connection is the only aspect of literature worthy of study are too obviously ominous to be ignored.

In the introductory essay in *Canadian Review of Comparative Literature*, Jonathan Hart does not speak of the situation of comparative studies in terms of a dramatic contrast between the death and decay in the West and a new birth and growth in the postcolonial world. Instead, he speaks of the "expansion" of comparative literature, by which he means the constant crossing of linguistic and cultural boundaries, "an increase in consciousness or self-consciousness about our methods and ideological assumptions and not some imperial project."⁶ What prompts comparatists to such self-consciousness is again literary theory from structuralism to deconstruction, from formalism to Marxism and feminism, from Roman Jakobson to Roland Barthes and Jacques Derrida. When he discusses the challenge to Western literature or traditional Eurocentric ideas, Hart also mentions "theorists of the subaltern, colonial, and postcolonial, such as Edward Said, Gayatri Spivak, and Homi Bhabha," as important forces behind the new waves of cultural critique and postcolonial theory.⁷ Here again, hardly anything is said about China, Japan, Korea, or East Asian literatures and cultures, even though many articles dealing with East-West comparative studies have appeared in *Canadian Review of Comparative Literature* in recent years, and other journals, notably *Comparative Literature Studies*, regularly feature such articles. This lack of attention to East-West comparative studies is not that surprising when we consider that the challenge to traditional approaches of Western literary studies comes, after all, from within the institutions of Western literary studies, and that theories of Orientalism and postcolonialism represent precisely some of the latest transformations of Western literary theory in those very institutions. This is quite clear in reading the Bernheimer report to the ACLA and the various essays in response to that report. They debate on the nature of comparative literature, its methodology and content, and they question whether it should be concerned with literature or with cultural studies, but nowhere is East-West comparative literature mentioned and discussed as a potential area of development. However, when I remark that East-West comparative studies have been more or less neglected by scholars in their review of the field, I am not saying that these scholars are being unfair or myopic, but acknowledging the marginal position of East-West comparative studies in a field that has traditionally been concerned with themes and concepts in European literatures and their relations and pointing to the tremendous potential of East-West comparative studies as a largely uncharted area.

I do not mean that the importance of East-West comparative literature is totally unacknowledged, nor do I suggest that this is a completely new area in which no work has been done. East-West, or more specifically, Chinese-Western comparative literature has been the subject of intense study and debate by scholars in Taiwan and Hong Kong since the early 1970s, and comparative literature as a new field of study also opened up in 1980 on the mainland. In the United States, East-West comparative studies have also found a few hospitable islands such as Indiana University at Bloomington. Conferences have been held, and many fine articles have been published in a number of journals dedicated to literary studies. The works accomplished by comparatists in Taiwan, Hong Kong, mainland China, and elsewhere provide a solid basis to build upon as well as many lessons to learn from, and the significance of such works cannot be doubted. Claudio Guillén, whose book is in my judgment the best and most nuanced introduction to comparative literature so far, not only generously acknowledges the importance of East-West comparative studies, but also declares that comparatists engaged in East-West studies "are probably the most daring scholars in the field, above all from a theoretical point of view."[8] Compared with the well-established comparative studies of European or Euro-American literatures, however, East-West comparative literature is still relatively new, and its viability is not without challenge from different quarters of the academy. "This type of investigation," as Guillén puts it, "would not have been regarded as legitimate thirty or forty years ago. Comparativism was then dedicated to international relations, to what Jean-Marie Carré called, unforgettably, *rapports de fait*. And even today quite a number of scholars tolerate nongenetic studies of supranational categories with great distaste or scant enthusiasm."[9] I am quite sure that distaste, skepticism, and even outright hostility are not unfamiliar to students of comparative literature, especially of East-West comparative literature.

The dismissal, or at least skepticism, of the very possibility of Chinese-Western comparative literature usually combines two quite different lines of argument: a positivistic one that points out the lack of any significant contact (*rapports de fait*) between Chinese and Western literatures, especially in premodern history, and a cultural relativist one that emphasizes essential differences and tends to see China as the opposite of what the West is conceived to be. Such a combination plus a highly "politicized" view of what literary study should be, for example, is what we get in a recent critique of Chinese comparative literature as "idealistic" and "utopian." If traditional sinology errs, according to the author of that critique, in resisting contemporary Western theory by holding on to a naive belief in reality and textual meaning that can be recuperated by philological means, then, Chinese-Western comparative literature errs in subscribing to the wrong kind of theory of formalism and humanism, while both err in hoping for an objective, neutral, and ideology-free discourse of literary study. "Chinese comparative literature, particularly of premodern literature," we are told, "is essentially a *utopian* project." It is "inscribed" in an "impossible disciplinary space" because, aiming to reveal some shared theoretical concerns or to gain some insights in comparative poetics, Chinese-Western comparative literature cannot "address the radical alterity of Chinese cultural objects."[10] But from what perspective, or in whose eyes, do Chinese cultural objects become objects of "radical alterity"? The radical otherness in this formulation obviously presupposes an outside point of view;

that is to say, it is from a position in the West that one can speak of the alterity of Chinese literature and gauge how radical that alterity is. To be able to make such a claim, however, one must also claim to know the totality of something as huge and complex as Chinese culture and literature, and also something equally huge and complex as the West and Western literature. Since it is unreasonable to expect such total knowledge, chances are that the "radical alterity" ascribed to Chinese literature and culture presented in such an argument is based on a caricature of that culture and an unrepresentative selection, if not second-hand reports, of its literature.

But if the "radical alterity" of Chinese literature and culture is admittedly a Western ideological construct, why should we take it for granted as if it were a true representation of some distinctively Chinese essence beyond question or comparison? I am also puzzled by the charge of utopianism and the repeated association of "utopia" or "utopian" with a naive, idealist avoidance of ideology, for surely utopia as the project or blueprint of an ideal society is nothing if not ideological and ideology-critical. Thomas More's *Utopia* may appear to be a fantasy, but as Dominic Baker-Smith observes in a recent study, it is a "political fantasy."[11] More's concern in that famous book, as Quentin Skinner reminds us, "is not merely or even primarily with the new island of Utopia; it is with 'the best state of a commonwealth.' "[12] To achieve that best state of a commonwealth, or to put it in a modern idiom, to establish the ideal social and political system, More in *Utopia* proposed, among other things, the abolition of private ownership and a lifestyle that can be called a simple model of communism. For the last two centuries, utopia and utopianism have often been related to the ideology of socialism. To be sure, Marx and Engels dismissed utopian socialism as naive and reactionary, as superseded by Marxism as the truly scientific theory of an ideal society, but many eminent Marxists in our time, notably Herbert Marcuse and Ernst Bloch, have retained the utopian vision as transformative and revolutionary.[13] On the other hand, utopianism has also been related to the state socialism in our time that became political reality in China, Eastern Europe, and the former Soviet Union, but as Krishan Kumar forcefully argues, though socialism may be utopian, utopia is much more than socialism, and the collapse of failed state socialism since 1989 does not necessarily spell the end of socialism, the end of history, and certainly not the end of utopia.[14]

In any case, if one cannot be ideology free, as David Palumbo-Liu, the author of the above-mentioned critique, insists, it would then seem truly "utopian," in the sense he uses in that critique, that is, being naive and naively wishful, to hope that every comparativist could be persuaded to abandon his or her "utopian" ideology and conform to the particular kind of ideology he recommends. This is not to say that Palumbo-Liu recommends a particularly bad ideology, but even a good ideology can become unbearably repressive when it is the only game in town, the only ideology allowed in intellectual pursuit. Indeed, that is precisely where utopia, which is by definition a good or ideal society with a set of detailed and usually mandatory rules or codes of conduct, turns sour and becomes repressive and positively awful: *corruptio optimi pessima.* To require subscription to that particular ideology as the precondition for franchising Chinese comparative literature would then lead to the opposite of an idealist utopia: the intolerance and coerced uniformity characteristic of a totalizing and totalitarian anti-utopia. To many Chinese, that highly regimented, ideological anti-utopia is the least attractive of all constructs in theory as it is in political reality, and utopianism has such real consequences in life that it can hardly ever be related to an ideology-free condition, a sort of political naïveté.

The obviously different understanding of utopia, ideology, and the like seems to me an indication of the very difference between comparative literature as it is generally understood in the West and Chinese-Western comparative literature we are trying to establish as a field of study, between what is currently of central concern in Western literary and cultural studies and what is apparently marginal for such studies. That difference is also implicitly present in Palumbo-Liu's critique because what he pronounces as impossible is not comparative literature in general, which is not only possible but has been well established in a "disciplinary space," but specifically "Chinese comparative literature." This is hardly surprising. The very effort to identify certain points or degrees of comparability between Chinese and Western literatures and cultures is likely on the one hand to arouse the suspicion and contempt of some sinologists or Chinese traditionalists who insist on the unique and incomparable nature of things Chinese, and on the other to meet with doubt and indifference from those theoreticians and critics who thrive on the discourse of difference and cultural relativism. Against all these odds, however, it is still worth trying to help promote cross-cultural understanding and tolerance in this fragmented world of ours through comparative studies of literatures and cultures. Is this utopian and idealistic in the pejorative sense that Palumbo-Liu uses the terms? If so, then one may as well embrace negativity, relativism, and skepticism as the only authentic view of the world, one may as well embrace Rudyard Kipling's hackneyed "East is East, and West is West" as some kind of a sacred truth and deny that humanity shares a common ground.

Perhaps the most eloquent refutation of the impossibility argument comes from Taiwan, Hong Kong, and mainland China, where comparative studies, and especially Chinese-Western comparative studies, have been established as a lively and burgeoning field of literary study. The best works of Chinese scholarship on premodern literature, philosophy, and the other aspects of the entire cultural tradition, as exemplified by Qian Zhongshu's *Tanyi lu* (Discourses on the literary art), *Guanzhui bian* (The tube and awl chapters), and his other critical essays, are often comparative in nature.[15] Although Qian's works cannot be neatly classified under the rubric of comparative literature, they discuss the problems and illuminate the features of Chinese texts in the light of other texts and texts from other traditions and thus set up an inspiring model for our comparative work. Not only has Chinese comparative literature become established in Taiwan, Hong Kong, and the Chinese mainland, but some comparatists have called for the formation of a "Chinese school." John Deeney advocates it in Hong Kong, many scholars on the mainland try to promote the idea, and more recently Chen Peng-hsiang, who first called for it in 1976, published an essay in Taiwan to expound the theory and strategies for the establishment of the "Chinese school" of comparative literature.[16] As discussions of the proposed "Chinese school" often make reference and analogy to the so-called French and American schools in comparative literature, it seems appropriate here to reflect on the old opposition between these two "schools" in the history of comparative literature, an opposition that needs to be understood in its historical context.

As many scholars have pointed out, the conventional labels of these "schools" are misleading, because they suggest the presence of specific programs and concerted efforts to implement them, which actually never happened. What did exist was the difference in emphasis, in methodological priorities, and in the very concept of comparative literature, but those changes constituted different paradigms for literary studies rather than particular "schools" of scholarship. Guillén prefers to indicate the changes by such terms as the "French hour" and the "American hour," and the temporal notion suggests some crucial modification in the concept of comparative literature before and after the Second World War. The French emphasis on influence, transmission, communication, transit, and so on was, as Guillén remarks, "based on *national literatures*—on their preeminence—and on the connections between them."[17] After the horrors of the Second World War had fully exposed the danger of nationalist sentiment and the patriotic ideologies underlying such sentiment, there emerged among intellectuals as well as the general public a widely shared desire to transcend the narrow boundaries of nationhood and to cultivate a largeness of mind, a greater appreciation of human life, and the spirit of humanism. When nationalism lost its allure in the postwar world, the older concept of comparative literature based on European national literary traditions and their relations also appeared inadequate and limiting. In the meantime, large numbers of writers and scholars who had immigrated to America were able to cut themselves off from the horrors of Nazi-invaded Europe and foster an intellectual life of new ideas, a new vision, a new concept of comparative literature and culture. "It is difficult for almost any European country to overcome the instincts of nationalism," says Guillén, who lived in the United States for many years himself when Spain was under the Fascist dictatorship of Franco, "whereas in America and above all in exile the concept of Europe arises naturally—from a distance—a vision of an entity, a break with the follow-the-leader mentality, apt innovations for the New World."[18] If the emphasis on national literatures, on the influence of one national heritage upon another, and its implicit ethnocentrism constituted the core of what Guillén calls the French hour, in the postwar atmosphere of humanism and intellectual cosmopolitanism, interliterary and interdisciplinary studies beyond national boundaries characterize what came to be known as the American school of comparative literature. That is to say, what Bassnett disparages as the "ahistoricity" of the American school was itself a product of historical conditions, and the rejection of nationalism was dictated by postwar realization of the danger and limitations of nationalism, ethnocentrism, and the various patriotic ideologies. The change in the concept of comparative literature and the difference between the French and the American "schools" are all part of the historical transformations in our times, but there was never a consciously formed French school, nor was there an American school. Like many other "schools" in literary history, such terms are often coined after the fact for the convenience of periodization or classification, but rarely represent programs meticulously carried out according to some studied plans and premeditated designs.

In that sense, then, whether there will be a particular "Chinese school" of comparative literature is almost an irrelevant issue, or at least not an urgent one. What is of consequence is the achievement of Chinese comparatists, their important books and essays, the intellectual fruit of their scholarly investigations and critical studies. Given the marginality of East-West comparative studies today in the eyes of many Western scholars of comparative literature, the most effective response to the challenge is not a call to form a particular school, but the solidity of scholarship, the significant result of intellectual pursuit from Chinese comparatists that cannot be ignored in any responsible consideration of comparative literature in general. In doing our work, we certainly have our own perspective, our own emphasis, and our own characteristics, but that is naturally determined by who we are and what we do as comparatists working with Chinese and other literatures rather than the result of a conscious effort at defining our works in terms of national character or a specifically Chinese cultural identity. Scholarship is ultimately a personal commitment. In the careful examination and critical study of texts, ideas, and traditions, it is often the work of a personality, the qualities of an individual mind, rather than its conformity to a collective way of thinking, that leaves the most enduring impression on us.

Guillén's notion of comparative literature, which is based not on collective or national but on "supranational" considerations, seems to me a suitable concept to start with in our effort at Chinese-Western comparisons. The notion of "supranationality" locates the point of departure not in national traditions or their interrelationships, but in the mediating ground beyond the "national" and even the "international." It guards against any abuse of scholarship for nationalistic purposes. As Guillén reminds us with Goethe, "There is no patriotic art and no patriotic science."[19] Dissociated from national literatures and their interrelationships, which are often understood in unequal, hierarchical terms of influence and indebtedness, center and periphery, or Western impact and Eastern response, comparative literature can now be placed between the extremes of a narrow-minded nationalism and an uprooted cosmopolitanism, and be understood as an effort to examine a set of problems between the local and the universal, the one and the many, and especially in East-West studies, as a set of theoretical problems arising in the basic issues of language, writing, and the reading of literature. Guillén offers three models of supranationality that lay the ground for comparison with reference to (a) "common cultural premises," or (b) "common sociohistorical conditions," or (c) "common problems in the theory of literature."[20] The first model includes comparative studies of works that share the same cultural background, Western or Eastern, but do not cross over. Much of traditional comparative studies of European literature falls under this category, and using this model, we may examine literary relations within the East Asian context among Chinese, Japanese, and Korean writers and their works, both the shared features of cultural premises and the differences or variations.

The second model of supranationality, the one that lays the ground for comparison with reference to common sociohistorical conditions, is interdisciplinary. Genre studies with a historical or sociological slant fall under this category.

The third model of supranationality, the one that lays the ground for comparison with reference to common problems in the theory of literature, is predicated on a theoretical framework, the identifying of a specific problem or problems that go beyond a single cultural background and the relative homogeneity of a given historical period. Necessarily transcending cultural boundaries and not limited to the investigation of parallel sociohistorical conditions, East-West comparative studies, says Guillén, "offer especially valuable and promising opportunities for investigations based on the third model."[21] That is to say, East-West studies necessarily form an alliance with the theory of literature. The three models in Guillén's book do not of course exhaust all possibilities, and we do not have to be particularly conscious of the application of a certain model in any actual comparison, but they do offer a useful grid, and the idea that East-West studies are closely related to the interest and concerns of literary theory provides a particularly firm ground for comparison in our effort to engage Chinese and Western literatures and cultures.

To be sure, any critical study of literature has its theoretical underpinnings, but because East-West comparative literature, especially when dealing with premodern works, stretches beyond the bounds of shared cultural premises and does not build on *rapports de fait* or the positivistic notion of source and influence, it looks especially to literary theory for a strong argument for its validity and values. Actual contacts and literary relations between the East and the West of course continue to offer possibilities for further exploration, but what makes such exploration new and truly enlightening is precisely a high degree of theoretical sophistication and the valuable insight it yields into the very nature and problems of East-West comparative studies.[22] It is certainly not fortuitous that the growth of East-West studies coincides with the development of critical theories. Given the importance of literary theory as the very foundation of East-West comparative literature, however, we cannot ignore the crucial question of the very real relationship between theory and the literary works we compare. This is an old question often raised but not solved. In one of the earlier reflections on the possibilities of Chinese-Western comparative literature, Heh-hsiang Yuan puts the question most astutely when he remarks that "the major problem facing those of us who adopt (and even adapt) Western critical theories in analyzing and evaluating Chinese literary works is applicability."[23] The relationship here is clearly formulated as one between Western theory and Chinese texts, and the tacit or explicit epithet for theory is indeed *Western*. This becomes a "major problem," some critics argue, because Western theory is culturally specific and therefore does not apply to non-Western texts. That may be so, but I take this to be the least of the problems, because what is theoretical about theory is precisely its potential to transcend cultural specificities and historical contingencies. It is this transcending quality—shall we say the theoreticality of theory?—that makes theory singularly transferable. Theories or ideas do travel, and that is why Guillén sees, quite rightly, literary theory as the basis or framework for East-West studies that often compare works that do not share a cultural background and were created under very different social and historical conditions. Therefore, I believe that the problem Yuan refers to does not come from the cultural specificity of literary theory but from the unequal relationship between Western theory and Chinese works. So long as the West supplies the critical theories and the East provides the texts for analysis and criticism, and so long as East-West comparative literature is thought to be just a matter of application, the problem will persist and replicate itself as the various Western theoretical concepts and approaches are tried out and applied to Chinese texts one after another.

What I am suggesting is that perhaps the very idea of application is what many comparatists have come to see as a major problem. The theoretical framework in Guillén's third model cannot be a ready-made Western product that hardly accommodates the situation of reading a non-Western text, but rather the framework must be examined in the very process of its production so that we understand the basic issues and phenomena from which theoretical concepts and approaches arise as responses. That is to say, rather than start with a theoretical framework with its specific devices and methodologies ready to be applied to whatever works and texts we read, we should try to identify and frame the theoretical problem anew each time by tracing the formation of theory back to some basic issues and phenomena, to the basic questions and cultural premises of language, grammar, expression, representation, textuality, reading, understanding, criticism, and interpretation. Such questions tend to be more general than specific theoretical formulations, and if they are also theoretical—and they are—perhaps we may say that they are prototheoretical: they raise questions of the first order that are common to different literary and cultural traditions and occupy the area of what Guillén calls "supranationality." In dealing with such questions, we are not applying any theory as a given or a ready-made a priori, but we come to a position that makes it possible to see where and how a theoretical problem arises, and to what extent it can be challenged, revised, and reformulated in the perspective of East-West comparative studies.

Let us take the question of parallelism discussed in Guillén's book as an example. As Guillén recapitulates it, parallelism is one of the basic issues in the conceptualization of poetry as well as one of its formal features. Roman Jakobson, Michael Riffaterre, Emilio Alarcos Llorach, James Kugel, Wolfgang Steinitz, and V. M. Zhirmunsky have all discussed it, and Guillén gives us a wealth of examples quoted from Russian epics, Castilian *romanceros*, Provençal love songs, Chinese *Shijing*, and Nahuatl ballads. In a historical study of diverse poems from the medieval period to the sixteenth century, Zhirmunsky discovers that parallelism becomes less and less important as syllable count and end rhyme gradually gain ground. Thus he comes to the conclusion that "the installation of the end rhyme as an autonomous and obligatory means of metrical linkage leads evidently at the same time to a retreat of parallelism and alliteration."[24] And indeed, in modern free verse, which has forsaken rhyme and quantitative syllable counting, as the examples from Walt Whitman, Vladimir Mayakovsky, and Vicente Aleixandre clearly show, parallelism or syntactic repetition seems to have made a remarkable comeback. All these seem to imply that parallelism and end rhyme are to some extent mutually exclusive. When we consider Zhirmunsky's theoretical formulation from the perspective of East-West comparative studies, however, it becomes highly problematic because parallelism and end rhyme are found together in classical Chinese poetry. As Yu-kung Kao and Tsu-lin Mei have argued in an important essay on the rhetorical features of Tang poetry, parallelism becomes the basic structural principle in Chinese poetry that supports Jakobson's theory of poetic function as "similarity superimposed on contiguity," even though Jakobson formulated his theory with Western examples in his mind.[25] Andrew Plaks also maintains that "the workings of parallelism seem to go farther in Chinese usage than in most comparable cases, perhaps even farther than in the poetics of the Hebrew psalms."[26] Probably because of "the predominance of dualistic thinking in Chinese philosophical discourse" and the "various formulae of Chinese bipolar logic, such as *yin-yang*, *kang-jou* and the like," Plaks finds parallelism not only in Chinese poetry, but in the dual constructions in prose works, novels, and dramatic works as well.[27] In Chinese literature, parallelism and rhyme coexist to such an extent that they play an important role even in genres other than the formally more stringent regulated verse (*lüshi*), as in the southern style *sao* or in rhyme-prose (*fu*), and they do not become mutually exclusive even in modern verse. This different correlation between parallelism and rhyme may have something to do with the monosyllabic and tonal structure of the Chinese language as distinct from the largely polysyllabic and accented structure of European languages. Guillén mentions the pervasive presence of parallelism in Chinese *sao*, *fu*, and "balanced prose" (*pianwen*), and realizes that "the phonemic function of the tones in Chinese permits a very complex formal counterpoint, not limited to the parallelistic framework [that is, as Steinitz or Zhirmunsky have understood it]," and he adds that "it is worthwhile to distinguish between different genres, styles, and historical periods if we do not intend to subordinate the variety of poetry to the unity of one poetics to an exaggerated extent."[28] Certainly we do not, but I want to suggest that we at least have some knowledge of the different possibilities in the relationship of parallelistic structure and end rhyme when we reflect on parallelism as a basic feature in poetry. To test Zhirmunsky's conclusion against Chinese examples is not to arrive at a universal poetics, but to guard against the possible danger of mistaking a Western theoretical formulation based on limited examples for a universal and universalized conclusion. What may be gained, then, is not a unified notion but a better understanding of the nature and formation of parallelism in different languages.

Parallelism of course provides an appropriate metaphor for comparative literature itself, because what we do in comparing works and concepts in different literary and cultural traditions is to line them up in two or more series and to work out their connections, similarities, contrasts, and patterns in mutual illumination, just as we read a parallelistic couplet in a Chinese poem. Texts, images, literary genres, or movements from two or more traditions are put together and fall into a meaningful pattern, just as words in the two lines of a couplet bear on one another in meaning, sound, tone, and grammatical function. Parallelism indicates that a poetic line never exists in isolated suspension but always forms a connection with another line and is thus inherently comparative in nature. It is an apt metaphor because the relation of the two lines, if we remember how it works in a Chinese couplet, is not a simple repetition or application: the second line never simply follows, imitates, or exactly copies what the first line proposes. The two parallel lines carry on a dialogue, raise questions and supply answers, and stand on equal footing; the couplet simply does not work if the second line does nothing but repeat the first. That is to say, East-West comparative studies cannot simply be a matter of application of Western theory or critical methodology to Eastern texts but must be based on theoretical issues that are common and shared by Chinese and Western traditions in different but comparable manifestations.

Once we realize that the simple application of a theory causes more problems than solutions, we will perhaps become more truly theoretical in the sense of being more self-conscious and self-critical about the theoretical assumptions we employ in our comparative studies. The biggest misunderstanding of comparative literature is to see it as the juxtaposition of two literary works or two discourses, the theoretical and the literary. More specifically with regard to Chinese-Western comparative literature, it is never simply the juxtaposition of Western literary texts or Western critical theories with Chinese texts or poetics. The comparative work is always something to be redefined through a rigorous study of the basic issue, a new set of problems that can be raised and explored only in the comparison of different works, texts, and theoretical notions. What Roland Barthes said twenty years ago about the change in the concept of language and the emergence of interdisciplinary studies may be modified to describe the kind of challenge we face in developing an East-West comparative study of literature. Interdisciplinarity, says Barthes,

> cannot be accomplished by the simple confrontation of specialist branches of knowledge. Interdisciplinarity is not the calm of an easy security; it begins *effectively* (as opposed to the mere expression of a pious wish)—perhaps even violently, via the jolts of fashion—in the interests of a new object and a new language neither of which has a place in the field of the sciences that were to be brought peacefully together, this unease in classification being precisely the point from which it is possible to diagnose a certain mutation.[29]

The kind of study we try to envision cannot be the simple confrontation or juxtaposition of sinology or Asian studies on the one hand and a Eurocentric comparative literature or Western literary theory on the other, it must be established in a third area, a mediating ground on which East-West comparative literature will acquire its own identity as different from either of the specialist branches mentioned above. To accomplish that task is a difficult challenge, but it is a challenge worthy of our efforts.

Chapter 2

The Utopias of Discourse: On the Impossibility of Chinese Comparative Literature

DAVID PALUMBO-LIU

The topic of this volume, which addresses a basic tension between those who might be called "hard-line sinologists" and those who promote the use of modern Western critical and theoretical terminology in the field of Chinese literature, is one of tremendous complexity. Not only do these issues have everything to do with the discipline we call Chinese comparative literature, they also inform Chinese studies, East Asian studies, and, indeed, overlap to a great degree with the general debate over the "state of the humanities."

Given this ever widening sphere of significance, in this essay I have necessarily both narrowed the focus of "the debate" and overgeneralized the case, yet I believe the main contours I sketch of this problematic are valid. My main goal is to show how and why the task of Chinese comparative literature, particularly of premodern literature, is essentially a utopian project. To understand its utopian nature one must first examine the discourses that have inscribed that impossible disciplinary space. Here is how I would characterize the main split.

"Sinologists" favor what they see as a purely neutral (i.e., non-culture-based, nonideological) "philological" project immune from the contingencies of interpretation, which takes recourse to the notion of a perfectly recuperable language. When applied to the act of criticism, this leads to a supposedly neutral recovery of literary works that "restores" the text in a way that vitiates any possibility of distortion or variance from some final truth embedded in the language of the text.

"Theorists," on the other hand, while arguing for wide latitude in the application of Western criticism and theory to Chinese texts, have yet to seriously address the radical alterity of Chinese cultural objects, which evolves from a cultural, historical, and linguistic distance that cannot be "disciplined" by either their faith in a pure "science" of the text (such as that which formalist poetics promise) or a hermeneutic regimen that seeks not so much to recover meaning from across that distance as to understand the text according to new critical conceptualizations.[1] To understand the utopian aspects of both these critical operations, we should first distinguish three key terms: "discourse," "criticism," and "theory."

Discourse and Topos

"Discourse" has its root in the Latin, "currere," which means "to run, move." The *Oxford English Dictionary* locates the earliest usage of "discourse" as "moving to and fro, conversation, discourse." The element of movement so crucial to the word is evinced in Elyot's phrase, "The naturall discourse of the sunne." Later, the word takes on a meaning particular to ratiocination, denoting an act of understanding, by which one *passes* from premises to consequences. For example, Wesley writes in 1788, "Discourse, strictly speaking, is the motion or progress of the mind from one judgement to another." Most important for the matter at hand, in 1864 Bowen notes that "discourse indicates the operation of *comparison*."[2] Thus, in *discoursing*, one moves from one topic to another in an orderly, logical fashion. Here it is important to underscore the necessary *orderliness* of discourse, that quality which isolates it from mere babble. From the essentially *verbal* performance of "discoursing" we derive the noun—the "orderly" logic that informs the verbal performance fixes it as a stabilized, and stabilizing, object—discourse.

It is very important that we be able to apply discourse to and in various spaces, and here there is an interesting overlap in the idea of *topos*, which may be linked to classical rhetoric's idea of *topoi*, or "topics," that is, a set of rhetorical situations that the orator is to entertain. Discourse then reaches across spaces (*topoi*) and verbal situations (topics), drawing things together under its analytic influence. Most important, discourse re-inscribes and *reconfigures* its object according to its mode of representation and analysis, and this mode of analysis necessarily involves a *comparative* act that draws out and bridges the local, logical relations between topics and *topoi*.

We now must ask what kind of critical or theoretical language is then able to "discourse upon" and thereby represent the Chinese literary text from the position of contemporary Western literary studies. What discourse is able to link the worlds of premodern China and contemporary Western culture—to translate that difference? I contend that given the presumptions of our dominant critical positions, such an "adequate" comparative critical discourse inhabits only that impossible space perceptible precisely at the moment of its failure to manifest itself in practice according to the logic of its own terms—it is *without* a space, that is, *u-topian*.

Criticism and Theory

To understand how this may be so, we must address the practice of criticizing and theorizing premodern Chinese literature, and to do that we must first distinguish between criticism and theory.

In very simple terms, criticism involves the evaluation of aesthetic effects and is text specific. Its resulting interpretive discourse is *mimetic*, substituting one object for another: the "hidden" aesthetic value of the original textual object is illuminated in the spectrum of its critical objectification.

Within its *mimetic* practice, literary *criticism* yields two possibilities—that of producing the textual object in a fullness available only through the critical operation, or else a revision that reconfigures the object in a way that realizes its immanent aesthetic significance. While the difference between these two critical modes may be a matter of degree rather than kind, criticism as revision is the main target of attack by traditional sinologists, who argue against the "distortion" of the meaning that such revision entails.

Theory involves a hypothesis regarding the mode of literary production. It is not text specific; it necessarily uses *texts* to ground its larger hypothesis, and its resulting discourse is *speculative*.

Within its speculative practice, *theory*'s idealist base is its attempt to bridge a hypothetical reality with concrete textualities, reducing literary production to a single predominant modality. And as such, for traditional sinologists, Western theory poses the threat of creating a hypothesis inadequately grounded in the reality of the Chinese text as they have construed it, a hypothesis that then has the potential for spreading a theoretical "virus" across all of Chinese literary studies.

Criticism, Theory, and the Case of Premodern Chinese Literature

Having made this rough distinction, we can now speak of the specifics of Chinese comparative literature. In the case of premodern Chinese literature, the task is profoundly difficult—for Western criticism in this instance seeks an object that is commensurate with a *radically* Other object that requires more "explanation" perhaps than less remote literatures. It involves a tricky balancing act—to criticize, comment upon the text, but not to "distort" it. Sinologists like Paul Kroll are explicit in their praise for those appliers of Western critical discourse who exercise "restraint."[3] (And in this particular case Kroll is praising Stephen Owen.) But now we must ask, how does one know when one has stepped over that "critical" threshold that marks off the "proper" critical act from that which departs from its mimetic function? When is the critical act productive of "genetically correlative" objects, and when are its products monsters? To answer this, there is simply nothing else to turn to than the text at hand in its "precritical," "pristine" linguistic state. Thus it is no wonder that the center of the debate is *language*.

This attention to language may be found in debates about how to translate traditional Chinese poetry. For example, we can look at Paul Kroll's critique of Stephen Owen's *Poetry of the Early T'ang* and Owen's response. Owen points out that their difference lies precisely in Kroll's belief that a word has one true meaning—an absolute center of meaning.[4] Traditional sinological literary criticism relies on such a notion of a "basic" language that can be reconstituted via rigorous philological effort. This project finds its roots in Orientalist philology, which sought to reinvent the Orient from the position of a privileged observer. Renan, for example describes himself "there, at the center, inhaling the perfume of everything, judging, comparing, combining, inducing—in this way I shall arrive at the very system of things."[5] We find here a sense of confidence based on linguistic mastery but, behind that, a *cultural* mastery—the ability of one "culture" to explain, analyze, critique, and represent another by way of an excavation of its "real" language. Through this philological regimen, one is able to stake out one's mastery of the Other and position oneself as the *necessary* conduit through which understanding must flow or, to stick with our notion of *discourse*, that discourse through which radically different spaces can be linked.

It is precisely such self-confidence, based on linguistic certainty and a presumption of cultural authority, that leads to a situation wherein, rather than any rigorous *critique* of the application of Western criticism to classical Chinese literature, the debate all too quickly becomes displaced, turning into a coy criticism of the *language of criticism* ("A grotesque *patois* compounded of Northrop Frye and Jacques Derrida which seems to be in fashion lately among many students of Chinese literature")[6] that supposedly provokes the same reaction in all clear-thinking individuals. In an important essay, Jonathan Chaves speaks of "the repulsive jargon which drives so many away from Deconstructionism [sic] *through sheer instinct*."⁷ But we are called upon to accept this *prerational* consensus without any sense of what it is exactly that should repulse us, other than the fact that it presents, to Chaves, an ideologically problematic viewpoint.

Another way that certain critical discourses are attacked in rather unscholarly ways is by claiming that all this is simply a passing fad (in the same review, Kroll dismisses these "fashionable western interpretive concepts").⁸ The rhetoric employed here is of dismissal, rather than of substantive critique (engagement in Western criticism is seen to be transient, it is used only by impressionable youths, its language is decidedly monstrous, i.e., having no intelligible category or form, meaningless). All this presumes that the history of literary criticism has indeed come to its final resting place, and that critical paradigms are set for life. We should try to better understand exactly what kind of critical paradigms have dominated premodern Chinese literary studies, and what the perceived threat to their critical hegemony is.

The most sustained criticism of the use of recent Western criticism and theory is found in an all-too-brief paper delivered by Jonathan Chaves at the 1990 Association of Asian Studies meeting and published in *CLEAR*. Chaves begins by noting that "[there are] *two* crises in the humanities: (1) The well-known one which consists of a general falling-off of interest in the Humanities; and (2) a less-recognized, internal crisis of the ideologization of the Humanities themselves, which indeed may be partially responsible for the loss of interest."⁹ This charge is crucial, for it brings forth the issue of ideology and the quest for a nonideological critical discourse. And the tension between the two informs the base of the utopian critical projects that are the subject of this essay.

Now the fact is, it is always easier to see someone else's ideology than it is to see one's own. One's own seems rather invisible, but is articulated in two ways: negatively (in the polemic negation of others as "ideological," we find an index to the ideological suppositions of the speaker); and "naturally" (ideology appears in statements such as "that is the way things are, have to be, will always be, need to be"). This latter mode of articulation removes itself from debate precisely because there is nothing to debate about—the "other" is, simply, wrong, and here, wrong because it is ideological.

Speaking of such attacks on theory, Paul De Man notes that "the question ... is not even one in need of discussion. For all people of good will and good sense, the matter has long since been settled once and for all. What is left is a matter of law-enforcement rather than a critical debate."¹⁰ Ironically, De Man's description of the pseudo-debate echoes this passage from C. S. Lewis quoted approvingly by Chaves:

Utopias of Discourse 41

> [These "Vigilant" critics find] in every turn of expression the symptom of attitudes which it is a matter of life and death to accept or resist. [The reader of such critics] must . . . accept their (implied) conception of the good life if you are to accept their criticism. That is, you can admire them as critics only if you also revere them as sages. And before we revere them as sages we should need to see their whole system of values set out, not as an instrument of criticism but standing on its own feet and offering its credentials—commending itself to its proper judges, to moralists, moral theologians, psychologists, sociologists, or philosophers. For we must not run around in a circle, accepting them as sages because they are good critics and believing them good critics because they are sages.[11]

While Chaves modestly does not claim sagehood, what is disappointing in his paper is that he really never gives us a good reason why ideology is (necessarily) "bad." In fact, it becomes clear that it is only that ideology with which he disagrees that is to be eradicated—the ideology he counterposes to it is of course acceptable. Ironically, that his own discourse is equally ideological is evident in its *replication* of exactly that rhetoric that he faults as "ideological" in others.

For example, Chaves claims that

> the one thread that appears to run through all the plethora of critical approaches today is a type of tendentiousness, on overly urgent desire to assert or prove the correctness of a certain theory, whose application will unlock the hidden truth—even should that truth turn out to be the quite dogmatic claim that there is no truth, or that we can have no access to truth, at least through language.[12]

With the exception of that final phrase (which I come back to later), everything that precedes it rather accurately applies to Chaves as well. Note the "urgency" behind his naming of the double "crisis" that afflicts today's academy, note too the tendentiousness, as Chaves neatly includes "*all* the *plethora* of critical approaches" in his sweeping indictment. How is Chaves's critique not as ideological and dogmatic as that which he attacks? While this sort of broadside might be appropriate for the rhetorical situation for which it was written, it is unfortunate that such accusations were not refined or developed for publication.

Interestingly, a recent article in the *Times Literary Supplement* repeats Chaves's discomfort over the "zealousness" in recent theory: "Theory is suspended between an explanatory zeal, a rage to uncover, to reveal, and a fetishizing of incoherence that attaches *moral* significance . . . to something which has to do with style. We need to move away from morality, and back to language." While Chaves would not eliminate moralizing, but simply switch from the "deconstructionist" brand to the "High Aesthetic" brand, both his essay and the essay in the *TLS* end up by directly or indirectly instantiating a "pure" critical language that must be protected from ideology. But to perform such a prophylactic act ultimately requires, as the *TLS* essay suggests, that "such a criticism . . . be aware that literature is its own best theory. It would let, as it were, literature interpret itself."[13]

The ideological base of such an assertion is rather clear: while pointing to a moment when literature interprets itself, and thereby obviates the critical act by restoring itself to itself, the *discourse* that links those two (now) falsely distinct objects is inherently ideological, since it lays claim to being the sole mechanism behind that perfect mimetic transaction. However, in such a case, it is not clear how such criticism is not solipsistic. This sort of operation is supposed to guard against what Chaves criticizes in Stephen Owen: "He has revealed something not about the poem, but about his own metaphysical position."[14]

But this again begs the question—how do we distinguish what the poem says from what it says *to us*? The only way to do so is to efface the reader/critic, and let the poem "speak for itself." This calls for an absolutely naive sensibility that believes in, again, a self-evident, unambiguous, and unmediated text.

Yet in Chaves's own work, both in translation and criticism, which I generally admire, there is a clear sense of what he considers the "way of poetry." In his important essay, "Not the Way of Poetry,"[15] it is hard not to recognize Chaves's own prejudices toward the notions of poetry he notes in his Song poets. Furthermore, in the famous debate on translating Mei Yaochen (involving Chaves, Richard John Lynn, and, *in absentia*, Edward Schafer, and published in 1977 and 1978 in the *Journal of Asian Studies*),[16] Chaves admits the opacity of medieval Chinese poetry to modern Western eyes, and thereby allows *himself* interpretive latitude: "My position is that it is *impossible* to *prove* that any one of these [English equivalents to a couplet by Du Fu] is necessarily the poet's intention. Therefore, as translator, I reserve the right to use any one of them, *without* being accused of paraphrasing."[17] We see here precisely that gray area that supposedly marks off "legitimate" interpretation from "illegitimate" paraphrase. While here Chaves is speaking of the act of translation, I suggest that the debate involves a similar struggle to ascertain the "right" to read medieval Chinese poetry in ways that necessitate the choice of a modern reader in extrapolating meaning—if "proof" is not forthcoming, then the translator has to make a choice based on his or her understanding of medieval Chinese poetic discourse. At some point this *necessarily* involves a subjective decision. Yet if we cannot "prove" intention, is it not only possible but necessary to posit meanings that appear viable to us? I return to this question of interpretation at the conclusion of this essay; here I simply wish to stress that the issues Chaves opens up are complex and often paradoxical.

A critical discourse that claims such neutrality ultimately leads to a situation wherein Chaves rehearses exactly the movement of self-reflectivity he accuses Owen of, that is, of "meeting only himself." In Chaves's scheme, the text speaks only of itself. But this is only a thinly veiled illusion, for of course, literature is materialized in critical interpretation. Only here the critical voice is muted, and perhaps for that very reason it is all the more ideological, since it would have us believe that it does not exist as anything other than "natural" to the text itself.

Ironically, again, Chaves comes to mimic his object of criticism—for his assertion of a poem's necessary condition of absolute self-referentiality echoes precisely the (commonly misunderstood) assertion of deconstruction that "there is nothing outside the text." The motive for such a closed circuit is clear—it would deny the intrusive and distortive critical process and remove the "text" from danger, preserving the hegemony of an idealized pre-critical mode of access.

For Chaves and others, the "threat" of criticism is only surpassed by the threat of theory, for while criticism is more modestly rooted in specific texts, theory has the audacity to lay claim to the entire mode of textual production.

Theory

What concerns conservative critics most, it seems, is the deconstruction of "meaning" as absolute and recuperable, either because of a new hermeneutics that argues for a multiplicity of aesthetic effects and ideological determinants, or because of deconstruction's unanchoring of the signifier. This attack on deconstruction is of particular significance, for if there is no meaning, then we have "deconstructed" exactly that semantic base upon which sinology founds itself and upon which it claims to provide access to the "basic meaning" of premodern Chinese texts. The vehemence with which traditional sinological scholars attack recent Western criticism and theory is thus overdetermined by the specific institutional history of "oriental" studies, which has always founded itself on its unique ability to present the "meaning" of the Orient in its particularized discourse.

But nearly all of the attacks I have read on deconstruction are founded on basic and often embarrassing misreadings of it from both the right and the left. For example, Derrida's project centers, not so much on destroying "meaning" (for to claim to do so would be to fall into precisely the kind of metaphysical discourse that Derrida attempts to expose), but rather on critiquing the tenuous mechanics of the production of meaning. Deconstruction can be a powerful analytical tool against exactly what its critics accuse it of fostering—fascism and totalitarianism. Nor is it true that Derrida exempts himself from deconstruction—he explicitly puts his key terms "under erasure," and his self-parody (which Chaves calls "clowning") is a reflection of his self-critique. It is his awareness of the dimensions of his project and the manner in which metaphysics has permeated *all* Western discourse.

Again, it is absurd to believe that deconstruction sets itself forward as a political tool (ironically, the Right excoriates deconstruction for being "political," while the Left critiques it for not being political enough), for deconstruction sees itself as eminently deconstructible. Gayatri Spivak notes:

> Deconstruction cannot found a political program of any kind. Deconstruction points out that in constructing any kind of an argument we must move from implied premises, that must necessarily obliterate or finesse certain possibilities that question the availability of these premises in an absolutely justifiable way. . . . Deconstruction also insistently claims that there cannot be a fully practicing deconstructor. For, the subject is always centered as a subject. You cannot *decide* to *be* decentered and inaugurate a politically correct deconstructive politics. What deconstruction looks at is the limits of this centering, and points at the fact that these boundaries of the centering of the subject are indeterminate and that the subject (being always centered) is obliged to describe them as determinate. Politically, all this does not allow for fundamentalisms and totalitarianisms of various kinds, however seemingly benevolent. But it cannot be foundational. If one wanted to *found* a political project on deconstruction, it would be something like wishy-washy pluralism on the one hand, or a kind of irresponsible hedonism on the other.[18]

It seems clear to me that most of what we find in such attacks on deconstruction betrays the fact that most of these critics have never read Derrida seriously. Rather, it is most likely the case that such attacks are based on popular descriptions and distorted excerpts from Derrida and others—a most unscholarly basis for received knowledge. (We can imagine at what point Jonathan Chaves's "repulsion" caused him to stop reading and begin trashing.)

Ultimately, the traditional position asserts that premodern Chinese literature is inherently *un-theorizable*, since according to the precepts of traditional sinologists, our only mode of access to it hinges upon a belief in the recoverable concreteness of a language, a true and adequate translation of the "original." To move from the security of such "concreteness" thus involves a chance that not only that "concreteness" but the very discourse that makes it possible can be evaded. Any attempts to theorize premodern Chinese literature threaten to denature it, to turn it into an object of discursive violence.

But can even such a "conservative" criticism be free of a founding abstraction—a *theory* of criticism, with which to legitimize it as the necessary and commensurate discourse adequate to the task of speaking of, discoursing upon, and recovering premodern Chinese literature? In short, how can it presume to speak of the illegitimacy of theory, since it has yet to theorize its own Truth? A necessary move for any critical project, since it must not only be able to address one specific text but also put forward the hypothesis that its discourse can treat a multiplicity of textual "cases."

From the Other Side

But traditional sinologists are not alone in coming to such an impasse—for many "theorists" of Chinese comparative literature have yet to find a discourse that can make the connections required of comparative literature East and West. Here I consider two approaches which represent the main critical methodologies.

Many tend to side-step the issue of "basic" language and the hermeneutics it makes possible, but in so doing they at once detach themselves from the grounding that such an idealization offers. One way some have found to recuperate that stability is to eradicate interpretive indeterminacy by doing away with interpretation altogether. For example, we have André Lefevre's "Some Tactical Steps Toward a Common Poetics," which attempts a "science" of comparative literature. He proposes:

> A distinction between "literature" on the one hand, meaning the actual production of literature, of the "category of texts considered worth treating in the way that literary texts are treated" and what I propose to call "metaliterature" on the other hand. Literature is a non-scientific discipline, which has as its goal to describe experience and, in so doing, to gain and share knowledge—a knowledge not necessarily, and often emphatically not equivalent to intellectual knowledge alone. To achieve this goal literature has at its disposal a repertory of procedures, "an imaginary inventory of all possibilities of literary creation." This inventory can be analyzed and argued about in an intersubjectively testable, i.e., scientific manner. . . . The inventory includes, among other elements, genre, form, mode, style, rhetoric, prototypical char-

acters and situations, the natural language in which the work is written with all its ties to the culture of which it is to some extent the repository, plot, symbol, motif, allusion, etc. Needless to say, this inventory cuts across both linguistic and national boundaries and is open to modifications. Indeed, changes in literary history may be accounted for in terms of modifications of the inventory.[19]

Such faith in the scientific objectivity of such stock-taking leads Lefevre to an openly utopian vision:

> The theory quite simply does not allow any room for any centrism of any kind, be it Sinocentrism or Eurocentrism.... The theory does away with the opposition between "national" and "comparative" literature. What is really, testably, Chinese in Chinese poetry, for example, is the system of forms, genres, that China has devised. Research into this system is also research into comparative, or even "general" literature, because it is research into the inventory, and because that inventory is, and cannot possibly not be, world-wide and therefore transcends national boundaries at the very outset.[20]

Nevertheless, the entire project begs a number of questions. For example, Who's taking stock? What counts in each of these categories? Are such categories universal, and if not, what good is it to say, for example, that traditional Chinese ideas regarding the function and essence of genre are different from Western ones, if we retain "genre" as a fixed term? Is there even any consensus about the category of literature?

Heh-hsiang Yüan's essay, "East/West Comparative Literature: An Inquiry Into Possibilities," stakes out a moderate position—one which attempts to sketch out the possibilities of East/West comparative literature while retaining the category of literature. But Yüan too is attracted to the idea of an inventory of categories, and the point here, as with Lefevre, is to achieve the kind of objective neutrality, the kind of ideology-free discourse that traditional sinologists like Chaves propose. He writes:

> Differing literary traditions more than often elude our apprehension. But if we accept divergence without imposing any value judgment, without any discrimination, cultural variety and differences would then only constitute interesting subjects for exploration rather than prejudices for exploitation.[21]

To achieve this, Yüan suggests:

> The specific purpose of formulating a definition in any subject is to narrow down the scope and content of what one is going to investigate. Two elements are, therefore, to be considered: first, certain basic criteria upon which

an examiner is to make his selection of the subject matter; the other, subsequent to the choice, *proper methodology* which will ensure the success of the investigation.[22]

Yet at nearly every point in his plan for Chinese comparative literature we are faced with the necessity to *reinscribe* a subject position that "neutral criticism" tries to bracket out. Again the stubborn questions arise: how are "basic" criteria arrived at? What is the proper methodology? I must credit Yüan with pursuing these questions in an extremely serious way, and the essay stands in my mind as one of the very best of its sort; nevertheless, its one weakness for me is its overly optimistic faith in the critical project's ability and will to elide value and, by extension, ideology.[23]

Yüan himself seems to acknowledge this indirectly when he points out the contradictory aspects of comparative literature and retreats to the activity of pure description advocated in different ways by Lefevre and Chaves:

> Whatever definition we adopt, an inherent contradiction in the nature of our discipline remains unresolved. The attempt to define the subject of comparative literature is aimed at narrowing down the scope of our pursuit in order to clearly define its objectives.... To resolve cultural and philosophical diversities which give birth to divergent views calls for the most flexible description and the broadest scope for our discipline.... These two contradictory tendencies have made the definition of East-West comparative literature very difficult, if not impossible. At this stage, we perhaps should not attempt to set a definition for East-West comparative literature; instead, we should only describe what we are doing.[24]

Nevertheless, Yüan cannot resist one final utopian vision, in which all these ideologically unbounded methodologies result in making comparative literature "a universal medium of communication."[25]

The utopian projects outlined here, which are found in both "camps," are utopian largely because they seek, perhaps with all good intention, to erase ideology, to remove it from both aesthetic and formalistic criticism and theory. It is precisely the accusation of being ideological that has been central in attacks on recent Western theory and criticism. But as Gayatri Spivak notes, "Utopias are historical attempts at topographic descriptions that must become dissimulative if attempts are made to represent them adequately in actual social practice."[26] The utopia of an ideology-free criticism must mask its own ideology in order to appear natural.

The point is *not* simply that "everything is ideological," but rather that it is crucial to understand how ideology affects the very constitution of critical discourse. We need to realize that our critical and theoretical discourses are not simply "there," but are articulated within specific disciplinary and institutional spaces, which affect our conceptions of texts, our ways of talking about them, and whether or not we are listened to. Literature is not a science, nor can it interpret itself.

I would like to very modestly venture a suggestion that rather than banish ideology (as if it could be safely sequestered away from our discourse), why not acknowledge its presence (for good or ill) and seriously try to account for its various relationships to aesthetics and theory? Such a project would postpone the utopian moment and make it possible to rigorously engage in an analysis of discursive formations—their constitution, function, and residual effects on our understandings of literature. In the case of premodern Chinese literature, one could, for example, revisit the question of the constitution of literature—what kind of function did literature play at different moments in Chinese cultural history? How did poems mediate experience, and how was "experience" validated by cultural ideologies? What kinds of "speaking positions" did poets occupy, and how did those positions find legitimacy? Turning to a *real* critique of the application of Western theory and criticism—what kind of historical moment do we inhabit that has made traditional sinology susceptible to change? What is the cultural, political, and historical context of this debate?

I am not suggesting that we can ignore philology and linguistics, quite the contrary. Among those employing Western theories to interpret Chinese texts are those who reduce the Chinese text to the status of mere allegory for some Western cultural phenomenon, bracketing out the historical materiality of the Chinese text in order to work such tropological transformations. Such dematerializing of the Chinese text opens it up to the same "Orientalist" operations that "anti-Orientalists" decry. But to make "language" speak in one eternally enshrined, nonideological critical voice is to ignore the fact that even the "traditional" critical paradigms were once "revolutionary." Matthew Arnold would have been horrified by New Criticism. If we attempt to territorialize Chinese studies as somehow apart from the contemporary revisions of humanistic studies, if we are satisfied with glib dismissals rather than sustained intellectual debate, then we *will* find ourselves speaking only to ourselves, and there will be fewer and fewer of us listening.

Comparative literature is presented with the tremendous opportunity to enter the debates about culture and its transnational negotiations; Chinese comparative literature in particular has arrived at a moment when it must *face* the crisis in the humanities, rather than attempt to retreat from it and into an ideologically innocent utopian space. The stakes are simply too high. Such an attempt reminds me of the conservative criticism of multiculturalism—as if not recognizing the validity of multicultural analyses in the academy could negate the *fact* of a multicultural world.

I close with two short comments. First, returning to Jonathan Chaves's criticism of Stephen Owen as engaging in potentially "totalitarian" criticism—criticism which seeks to dehumanize—I find it remarkable that Chaves would castigate Owen for taking Green Pearl's death in Du Mu's famous "Golden Valley Garden" as an "act of poetic violence," when, according to Chaves, "generations of Chinese readers have seen [it] as a delicate compliment to the beauty of [her] death."[27] I would say that it is precisely such an *aesthetization* of life that makes totalitarianism possible, as it *anesthetizes* us into celebrating the "beauty of death" while ignoring the circumstances of dying. And to suggest that we should limit our critical analyses to simply reaffirm what others have said in the past is also totalitarian and culturally hegemonic.

Thus, rather than dismiss modern theory and criticism entirely without first seriously addressing its various forms of ideological construction, thereby vacating it of ethical and political significance, we should seek out ways that such inquiries can *connect* our work with the larger intellectual life, and indeed, to the contemporary world. As Terry Eagleton has put it:

> Critics who find such pursuits modish and distastefully newfangled are, as a matter of cultural history, mistaken. They represent a contemporary version of the most venerable topics of criticism, before it was narrowed and impoverished to the so-called "literary canon." Moreover, it is possible to argue that such an enquiry might contribute in a modest way to our very survival. For it is surely becoming apparent that without a more profound understanding of such symbolic processes, through which political power is deployed, reinforced, resisted, at times subverted, we shall be incapable of unlocking the most lethal power-struggles now confronting us.[28]

Finally, I would like to say that it was none other than that eminently "sinological" of scholars, Edward Schafer, who introduced me to a book entitled *Sade, Fourier, Loyola*, by that eminent poststructuralist thinker, Roland Barthes, in a graduate seminar on medieval Chinese poetry. It is precisely that sort of willingness to intelligently explore critical discourses that we need now.

Chapter 3

Canon Formation in Traditional Chinese Poetry: Chinese Canons, Sacred and Profane

MARK E. FRANCIS

> As each follows his own preferences, critiques all differ. The Zi and the Sheng flow indiscriminately; the vermilion and the purple vie with each other. Debates turn disputatious, and there is no reliable standard.
>
> —Zhong Hong, "Preface to Shipin"

The critical concepts of literary value and canonization are by now well-established concerns in contemporary scholarship in the fields of European and American literatures. Only recently and rather tentatively have these topics begun to be explored with respect to the reception of Chinese literature, however. The very term "canon" is seldom applied in any rigorous fashion to Chinese literary history, although offhand remarks about the so-called Confucian canon or the standing of the canonical poets of the Tang, for example, perhaps seem routine enough. This essay attempts to push further at the idea of canon as a delimited and highly applicable concept for organizing our understanding of the history of Chinese literature and its criticism.

Since the basic terms and most fundamental historical parameters of the subject are not yet fixed, my treatment necessarily begins with an overview of the general nature and salient traits of those collective bodies of religious, philosophical, and literary exemplars which we may with confidence call canons and classics, with some attention given to the relationship between the two terms. A brief treatment of the Western cultural traditions followed by a comparative consideration of the Chinese case at the same level of generality should be sufficient before I move to an investigation of the shaping of the Chinese poetic canon during the ancient and medieval eras.

The rationale of concentrating on the formation of the poetic canon during these periods, to the apparent neglect of other genres as well as the criticism of the late imperial and modern eras, are multiple. Poetic exemplars were the original and virtually definitive material formulations for the classical Chinese literary canon as a whole. As such, they were distinguished both from the "sacred" philosophical and religious texts of the Confucian, Daoist, and Buddhist corpuses, as well as from the unenshrined legacies of "low" genres such as fiction and drama. The authorized *poetic* anthology, a mechanism represented first by the *Shijing*, imitated by the *Chuci*, echoed in the *Wenxuan*, and later still repeated again by the *Three Hundred Poems of the Tang*, played a central role in the canonizing process. Other, secondary factors in the process were the authorizing power of ancient editorial precedents, the force of inherited values generally, and the crystallizing sanction of the state.

Classical Chinese poetic canons—here, the plural is imperative—patently embody a cultural principle and historical reality that characterizes the broad patterns of Western and Chinese literary value alike: a principle which Barbara Herrnstein Smith, for one, has called an orthodox recognition of the "contingency" of literary value within the canonizing process. This principle may be understood as the acceptance and preservation of a cultural space for "canonical" divergence—a tolerated "heterodoxy"—alongside the "orthodox" curriculum. Chinese poetic canons adhere to this principle both within the approved anthologies themselves and on their external "margins" in the form of more problematically regarded, but equally influential, anthologies (e.g., the *Chuci*, the *Yutai xinyong*).

Canons in Traditional China

By definition, the idea of a literary canon makes strong assumptions about the uniqueness and exclusivity of the body of privileged texts to which it refers. This holds true whether one chooses to decry the exclusive power of a canon or to justify its existence. Wherever the concept of a canon is pursued through its manifestations as a concrete phenomenon, however, these assumptions of uniqueness and closure are challenged by the discovery of variation and substantive change. The tracing of additions and deletions over time to the supposedly fixed list of exemplary works, and the locating of a contemporaneous countercanon, equally imply the existence of a plurality of *canons*, which in all cases must be historicized and relativized within the framework of a temporal process. Barbara Herrnstein Smith suggests something of the multisidedness of this process: "The normative mechanisms within a community that suppress divergence and tend to obscure as well as deny the contingency of value . . . will *always* have, as their counterpart, a countermechanism that permits a recognition of that contingency and a more or less genial acknowledgment of the *inevitability* of divergence."[1]

What is now called the canon in Western literary studies was formerly understood rather more loosely as "the classics." The use of the term "canon" as a substitute for "classics" to refer to purely belletristic writings is clearly a move motivated by the desire to appropriate the connotations of sacrosanct authority and fixity from the collections of revered religious, philosophical, and historical writings which previously had exclusive claim to the word. Yet it is only from the perspective of our own age, remote as it is from those eras when the long-evolving traditions of Judaism and Christianity became fairly fixed, textually speaking, that the sacred canons can appear to be so closed and unique. In reality, sacred canons are always subject to the same historical vagaries of change and development as belletristic canons—they are generally perceived as more stable, and invested with greater authority, than literary canons only because of their more ancient origins, their religious associations, and the ossification of the institutions in which they have been formulated and transmitted. Literary canons differ from sacred ones in other significant ways: the social base of their authority is wholly secular; their texts carry no metaphysical sanction; and their readers include persons whose main intention with respect to the text is to move beyond the role of custodian or student, to emulate and expand on the inherited model in the capacity of *writer*.[2]

The foregoing observations have been framed with the Western tradition of "canons" and "classics" foremost in mind; such terms are, after all, culture bound. Nonetheless, in Chinese civilization, the situation is roughly analogous—albeit some interesting divergences appear in the details. The Confucian *jing*, variously translated as "classics," "canon(s)," and "constants,"[3] enjoy an ancientness, status, and cultural role comparable to that of the biblical canon. The Confucian *jing* underwent a lengthy and complicated process of development and institutionalization, involving textual disputes, competing efforts to standardize commentaries and subcommentaries, debates concerning the relative merit of the various *jing*, and cumulative expansion, before reaching their present form during or after the Song dynasty.[4] In addition, there is a clear and all-important boundary between *jing* and what we could call "classic" works of Chinese belles-lettres. Finally, although it is true that *jing* are not sanctified by claims of divinely inspired authorship, as are the Torah, the New Testament, and the Koran, they are nevertheless privileged by their association with legendary cultural heroes such as Confucius and the Zhou dynasty rulers—mundane authorities who arguably carry an equivalent suasive force.[5]

Despite these broad similarities, the Chinese tradition remains distinctive in several crucial respects. First, the Confucian canon is, in actuality, but the most established and influential of *three* "canonical" corpuses in traditional

Chinese civilization: Buddhist and Daoist canons do exist, and these are also called *jing*. Second, the canonizing institution of the Confucian corpus was the Chinese imperial state, not an ecclesiastical body, a characteristic that distinguishes it both from the holy texts of "the peoples of the Book" and from the Buddhist and Daoist canons. While the traditional Chinese state had significant ritualistic dimensions, most of which were "Confucianized," the *jing* themselves are generally thought to have served its purposes mainly in non-ritualistic functions, in terms of legitimizing ideology, educational curricula, and recruitment methods.[6] Third, works in the Confucian canon were treated not only as constant sources of moral knowledge and inspiration but consistently also as models and sources of a variety of materials for active literary composition, both arguably to a far greater extent and certainly for a longer duration than the King James Bible. Fourth, the Confucian *jing* from the very start have included one particular text that has always been understood in some sense as a specifically "literary" composition, that is to say, a text with "aesthetic" as well as educational and moral functions. Far from being a mere resource for literary writers, this work has also served as a paradigm and precedent to be invoked to justify specific literary agendas and the very role of literary writing in Chinese society. The *jing* in point is the *Classic of Odes*, or the *Shijing*.

The Shijing as a Canonical Text

Within the Confucian canon the *Shijing* has occupied a secure, even lofty, position. One source of its prestige is its sheer antiquity; it is among the oldest of all extant works in Chinese. The ancient folk songs and court poetry in the *Shijing* are an indisputable and integral part of the legacy of the Zhou dynasty, the formative age of Chinese civilization.[7] The *Shijing* has therefore been duly revered as one of the foundation stones of Chinese culture and has traditionally shared the aura of the socially perfect Golden Age thought to have produced it.[8]

In fact, however, it was only long after the Zhou that the canonical label of *jing* was applied to "the Odes" (as Confucius himself is always portrayed as referring to them), most notably by the late Warring States philosopher Xunzi. Regarding the Odes as paradigmatic expressions of proper thoughts and feelings by morally accomplished individuals, Xunzi promoted their study and interpretation as "normative" texts, making them the central focus of a "Confucian" curriculum. Only from this period on did the Odes begin to approach the function of a canonical work in the Western sense, and fulfill the meaning of the Chinese word *jing* as "vertical threads," or part of the normative warp, on the loom of civilization, through which other cultural elements were interwoven.[9]

The status of the Odes as *jing* was institutionally confirmed by the authority of the Han dynasty, which by imperial imprimatur brought the *Shijing*, together with the *Shujing*, *Yijing*, *Liji* (Classic of rites), and *Chunqiu* (Spring and autumn annals), under the rubric of the "Five Classics" (*Wujing*) and made it an indissoluble part of the Confucian state's legitimizing ideology and bureaucratic culture. Prior to the establishment of the Han reign, the Odes are assumed to have been accorded "canonical" respect by the Confucian school; besides their educational role, they played a part in Confucian (*ru*) ritual functions in which they were sung to music (hence, the English translation, "Odes"). For some time prior to the age of Confucius they seem to have served as an element of elite education, since they are described in the *Zuozhuan* and *Lunyu* (*Analects*) as a privileged source of felicitous diction and general knowledge.[10]

The association of the *Shijing* with Confucius was formed so early and firmly—encouraged by the *Analects*, through allusions to the Odes and advocacy of their study by the Master, and by the tradition that Confucius "edited" the *Shijing*, selecting only those Odes "which could enact propriety and righteousness"[11]—that the special status of the work could never be seriously threatened once Confucianism became state ideology. Still, the *Shijing* had its detractors in the post-medieval age, particularly during the Song dynasty, when scholars and ethical thinkers challenged the text on normative grounds. In a development that Steven Van Zoeren has called "the discovery of depravity in the Odes,"[12] the classical attitude that attributed normative value to the *Shijing* as a whole (the tradition established by Xunzi and the Han Confucians) was modified under the pressure of exegetical progress into a new understanding which acknowledged that certain of the poems in the anthology must represent "noncanonical" emotions and intentions. The poems in question were pieces whose surface readings had always suggested erotic themes or emotional excess, but which in the era of Xunzi and the early empire had been effectively rationalized by allegorical means.[13] By the time of the Song, the allegorical interpretations had become so problematized that another justification for the designation of the texts as canonical became necessary. The profoundly influential Zhu Xi promoted the idea that Confucius had included morally nonparadigmatic poems in the *Shijing* purely as negative examples, which should not be allowed to claim a reader's main attention. Subsequently, some of the so-called debauched odes (*yinshi*) were excised from at least one edition of the *Shijing*.[14] Zhu Xi also incorporated into his criticism of the *Shijing* (as well as that of other poetic works) the idea of "changed" or "deviant" poetry whose non-normative nature is a reflection of moments when both society and poet depart from orthodox models: that is, when the age is troubled or disordered. According to this view, whole sections of the *Shijing* can be regarded as non-normative because they were composed in non-normative times, namely, only after the Zhou government and culture were in decline.[15]

Owing to these developments in the Song, the relative importance of the *Shijing* in the Confucian curriculum must have declined, especially as the "Five Classics" of the classical and medieval periods were eclipsed by the "Four Books" of the later empire as the basis of both general instruction and the civil service examination system.[16] But the canonicity of the *Shijing* could not be withdrawn, and the inclusion and centrality of the privileging *Analects* among the "Four Books" assured continued sanction of the Odes by the Master (an authorization echoed by the *Mengzi* [Mencius], a second element in the quadripartite post-medieval realignment).

The Shijing as a Literary Classic

In addition to its educational and bureaucratic functions as an element of the Confucian canon, the *Shijing* has also fulfilled roles that we would regard as being duly bound up with its nature as a "literary classic." These aspects of the *Shijing* are connected with its universal recognition as the "embodiment" of the Chinese lyrical tradition. They include its designation as the point of origin of the long-lived *shi* genre; its use as a source of concrete compositional materials and techniques; its function as a more abstract model and precedent for the practice of lyrical expression in general in Chinese society; and its eminent position in the various debates and schemes of Chinese literary thought.

To call the *Shijing* the fountainhead of Chinese poetry is a cliché. The cliché conveys two historical realities about the literary nature of the *Shijing*: first, that the book comprises China's earliest known poetry, and second, that this poetry is considered to have continuously influenced in a formative way a significant amount of later Chinese poetry. There is little to dispute in either of these statements. While the poetics of the *Shijing* is assumed to represent the culmination of a compositional tradition far more ancient than the anthology itself, and the individual poems are presumed themselves to have undergone a lengthy process of refinement from their ultimate origins, "the Odes" that have been preserved are all of the earliest tradition known to us. As for the view that the Odes have strongly determined the shape and content of subsequent Chinese poetry, this has always been the common understanding.[17]

That continuities exist between the *Shijing* poetry and the *shi* of the later dynasties in terms of prosody, themes, imagery, and other techniques is a readily observable fact. Precise generic histories may qualify this rather general statement—for instance, the extent to which the *shi* forms in the *Classic of Odes* may be thought of as genuinely "active" compositional models for the post-Zhou era would seem to be a debatable issue—but the qualifications need not contradict the essential validity of the notion that the *Shijing* stands at the head of a vital and unbroken lyrical tradition to which it has always contributed a certain amount of basic form and content.

The prevalence of general histories of Chinese poetry that treat the *Shijing* poems as constituting something of a perennial generic standard to be traced through the ages in terms of its further development or decline is a reflection of genuine historical continuities, as well as perhaps questionable theoretical or (broadly speaking) political biases.[18] Whether or not it can be agreed the *Shijing* had discernibly lost its usefulness as an effective compositional model by a particular point in time, it is clear that in all ages it continued to be looked and drawn upon as an *ideal* for lyrical expression. As a highly authorized and glorified precedent, it was often invoked by writers and editors as a general model and theoretical justification for the writing and collection of new poetic works per se. In this regard, writers and critics surely were taking advantage of the *Shijing*'s dual function as both canonical text and literary classic.

The enduring "double life" of the *Shijing*, as Stephen Owen calls it, is a constant aspect of the history of the Odes.[19] Although it is widely recognized today that the individual poems in the anthology had disparate and certainly in many cases nonideological or "ethically neutral" origins (we may share the view of Zhu Xi on the non-normative ultimate sources of the "debauched odes"), their received history is tied to the idea of an integral text which is associated with the editorial auspices of the Zhou state and Confucius.[20] The poems are therefore not traceable back to any *historical* point when their literary functions were clearly separate from the political and ritualistic uses that were made of them.

The dual aspects of the *Shijing* did not reflect a necessary contradiction in Chinese society between moral authority and purely aesthetic concerns, as Western readers might venture to assume. It has often been observed that a major stream of Chinese thought—indeed, probably the mainstream—views moral and aesthetic functions as complementary or reconcilable. Such an attitude informs the entire commentarial tradition of the *Shijing*; it was attributed to Confucius, and we find it in the "Great Preface."[21] Although many traditional Chinese critics and philosophers insisted on the integration of moral and aesthetic values in the practice of literature, the reality of that practice was more complicated. Concerning the *Shijing* specifically, as Owen has put it, "There was always some tension between the clear and natural surface of the text and the weight of moral interpretation attached to it."[22] The tension in the *Shijing* had the potential to be exploited either way: either as an unimpeachable authorization for the existence of belles-lettres in Chinese society—particularly, for the compositions of writers who were not primarily motivated by or concerned with the explicitly normative functions that had been assigned to the *Shijing* and to literature as a whole—or as a constraint on practicing poets and litterateurs to maintain the moral seriousness of the model that justified their writings. In the latter case, the intent was to absorb creative literary activity into the sphere of canonical standards and concerns; in the former, to invoke canonical associations for purely literary purposes.

Even so unconventional and free-spirited a poet as Li Bo made public acknowledgment and use of the legitimizing tradition of the Odes. By its title, form, and contents, his poem series "Ancient-Style Airs" (*gufeng*), for instance, invokes the model of the *Shijing* and a genealogy of orthodox composition. In a direct comparison with the *Shijing*, the first poem begins: "The Great Odes are long unsung. / When I am gone, who will be able to carry on?" There follows a capsule literary history of the ebb and flow of "the high tradition" that ends very safely and self-satisfactorily with the restored glories of the current age and a final gesture of identification that unabashedly alludes to the cultural role and ideals of Confucius:

> To edit and transmit is my ambition
> That through a thousand springs the glory may shine on.
> If I achieve the Sage's intention
> I'll lay down my brush before a captured unicorn.[23]

As if to dispel any doubt about the seriousness of his commitment to orthodox attitudes, Li Bo's "Ancient-Style Airs" have been placed, if not by his own self-interested hand, then by legitimizing editors, prominently at or very near the opening of major editions of his works.[24]

The example of Li Bo may well be among the most patent and extreme, but then Li Bo perhaps had to account for a greater than usual amount of unorthodox writings and dubious behaviors. Other poets could associate themselves with "the high tradition" through less dramatic methods, perhaps simply by working within the boundaries of the *shi* genre and keeping to its most approved metrics, themes, and diction. Yet poetic genre was not the sole legitimizing authority in terms of the category of form for practitioners of belles-lettres in traditional China. Even more influential in the "canonization" of Chinese literature, many would argue, was the concrete paradigm of the select anthology, one supplemented with prefatory and other commentarial materials that explicitly address the issue of value.

At this point, before we explore further the development of the anthology as a canonizing institution in Chinese literary culture, some justification may seem necessary for the apparent identification of Chinese literature or belles-lettres with poetic genres. It has been suggested that of all the texts in the Confucian canon, only the *Shijing* was treated as a continuous model for a specifically "literary" kind of writing. In comparing the role of the *Shijing* with that of the other classics, it must be acknowledged that the latter were certainly capable of what we could call belletristic functions, since they were used by poets as supplementary sources of allusive phrasing, at least, if not of specifically literary devices such as metrics and topoi, and by essayists and other prose writers as more immediate stylistic models. Nevertheless, their direct influence on later writings in terms of exemplary generic form is negligible. The other Zhou classics included a book of divination (the *Yijing*), ritual texts (the *Liji* and associated documents), and laconic annals and pronouncements (the *Chunqiu* and *Shujing*). None of these provided very strong generic models for later writers: the composition of divination and ritual texts was not among the regular literary activities of the educated, and while history was both a serious concern and a living genre among the cultural elite, its paradigm was actually established in a much more elaborate and secular form by the Han historians, above all by Sima Qian, who was a highly estimable figure but unlike Confucius (who could be portrayed as the last embodiment and upholder of Zhou culture) never a canonical source in the quasi-sacred sense.[25] Chinese historical writing remains distinguishable from what I am calling belletristic writing also by its very strong official functions and formal associations with the court, and by its factually discursive style, which stands in contrast with the more expressive and descriptive, not to mention often highly personal, qualities of the *shi* and other verse forms.[26]

As for the nonpoetic genres of "creative" or belletristic writing (drama and fiction), which developed much later in China, it is a truism that poetry was always privileged above them by the orthodox. One need only be aware of the vernacular character of those forms—their lack of representation in the Confucian canon, their absence from the bureaucratic culture of the imperial state in terms of educational curricula and civil service examination materials, and the popular social contexts of their performance and "readership"—as compared with the institutional history of the *Shijing* to realize why this was so.[27] The same factors that kept nonpoetic genres at the bottom of the literary hierarchy also operated among the subcategories of the genre of poetry against "lower forms" that were so defined by their marginal or popular origins and unorthodox form and content.

The "Other" Classical Anthology

The *Shijing* is the only canonical Confucian work—the only *jing*—that also functioned equally as a classic belletristic text. However, as important as the *Shijing* was in the shaping of the Chinese lyrical tradition, there was another early collection of poetry which enjoyed nearly as great a status and influence in Chinese literary history, if not in canonical scholarship and official court functions:

> For Chinese poetry has a dual ancestry, a Northern and a Southern.... The Southern ancestor is less ancient than the Northern one and can, in a very roundabout sort of way, be derived from it; but the differences between them are so great that it is more convenient to think of them as two separate sources, contributing in equal measure to the new kind of poetry that began to emerge in the second century A.D. The Northern of these two ancestors is *Shijing*, the "Book of Songs"; the Southern one is *Chuci*, the "Plaints of Chu" or "Songs of the South." In these two anthologies is contained all we know of ancient Chinese poetry.[28]

Despite distinct differences in metrics, style, imagery, and subject matter, the *Chuci* is comparable to the *Shijing* in several ways. Like the *Shijing*, it is a collection of select compositions that represents an entire poetic tradition necessarily both more ancient and more extensive than the particular items anthologized. This "Southern" tradition also had early ritual and political associations; but since classical times its legacy has been mainly poetic. The first edition of the *Chuci* known to us, the second-century compilation of Wang Yi, an admirer of the *Chuci* and an imperial librarian of the Later Han dynasty, includes prefatory material and commentary that expressly address the issues of authority and value in the collection. As for the statement that the *Chuci* can be indirectly "derived from" the *Shijing*, it is assumed that the poets of the *Chuci* composed their works in a literary milieu that was informed by the "Northern" (or proto-Confucian) habit of interpreting poetry allegorically.[29]

Regardless of the circumstances of its original composition, during historical times the *Chuci* became enveloped by the same normative hermeneutics that the Confucians had attached to the *Shijing*. The attachment of Confucian values had begun in earnest clearly by no later than the Later Han edition of

Wang Yi. All too aware that the *Chuci* "belonged to no canon, dealt in matters that were outlandish and unorthodox, and originated outside the area of sanctified Western Zhou tradition,"[30] Wang Yi sought to bring this poetry into the good graces of Confucian orthodoxy by deliberately linking it to the tradition of the Master and to the *Shijing*. In his preface, for instance, Wang Yi compares the adversities of Qu Yuan, the central poetic figure and alleged composer of most of the major pieces of the anthology, with the frustrations of Confucius, placing the poem "Encountering Sorrow" (Lisao) on the same exalted level as the *Shijing* and the *Chunqiu* (both *jing* were supposedly edited by Confucius). Wang also claims that the *Chuci* "bases itself on" the Five Classics. In addition to these deliberate canonical associations and genealogical claims, Wang Yi defends the character of Qu Yuan against Confucian critics of his behavior in terms of the virtues of loyalty, integrity, and proper conduct, establishing a normative value for the text per se. Despite these legitimizing moves—or, indeed, in concert with them—Wang Yi acknowledges that to designate the *Chuci* as *jing*, as had been done during the first century (and which presumably played a large role in inciting the Confucian critics) was not proper.[31]

Before Wang Yi, Yang Xiong had attacked Qu Yuan's character because the poet reputedly drowned himself, an action that was not merely unorthodox, but counter to the example of Confucius (a point which Yang makes explicitly). To the Han historian Ban Gu, Qu Yuan was a selfish man who lacked broad wisdom; and even if he had outstanding literary talents, as the *Chuci* demonstrates, the poems associated with him are not comparable to the Odes and could never serve as "constants" (*jing*).[32] After Wang Yi, critics usually viewed Qu Yuan as a more worthy, even "heroic" character, and were always impressed by the high poetic talent of the *Chuci*. Nonetheless, they were content to see the *Chuci* remain at a subcanonical level. For instance, in the Six Dynasties period, Liu Xie, in *The Literary Mind and the Carving of Dragons*, reviews the opinions of the three Han writers, commenting that "both in commendation and in censure all have been arbitrary, and both their blame and their praise have been exaggerated."[33] Liu Xie's own more "discriminating" appreciation surveys the diction, style, and imagery of individual passages in the *Chuci* in order to determine which of their formal details are orthodox—that is, in harmony with the methods of the *jing* (primarily, the *Classic of Odes*). Where they are not, he calls them "strange," "fantastic," "exaggerated," and "of licentiousness and excess."[34] Liu Xie highly praises the "spirit," "talent," "beauty," and expression of the *Chuci*, but makes it clear that he elevates the work as a literary classic, one to be read and emulated with care and qualification, rather than as a fully normative canonical text: "We know, indeed, that its style cannot compare with that of the literary works of the Three Dynasties, and yet it is fuller of the qualities of *feng* and *ya* than that of the literature of the Warring States period. Though a ruffian in the realm of *ya* and *sung*, it is a hero in the land of poetry."[35]

After the Han, the *Chuci* tended to be treated as an esteemed literary classic whose unorthodox origins, associations, and methods inspired the poetic imagination, but denied it the truly canonical status enjoyed by the Odes. Zhu Xi's comments are typical of the ambivalence toward the anthology shown by later Confucian moralists and scholars:

> As far as the character of Qu Yuan is concerned, although his intention and behavior might have exceeded the standards set by the *Zhongyong* (The doctrine of the mean) so that he is unsuitable as a model, nevertheless all that he was and did came from a sincere heart that was loyal to its ruler and loved its country. As far as his writings are concerned, although the meaning of his words might tend to be unrestrained and demonic, and hatred and resentment so welled up in them that they are inappropriate as moral teachings, nevertheless all of them are the product of the most honest sentiments of profound concern and sad worry—which he could not stop from feeling in spite of himself. Because he did not know that he should study in the North and so seek out the Way of the Duke of Chou and Confucius, he merely galloped around in the corrupt vestiges of changed (*bian*) airs and changed elegentiae.[36]

Zhu Xi criticizes both the moral qualities of Qu Yuan the man and the poetic qualities of the *Chuci* poems, describing a failure to replicate behavioral and poetic norms which are necessarily implied by one another. Further, Zhu Xi confines Qu Yuan within a doubled sociohistorical heterodoxy that is defined by the unsanctioned traditions of the non-Confucian South, taken together with the decline of Northern paradigms as represented in the "changed" *shi*. Literary historians, on the other hand, expressed a similar ambivalence by fitting the *Chuci* into the more general pattern of periodization schemes based on the alternation of "golden ages" and eras of decline, and judging the *Chuci* as a high-water mark in the mainstream of Chinese poetic expression that nevertheless also represented a distinct downturn from the glorious age of the Odes.

Such seemingly balanced views ignore or downplay the uncommonly significant role actually played by the *Chuci* in Chinese literary history and culture. According to David Hawkes, in terms of prosody, each of the two main forms of poetry in the *Chuci*, the Song-style and the *Sao*-style, was highly influential in determining the metrics of later Chinese poetry:

Chinese critics sometimes speak of the *Ch'u Tz'u* as the ancestor of Chinese poetry. This is partly because the *tum tum tum hsi tum tum* line of the Song style gave way in time to the regular pentasyllabic, which became one of the favorite media of Chinese poets throughout the ages. This is the metre in which were written many of the T'ang poems.... The Sao-style poem was developed, not surprisingly, into a sort of essay in rhymed and rhythmic prose called a *fu*. It had perhaps as important an effect on the development of Chinese prose as the Song style had on Chinese poetry. But its influence on later poetry, too, was considerable.[37]

This version of Chinese poetic genealogy complicates the claim that the *Shijing* is the obvious and undisputed progenitor of the Chinese lyric.[38] It is undisputed that the *fu* form was more popular than the *shi* during the Han dynasty, when the *fu* was put to serious use by the most famous poets and literati of the court. Those who concerned themselves about its orthodoxy, or lack of same, at times attempted to legitimize the genre by tracing a false lineage back to the *Shijing*, in connection with which the identical term *fu* had been applied quite differently (for example, in the Great Preface) to describe imagistic or musical details of the *shi*.[39]

The impact of the *Chuci* on the course of Chinese literary development was not limited to prosodic influence. It supplied later writers with a rich source of poetic situations, imagery, diction, and allusions. Its themes of mistreated loyalty, unrecognized talent, and exile had a perennial appeal for poet-officials whose real-life situations might at any time come to resemble those of Qu Yuan. The encounters with divine beings and fabulous creatures portrayed in the *Chuci* may be considered the antecedents of works on similar subjects by Cao Zhi, Li Bo, and the Late Tang poets. Itself modeled on the *Shijing* as a collection, the *Chuci* contributed to the establishment and definition of the poetic anthology as the effective canonizing agent of belles-lettres in traditional China. It added to the example of the *Shijing* its own prestige, joining it in the formation of a cumulative precedent.

In the same way that Daoism has been regarded as a philosophical and religious foil to the rational and humanistic tradition of classical Confucianism as a general cultural phenomenon and force, the *Chuci* may be thought of as the balancing complement to the restrained, this-worldly, and socially conscious "classic" poetry of the *Shijing*. As such, the *Chuci* offered effective poetic alternatives for Chinese readers and writers, fulfilling the role of a tolerated literary heterodoxy that, in Herrnstein Smith's terms, may be conceived of as a larger "*counter*mechanism" that demonstrates "more or less genial acknowledgment of the inevitability of divergence" in Chinese literary culture.

Later Classic Collections and Poetic Canons

The *Shijing* and the *Chuci*, China's most ancient and revered literary anthologies, provided classical Chinese poetics with a complex, pluralistic (even "binary") foundation. This is true not simply in a formal sense: beyond their influence on metrics and other conventions of composition, their paradigmatic precedents strongly influenced the nature of the canonizing process in Chinese literature, shaping its format and setting the terms of its critical discourse. Indeed, subsequent to the early imperial period, in the medieval era, a striking parallel to the *Shijing-Chuci* interplay of canon and countercanon was to develop.

During the fourth century, some two hundred years after the fall of the Han, the compiling of new anthologies began in earnest. Literary collections became highly popular during the Six Dynasties period (220–589), establishing a mode of literary activity that continued in great abundance and variety through the Tang (618–907) and subsequent dynasties. Only two belletristic collections survive from the Six Dynasties era; ten from the Tang are now extant. Several scholars maintain that these anthologies constitute the most pertinent materials available for the task of understanding the dynamics of value and change in Chinese literary history in their ages—far more crucial, in fact, than the purely critical or "theoretical" works which also began to be produced during the post-Han era and important examples of which also survive.[40]

The post-Han belletristic collections have been described as performing the following critical functions: (1) valorization, or preservation and propagation, of model examples in terms of genre, style, and "taste"; (2) historicization, by the construction of literary chronologies and genealogies; (3) interpretation, or the determination of meaning in the texts selected; (4) generic criticism; and (5) "canonization" of individual poets, through degree of representation, ranking (by either explicitly moral criteria or "aesthetic" standards), and commentarial assessments.[41] Each of these functions to some extent reflects the original format and standards or the effective legacy of the *Shijing* and the *Chuci*. The two ancient anthologies were, of course, valorized selections intended and regarded as normative models worthy of preservation. Their internal organizational principles included generic division and, within the generic divisions, arrangement by (in the *Shijing*) geographical location, or (for the *Chuci*) by poet, chronologically. Their attached commentaries variously attempted to fix interpretation; set aesthetic and moral criteria for criticism; and determine the relative canonicity of the individual compositions (beginning with Zheng Xuan's negative notions about the "changed Airs").

Of the two anthologies that have been preserved from the pre-Tang period, the *Wenxuan*, or "Selections of Refined Literature," as David Knechtges has translated the title of the collection, is decidedly the more orthodox of the pair. Knechtges judges the *Wenxuan* to be the effective model for the major literary collections in China after ancient times. He indicates the primacy of the *Wenxuan* by pointing out that it is the oldest surviving Chinese anthology organized by genre (a significant organizing principle of later collections), citing other scholars who refer to the *Wenxuan* as "the Chinese Anthology" or "the Anthology par excellence," and designating the *Shijing* and the *Chuci*, in contrast, as "protoanthologies." In addition, Knechtges relates the popularity and practical importance of the collection to success in the imperial civil service examinations a full five centuries after its compilation during the Song dynasty, when members of the scholar class circulated the saying: "The *Wenxuan* thoroughly done, / Half a licentiate won."[42]

The *Wenxuan* consists of pieces in thirty-seven different genres, including many categories other than poetry, such as edicts, memorials, letters, eulogies, treatises, inscriptions, and epitaphs, demonstrating that the title and purpose of the anthology relate to belletristic writing (*wen*) in the broad sense. However, as Knechtges notes, history, philosophy, and humor are not represented in the *Wenxuan*, and the treatment of certain categories is "less general" than elsewhere (for example, than in Liu Xie's contemporaneous critical treatise, *Wenxin diaolong*). Further, "If one were to identify a principal emphasis of the *Wenxuan*, one would have to say it is without question the poetic genres." Of the latter, the vast majority of works are in the *fu* or *shi* forms; the *fu* predominates, both in sequence and in bulk. According to Knechtges, "The importance of the *fu* and *shi* is also reflected in the fact that they are the only genres divided into subgenres."[43]

The *Wenxuan* was expressly intended to preserve the "best" examples of compositions, from the Han to contemporaneous times, in each of the thirty-seven genres that it encompasses: to "omit the weeds" and "collect only the purest blossoms."[44] The compiler of the *Wenxuan*, Xiao Tong, crown prince of the Liang dynasty, directly sets out the criteria of selection in his preface. Following opening statements about the nature, purpose, and genealogy of literary composition, Xiao Tong proceeds with a catalog of the represented genres, defining the specific expressive function and model form of each. It is this central concern with properly matching available forms to the writer's purpose and subject that leads modern commentators to call the *Wenxuan* a text in early Chinese genre theory, one that promotes generic classification as

Chinese Canons, Sacred and Profane

both an organizing tool for anthologies and as a set of criteria for the assessment of an individual poet's works in terms of his conformity with and technical expertise relative to established generic models.[45]

The preface pays reverence to the canonical anthology of the ancients, the *Shijing*, by invoking continuity with its sanctioning paradigm. But it also justifies literary change or "deviation" as natural, progressive, and appropriate: "Continuing the process increases ornament, / Changing the basic form adds intensity."[46] Xiao Tong recognizes a historical shift in the role of the *fu* but locates the genre in a proper orthodox lineage:

> As we come to the writers of the present,
> Who differ from those of the past,
> That form of the ancient *Songs*,
> Now has solely assumed the name *fu*.[47]

In a more subtle gesture of legitimation that acknowledges the *Wenxuan's* debt to the *Chuci* tradition, the compiler also praises Qu Yuan as one who "embraced loyalty and trod the path of purity."[48]

The second surviving Six Dynasties anthology, the *Yutai xinyong* (New songs from a jade terrace), seems to be a different kind of literary amalgamation entirely. Set alongside the *Wenxuan* it makes for a study in contrast at least as striking and suggestive as that offered by the pairing of the *Chuci* and *Shijing*. Its English translator, Anne Birrell, calls it a collection of love poems put together explicitly "to give pleasure rather than instruction." Moreover, in the book's preface, Birrell finds a deliberate "tilting at dour academics who managed to find moral meaning everywhere," disclaimers of canonical seriousness, and "an urbane acknowledgment that art is lightly to be pursued for art's sake."[49] Birrell also advises the reader that despite the apparent frivolity of its content and purpose, "This anthology will provide a necessary link between the more familiar landmarks of ancient China and the later medieval period of the T'ang Dynasty. Clearly, much of the originality claimed for T'ang poetry has to be put back where it rightly belongs—among the poets of the Southern Dynasties."[50]

The *Yutai xinyong* was edited by the court poet Xu Ling under the sponsorship of Xiao Gang, the brother of Xiao Tong who became crown prince and then emperor of the Liang after Xiao Tong's premature death. Xiao Gang contributed many poems to the *New Songs*, and his literary court is credited with the development of "Palace-Style Poetry," or *gongtishi*, "a new form of love poetry" that features the glamorous ladies and sumptuous decor of the palace boudoir. As Birrell tells us, Xiao Gang's commissioning of Xu Ling "to garner the gems of the earlier tradition of love poetry and glean the finest contemporary models ... was instrumental in immortalizing this new form of verse."[51]

Xiao Gang's views on literature were not orthodox. He is considered to have "asserted the independence of literature from the Classics, and the inappropriateness of literature as a guide to conduct," and is seen as being critical of "the blind imitation of classical models and the enshrinement of orthodoxy at the expense of the spontaneous beauty of expression."[52] The rise of Palace-Style poetry, as a whole, has been seen as "essentially a reaction to the traditional view of poetry as a vehicle for moral instruction."[53] In light of this, it is hardly surprising that Xu Ling's preface does in fact seem to tweak the orthodox tradition. One way it does so is through the ostensible location of its intended audience among the perfumed ladies of the palace, for whom the new verse "Can / Act as soothing herbs / And ease the malady of sorrow."[54] Certainly the Preface makes no pretense to finding canonical justification in the example of the *Shijing*:

> I have selected and set down love songs
> To total ten scrolls.
> They could never rank with the *Elegentia*,
> Nor hyperbolically be compared to the *Airs*.
> The relation between the Jing and the Wei
> Is exactly thus.[55]

The allusion to the proverbial Jing and Wei rivers (one runs clear while the other is muddy, yet, though their courses flow together for three hundred leagues, their qualities never become mixed) encapsulates Xu Ling's apology for non-normative poetry. By first disclaiming all but the most modest purposes for the *New Songs* poetry, and then arguing that the unorthodox will not impact the purity of the "high tradition," he has made a clever case for the coexistence of the heterodox alongside the normative.

Despite Xu Ling's (probably false) modesty, the *Yutai xinyong* enjoys a definite literary importance. Together with the *Wenxuan*, it survived all other contemporaries. During the Tang and Song dynasties, while its orthodox "brother" served as a sanctioned model for students, poets, and editors, the *New Songs* exerted an intermittent but continuous influence on the style, imagery, and themes of more private or less official writings. Inevitably, Palace-Style poetry became subject to the same allegorizing and moralistic interpretations that had been applied to the *Chuci* and the *Shijing* before it.[56] Still, in orthodox literary histories, the *Yutai xinyong* became identified as the standard negative exemplar of the "tones" and general style of an age of regrettable decline, especially as judged relative to the allegedly more substantive poetic accomplishments of the dynasties which preceded the Liang. In particular, poets of the Jian An age, which includes the last period of the reign of the Han together with the short-lived Wei dynasty,[57] were looked back upon by writers and critics of the Tang and later times as the postclassical writers most worthy of emulation.[58] Although verse by the canonized Jian An poets is amply anthologized in the pages of the *Wenxuan*, the *Yutai xinyong*, nevertheless, also includes examples of their works.

The Tang poetry of Li Bo, in its diverse loyalties, may serve to illustrate some of the ambivalence of the Southern Dynasties legacy. One of Li Bo's most famous poems is "Yujie yuan" (The plaint of the jade stairs), a brief masterpiece in the subgenre of poetry about glamorous and lovelorn palace women that is completely in the *Yutai* tradition. But the same poet's more discursive and judgmental treatment of the legacy of Palace-Style poetry in "Ancient Airs: No. 1" is a case of studied contrast:

> Although eras of glory and decline come in constant alternation
> The Classics are truly completely gone.
> Since the age of Jian An:
> An ornateness not worth treasuring.[59]

The Tang and After

The ten surviving anthologies of the Tang dynasty display a diversity of content, organization, and critical bias.[60] Whether their diversity is merely apparent—perhaps simply the result of circumstances of preservation and transmission that were random or accidental—we cannot know. But some scholars believe that the Tang collections are a reflection of a general period of genuinely diverse cultural and poetic practices. According to Pauline Yu, "The very variety of aims and criteria evident in these Tang anthologies, which represent about one-fifth of the total number whose compilations have been recorded, suggests a tolerance for a diversity of critical tastes that was paralleled . . . by a pluralism in other arenas of intellectual and cultural activity during the dynasty."[61]

Their diversity notwithstanding, certain common features and recurrent concerns are evident among these Tang collections.[62] One example is an editorial awareness of the temporal and cultural remoteness of the orthodox poetry of the past—the poetry of the *Shijing* and the Jian An era. Another highly pertinent detail is the lack of legitimizing sponsor. None of the Tang anthologies is associated with a revered and larger-than-life cultural figure, as the *Shijing* and *Chuci* were. Only one is the issue of an imperial commission—and that one manifestly is neither comprehensive nor historically minded[63]—although both the *Wenxuan* and *Yutai xinyong* were official productions. Such factors underlie what Yu identifies as a lack of self-confidence and a fixation with self-justification among the Tang anthologists:

> Many of the Tang anthologies extant ... not only choose to emphasize their direct links with and emulation of the principles of the *Classic of Poetry* [the *Shijing*], but also seem to be much more concerned with legitimating the status of the poets whose works they are collecting.... As a result ... in both the prefaces that are appended to most of them, as well as the remarks on poets that also sometimes appear, we can detect a much more vigorously polemical—both offensive and defensive—stance than is evident in their predecessors [the anthologies of earlier ages].[64]

We may indeed interpret such editorial anxiety and contentiousness as not merely critical currents associated with the lack of any potently authorized and authorizing agent on the model of the earlier anthologies—but, rather, as direct symptoms of that condition. Although their "argumentative mode also reflects the fact that many of them claim to be directly opposing the prevailing tastes of their day, which, needless to say, changed over the course of the dynasty," and such argumentativeness may be inherent in a poetry in which "there was considerable diversity of taste," it was all too obvious that none of these surviving Tang anthologies was "blessed with the conviction of the *Wenxuan* that it is enshrining masterpieces or authors on which widespread agreement exists as to excellence and which must simply be selected from some larger group." Therefore, "they all argue, and sometimes quite desperately, for the value of what they are collecting."[65] For all their concern with legitimacy, the Tang anthologies most resemble the least orthodox of the earlier surviving collections—the *Yutai xinyong*—in their focus on a single form, the work of contemporary poets, and what may be termed an oppositional poetics. These characteristics went hand in hand with a classificatory scheme based on poet, rather than genre.[66]

The absence of an authoritative Tang anthology for the men of the Tang meant continued reference to earlier models. The poetic debates of the Tang, of which these surviving anthologies are one aspect, were typically cast in terms of a bipolar opposition between the allegedly more ornate and superficial poetry of the Southern Dynasties (i.e., Palace-Style and court poetry generally) and the supposedly more direct and morally substantive poetry of the Jian An and earlier styles. The rejection of the practice of the recent past and the idealization of a more remote tradition that had suffered a decline is associated with the ideals of *fugu*, "return to antiquity." While early Tang poets and critics had promoted the concept, it was not until the Mid-Tang—a period of acute political and social crisis—that a true *fugu* movement developed and spread. That literary cum cultural movement is regarded as being of a piece with major intellectual and cultural changes that affected traditional Chinese society as a whole, beginning in the Late Tang and early Song. We can characterize this shift in part as one of increasing orthodoxy in all aspects of Chinese life.[67]

It has been suggested that poetic orthodoxy either returned with a vengeance or first became formidably entrenched in the Song and subsequent dynasties, principally for the same reasons that religious and philosophical culture became less heterogeneous after the Tang: according to Pauline Yu, "Orthodoxies in, for example, Confucian doctrine and hermeneutical practices and the visual arts were taking shape, so canons of poetry were being defined."[68] But it was the poetry of the Tang itself that figured most prominently in literary canon formation in later dynasties—perhaps because for the poets and readers of the Song, the poetry of the Tang remained close enough to serve as accessible and useful models for study and composition, but had already gained a distance and an edenic aura as a concluded period of accomplishment by which the works of subsequent eras could be assessed.[69] The distance also allowed the fractious differences in Tang poetics—its contentious diversity—to be subsumed, and made more opaque, by the collective reception of "Tang poetry," for those who preferred a less heterogeneous heritage. Appropriately enough, for most readers of Tang poetry in the concluding century and a half of the empire, and the twentieth century, the enduring legacy of the "golden age" of Chinese poetry is strongly associated with a single unitary collection, the *Tangshi sanbai shou* (Three hundred *shi* of the Tang).

After the Tang, the anthology remained the premier canonizing institution for Chinese poetry. For the most significant anthologies, poetic form and chronology were again the basis of organization. This is eminently true of *Three Hundred Shi of the Tang*. The *Three Hundred Shi* was first published in 1763 or 1764 under the obvious pseudonym of "The Retired Scholar of Fragrant Pool" (Hengtang tuishi), but is now known to have been compiled by the Qing scholar-official Sun Zhu. Sun's modest preface maintains that his anthology is "but a family reader for children, though it will hold good till one's hair is white." The editor's inclusion of three hundred pieces (more or less) is justified by reference to a common saying, "Having mastered three hundred Tang poems, one learns the art of poetry." We can merely speculate whether the fact that his collection became a standard textbook of Tang poetry for all subsequent generations was aided by his (again, perhaps merely apparent) modesty. The commonality with the *Shijing* in terms of number of poems included has been duly noted before, mainly in terms of "model" or "inspiration"; I would stress the possibility of a deliberate invocation of the authorizing force, subconscious or otherwise, of the older anthology.

Three Hundred Shi of the Tang is thought to have been based on anthologies compiled by Shen Deqian, a Qing official and literary figure who promoted a poetics based on classic models as well as morally didactic content, known as *gediao*.[70] Shen Deqian was one among many orthodox critics of the later empire who regarded the so-called High Tang as the ideal age of the poetic past. However, he believed that the Tang produced both orthodox and depraved poetry—the latter, especially, during the Mid- and Late Tang years—and that "to discriminate in discarding and retaining is the sole task of the compiler."[71] His anthologies therefore exclude, for example, the ornately erotic *wutishi* (poems without title) by Li Shangyin, some of which *are* included in *Three Hundred Shi of the Tang*. Shen Deqian's collections and criticism make the *Three Hundred Shi* seem by comparison more eclectic and moderate—a compromise survey. Sun Zhu claimed he had made his choices on the basis of popularity over the centuries. The success of the *Three Hundred Shi* as a canonical text has been attributed to its broad appeal to scholarly and unrefined readers alike. We may wish to consider also its "genial acknowledgment of the *inevitability* of divergence."

With respect to the powers and vicissitudes of canonization in Chinese poetry, we should not leave off on the subject without commenting on the status of the most acclaimed poet of the past thousand years. Within Shen Deqian's collections, the Tang poet "retained" by the greatest number of pieces is of course Du Fu, as in the *Three Hundred Shi*. However, in all the diversity of the surviving Tang anthologies, Du Fu—since the medieval period universally regarded as the model poet of a model poetic age—is barely represented. This fact should serve not merely to underline the divergent purposes and standards of the Tang anthologists, or the gap between contemporary and ultimate poetic reputations. It illustrates, as well, by negative example, the potent role of those fortunate editors of both early and later dynasties who could make claims to comprehensive and, especially, officially sanctioned or "orthodox" standards, and thereby invoke an authority which we can only call, "canonical."

Part Two

Gender, Sexuality, Body

Chapter 4

A Feminist Re-Vision of Xu Wei's *Ci Mulan* and *Nü zhuangyuan*

ANN-MARIE HSIUNG

Women are frequently represented in Chinese literary works as passive, self-effacing, and submissive, a representation that supports the Confucian patriarchal power structure. Although Confucian patriarchy subjugated women to men through gender hierarchy and its doctrine of separate spheres, the early Confucian philosophy based on Chinese cosmology held a largely reciprocal view toward the relationship between *yin* and *yang* or women and men. Dorothy Ko calls this inconsistency the "inherent conceptual ambiguity" in the Confucian tradition.[1] The development of Chinese patriarchy, especially Neo-Confucianism, which became an orthodoxy in the Ming dynasty, forced a greater constriction on women or the *yin*. The view of Zhu Xi, the foremost Neo-Confucian scholar, that "*yang* often also comprises *yin*, but *yin* cannot comprise *yang*," was pervasive in the Ming era.[2] Yet interstices existed within this didactic tradition, and practice did not always correspond to prescription. As a result, there was space for women to negotiate and maneuver toward their perceived interests without outwardly provoking the guardians of the prevailing system. The Ming playwright Xu Wei's works provide a vivid example that illustrates the complexity and ambivalence of the Confucian gender system.

In Xu Wei's plays *Ci Mulan* (Female Mulan) and *Nü zhuangyuan* (Female first-place scholar), not only does *yin* comprise *yang*, but women also excel men in the male sphere. Those plays, which show women taking up men's roles and assuming male strength in order to overpower and outwit men, might be

73

termed "subversive." Subversion here is understood as behavior or the expression of views that oppose orthodox ideology or prescribed social norms. As defined by Michael D. Bristol, subversion represents "the articulation or 'becoming visible' of any repressed, forbidden or oppositional interpretations of the social order."[3] Although in literature subversion often ends with containment,[4] to regard subversion as "always" contained or "self-defeating" is to deny the importance of subversive representations in literary works. In Xu Wei's two plays, it is true that subversive features are eventually contained by the Confucian system, but on numerous occasions they also oppose the dominating structure. Such opposition can be regarded as a sort of "counterculture" that points to an alternative without posing a "serious threat to orthodox hegemony."[5] The process of subversion, nonetheless, forges a broadened perspective on women and challenges what patriarchy used to take for granted.

Known as the most talented and versatile scholar in the late Ming period, Xu Wei is sometimes said to have promoted pro-feminist views by advocating women's rights or equality between the sexes in *Ci Mulan* (ca. 1556) and *Nü zhuangyuan* (1577–79).[6] In *Zhongguo wenxue fazhanshi* (History of the development of Chinese literature), Liu Dajie remarks:

> *Ci Mulan* and *Nü zhuangyuan* are two plays that respect and stress women's rights. Against traditional thought, which regards men highly while despising women, they praise women's wisdom and quality, rendering them in lovely images. Xu Wei feels that women also have character, intelligence, and strength.... For instance, Mulan's martial arts allow her to serve the country, while Huang Conggu's learning qualifies her as a government official.[7]

There are insights in Liu's evaluation of Xu Wei. Obviously, these texts appear to celebrate women's unusual abilities, but to view Xu Wei as a promoter of "women's rights" seems to go too far. This view fails to consider Xu Wei's personal disposition and the historical context in which he wrote. Since a literary work functions in part "as a manifestation of the concrete behavior of its particular author,"[8] to investigate Xu Wei in his specific cultural, historical conditions becomes crucial to our understanding of his plays. In this study, I first examine Xu Wei's representations of women in *Ci Mulan* and *Nü zhuangyuan*, placing his subversive features against Confucian constructions of gender in patriarchal society. Then, I examine Xu Wei's distinctive personality and literary style within the context of the sociohistorical milieu of his life.

Chinese dramatic representations encode ideological meanings and usually serve to perpetuate a patriarchal ideology, especially in male-authored texts in the premodern era. Xu Wei's dramatic texts echo the dominant voice of a male-centered society; at the same time, however, they also feature a displacement of gender roles that can be read as questioning certain gender assumptions in Chinese patriarchal culture. In a broad sense, Xu's representations of women in the two plays correspond to the literary tradition of the Amazon, for one woman character literally puts on armor to fight the male enemy, and the other woman character outwits her male counterparts.

Ci Mulan and *Nü zhuangyuan* both offer women who clothe themselves as men in order to achieve what they cannot as women. These two characters resemble Shakespeare's comic heroines who also disguise themselves as men to obtain freedom of action and speech. However, while sexual attraction plays a major role in Shakespeare's plays, in which the heroines don male attire to be near the men they love or to maintain a desirable status,[9] the cross-dressing Chinese heroines in Xu Wei's plays seem to have no sexual interest in men. The heroines dressed as men in Chinese drama closely resemble the "superior woman" (who also dons male clothing in order to outdo a man or men) of Chinese fiction, whom Keith McMahon describes as sexless.[10] In *Ci Mulan*, the heroine, Mulan, is portrayed as a filial daughter who feels it is her responsibility as the eldest child to take over her aged father's onerous duties on the battlefield. In *Nü zhuangyuan*, the heroine, Chuntao, who has led a poverty-stricken life in the mountains with an elderly nursemaid since the age of twelve when her parents died, thinks that the only way to survive is to disguise herself and compete in the male world. Both heroines excuse themselves for taking up male identities on the grounds of expediency (*quan*), to adopt Mencius's phrase about "the uncle rescuing the drowning sister-in-law" (*shuyuan saoni*) when there is no other choice.[11]

The gender reversal in Xu's texts does not stop at cross-dressing; the disguised heroines are also armed with a "masculine" spirit or capacity that equals or even exceeds that of men. The women represented here are neither passive nor self-effacing; rather, they are determined and assertive. Their masculine traits emerge when they decide to take on male identities. After purchasing a military outfit to take on her father's military role and his name, Hua Hu, Mulan questions, "To erect the earth and support the heaven, why is a 'macho guy' [*nan'erhan*] needed?"[12] Mulan does not consider a woman less capable than a man; indeed, what she undertakes is in fact the role of a surrogate son. She trusts her ability to fight because she is the eldest child of a military officer and has been practicing the martial arts since she was a child. This might be an uncommon experience for women of premodern times, but it was certainly not unprecedented among girls raised in northern China. As Mulan puts on her military accessories, she transforms herself from a young woman weaving at home to a military officer eager to fight. Thus she sings as she anticipates glory while practicing with various weapons and riding on horseback:

> This sword!
> It's so long since I've drawn it, . . .
> Just now when I raised it up and flipped it through the air
> It was like olden times.
> Why doesn't my hand ache,
> The hand that has grown accustomed to
> > threading an embroidery shuttle?
>
> . . .
>
> (Pantomimes mounting the horse)
> In the deep mountains I can capture alive a monkey;
> With one shake of reins I can trample flat the fox fortress.
> Not until I return home
> > shall I reveal myself as a girl so lovely [*nüduojiao*];
> When I am sitting in the saddle,
> > who will not call me a Hero [*yingxionghan*]?[13]

Mulan's vigorous spirit and bold anticipation of her future glory demonstrate an active masculine energy. Here she has unconsciously identified herself as a hero worthy of admiration.

As for Chuntao, she is even more self-confident than Mulan when she decides to compete in the male world, since she has concentrated much of her eight years' mountain life on study, though without neglecting her embroidery and needlework. Her lines demonstrate her self-assurance at her intellectual ability:

> I was born wrong as a woman to learn all the woman's work. Talking about my intelligence and learning, which can "hang onto a dragon" [*panlong*], I am sure to have my name listed as a top success leading all other men. . . . It is not that I brag about myself. If I can disguise myself to compete with men, I am sure to win first prize in the imperial examination without difficulty.[14]

Such unyielding, competitive spirits are by no means traditionally feminine. Chuntao expresses her desire to be a man in order to prove her literary ability and to earn a living. With such words, Chuntao proceeds to put on her father's robes and goes one step further to create a male identity by renaming herself Chonggu, a very masculine name.

Mulan's and Chuntao's departures from traditional "femininity" undermine conventional representations and gender ideology concerning the nature of women. Their cross-dressing reveals the mobility of gender as manifested by signs of clothing and naming, for these signs are coded with social and ideological meaning and affect not only one's gender behavior but also the gender codes attributed to the bearers of these signs. Evidently, Mulan's and Chuntao's "immodest" remarks deviate from mainstream representations of women as well as from premodern social expectations for women. According to the Confucian doctrine of separate spheres, women are supposed to stay within the domestic realm, while the outside world belongs to men. Women's submissiveness to men and their humbleness in speech are heavily stressed by Chinese patriarchal society, in which male supremacy is codified by rules of propriety and supported by social convention. In her *Nü jie* (Admonitions for women), Ban Zhao reinscribed women's conduct as "Three Obediences and Four Virtues" (*sancong side*), a formula that shaped Chinese women both in life and in literary representations for almost two millennia. According to the "Four Virtues," women are supposed to refrain from sharp and clever speech, to conceal their intelligence, and to avoid competing with others.[15] The representations of Mulan and Chuntao challenge these virtues, and their actions clearly oppose the dominant social mores.

When these two "masculinized" heroines engage in activities then considered exclusively male, they outperform their male competitors. Mulan is highly decorated and receives an official title for her success on the battlefield. Yet the assumed "masculine" activity of fighting is nothing unnatural to her, as she remarks on the award, "I killed bandits and captured their leader, being a woman who masquerades as a man. I get credit without much effort."[16] Chuntao, in her new identity as Chonggu, not only outwits men and wins the highest official title for scholars, *zhuangyuan*, she also serves in government for more than three years and handles with success a number of tough cases that her male colleagues could not resolve. Chonggu regards her official post as a good opportunity to develop her administrative abilities and to benefit people. It appears that, in time of need, Mulan's and Chonggu's "masculinity" emerges (both in spirit and in deeds) as part of their innate capacities—it is as familiar to them as their needlework. Male disguise enables them to express parts of their nature suppressed by a male-dominated society under a narrowly defined code of femininity. Obviously, women in male attire do not become men, but they become more developed and complete women.[17] A developed woman is not inferior to men; she is in some cases even superior to them.

These instances of gender inversion and women's superiority have led critics like Liu Dajie to conclude that Xu Wei was a pro-feminist writer who stressed women's rights. We should remember, however, that the concept of "rights" was not an issue in premodern society. There is no place where Xu Wei suggests that women could obtain opportunities in society without resorting to disguise. In addition, Xu Wei's affirmation of competition both on the battlefield and in civil examinations perpetuates what were traditionally considered masculine values. The heroines' unconventional deeds and thoughts have a regional and personal basis. Despite traditional social expectations of women, Mulan's skill in the martial arts was not uncommon for a northern girl raised in a military family. A masculine spirit could be characteristic of a northern woman, as shown in much Chinese historical literature.[18] A southern girl born in a literati-official family, Chuntao lived without parental supervision after the age of twelve. Her life in an isolated mountain cottage shielded her from mainstream gender ideology enforced in family and society, and further led to her determination to invert gender norms in time of need.[19]

Xu Wei renders his heroines' reversal of gender roles socially acceptable by giving them adequate motivation and by making them comply with patriarchal attitudes in their female roles. Although they display an unyielding spirit and superior "masculine" abilities in their male roles, the heroines conform to the norms of patriarchal society in their female attire or female identities. The texts indicate that marriage, regarded by Confucian patriarchy as a woman's proper destiny, remains the dominant concern for Xu Wei's heroines. Loosening her bound feet to put on male shoes, Mulan for a moment is worried about decreasing her desirability, but she soon comforts herself with a home remedy that will make her feet even smaller. Marriage also come to Chuntao's mind when she considers entering the male world in disguise, although she decides to take marriage less seriously for the time being. Moreover, when the identities of both heroines are revealed, they resume their traditional female roles unquestioningly.

Surprisingly, Mulan and Chonggu appear *even more* feminine and conventional when they return to their female roles than they did before they assumed male guise. It is almost as if each of them now desires to compensate for their acts of gender subversion. Their views become even more conventional and their gestures even more feminine soon after they change back to their female identities. Once she is home in female attire, Mulan justifies her deeds to her male companions, remarking that men and women in fact should not even touch each others' bedding, but that under the circumstances she had really had no other choice but to adopt the expedient measure of disguise. She readily accepts her parents' arranged marriage and appears rather bashful by turning her back when encountering her husband-to-be. As for Chonggu, when her female identity is revealed and she is asked by her supervisor, Prime Minister Zhou, to be his daughter-in-law, she kneels down in shyness, saying, "with my deed of cheating, I feel so ashamed in front of you for even this one moment. If I become your daughter-in-law, I will wait on you all my life. How shy I would be!"[20] Since Mulan's and Chonggu's independence and "masculinity" lie in their detachment from their female roles, an increased degree of dependency and femininity resurfacing in their reattachment to such roles displays a dramatization, or exaggeration, of the existing social norms.

These displays of modesty and humility, considered desirable feminine "virtues" in patriarchal society, point to the way the dominant ideology contains potential subversion. These later acts soften the masculine power the heroines have obtained in their male identities. Although their disguises have made Mulan and Chonggu more developed women, their contrasting behaviors in male and female identities foreground the construction of femaleness as a site of self-sacrifice and weakness. While dutifully performing their male roles, these women are fully aware that they have run the risks of never marrying, of being considered wanton, and of being accused of the crime of deceiving the emperor. When they return to their female identities, they willingly act out female submission, as if they were fully persuaded to redeem their acts of disguise. The comedic character of the plays reduces the possible risks and turns the heroines' concerns around in their favor. Tension surfaces briefly when Zhou pretends that Chonggu's disguise has deceived the emperor and has made her culpable; but this is only a pretense because he actually intends to make her his daughter-in-law (after discovering that she is a woman), altering his original intent to recruit "him" as his son-in-law. Chonggu's immediate submission pleases Zhou and dissolves the tension caused by her subversive acts. Above all, the emphasis of the heroines' maintenance of virginity further satisfies the Confucian norms, making them appear worthy of appreciation. This perhaps has to do with a patriarchal attitude popular since the Tang and Song periods, which frequently associates talent in women with licentious conduct.[21] To present his heroines positively, Xu Wei had to ensure that they were perceived as chaste.

Virginity in fact is an underlying issue in these two texts, for both show that, in Kirsten Hastrup's words, "[a woman's] purity becomes somebody else's concern as well as her own."[22] Before taking off, Mulan eases her mother's concern by promising to return as a virgin. It is what she is proud of when she comes home in twelve years: "It is not that I brag about myself as pure gold or blazing fire, but I am like a lily in muddy water."[23] Likewise, as Chonggu is to be Zhou's daughter-in-law, it is the confirmation of her virginity that makes her doubly adorable to her father-in-law. Chonggu's old nursemaid Huang Gu, who is disguised as a male servant, is brought to the scene to testify for her lady's "purity." When questioned about Chonggu's virginity, Huang is eager to unmask and present herself as Chonggu's sole companion since the latter was a baby. Zhou is relieved and almost thrilled when he hears Chonggu's clarification that "with Huang I entered a deep mountain like celibate monks and nuns. For ten years I buried myself in poetry and books. All along she was my only company. Not even for one moment did a male servant replace her."[24] Zhou's immense excitement at Chonggu's being "thoroughly pure and clean" reveals a male-dominated society's expectation for a young woman.[25] The familiar double standards are operating here. The purity and virginity of men is never an issue, but it is a primary concern for women and a criterion by which they are judged.

Nonetheless, Xu Wei rejects the idea that "women without talents are virtuous"—a prejudice derived from Chinese male-centered society and prevalent in the Ming dynasty. It is true that traditional Chinese society has long placed "virtue" (*de*) above "talent" (*cai*); to make these two mutually exclusive, however, is a patriarchal attempt to manipulate and control women. The question whether a woman's "talent" would endanger her "virtue" had been much debated among orthodox Chinese scholars.[26] Xu Wei insists through his plays that talent and virtue in a woman can be mutually reinforcing. This view reveals another dimension of Chinese tradition—its syncretism (or nonexclusiveness)—a characteristic evident in traditional Chinese philosophy. In these plays, we find that women's talents and abilities, rather than being detrimental to them, enhance their images as they reinforce the prevailing social values of filial piety and female virginity. Talent and strength, though not necessarily essential for these women, serve as decorative accessories that increase their value in the marriage market, as long as they comply with patriarchal rules.

Gender subversion is only temporary in Xu Wei, for the overriding theme remains the reward of virtue. In these two plays, the heroines' gender reversals are represented as only temporary. Despite Mulan's physical strength and superiority in the martial arts, which could be an asset for her country's military forces, she returns home to marry. Chonggu's official post is also to be abandoned upon her marriage, no matter how talented and capable she is. Both women will spend the rest of their lives waiting on their parents-in-law and husbands, with no further exercise of their valuable "masculine" strength and abilities. Nonetheless, to become "a dutiful wife and loving mother" (*xianqi liangmu*) has been what they were aiming for all along, especially in Mulan's case. No doubt an internalization of patriarchal ideology is in effect here. As Dorothy Ko notes, "The enormous respect that the Confucian tradition bestowed on her as mother . . . brought power, comfort and self-esteem. . . . [It motivates] generations of women to conform to the norms of female virtue."[27] Both heroines treat their masculine roles as transitory, rather than any sort of long-term self-fulfillment. After receiving her military rewards, Mulan sings: "When you think of it, ten thousand sorts of things are but illusion. What accomplishment can I boast of?"[28] Even though Chonggu sees her official position as enabling her to develop her talents of supervision and administration, she readily ends her public career to embrace her domestic role, as indicated in her sister-in-law's song: "My groom turns into my sister-in-law, who enters the kitchen and sends for me to taste her cooking before presenting it to her parents-in-law."[29] The text does not show much change in Chonggu's original objective; since she voiced in her earlier statement to her nursemaid that she would quit her official post after earning enough money, we can assume that marriage to a promising scholar is her goal just as it is Mulan's. For both heroines, their masculine roles appear to be necessary transitions, which allow them to attain the status they subconsciously long for—to settle in marriage and fulfill their assigned social roles as wife and mother. This process—from (unfulfilled) maiden, to destabilization (a need for male disguise), to restoration of the social status quo in marriage—appears as a typical comedic plot.

Although Confucian patriarchal ideology dominates these texts and contains the subversive acts, the heroines' facile change of gender roles sheds light on the construction of gender itself. Xu Wei's representation of gender reversal challenges the patriarchal dichotomy that assigns "masculinity" and "femininity" respectively to man and woman, and claims that such differences are based on biological destiny.[30] Xu's plays suggest that gender identity is a sociocultural construct that exists in the masquerade of masculine and feminine roles. When the heroines put on male dress, they are no less masculine than men; yet, when they change back to female dress, their femininity emerges even stronger than before. These changes dovetail with de Beauvoir's famous line that women are not born but made. They reveal that gender, as Teresa de Lauretis notes, can be construed as an effect of language or as imaginary under the concept of sexual differences. In an attempt to unravel this notion of gender as a construct, de Lauretis adopts Michel Foucault's theory of sexuality and argues that "gender, too, both as representation and as self-representation, is the product of various social technologies ... and of institutionalized discourses."[31] In other words, society provides a set of norms of masculinity and femininity for men and women, who become gendered through the sex-role socialization of speech, daily life, and social relations. To quote Maureen Robertson, "These specific patterns of difference are ideologically founded and are actualized and sustained in social behavior."[32] Mulan and Chonggu have learned their expected female roles and must have also observed what is expected of male roles within their families. For instance, they seem to have taken their fathers as role models in their male identities—one as soldier, the other as scholar-official. In their female and male costumes, they embrace different gender identities as well as separate codes of behavior. They satisfactorily meet and even exceed expectations in their new identities. To recast Judith Butler's question, we may ask: Are their acts in cross-dressing "the imitation of gender, or [do they] dramatize the signifying gestures through which gender itself is established?"[33] Mulan and Chonggu probably do both. Their dramatization of the established gender codes makes the process of social construction of women obvious, and thereby calls into question the patriarchal dictates.

The examples of Mulan and Chonggu can be read as manifesting the gender fluidity and "androgyny" featured in traditional Chinese philosophy. In Chinese cosmology and natural philosophy, *yin* and *yang* are interactive and mutually penetrating, and periodically, each takes ascendancy over the other.[34] Regardless of Mulan's and Chonggu's readiness to settle for their assigned female roles as wives, their ability to cross the boundary and even outperform men in the "male" sphere indicates their androgynous character.[35] Their masculine potential, largely repressed by patriarchal society, outplays the "real" men when opportunities arise. This representation subverts *yinyang* duality stressed by Chinese patriarchy and suggests that the common Chinese assumption of female inferiority is a patriarchal tactic adopted to boost male supremacy. From a feminist perspective, the obvious androgynous aspect of these representations of women subverts the dominant ideology because, to some extent, they undermine the "patriarchal master narrative" by shaking the notion of a fixed gender identity.[36] Paradoxically, by having the heroines assume masculinity in male roles and femininity in female roles, these women appear to move from one fixed identity to another.

Xu Wei's *Ci Mulan* and *Nü zhuangyuan* were bold and unconventional in his day. My textual analysis shows that these plays raise some feminist issues, but it would be simplistic to assume that the author intended to support women's rights or sexual equality. Because these two plays are collected with two others under an extraordinary title, *Sisheng yuan* (Four shrieks of a gibbon), indicative of grief and most likely the author's personal outcries as well, there seems to be a close relation between the author's life and his plays. Although his life may not be directly linked to the reason why he wrote these plays, Xu Wei nonetheless appears to be one of the literati authors who gave their works an autobiographical bent, a literary trend that dates back to the sixteenth century.[37] To investigate the relationship between the author and his plays, it is necessary to place Xu Wei within his sociohistorical context. We may draw on aspects of Xu Wei's official career, life experiences, and literary ideas in order to better understand the subversive features in his *Ci Mulan* and *Nü zhuangyuan,* and to better determine whether Xu Wei could have possessed any pro-feminist ideas. The impact these two plays might have exerted on real-life women may also illustrate the intensity of their subversive effects.

Diverse cultural forces along with social changes in sixteenth-century China certainly affected Xu Wei as a person and writer. Neo-Confucian ritual propriety still remained dominant in this period, although it was not as powerful as it had been during the early Ming. Social concerns regarding female chastity and seclusion were pervasive, but the school of Wang Yangming, with its broadened human concern and an ideal of sagehood that could be attained by both men and women, was gaining popularity. Xu Wei was one of the distinctive scholars influenced by Wang Yangming. On the basis of this school of thought, he developed a unique style as a dramatist, poet, painter, and calligrapher and aspired to excel in the three major philosophical disciplines of Confucianism, Taoism, and Buddhism.[38]

An economic boom in Xu Wei's time expanded education and reduced the gulf between officials and commoners, but the path to officialdom still remained a major goal for scholars.[39] Xu Wei's repeated failures in the imperial examinations—the ladder of upward mobility for scholars—might have been the result of the increased competition because of the expanded educational system. Denied official advancement, he abandoned himself to liquor and released his frustrations through extensive traveling. Since it was the despotic system of the imperial court that forced most scholar-officials into conformity, his exclusion from this system could have permitted him to indulge in a carefree, unrestrained mode of thinking and behavior. Thus, while the literary representations by scholar-officials tended to conform to dominant gender representations, Xu Wei, as Maureen Robertson puts it, was more likely to "articulate [his] 'otherness' within the accepted discourse ... through a 'mixed process of acceptance and resistance,'"[40] as did other writers who did not enter mainstream officialdom and therefore remained a subordinated group in society.

Xu Wei's personal life was as disastrous as his performance in the civil examinations. The most traumatic and dramatic events in his life came during his middle age, right after the downfall of his patron, Governor-general Hu Zongxian.[41] Xu Wei suffered an emotional breakdown and attempted suicide several times, once cracking his head with an ax, and another time piercing his ear with a long nail.[42] He writes in one essay, "upset by current affairs, I was afflicted with derangement."[43] His most egregious act was the slaughtering of his (third) wife because he thought she had been unfaithful; for that he spent seven years in prison. His brief "joyful" years were probably those he spent with his loving stepmother and his first wife before their deaths.[44] These were his early, formative years and might have led him to develop a positive view of women.

As indicated in his autobiographical records, Xu Wei was self-conscious and notably eccentric.[45] The lavish love from his stepmother in his childhood may have contributed to the development of his strong sense of self, whereas the absence of a father probably affected his superego formation.[46] He often went his own way, regardless of social conventions. In his later years, for instance, he rejected the company of illustrious officials and the rich, but would go to a wine shop and invite lower-class people to drink with him. His keen sense of self and his nonconformist character could in part have stimulated his unique creativity in literature and the arts.

Xu Wei's deviations from social norms do not mean that he was free of patriarchal prejudices. The murder of his wife seems to have been the by-product of a male-dominated society that stressed female fidelity. Although some have excused his murder on the grounds of insanity,[47] Xu Wei's violent act reveals the patriarchal double standards that he had inherited. Like most other literati of his time, he frequented brothels, but his wife's alleged illicit affair became a "crime" punishable by death. The different standards of sexual behavior suggests that Xu Wei's emphasis on virginity in the two plays discussed above reflects his own male-centered view of women, a view that assumes men's absolute right to control women's sexuality.

Nonetheless, as a social outcast, Xu Wei seems to have been less confined by Confucian orthodoxy. He explored various arts, skills, and issues and often crossed the boundaries of Confucianism, Taoism, and Buddhism. This might have broadened his perspective on women. He wrote in his own obituary, "When integrity is not in question, I am not bound by petty Confucian morality."[48] He followed his heart's call without setting any limits on himself. Not only did Xu Wei's various talents and skills reach fruition and mastery in his later years, but he also came up with original insights about such diverse issues as military strategy and Ch'an Buddhism.[49] His superior talents in literature, painting, calligraphy, music, swordsmanship, and horsemanship, to name just a few, are reflected in varying degrees in Mulan and Chonggu.

As a commoner who had traveled extensively and was widely involved in religious practice,[50] Xu Wei was possibly aware of or influenced by the developing folk religions of that time. These folk religions, in which women played a major role, taught that the world had been created by a mother goddess (*wusheng laomu*). This ideal of a mother goddess introduced a vague notion of parity between the sexes and generated quite a number of female religious leaders and disciples, some of whom even participated in revolts during the later Ming.[51] Although there is no evidence that these religions influenced him directly, Xu Wei's dramatic writings about female leaders in martial and civil fields echo this growing popular trend.

What Xu Wei witnessed in his trips to the southern coastal areas and to the north also seems to have surfaced in his dramatic creations. Xu Wei's grief about what southern women had suffered at the hands of the *wokou* (Japanese pirates) and his impression of the masculine strength of northern women may have inspired his writing of *Ci Mulan*.[52] Xu Wei certainly approved of strong women, but his other writings (such as poems and essays), in which he exalted chaste women and women who killed themselves to avoid rape by the *wokou*, indicate that both his act of uxoricide and the stress on virginity in his plays are no accidents.[53] Of course, the incident of wife-killing alone is not sufficient to prove Xu Wei was a misogynist.[54] For Xu Wei, chastity for women is a cultural value taken for granted, just like loyalty is for men. In fact, he himself attempted suicide after the downfall of his patron. Since husbands and wives were not separable in traditional Chinese thought, the violence Xu Wei committed against his wife might be linked to the violence he aimed at himself in his attempted suicides.

Xu Wei's literary views rebelled against the canon of his time, which emphasized an imitation and revival of the ancients (*nigu*, or *fugu*). Following Wang Yangming's precepts about "attaining innate knowledge of goodness" (*zhi liangzhi*), Xu Wei advocated personal expression and stressed "original character" (*bense*). He placed importance on a writer's ability to break from traditional bondage and to create a new style of expressing the self.[55] Xu Wei's literary creations appear to exemplify his own theory.

Not widely recognized in his lifetime, Xu Wei attained national fame posthumously when his manuscripts were accidentally rediscovered by Yuan Hongdao. Yuan, the leader of the Gong'an school (*gong'an pai*), opposed the "imitation movement" (*fugu yundong*) that had dominated most of the Ming period.[56] He saw Xu Wei as a pioneer, an inspiration for the Gong'an school.[57] Yuan's biography of Xu Wei included these lines: "He did not follow our current trends and looked down upon the leaders of our present literary circles. Therefore his name never reached beyond Zhejiang province. What a pity!"[58] Yuan's assessment illustrates that Xu Wei's writings were "against the grain" of his time.

Xu Wei's subversive constructions of women in *Ci Mulan* and *Nü zhuangyuan* may partly reflect his unconventional aesthetic views, but they are also products of the emerging tolerance and diversity in sixteenth-century Chinese culture. The story of Mulan, dating from much earlier, was recorded by Lü Kun in his *Guifan* (The precepts of the women's quarter), where he affirmed the use of expediency, praised Mulan's integrity to maintain "purity" (*qingbai zhicao*), and regarded her as a *junzi* (person of integrity) worthy to be his teacher.[59] Late Ming literati Tian Yiheng and Xie Zhaozhe reported two girls disguising themselves as men—one to avoid being arrested by rebels, the other to pursue a living as a merchant. Tian called them chaste women of his dynasty and eulogized them for remaining virgins for years in their male roles.[60] Li Zhi, furthermore, insisted that both men and women possessed intelligence which should be allowed to develop.[61] These were by no means the mainstream writings of the period, yet they reveal a flexibility that allowed space for alternative views.

While this emerging sociocultural ambiance could have nurtured Xu Wei and encouraged him to depart from Neo-Confucian orthodoxy, his personality and life experiences would have had a more direct influence on his unusual representations of women. One common theme in these two plays related to Xu Wei's own experience and style can be found in the main characters' defiance of traditional roles. The depiction of heroines who follow their hearts to cope with their impending crises in an unorthodox manner echoes Wang Yangming's "innate knowledge of goodness," a cornerstone of Xu Wei's literary theory. Some critics contend that Xu Wei's *Nü zhuangyuan* indicates a repentance for his wife-murder;[62] though we are not sure how regretful he felt for such a deed, it is quite likely that in dramatic creation Xu Wei underwent a subconscious overcompensation for the act of uxoricide. Since Xu Wei's writings contain memorials to his first wife and say nothing about the one he murdered,[63] the murder might have become a repressed memory which only surfaced in his extensive exaltation of women in his plays. This process can be termed "autobiographical redemption" or self-healing for traumatic experience, for it allows the author to attain a "narrative self-transformation."[64] Similarly, in view of Xu Wei's repeated failures in his official career and his aspirations for success, I think Xu Wei is projecting his own dreams onto Mulan and Chonggu. Xu Wei not only displays his various skills and talents through these heroines, but he also makes them achieve what he has been denied. Unable to achieve any higher social position, Xu Wei has been marginalized and "feminized" by male society. Through his creations of talented women, who reach a high standing and success in officialdom, Xu Wei's own wishes are fulfilled vicariously.

Furthermore, as a nonconforming dramatist, Xu Wei's elevation of women's strength and ability fits well with his character. His representations can be seen as part of his revolt against social conventions, which specified women as house-bound and inferior to men, and which viewed talent and virtue in women as mutually exclusive. Xu Wei's search for novelty in literary expression enhanced his subversive representations of women. Wang Jide, a famous drama critic who once studied with Xu Wei, wrote this assessment, "Master Xu's *Sisheng yuan* is one of the most marvelous and unusual works of literature in the world. The northern style of Mulan, contrasted with the southern style of Huang Chonggu, is a marvel among marvels."[65] Becoming a "marvel among marvels" (*qizhong zhiqi*), rather than a promoter of women's rights, might have been Xu Wei's motivation in his literary endeavors.

Pro-feminist concepts are not evident in Xu Wei's personal life, nor in his sociohistorical context. He might have harbored some vague notion of parity between the sexes that existed in folk religions and among a few liberal scholars. It is a mistake, however, to link Xu Wei's works with women's rights or sexual equality. Moreover, the containment of subversive acts clearly appears toward the end of Xu's plays, after the heroines' identities are revealed. Such containment reveals the author's patriarchal heritage and perhaps his willingness to fulfill some of the social requirements of his time, as he was inescapably a social being in a patriarchal culture. As mentioned earlier, one may argue that Xu Wei is a writer marginalized under the dominant discourse who expresses his "otherness" through an interplay of resisting and consolidating the official ideology.

Nevertheless, if Xu Wei expresses as much of his personality in his writing as he claimed, his attitude toward women is at least affirming rather than despising, although his murder of his third wife because he suspected her of having been unfaithful more or less reflects his double standards in sexual behavior. It is too far off the mark to regard Xu Wei as speaking against the oppression of women in Chinese feudal society, as one contemporary biographer of Xu Wei suggests;[66] yet to suppose that Xu Wei cynically views those who enter officialdom as being as insignificant as women, as is claimed in *Quhai zongmu* (The compendium of drama), seems to be an equally fallacious, extreme position.[67] Officials under the despotic Ming rule were "feminized" to some degree; yet rather than use the image of a female official as a metaphor for officials in general, Xu Wei affirms his heroines' "masculine" capacity. Male novelty-seeking fantasies might permeate these two plays, for the literati did sometimes get fed up with images of weak women. Xu Wei, nonetheless, exalts these two heroines in various aspects and makes them almost ideal by both unconventional and traditional standards. Dissatisfied with current affairs and the system of male society, he unconsciously turns his favor to the socially repressed women, thereby making connections to himself and finding solace in the process. In *Nü zhuangyuan*, Xu Wei praises women's strength through the words of Prime Minister Zhou—"Achievement such as Mulan's is heroic; it is honor rather than shame"[68]—and through the line that Chonggu and her husband sing at the end of the play—"To whom do the good things in the world belong? They are in women rather than in men."[69]

In sum, the force of containment working against the threat of subversion creates an ambivalence in Xu Wei's representation of women in *Ci Mulan* and *Nü zhuangyuan*. On the one hand, the heroines' subversive acts reveal gender mobility, thereby undermining the fixed gender ideology asserted by patriarchal society and, in a sense, valorizing Virginia Woolf's observation that "in every human being a vacillation from one sex to the other takes place, and often it is only the clothes that keep the male or female likeness."[70] The containment of female subversion in these plays also reveals the patriarchal device of keeping women in place through an ideological control of images of femininity. On the other hand, while masculinity occurs mainly in women identifying with male roles, femininity surfaces and resurfaces in female roles, perpetuating the gender dichotomy through which patriarchy divides men and women. The containment of women's transgression through a voluntary return to the assigned role at the end also turns into an affirmation of the patriarchal system.

Despite Xu Wei's unconventional exaltation of women's undiscovered abilities (in male outfits)—unconventional in that it resists the predominant notion of female inferiority—on a deeper level he is reinforcing the rigidity of the patriarchal order, which assumes that women have no access to social recognition except by "becoming" men. Xu Wei's representation of women in *Ci Mulan* and *Nü zhuangyuan* in this sense is both liberating or enabling and limiting or oppressing. These women do momentarily cross or transgress the boundary of the male-centered social norms (e.g., the separate spheres) and break away from the dominant ideology, but Xu Wei's plays remain fundamentally rooted within a patriarchal value system.

Xu Wei's dramatic representation thus imparted mixed messages, which produced ironic or even subversive social effects. Not only did such representation become part of forums valorizing women's talents and enhancing their enlarged sphere, but it was also exemplified to a greater extent by seventeenth-century learned women, such as Huang Yuanjie and Wang Duanshu.[71] Like Mulan and Chonggu, Huang Yuanjie and Wang Duanshu traversed their domestic boundaries and proved themselves superior to many men; they in fact stepped beyond dramatic representation to become "career women" without resorting to male disguise. To justify her public role, Wang Duanshu cited the example of Huang Chonggu as her model. The irony or ambivalence, similar to that of Xu Wei's plays, lies in these women's apparent transgression of the dominant gender ideology on the one hand, and on the other, their embrace of Confucian familial morality, which they and others used in their defense. Even though their remaining entrenched in domestic identities might be seen as strengthening the prevalent gender system,[72] I would argue that to appeal to Confucianism is an inevitable transitional tactic for social justification, since these women's behavior had gone beyond the existing norms. They should be regarded, therefore, as further testing the gender fluidity and acting as members of a new social order in the making. The appearance of such boundary-crossing of talented women after Xu Wei's dramatic representation, no matter how closely or loosely they are linked, indicates a transformation of Confucian order and a possibility of dramatic social effects centered around subversion and consolidation.

Both Xu Wei's heroines and the seventeenth-century "career women" display a complex and ambivalent working of the Confucian gender system. These women embody at once the dichotomous *yin-yang* gender roles prescribed by increasingly stringent patriarchal Confucianism and the flexible, tolerant *yin-yang* relations suggested by early Confucian philosophy.[73] Their adoption of expedient measures, which enables them to deviate from prescribed norms without undermining the dominant social structure, is justifiable in terms of the Confucian doctrine. It is such conceptual ambiguity in Confucian tradition that enables these women, fictional or real, to be enveloped in Confucian values even as they challenge them.

Xu Wei's *Ci Mulan* and *Nü zhuangyuan* show that gender inversion in dramatic literature may be temporary, yet the subversive process itself can be significant. The cross-dressing of Mulan and Chonggu evokes women's power and potential, as well as the author's personal, cultural dislocation, and his novelty-seeking disposition. The gender specifications in the titles, *Ci Mulan* and *Nü zhuangyuan*, are particularly revealing. "Ci" (female) is used to modify Mulan, a girl's given name that has acquired a masculine association since the folk song of Mulan first appeared in the Northern Wei dynasty (386–534); "nü" (female) and "zhuangyuan" (a term referring to men) are in fact mutually exclusive. These titles bring attention to women's power and intelligence and display novelty or marvel (*qi*), which invites readers and audiences to pause and reconsider women's abilities. These titles thus symbolically unsettle the patriarchal formulation of the "natural" status of sexual differences. In conclusion, we may say that without posing real threat to the hegemonic orthodoxy, Xu Wei's representation of disguised women calls gender ideology into question, broadens the possibilities available for women, and to an extent subverts the dominant gender structure of power.

Chapter 5

Gender, Subjectivity, Sexuality: Defining a Subversive Discourse in Wang Anyi's Four Tales of Sexual Transgression

HELEN H. CHEN

From feminism's inception in China at the turn of the century, writers have woven it into the grand narrative of nation building.[1] Since the liberation of Chinese women was seen as symbolizing the liberation of the weak, the poor, and the underprivileged, women's freedom was seen as an imperative for the construction of an independent and modern country. However, the ideological state apparatus has largely perpetuated this gender identity as a symbol of the socialist myth. While the Communist Party claims to have liberated women from the fetters of feudalism and Neo-Confucianism and to have instituted equal voting and working rights for women,[2] and while women are empowered constitutionally and supposedly enjoy political and economic freedom, their independence, to a great extent, is predicated on their submission to the state apparatus.

In reality women enjoy little personal freedom and individuality, since both concepts are condemned as "bourgeois." Gender discourse in China since 1949 has been subsumed under the public discourse on class, state, and the Party that defies gender differences and biological determinism. In this vein, women's identity is first and foremost a class-revolutionary one that denies the autonomy of an individual, much less a gendered female. The term *funü jiefang* (the liberation of women) is utilized by the Communist Party to mobilize the female half of China's population to serve the state, by situating and constituting a collective *funü* consciousness and suppressing individuality and femininity.[3]

I am not endorsing, however, a mainstream feminist consensus that a liberated woman has to be individualist and feminine, nor do I mean to exaggerate the role of the *fulian* (All-China Women's Federation) in the institutionalization of Chinese feminism.[4] But I do intend to argue that the suppression of the individuality and femininity of the Chinese woman can be seen as a form of political oppression that is no less atrocious than the Party's other notorious political campaigns to monopolize ideology. Moreover, women suffer the double oppression of communist ideology and Neo-Confucian ethics. While women must measure up to men by being "iron ladies" who "hold up half the sky," they must also live up to traditional cultural constructs of *xianfu* and *xiaonü*—they must be self-sacrificing and submissive mothers, wives, and daughters. In this light, the criticism made by historian Marilyn B. Young is apt, though perhaps overgeneral. She points out that the double oppression confines Chinese women to role-playing in society rather than biological sex: "Here Chinese socialism and Chinese culture are braided together, collectivism reinforced by feudalism, an anti-individualist class perspective by an older vision of fixed social estates."[5]

The discourse of sexuality in post-1949 China is a discourse of repression through which a variety of institutions such as law and ideology claim authority, and thus sexuality becomes an object of analysis and concern, of surveillance and control. By claiming control in such a fashion, these institutions ascribe political and ideological powers to sexuality that have little to do with its innate nature. The discourse of repression regards the physical aspect of love, *yu*, as a bourgeois entity and a private issue that is subsumed under public discourse.[6] If the Party's purist ideology in the early fifties was meant to build a strong society with moral virtue, its puritanical nature reached inhuman proportions in the following decades. As cultural critic Jianying Zha explains: "Viewing sex as sign of bourgeois decadence and something that would erode revolutionary purity and military morale, the communists promulgated a stiffly antibody, antiflesh, antisexuality attitude. They systematically eradicated all palpable signs of bodily interest and institutions of carnal pleasure."[7] The representation of sexuality portrays *yu* as dirty and destructive, subversive and demoralizing, leaving only the reproductive function as a positive aspect. Such an interpretation has dictated and distorted people's behaviors and their creation of art and literature. During the Cultural Revolution, not just *yu* but romantic love vanished from Chinese literature.[8] While in the West, romantic love may be viewed by some as a discourse of illusion, in the Chinese context, romantic love does not carry a cynical overtone and signifies more than a vision of idealized love, because the attainment of romantic love usually suggests individuals' triumph over restrictive moral, political, or religious codes.[9]

The discourse of sexual repression inscribes the biological implications of women's gender within the social implications of class; it condemns women who pursue sexual freedom as bourgeois and hence counterrevolutionary, because the sexual behavior of women is perceived as a conscious expression of their political stance. Consciousness of female gender is not only repressed but also neutralized, through the exploitation of female sexuality—an exploitation achieved by denouncing their femininity and promulgating gender neutrality. Female identity is contingent upon the communist subordination of all social distinctions and is inscribed within a revolutionary discourse. Consequently, the consciousness of Chinese women can be contextualized on historical, institutional, and ethical grounds only.

To seek artistic autonomy from the hegemonic discourse that subordinates personality, emotion, and subjectivity to morality, rationality, and intellect and subjects characters to the signifiers of enforced official thinking and mentality, Chinese women writers in the post-Mao period have fought hard to demystify the standardizing discourse of Chinese women as a metaphor of the nationalist and socialist myth. In male writers' works of the early 1980s, women characters are largely working-class women with minimal education, who serve as objects of male fantasy or as devotees to men's careers and causes. In contrast, women writers do not eulogize women in supporting roles, and the women characters in their works are largely intellectuals. Although prize-winning stories by women writers, such as Chen Rong's "Rendao zhongnian" (Middle-aged people, 1980), Bing Xin's "Kong Chao" (Empty nest, 1980), and Ye Wenling's "Xin Xiang" (Xin Xiang, 1980), reinforce the official paradigms of ideal women as devoted and self-sacrificing wives or as ambitious and successful professionals, the most fruitful works, such as Zhang Kangkang's "Beijiguang" (Northern lights, 1981), Zhang Jie's "Fangzhou" (The ark, 1982), and "Ai, shi buneng wangji de" (Love cannot be forgotten, 1980), depict the frustration and despair of intellectual women in their often futile search for self, for unfulfilled love, and for moral support in a male-dominated society. It is little wonder that these writers are likely to cause controversies and elicit criticism from conservative critics, since they challenge the official notion that women enjoy the freedom to love and marry in a "liberated" society.[10]

Post-Mao Chinese writers seek to break the silence of condemned romance and to re-enter the emotional world. As a result, narratives of romance and sexuality provide the means to explore humanity. Writers were initially cautious, trapped in their portrayal of love as only spiritual or platonic, and ventured into the world of romantic and physical love gradually. Still, their initial maneuvers were charged with political overtones and did not go beyond protesting the destruction of family and the suppression of romance by ultra-left politics.

For example, in 1980, Zhang Jie's novella "Love Cannot Be Forgotten," which psychologizes a married woman's unfulfilled love for a married man, stirred a controversy not only on the legality of a loveless marriage, but also on the morality of extramarital love. Although the two idealists of Zhang Jie's work have known each other for more than twenty years, they have been together for no more than twenty-four hours. Despite the Platonic nature of their relationship, they are forbidden by law and morality to unite. The only love token from the man is a complete collection of Chekhov—a spiritual gift, but charged with passion—which signifies their spiritual bonding. Although they love each other with a power that is "stronger than death" and feel that they "completely possess each other,"[11] they do not have the courage to leave their loveless marriages.

Zhang Jie is the first post-Mao Chinese writer who questions the sanity of loveless or commercial marriage under socialism. She asks whether the legal bond of marriage is enough to make a marriage work, and whether, if love alone cannot unite two lovers, something stronger than law and morality might accomplish the deed. However, though Zhang Jie calls into question fundamental underpinnings of the superstructure of the Neo-Confucian and Maoist ideologies that privilege the homogeneity of family and make it a model for submission to the state institution, she does not probe further into the problem. She weakens her romantic and idealistic stance by foregrounding the spiritual aspect of love and avoiding the problematic site of desire. She simply puts the blame on the flaws of socialism and proposes a utopian vision of the communist society in which marriage and love will be inseparable.

The first Chinese writer to address sexuality directly in the post-Mao period is Zhang Xianliang, a male writer whose early works chronicled the romances between an educated male Rightist and a sympathetic, uneducated country woman in such works as "Tulao qinghua" (Romance in prison, 1981) and "Lin yu rou" (Soul and flesh, 1980). In "Nanren de yiban shi nüren" (Half of man is woman, 1985), Zhang condemns the repression of sexual desire by the communist regime and the ensuing abnormal sexuality of political prisoners. But his focus centers on the disastrous effects inflicted by repression, rather than on the nature of human sexuality itself.

While Zhang and most other writers during this period describe how the political and social environment distorts sexual desire and human nature, and project sexuality as a metaphorical site where political and ideological implications are interspersed, Wang Anyi tackles the problematic of sexual difference as an immediate reality rather than as a signifier of social and ideological entities. She defies the social emphasis on reason and morality over desire and emotion and reinterprets human sexuality from a feminist perspective in her fiction, particularly in her romance trilogy (*sanlian*)—"Huangshan zhi lian" (Love in a wild mountain, 1986), "Xiaocheng zhi lian" (Love in a small town, 1986), and "Jinxiugu zhi lian" (Love in Splendor Valley, 1987), and her more recent work "Gangshang de shiji" (A century on a small hillock, 1989). In light of her thematic choices and stylistic features, these works might more appropriately be termed "tales of sexual transgression" than "tales of romantic love." In dealing with sexual taboos such as adultery and illicit sex, Wang Anyi transgresses against the orthodox mode of gender discourse: she reappropriates male/female stereotypes, and in the process problematizes and subverts conventional gender tropes. By integrating the language of morality with new languages of sexuality and sexual and gender difference, and slipping elements of the feminist discourse into traditional story-telling, Wang Anyi realistically portrays love and sex, not only paying tribute to the power of emotion and love in a repressive regime, but also stripping off the dehumanizing layers of Maoist discourse—those of scandal and moral despotism.

Previously known for the exquisite images and lyrical idealism in her autobiographical works of the early eighties—such as "Yu, shashasha" (Rain, shashasha, 1981)—works which revolve around an ingenue Wenwen's pursuit of romance and the meaning of life,[12] Wang Anyi embarked on changing her sentimental style into an objective depiction of the world. In 1983, Wang Anyi and her mother, Ru Zhijuan, an established writer, spent four months at the International Writer's Workshop at the University of Iowa and traveled across the United States. Her experiences in the United States showed her a completely different cultural environment and radically changed her outlook on Chinese culture, philosophy, ideology, and aesthetics. In an interview with students of the Chinese Department at Fudan University, she said, "Everything in America is the opposite of everything in our country. Americans have different views of history, time, and people from the Chinese. So when I look back on China, I see something very unusual in the seemingly ordinary life."[13]

Indeed, she sees something very significant in human desire and sexuality and attributes her change from perceiving sexuality as ideologically subversive largely to the influence of Western films and literature. While in Iowa City, Wang Anyi saw the film adaptation of D. H. Lawrence's *Women in Love*. For the first time she found that sex could be represented as naturally beautiful and formally aesthetic.[14] At about the same time, she was influenced by the naturalistic and aesthetic treatment of sexuality in D. H. Lawrence's *Lady*

Chatterley's Lover and Marguerite Duras's *The Lover*. She realized that human sexuality, being natural and instinctual, deserved thoughtful examination, not categorical condemnation.

The fundamental difference between Wang Anyi's fictions of sexuality and those of other post-Mao writers lies in her determination to write about sexuality itself, rather than its sociological implications.[15] In an interview with Wang Zheng, a Chinese scholar studying in the United States, Wang Anyi did not hesitate to declare the thematic purpose of her romance trilogy: "I actually think that my description of sex is beautiful. What my readers find unacceptable is that my description of sex is no more than that . . . making sex the end, the theme of the writing. That is what I did in my three novellas. People say I am making a fuss over something that is not important."[16] The depiction of sexuality in fiction is important to her, because for a serious writer, the depiction of people without their sexuality cannot provide an insightful account of their lives and cannot penetrate the heart of human beings.[17] Sexuality in Wang Anyi's works is a metaphor for human behavior and relationships in general. She studies the biological and hereditary nature of sexuality and explores the grounds and reasons behind sexual behaviors. She also explores the conflict between natural desires and the traditions of society and culture and the tragedies caused by that conflict. Through sexual relationships, her characters discover or redeem their subjectivity, their gender and sexual consciousness.

By characterizing sexuality as natural and instinctual, as a cathartic force that purifies corrupted souls, Wang Anyi convincingly constructs an alternative value system where "the irrational" plays authoritative and legitimate roles. The destructive force of sexuality—embodied in death and degeneration in "Love in a Wild Mountain" and "Love in a Small Town"—loses its grip in her later works "Love in Splendor Valley" and "A Century on a Small Hillock," in which the constructive aspect of sexuality—embodied in its aesthetic beauty and salvific power—emerges to triumph and dictates the tone. In short, she brings sexuality into a discourse in and of itself. Thematic attraction aside, Wang Anyi sees sexuality as a life force that possesses aesthetic value, and she is arguably the first and best contemporary Chinese writer to capture the essence of sexuality in a graceful manner. By the same token, she has freed herself not only from the evasive or moralizing method of repressing or condemning sexuality, but also from the sensationalist method of trivializing sexuality and catering to the lowest common denominator of mass readership.

"Love in a Wild Mountain": Rewriting Seduction and Adultery

Sexual politics in China has always been prejudiced against women, requiring them to be responsible for both their own sexuality and that of men's. Whether women are the seducers or the seduced, they are punished much more severely than men. The sexual politics of Maoist China went so far as to denounce adulterous women as class enemies poisonous to the revolutionary cause.

In the politically moderate environment of the post-Mao era, Chinese literature has sought to diversify the monolithic discourse on adultery. Each breakthrough has raised the eyebrows of the conservatives. It surprised nobody that Zhang Xiaotian's novella "Gongkai de neican" (Inside information made public, 1982), which describes an adulterous young woman who uses sex to go abroad without criticizing her views on love and marriage, was condemned as bourgeois liberalism.[18] Although his portrayal of the opportunistic woman is consonant with orthodox morality, Zhang raises the question of whether sexual freedom has a place in a socialist country.

In the following year, Dai Fang's short story "Tiaozhan" (Challenge, 1983) seriously tackled the subject of adultery. It shocked the country with its depiction of adultery as morally justified, and with its positive portrayal of the woman as seducer. It tells of a love affair between two intellectuals, both married, who meet and fall in love while traveling on a ship. The male protagonist's wife has transferred her interest in him to their daughter; moreover, romance has disappeared from their relationship. Marriage has become a burden instead of a joy. He is torn between the moral standards that his mother instilled in him in his early childhood and the "monster," as he calls passion, that torments his body and soul; between a seemingly safe haven of marriage and "the spiritual unfaithfulness, which, since he married, has almost consumed all his endurance"; between the peacefulness of marriage and the passion of love.[19] While Zhang Jie identifies love with spiritual understanding, Dai Fang identifies it with burning passion. He wonders whether man's pursuit of love and happiness can ever be immoral. Although it is the female protagonist in Dai Fang's story who initiates the affair, she is not condemned as sexually loose, but is portrayed positively, as maternal and loving, "look[ing] at him as if a weather-beaten old woman were looking at an innocent, funny and lovely small child," and possessing an "estranged, trembling passion."[20] Despite the guilt, he does not return to the arms of his wife and daughter to resume his spiritual unfaithfulness, but walks toward the woman he loves to pursue moral happiness.

Adultery in Wang Anyi's tales of sexual transgression is not merely described as a moral, ideological, or political issue, but figures prominently as an aesthetic, humanistic, and gender-related issue. She pits subjectivity against patriarchal institutions and power, and against the dominant culture, in which gender differences are denied and obliterated. In doing so, she contests the limits of sexual and gender inscriptions within the mainstream discourse of power. She pinpoints adultery as a way to redeem individuality and creativity, and a way to freedom from the shackles of tradition. She presents marriage not as the embodiment of the ideals of faith and stability but as either brutal or boring, to the point of inhibiting creativity, diminishing gender awareness, and alienating individuality. Her works toy with the idea that marriage signifies a backstage, while the love affairs act as the center stage for personal fulfillment, the climax of creation, and the transformation of subjectivity.[21] In her depiction of extramarital affairs, the style is not incriminating and intimidating, but sincere and insightful.

In "Love in a Wild Mountain," Wang Anyi defines seduction not as subversive, but as arising from a natural desire. She sees adultery as a form of human relationship and attempts to justify it morally with her idea of fate: two people madly in love cannot really govern themselves because their fate has already been written by who the lovers are before they meet and by when and where they meet. She devotes nearly two-thirds of her novella to narrating the two protagonists' lives before their first meeting. Her narrative punctuates the illusion of present time with a sense of the omnipresent past.

"Love in a Wild Mountain" describes a love affair between two people who are both bored with their marriages. While "He," a passive, effeminate man who succumbs to fate and has always been controlled by his elder brother, his mother, and his wife, needs space to get rid of his inferiority complex and to mature, "She," a beautiful, strong-willed woman who has always manipulated people—especially the opposite sex, excepting her husband—desires to act out a play of conquest and submission. The love affair, however, ends on a note of tragedy: succumbing to social prejudice and pressure, the woman decides that they should commit suicide on a wild and barren mountain. Nevertheless, Wang Anyi honors the transformational power of sex that changes the protagonists' characters: for the first time in his life, "He" becomes determined to take responsibility for his own life, and "She" changes from an artful and egoistic gambler and player of the love game to a devoted and selfless lover.

Wang Anyi employs the image "huangshan" (wild and barren mountain) to suggest that the love between "Him" and "Her" is not only wild (i.e., uninhibited and unfettered by morality, shame, and responsibility) but also barren (i.e., an aborted and fruitless love affair suffocated by their weak wills and social prejudices). She enriches the symbolic and ironic meaning of the novella by alluding to the classical Chinese novel *Pilgrimage to the West* (Xiyouji):

Wang's barren "huangshan" stands in contrast to the famous "huaguoshan" (flower and fruit mountain) with abundant greenery, flowers, and fruits. Sun Wukong, the hero of "huaguoshan," rebels against heavenly laws and rules; likewise, the heroes in "Love in a Wild Mountain" rebel against traditional morals. The "huangshan" image symbolizes the cultural constraints of repression and oppression in a larger context.

To pinpoint the different stages of life in the lovers' relationship, Wang Anyi underscores the images of sounds and odors. The sound images conjure an atmosphere predisposed for the love tragedy: the music of the cello whimpering, the siren from the dock whining, and the heartbreaking *erhu* (a traditional Chinese musical instrument) melodies from the bushes, the echoes of cello and siren reverberate in a haunting manner. Olfactory images convey the intensifying attraction between the lovers. At the beginning, it is the woman's flirtation and her "very pleasing" smell enhanced by a fan that put the man under her spell. Likewise it is his smell that excites her: "Looking at his back, she saw the white vest through the polyester shirt, a mark of sweat on his back wetted his vest, and through the vest his shirt, and the shirt was glued to his back by the sticky sweat. Gradually and interestingly the mark grew bigger and bigger."[22] Her desire grows stronger with the expansion of the sweat mark, "so she got up, with deep satisfaction, and left without saying goodbye."[23] Finally it is the reminder of his smell that makes her realize that she has fallen in love with him. She and her husband are taking a nap together when "slowly they began to sweat—wet and slippery sweat. Her hands were stroking the back of her husband, his sweat got her palms wet. And that reminded her of 'His' sweat, which suddenly seemed a sacred smell to her. Men were very different, she was lost in her thought and could not sleep at all."[24]

Although she denies that she is a feminist in the Western sense, Wang Anyi's gender views differ radically from the conventional stereotypes of strong men and passive women:

> In China, women always appear to be weak, always to obey the will of another person. But in fact, women are strong and use this means of obedience to reach an end that involves conquest.... Chinese men are passive but like to think of themselves as aggressive.... Chinese men have always been pampered by society and by women. So they have very weak wills.[25]

This idea is present in "Love in a Wild Mountain": the images that are associated with the women are conventional male stereotypes, and the images that are associated with men are conventional female stereotypes. The female characters are strong-willed, aggressive, and independent. While "His" wife's "strong heart and wide vision can take any weak souls under her wing," "He" is passive and diffident, "far too weak in both physique and spirit."[26] Toward the end of "Love in a Wild Mountain," the images of "He" and "She" appear heavily Freudian: "She" is the mother figure that "held him as if he were a baby," "He was holding fast to her neck, his soft arms circled tightly around her neck. He felt as if he were holding his mother's neck at a very early age."[27] The sexual feelings she arouses in him are purported to be as nurturing as maternal love. It is ironic that in falling for her he rescues himself from the power of his wife, his mother, and his elder brother, only to find his doomed final resting place in the merciful arms of his mother-like lover.[28]

To understand Wang Anyi's thesis of the male/female relationship, one needs to examine her essay "Man and Woman, Woman and City" (1986), in which she contends that the feminization of men should be conceived as a form of the cultural unconscious. She explains from a sociological point of view why Chinese women are stronger than men and why men tend to look for maternal figures in relationships. Whereas men are "pampered by heaven"—by society and its institutions and systems—they need more maternal love than women do to mature; women surpass men in character as they grow stronger in their continuous and lonely fight against adversity and prejudice.[29] Physiologically, Wang presumes, women must be superior to men because life starts within women's bodies, so they are able to understand life from within. By contrast, men use mind alone to comprehend the world. Cut off from life, men entrust their ideals to the outside world and pursue fame and fortune, filial piety, and family. Intertwined with life and relieved from social obligations of success, women create and perfect their inner world, and when called devote their heart and soul to love.[30] Likewise, as far as historical, political, and economical factors are concerned, Wang surmises that men have borne more burdens and responsibilities than women in China's long history of feudalism.[31]

Wang foregrounds the world of female subjective consciousness by focusing on the female presence, instead of the conventional scenario of female sexual dependence on male initiation. This amounts to a revision not just of images of women but of the very relationship of women to those images in the first place. It is always women ("She" and his wife) who take the initiative in sexual acts in Wang's stories. For instance, in the sweat scene of "Love in a Wild Mountain," "She" seduces "Him" by sucking a phallic symbol, a popsicle: "She was happier to see that he became so fidgety. She slowly sucked the popsicle, her tongue pressed closely to it, melting it drop by drop till it turned into sweet cool water in her throat. She tucked the little bamboo stick between her teeth and patiently waited for him to turn around."[32] By foregrounding female sexuality, Wang Anyi uses her narrative not only to oppose the deeply ingrained myth of female passivity but also to break down norms of representing female sexuality. Women have been either appropriated as objects of desire, with their subjectivity at stake, or accused of being morally subversive, of manipulating the desire of men and their own desire to a degenerating end. But in "Love in a Wild Mountain," the heroine as seducer is morally justified and aesthetically formalized by the fact that "She" is making an individual choice to obtain freedom from the shackles of social inhibitions.

Because she is acting consciously, the image of the female in the sex scenes is aggressive, assertive, and passionate, whereas that of the male is passive, effeminate, and cold: "He embraced her hot and steamy body, she embraced his icy cold body, they couldn't utter a word. . . . His slender fingers lightly stroked her neck, as if cold dew drops were rolling slowly down. She had never experienced such cool tenderness, which ignited her fiery passion. He felt suffocated, as if surrounded by flames."[33] Wang Anyi uses parallel phrases and sentences to build a poetic rhythm of the communion of passion. She ends the rhythm, though, with a narrative intrusion immediately following the sex scene, which, with adverbs clamoring for sensation, undermines the holiness of the passion and the effect of the naturalistic beauty of the writing: "This is happy suffocation, oh, they are so, so happy. Oh, Heavens, they are so, so sinful."[34]

Wang Anyi may have introduced new images and concepts of sexuality into contemporary Chinese literature, but that does not mean that she does not succumb to traditional, moralizing images and concepts. Elsewhere in the novella, "She" sees virginity as a virtuous property of women. Although she likes to flirt and play games with men, she will not sacrifice her virginity before her marriage, because she considers it "the most precious magic weapon" that she cannot afford to lose.[35] References to love affairs as biblical symbols of evil and sin are dispersed throughout the work. The lovers take their punishment as destined, fearing that they have committed the crime of "stealing the forbidden fruit."[36] The end of the story, where the lovers' deaths symbolize the punishment for their socially transgressive crime, reinforces, rather than disrupts, traditional morality, which the novella strongly criticizes.

"Love in a Small Town": Mixing Shame and Desire

In order to understand Wang Anyi's approach in "Love in a Small Town," it may be illuminating to compare Wang with another writer, Zhang Xian, who is one of the first post-Mao writers to depict socially transgressive sexuality. Zhang's novella "Bei aiqing yiwangde jiaoluo" (The corner forgotten by love, 1980) describes the love tragedy of two teenage peasants during the Cultural

Revolution. In this story, the girl commits suicide after the couple are caught and humiliated. Zhang's portrayal differs from Wang's in two fundamental ways. First, Zhang's story renders the heroine the object of the male gaze and fantasized desire, while the male gaze in Wang's stories plays different roles. Second, Zhang Xian uses sexuality as a broader political metaphor and avoids confronting the issue of teenage sexuality, an issue Wang Anyi tackles in "Love in a Small Town." In a story of desire, Zhang undermines the instinctual aspect of sexuality and the role of desire in human relationships by blaming the barren spirituality of the lovers, who are unable to control their desire: "A primitive instinct was raging flames in the blood of these materially inadequate, spiritually barren, yet physically strong young people. Traditional morality, rational dignity, criminal danger and a girl's sense of shame, everything and everything else, were all burned to ashes at this very moment."[37]

Instead of using teenage sexuality as a backdrop for political turmoil, Wang's "Love in a Small Town" foregrounds the sexual awakening and eruption of two dancers, "He" (from ages 16 to 28) and "She" (from ages 12 to 24) in a small town's local theatrical troupe. Wang Anyi explores the tension between morality and desire, repression and rebellion, shame and ecstasy. She investigates how the powers of desire can either release one from social and personal inhibitions or dominate and destroy one's psyche and behavior, and how the liberation of desire imbues life with beauty and meaning. While the teenagers' attraction to each other grows stronger during routine dance exercises, they blame their bodies for sexual arousal. They fall in love—yet their love is bonded by nothing other than sex. They do not know how to nourish their relationship other than through sex. Their shame about their indecent behavior, their fights caused by that shame, social stigma, and public criticism bring their love to a sad ending. "She" becomes a single mother with illegitimate twins; "He" marries another woman and turns into a wife-beating alcoholic and gambler.

One of the most frequently used sexual images in Wang's tales of sexual transgression is that of a baby, who embodies the pure, instinctual, and vulnerable aspect of sexuality. In "Love in a Small Town," when "She" develops a "pampering" feeling toward her body, she can "sleep [as] soundly and sweetly as a baby."[38] Wang Anyi not only conveys through this image the character's affection for her body, but also suggests she is naively unaware of her body as a sexual entity. Both "He" and "She" think of sex as "dirty ecstasy" and their bodies—carriers of desire—as shameful. They are a couple of "unheeded children with unknown sexual desire."[39] Nobody cares for their tormented souls, and they know nothing of how to channel their irrepressible feelings, the guilt and shame of which is captured vividly in the recurring images of sweating, bathing, and washing their bedsheet and bedspread. To torture their innocent bodies, they overdo dance exercises: "She" throws herself heavily to the floor and repeats the painful routine with no hope of success; "He" distorts his body to unimaginable shapes and "pretentiously" stands on his hands for twenty minutes to punish his body whose carnal desire is no longer under the control of his soul. Yet their overwrought bodies actually demand more attention and only further arouse their mutual sympathy and sexual desire. The excessive sweating during the exercises and the subsequent baths do more than just wash the dirt from their bodies: they connote their need to cleanse the dirty desire from their minds. Even washing the dirty bedsheet and bedspread, which wrap up her "sinful" body, indicates her desire to purge shame from herself.

The narrator in "Love in a Small Town" is as problematic as the narrator in "Love in a Wild Mountain." The narrator's moralizing rationalization stands in sharp contrast with the passion celebrated in the sexual images. For instance, after their first encounter, the narrator likens the teenagers' sexuality to "seeds" of "sin," "filth and mire," and "forbidden fruit," and implies that as ignorant as they are, they cannot conquer the forces of nature.

In the end, it is "through the violent purgation of sexual desire" that she becomes "cleaner and purer than ever before."[40] Motherhood releases her from the obsession of libido and bestows on her the peace of mind. The "simple-minded" woman, who has "thick thighs, fat buttocks, broad shoulders, and a round waist," surpasses the man who is "wise and rational": "Her heart was as crystal clear as a pond of water, she has never achieved such a bright and clear state of mind before. The burning fire that had tortured her for so many years was finally extinguished. She was unexpectedly resurrected in the flame of desire."[41] The conclusion of the story undermines the sacredness of desire by opposing desire and maternal love. It validates the reproductive function of sexuality while denying any validity to its passionate eruption. Still, Wang Anyi's endorsement of motherhood differs sharply from that of the Party, in that she extols the natural and instinctual aspect of maternal feelings whereas the Party subsumes motherhood under the nationalist discourse so as to perpetuate the socialist myth. Overall, Wang Anyi's portrayal of illicit sex disrupts the moralizing sexual codes. Since the sexual ignorance portrayed in "Love in a Small Town" symbolizes the apathy and insensitivity in the national psychological makeup, sexual awakening suggests a rejuvenation of national culture.

"A Century on a Small Hillock": Resurrecting Passion and Love

Another *zhiqing* writer would have made the story "A Century on a Small Hillock" just another tale of the suffering *nüzhiqing*. (*Zhiqing* were high school students from the urban areas who were forced to work in the countryside during the Cultural Revolution; *nüzhiqing* means "female *zhiqing*.") The rage of the young generation of writers over the victimization of *nüzhiqing* is an outcry against the rape of women, and against the exploitation of desperate women, whose only means to change their fate is their body. In a larger context, this rage is in response to the exploitation of youth and idealism by Mao and his ultra-left politics.[42]

"A Century on a Small Hillock" begins with a conventional plot of *zhiqing* fiction. Eager to leave the poor, backward, and boring countryside, Li Xiaoqin seduces Yang Xuguo, a married man and the head of the village, in the hope that he will recommend her for work in the local capital she was originally from. Yang Xuguo has no intention of recommending her transfer but nonetheless develops a sexual relationship with her.

Wang Anyi is unique among the writers who have dealt with this subject in that she does not simply end her story with a presentation of sexual exploitation or a criticism of the morality of the two people. She does not cater to the misconceived traditional morals that condemn without investigating and understanding. Instead, she constructs an imaginary cultural space that valorizes a moral and sexual context different from that of other writers. She transcends the seduction and exploitation plot, widens her thematic dimension, and develops the story into an exploration and fulfillment of love and passion. Moreover, she describes how passion transforms two mean-spirited people into affectionate and decent human beings capable of loving and caring. After the sexual liaison is exposed, Li is exiled to a poorer, more isolated village on a hillock, and Yang is arrested and sentenced to reeducation through hard labor. Yang then risks his life after his release to see Li on the hillock. Their love overcomes the fear of shame and punishment. They spend seven days and nights together with the "passion of desperadoes" and thus "create a paradisiacal century."[43]

"A Century on a Small Hillock" celebrates the salvific power of sex and love through images. For instance, the image of purging that appears in "Love in a Small Town" reappears here. Sex purges the feelings of fear and shame from the lovers' minds. On a more concrete scale, the salvific power of sex and love transforms Yang from an obscene and indecent man into a worshiper of feminine beauty. His gaze on Li as an object is transformed into his worship of her as an embodiment of aesthetic beauty, and his admiration for a love goddess purifies his carnal desire: "He was unable to show off his sexual prowess, every bit of him turned into a pure little boy."[44] Finally, the rejuvenating power of sex and love leads to his full physical transformation. Before they meet, he is an ugly man whose "dark brown skin was spotted with morbid scars"; but the galvanizing joy of sex creates a new and radiant Yang with smooth skin: "His coarse and numb calluses were made soft and sensitive by the caressing of [Li's] smooth body, as if he were a child again."[45] In this story, the seductive woman, as embodied in the traditional image of snake, does not just evoke fear in man, as found in conventional representation, but also evokes awe and admiration. Woman as the mother figure in "Love in a Wild Mountain" is elevated to the goddess figure in "A Century on a Small Hillock." It is culturally significant that Wang Anyi gives sexuality a transformative power and challenges the ideological constraints of the hegemonic culture that condemns woman's sensuality. Li Xiaoqin is embodied as the creator, whose ravishing beauty inspires and reincarnates a new Yang in body and soul. The traditional story of "beauty and the beast" is transformed into a celebration of creation and rebirth, love and passion.

The sexual images in "A Century on a Small Hillock" are more complex than in Wang Anyi's other works. In the first sexual encounter between Li and Yang, the sexual images project purity as well as conventional bias. "She innocently lifted her hand toward him like a newborn baby, her pure white arms circling around his withered and black body like a snake."[46] Wang then portrays Li as a complex character of childlike vulnerability and evil seductiveness, that of "a demon from underground" and "a vengeful spirit."[47] Li Xiaoqin and Yang Xuguo's third sexual encounter occurs on a snowy night when Yang uses a quilt to spirit Li into a barn. "[He] carefully opened the quilt as if he were opening swaddling clothes. . . . [She] was as peaceful as a baby. . . . He held her carefully as if she were a precious golden baby."[48] Here Wang Anyi reveals the complexity of Yang's character, who exploits Li's body as well as treasures it, but whose feelings seem to have overcome, or at least overshadowed, his dishonesty during sex. The image of Yang as a child appears when he grows afraid of the punishment for the sexual liaison and goes into hiding in his mother-in-law's house, where he curls his lean body "like a suckling child," despairingly waiting for the judgment day.[49]

Other important sexual images in "A Century on a Small Hillock" are those of creation and death, exemplified in the phrase "the passion of desperadoes."[50] In the first sex scene, Yang is morally confused, sexually intimidated by Li's attractive body and daring advance, and as afraid as "a dog without backbone," "as if he were dead," "and his eyes betrayed the radiance of death."[51] Li is also haunted by images of death: "She felt that death wasn't that terrible, death was just like a bout of madness. Her tragic laughter was buried by mud, she seemed to have seen green grass growing out of her grave and the rise of the blazing red sun."[52] She is afraid of death for reasons that differ from Yang's: she fears that her effort to get herself out of the countryside might prove futile and destructive, as if she were burying her future by doing so. On their second night on the hillock, Yang cries out death threats: "I want you to die," his voice dripping with blood at the time of climax, and Li responds in the same way. Yet the threats reveal the playfulness of the sex game rather than any inherent morbidity. The unifying image of life and death, however, figures prominently toward the end of the story, when the previously mean-spirited lovers are resurrected from the sea of love and surging waves of passion, reincarnated as the god and goddess of love. Their sexual enlightenment signifies a deepening and a confirmation of their contact with the natural and aesthetic world, out of which arise new ways of living, new ways of loving each other:

> Passion was surging tidal waves in their bodies, their rhythms were so in tune that they resembled a seamless heavenly robe. They never missed a step and could reach a harmonious state effortlessly. Their passion lasted so long that one tide was always higher than the other. They were like two unfailing surfers, playing to their heart's content, singing toward the climax without hurry, and created a paradisiacal century at the turbulent instant.[53]

Indeed, "A Century on a Small Hillock" represents Wang Anyi's mature artistry. Unlike the titles of her previous tales that assign meanings to places only, this one sets the tenor for the emotional ambiance of the novella by alluding to the tension between the flux of time and the eternity of an isolated corner, which is symbolic of the backwardness of traditional culture. "Century" suggests not only timelessness, for the lovers rebel against the historical milieu that looms in the background, but also a new era—they create an alternative world that glorifies the sensuous body, that pits itself against the orthodox moral prescription that associates desire with subversiveness.

"Love in Splendor Valley": Reconstructing Gender and Female Subjectivity

"Love in Splendor Valley" is not just another tale of an extramarital affair, but rather "a woman's story."[54] Similar to "Love in a Wild Mountain," the female protagonist needs a new stage on which to act out her feelings because she is suffocated by her marriage and bored with her "detached, impatient and indifferent" husband.[55] "She" yearns for peace with herself, serenity of mind and lucidity of thought, none of which she can share with her husband. While attending a literary seminar in Lu Mountain, "She," an editor, falls in love with a writer. In this instance, spiritual understanding, more than gratification of physical desire, forms the foundation of the relationship.

This story, unlike Wang's realistic portrayals of sexual transgression, evokes surrealism: it can be read as a female editor's imaginary, spiritual dialogue with a male writer, since it is triggered by her intuition, is complicated by a mysterious atmosphere, and alternates between realism and surrealism. Although the story employs a third-person narrator, who knows nothing of the male writer except through the female editor, the narrator acts as the editor's friend, shadow, defender, and speaker of her psychological state. In other words, it is through the editor's point of view that the writer's story is mediated and reconstructed; it is through the female vision that the male character achieves coherence and meaning. This narrative strategy foregrounds fictionality and undercuts the illusion of realism, a technique that may be considered as exhibiting the experimental spirit and reflexive mobility of Wang's feminist approach, which must constantly transfigure her progressive outlook.[56] In problematizing the reliability of the narrative, Wang Anyi implies that sometimes fantasy is more important to a person's self-esteem than reality, or, as she explains in an interview, that since love is sometimes one person's affair and one person's show, she deliberately makes the image of the male writer blurred and insignificant to accentuate the woman's self-esteem.[57] Thus, "She" can work herself into physical ecstasy and spiritual peace through her imagination, will, and calculation. The female protagonist combines the contradictory progressive and traditional images. She does not intend to subvert an unhappy marriage with an extramarital affair; rather, she imagines, produces, and wills the affair to re-create her selfhood, which has been stultified by marriage, to readjust a psychological balance of her married life, and eventually to succumb to the marriage institution against which she has rebelled.

Wang Anyi highlights the female protagonist's psychological state by pitting the image of her isolated home against that of the open space outside. Sick and irritated at home, she loathes the suffocating space of the dirty staircases: "She is so thoroughly familiar with her home that nothing could excite her curiosity and interest. She understands everything without paying any attention. Her life begins only after she walks out of her home. Home is like the backstage of life, nothing but a preparation for real life."[58] Wang Anyi depicts the serenity of the protagonist's psychological state in the images of clarity, such as water, since the novella turns on her achieving a balance of mind. Once she gets outside her home, her heart is as bright and clear as a pond of crystal clear water, and she wants to be a "peaceful" person. The sunshine outside her home is "streaming down" and "transparent"; the white cloud in Splendor Valley is "transparent" and the water is "green and clear, without any dirt."[59] Once outside her home, her heart feels "clear and bright" as if "a bright mirror were shining high above."[60] The literary seminar she attends represents a refreshing change from her tedious editing job, and she is inspired by the literary talk, "as if running water were flowing continuously" through the dried-up land of her spirit.[61]

The story addresses the loss and recovery of femininity. She loses her awareness of her gender after she gets married because she soon decides that learning the naked truth of the opposite sex requires no further effort or familiarity, which hence makes her own sexual consciousness insensible. She can no longer appreciate her husband as a man and herself as a woman. She does not recover her gender consciousness until she meets the writer, whose attention awakens her dormant and suppressed instincts and makes her recapture the strangeness of the male gaze. This gaze does not render the heroine a mere object of desire; rather, it affirms her identity as both an attractive female and an independent, intelligent professional woman, reestablishing both the confidence and the consciousness of gender that she needs to recapture her self-esteem. The gender relationship is represented as intricately intertwined, as well as free of domination by either partner, and as being constantly challenged and redefined. Even the images of Splendor Valley, along with its mist, fog, and white clouds, is found to "symbolize the unfathomable depths of self, which dissolve, transform, and consolidate" "a world of imagination, dream and fantasy, in which the self becomes fluid and capable of change and reconstruction."[62]

Despite Wang Anyi's unprecedented account of gender representation in "Love in Splendor Valley," one cannot fail to take note of the contradictory nature of her feminist approach: on the one hand, "She" is an independent, intellectual woman who stages her own show; on the other hand, she admires the writer as if he is her professor whom she loves with a high school student's shyness and innocence.[63] At the beginning and the end of "Love in Splendor Valley," Wang Anyi pinpoints the woman's elegance as being that of "an unmarried virgin."[64] This raises questions of whether the experience in Lu Mountain has changed her insecurity, whether her sexual and intellectual identities have matured or remain as vulnerable as before. It also undermines Wang's feminist stance and mirrors the conclusion of her mostly insightful analysis of men and women in "Man and Woman, Woman and City." The essay suffers a shortsightedness when she submits that gender differences, however unreasonable, are natural [and not socially and ideologically constituted], therefore one must acknowledge them and fight for gender-specific happiness. She points out that women unconscionably desire the protection of men even if women become completely independent.[65] In "Love in Splendor Valley," although "She" seems to have enjoyed a new life after leaving her home, ironically, regardless of her newly acquired consciousness, home—the place that suffocates her individuality—is where she belongs. Nevertheless, Wang Anyi's ability to grip, stir, and unsettle stems not so much from how her stories end as from the complexity of understanding from which their significance is artistically realized and projected as a whole.

In an age of transformation, sexual desire—once a cultural taboo, a symbol of repression and a virtually undeveloped field—becomes a fertile ground for contested meanings and ideologies, a vehicle for writers to challenge dominant discourses, to test new theories of all kinds and to discover new possibilities in human relationships. Although it is debatable that "all master narratives" of the Maoist era have disappeared,[66] the tide of cultural fluctuation and fermentation rides on the surging waves of new master narratives that reevaluate *yu*. One ironic bend in this postrevolutionary, post-"cultural-reflecting" (*wenhua fansi*) and, indeed, "postmodern" era lies in a disturbing trend of a specific cultural imagination that finds *yu* to have expendable commercial value at the intersection of booming capitalism and residual socialism. This trend thrives on exploiting *yu*, *yu* expressly signifying the juxtaposition of material and sexual desire, of wealth and fantasy, which has made its inroads not only in popular culture (e.g., the glamorization and glorification of the new elites, a celebrity "class" of businessmen, sports and film stars, popular singers, and fashion models) but also in fiction that capitalizes on the *exploitation* rather than the *exploration* of socially transgressive sexuality (e.g., Jia Pingwa's *Feidu* [Ruins of the capital, 1993]).[67]

The exploitation of sexuality, however, should be seen as part of the trend that gravitates toward commercial literature. At a time when literature loses its power to shock and challenge, the booming capitalism has consumed, overwhelmed, and commodified many writers, forcing them to redefine their role (be it commercial, literary, entrepreneur, or any combinations of the three) and negotiate with the tastes of the market. Wang Anyi is one of a few writers who swims against the tide and consciously safeguards her artistic integrity.[68]

Wang Anyi's exploration of gender politics and sexual psychology does not end with the four tales of sexual transgression; rather, she has continually intrigued readers with more ambitious works. Compared with these four tales of sexual transgression, the representation of passion and desire in her later works is rather subdued. Yet they point to a new height in her career that "transgresses" the expectations of critics: she contests the boundaries of sexuality and gendered relationship not just in realistic, humanist and sexual terms, but also in modernist and postcolonial perspectives. The subjects of her recent fiction range from the power of spiritual bonding in love ("Shensheng jitan" [Sacred altars, 1989]); to the contest among sisterly love, motherhood, and marriage ("Dixongmen" [Brothers, 1989]); to manipulation and victimization of innocent women by a political victim—a male Rightist writer ("Shushu de gushi" [The story of the uncle, 1989]); from sexual crimes and degeneration in an age of economic reform ("Mini" [Mini, 1990]) to sexual economy in a postcolonial age ("Xianggang de qing yu ai" [Sentiment and love in Hong Kong, 1994], and "Gexing riben lai" [The singer from Japan, 1992]).

Her latest novel, *Changhenge* (Song of everlasting sorrow, 1995), which records the tragic life of "Miss Shanghai" Wang Qiyao, spanning from the decadent years of the late forties to the economic reform of 1985, not merely presents an antiromantic critique of the delusion of glamour and beauty but also alludes to the glamour girls in the nineties, who, ironically, are the envy of Wang Anyi's many female readers. However, despite the deceiving force of *yu* entangled in greed and gender politics that demeans her, the heroine is not debilitated; rather, she rises above adversity through her resilience.

The new orientation in Chinese literature calls attention to the fact that women's liberation in contemporary China faces serious challenges in the new historical milieu. Although some women have taken a share of the recent economic success and gained personal freedom because of financial stability, the majority of Chinese women still suffer from job discrimination, and a large number of them have either been ordered or otherwise induced to leave the work force. The new form of repression of women—ironically made possible partly by the resurrection of femininity, which is not so much a way of self-expression as a way to fame and wealth—emerges as a result of the degenerate and corrupt cultural worship of *yu*. However, precisely because the painful memories of political and sexual repression are not easily forgotten, and in fact repression as such still persists, the Party has tolerated the representation and production of *yu* as disposable commodity, hoping that the public's memories of repression will be suppressed and submerged under a frenzied and delirious craving for *yu*. In this light, Wang Anyi's four tales of sexual transgression may even challenge this new dominant discourse that commercializes *yu*—not without, however, a political and ideological twist. In conclusion, her investigation of sexuality from the artistic, humanist, and gendered perspectives sets a high standard for depicting *yu* in the fin de siècle.

Chapter 6

Consuming Asian Women: The Fluid Body of Josie Packard in *Twin Peaks*

GRETA AI-YU NIU

"*Welcome to Twin Peaks*"

The generative premise of the television series *Twin Peaks* is the mysterious and brutal murder of a young white woman, high-school "homecoming queen" Laura Palmer in the town of Twin Peaks, Washington. In the first season, the network foregrounded the mystery of her murder with the catchphrase "Who killed Laura Palmer?" The gradual discovery that Laura's father sexually abused and finally killed her and the theme of father-daughter incest propels the series through its first season and into its second (and last) season. Laura Palmer was, as one character puts it, "full of secrets," and delving into those secrets is central to the series. On the other hand, the equally mysterious life and death of another woman character, Josie Packard, never seemed to motivate the plot in the same way. Portrayed by the Chinese American film star Joan Chen (Chen Chong), Jocelyn "Josie" Packard is an anomaly in the small town primarily inhabited by white individuals who are born, raised, and remain there to reproduce families.[1] Josie moved to Twin Peaks from Hong Kong only six years earlier.

Focusing on the figure of Josie Packard enables us to examine the relationships the series constructs between fluidity, consumption, and Asian women's bodies. In the character of Josie Packard, the series addresses the issue of a larger Pacific Rim community and the problem this raises for the production of an American national identity. *Twin Peaks* attempts to define national boundaries by critiquing Asians and Asian Americans, particularly people from Japan and Hong Kong, for their recent consumption in the Pacific Northwest and for being in a position to consume U.S. territory.

According to Edward Said, Orientalism presumes to represent, to speak for, the Orient, to elucidate the mysteries of the Orient for the sake of Western readers.[2] The orientalism of *Twin Peaks* presents Josie as not just a mystery to be solved, but as mysterious as such. *Twin Peaks* orientalizes Josie's sexuality and privileges the external as the truth about her, reducing her character to a mere visible surface. Through her, the series invokes national and racial differences to define and distinguish proper forms of femininity. By identifying proper femininity with domesticity, it reclaims regional Pacific Northwest concerns for nationalistic and xenophobic purposes and generates narratives of the domestic versus the foreign, the national versus the outlandish or exotic. The series accomplishes these narratives through "consumption," by conflating the individual body of Josie Packard and the political economy (social body) of Hong Kong.[3] In this twentieth-century U.S.-style orientalism, which draws on but differs from Edward Said's conceptualization of Orientalism for Great Britain, France, and Germany in the eighteenth and nineteenth centuries,[4] Josie Packard is represented as being consumed, not only by others, but also by herself, and ultimately, by her own body.

The financial backers and producers of *Twin Peaks* trusted that certain topics once considered primarily of regional concern to the Pacific Northwest were worthy of national interest. *Twin Peaks* is set in a region not previously represented on national television. Small towns have always had a place on television.[5] Focusing on a small community of characters, many of these melodramas use their settings almost tangentially, and often territorially; location is reduced from city, state, or nation and domesticated so that the home is the primary site of complex emotions for the characters.[6] One of the main differences between these other dramas and *Twin Peaks* is their focus on a group of characters. *Twin Peaks*, on the other hand, was deeply interested in both a group of characters and their relationships to a specific region. One of the most salient points of *Twin Peaks* is that it demonstrates again and again that the local setting, in this case this town, is perverse.

Consumption

The series subsumes a history of United States anti-Asian immigration policy with Josie serving as an exemplary representative of Hong Kong. She has settled in the United States without any legal difficulties. After the June 1989 government attack on the pro-democracy protesters in mainland China, increasing numbers of Hong Kong applicants sought to establish residency abroad before July 1997, the end of Great Britain's lease and "return" of the island and Kowloon territories to the mainland.[7] In the 1980s and 1990s Pacific Northwest, particularly in Seattle and Vancouver, the number of immigrants from Hong Kong, of transplants from California, and other Asian Americans grew. Josie's immigration makes no references to the politics facing Hong Kong residents in the late 1980s. The surprise here is not that a woman from Hong Kong is acquiring land in the Pacific Northwest, but that she is not doing so closer to, for example, Vancouver or Seattle, where other Asians are settling: she is not presented as a member of those communities or families. In this context, *Twin Peaks*'s representation of a woman from Hong Kong living in the Pacific Northwest who is both an inveterate consumer and someone consumed (i.e., used by other characters) is highly charged. This preoccupation with the Pacific Northwest in *Twin Peaks* seems troubled about the region's connections to the Pacific Rim, particularly the economic and social implications of the presence of individuals from Asia, and only peripherally concerned about the local and international lumber industry. Maintaining trade relationships with Japan and Hong Kong does not seem especially desirable for this town despite the fact that the town itself was largely founded around a sawmill. Instead, *Twin Peaks* displaces the region's economic concerns onto Josie and resolves the ambivalent relationship Twin Peaks has with Hong Kong and China with her death.

Twin Peaks is deliberately labyrinthine, with enigmatic clues dropped along the way in the tradition of the mystery genre. The frequent doublings of character, the minute details, the multiple and complex plots distinguished this series from other late 1980s and early 1990s prime-time programs and pointed to a different direction for subsequent programs.[8] Rather than offer a flattening linear narrative, I will describe only the salient details of scenes specific to Josie and to my argument about fluidity and consumption. The television series met with astounding success and was marketed in the hopes of generating a dedicated, even cult-like, following.[9] The two-hour pilot of *Twin Peaks*, which ABC featured as its Sunday night movie on April 8, 1990, was the highest-rated television movie of the season.[10] An estimated 20 million viewers saw the pilot in which Josie Packard, as the first character introduced, served the critical function of defamiliarizing an otherwise too-familiar representation of an outdoor environment that U.S. viewers already associated with the Pacific Northwest. The opening credit sequence begins with shots of a sawmill, log-cutting machinery, a waterfall, mountains, and a signpost identifying the location—the town of Twin Peaks in the state of Washington. Following the credits, there was another outdoor scene: a long shot of a large wooden

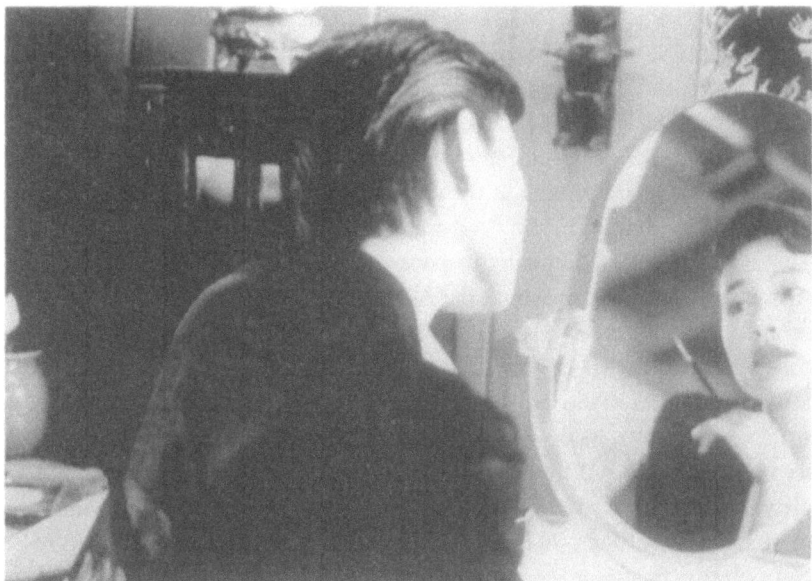

Figure 1. Twin Peaks: Josie Packard gazing into a mirror. Photo © 1989 by World-vision Enterprises, Inc. All rights reserved.

house. The pilot disrupts the familiarity of these representations of the Pacific Northwest as natural and uncultivated in the next scene of the interior of the house. The camera pans from the sleek, black ceramic figures of a dog and a duck sculpted in a stylized fashion to the sleekly stylized head of an Asian woman who is gazing at her face in a mirror (see figure 1). The woman is presented as an object of luxury, art (though not a singular piece of art but a mass-produced one), and perhaps affection, akin to that bestowed on glossy animals. The camera first shows her face framed in the mirror, then the back of her head and her reflection. She has just finished applying her very bright red lipstick, and yet continues to gaze at her reflection while she hums. By the camera angle we can tell that Josie is looking, not at the viewer, but at herself. In contrast to the natural splendors of a waterfall, the splendor of this woman mobilizes an artistry that is recognized as feminine and artificial: hair gel and cosmetics. In contrast to the "nature" suggested by the opening credits, this initial setting is intimate, domestic, and feminine. While it is unprecedented for a major network pilot to introduce an Asian woman as the first character, this scene also sets up a model of the gaze.

Nothing about the opening credits draws on recognizable Orientalist themes, but in the scenes immediately following, orientalism in the form of consumption is at work. By linking orientalism to consumption I have a particular model in mind. Edward Said describes what he terms Orientalism as a practice applied by Western scholars to represent Eastern cultures, what in the United States today is called "the Middle East," as passive rather than active, sensual rather than logical, feminine rather than masculine, timeless rather than progressive. Beginning in the mid-twentieth century, the United States practiced Orientalism in the Far East, or Asia. For this essay, orientalism describes a particular colonizing discourse of consumption, specifically, narcissistic consumption in which the Asian body is associated with dangerous or unproductive forms of consumption. In *Twin Peaks*, Josie's consumption collapses in on itself; her consumption practices form a closed circuit. Mark Seltzer notes that in the face of the culture of consumption which privileges artificial wants over natural needs, figuring consumption in terms of the body seems contradictory.[11] In other words, although the culture of consumption disavows bodily and material needs in favor of excess, consumption continues to be figured on the body in terms of eating, disease, and sex. The culture of consumption speaks of the economy of the social body in terms of individual bodies. While the series parodies itself, remarking on television consumption habits through the favorite soap opera of town inhabitants, *Invitation to Love*, the character Josie Packard's consumption habits are not given much room for play. The program introduces Josie as the primary consumer of her own image, displaying her narcissism to the viewer. One's identification with the image in the mirror is, as Homi Bhabha notes, also recognizing one's alienation from that image. This relation and alienation forms the basis for narcissistic and aggressive identification.[12] *Twin Peaks* presents Josie's narcissism as inaccessible to the viewer. The camera bestows an erotic charge on the tableau of her face in the mirror using soft, muted lighting to display Josie gazing at herself after she has finished applying her makeup. Since the camera angle does not offer spectators surrogate identification through Josie's point of view, it forces viewers to consume not only her image but also the spectacle of her consuming her own image, to consume voyeuristically.[13] At first it is not clear what position Josie holds in the town or the series *Twin Peaks*. The ambiguity of her presentation is also a marker of the ambiguity of the character.

By presenting Josie as a woman to be looked at, the series encourages viewers to share in the fascination that several male characters have with Josie. By positing a link between Laura's murder in Washington and the murder of Teresa Banks, a young woman in Oregon, *Twin Peaks* introduces a major character, FBI special agent Dale Cooper (Kyle MacLaughlin), and launches the federal investigation around which the series revolves. The authorities focus on the similarities in the crimes and the victims, delving into the women's lives to reveal that both Laura and Teresa were sex workers and colleagues. Cooper's introduction to Josie is the first spoken narrative the audience hears about her. At a town meeting where Sheriff Harry S. Truman (Michael Ontkean) explains what he knows about Laura Palmer's murder to the "town leaders," Cooper asks Harry about characters present.

COOPER: Who's the babe?
HARRY: That's one of the most beautiful women in the state. Mrs. Packard.
COOPER: Packard Saw Mill?
HARRY: Yup.
COOPER: Where's Mr. Packard?
HARRY: Died in a boating accident last year. Andrew Packard practically built this town. Brought her over from Hong Kong six years ago. Left her everything, which didn't exactly please his sister.

Cooper's first question and Harry's response are comments on Josie as a desirable object of the male gaze. In this conversation, Cooper might as well have asked not who she is but where she is from (or the variant, what her ethnic background is). The series strongly implies that not only is she from Hong Kong but she is a native of Hong Kong. It seems that aside from Josie and Cooper, every other character in the series is a native resident of Twin Peaks. The operating assumption is that Josie is not local regardless of how many years she has lived in the town, and that she did not migrate herself, she was imported, "brought over" under someone else's agency.

Though the series never revolves around Josie in the way it revolved around Laura and her murder, many similarities between the two are worth examining. In the initial depictions of Josie and Laura, *Twin Peaks* offers similar modes of representation. Josie is the Other to Laura's immediately recognizable "local" face. Crucially, the structure of the scene of Josie at the mirror teaches the viewer how to approach the next close-up shot of a woman's face. A few scenes later, the camera fixes on an extreme close-up of the corpse of Laura Palmer (Sheryl Lee), her face framed in clear plastic, hair wet, lips and eyes closed. Wrapped in a plastic sheet, naked, she has been washed up on shore and found by Pete Martell (Jack Nance), Josie's brother-in-law. The shroud-like plastic sheet doubles as a body bag. Offering a different spectacle which aims for a similar effect to Josie's close-up, the program presents another mystery, thereby associating the spectacle of Josie with the spectacle of mystery: a dead woman's face. The camera lingers on Laura's ashy-white face, accompanied by narrative from the medical authority of Doc Hayward, "Oh my God, Laura" and the legal voice of Sheriff Harry S. Truman, "Laura Palmer." The camera's extended and eroticized shot of Laura Palmer's face is a moment of painful misogyny that diverts attention away from the brutality of her death; her body has been stripped naked, wrapped in plastic, and tied with string before being pushed into the lake. The misogyny of this scene is not located in the display of a woman's corpse, but in this particular display in which Laura's face is strangely pristine, not bruised, bloated, or scratched, but irrefutably dead. Laura's face becomes the object of fascination that propels the narrative. There is no access to identification with Laura's position; she is dead, her eyes are closed and she is not looking at the viewer, so the viewer can safely look at her. In contrast to Josie's close-up, in the close-up shot of Laura, any traces of cosmetics are washed away from a face whose lips are tinged blue, a face now made-up with grains of sand. As a mystery, one of the program's premises is the promise of uncovering information that is not publicly available, but might be in a future episode.[14] Josie Packard offers mystery not because she is dead but because she is an "exotic" Asian woman or, more traditionally, the "inscrutable oriental."

Josie's relationship to the other characters is overdetermined by a past that is never visually represented. In the second season, in a statement which is very much like a monologue, Josie produces herself in a confessional mode as a daughter sold by her relatives.[15] She has ostensibly unwillingly left Twin Peaks for Hong Kong, and although she does not tell Harry so, she means to protect him. Josie appears in the middle of a lightning storm at Harry's home. She collapses into his arms, they fall to the floor, and the scene ends with the two kissing each other. The following morning, Harry wakes her, insisting that she tell him the truth. Josie says:

> The truth. I used to work for a man in Hong Kong. His name is Thomas Eckhardt. He helped me. He took me off the streets when I was sixteen. When you're from a poor family sometimes they sell their female children. I was lucky. He taught me about life, about business. He was my father, my master, my lover. When I met Andrew Packard I was already afraid of my life. Andrew was also a business partner. When Andrew asked me to marry him I said yes.

By telling the story, Josie adroitly invokes the sympathy of Sheriff Harry Truman, playing on his reading of her as a helpless Asian woman to elicit a "manly" desire to protect her. Although Josie explains that Thomas Eckhardt took her off the streets, it is not clear that he did not at the same time install her in a brothel. In other words, Thomas Eckhardt may have been her pimp. In her own words, she considered herself fortunate to be rescued, taught, and cared for by Thomas, at least for a while. Josie's stated relationship with Thomas Eckhardt, her father, master, and lover, resonates strongly with Laura's relationship with her father. The similarities offer a way to view the two women and their situations as the same, rather than as culturally specific. The series can present the incestuous relationship between Josie and Thomas as possible by extension since father-daughter incest is a foundational fiction for *Twin Peaks*. Josie never fully escapes this early position as the object of exchange, not a subject involved in the exchange. Later in the program Andrew Packard (Dan O'Herlihy), who it turns out escaped the death Josie planned for him, returns and explains that he "rescued" Josie from Hong Kong in order to carry out his plans for revenge against Thomas. *Twin Peaks* balances the implications of Andrew's open confession of his plans for Josie with her own confession of being sold by her family. The program depicts Josie's confession as the worst possible experience, a worse betrayal than anything that could possibly follow. By comparison, the treatment by her sister-in-law Catherine Packard Martell (Piper Laurie) and husband Andrew can never be as terrible as the treatment by her biological family. Josie's tale mobilizes the notion that "they" do not value human life, that of women and girls in particular, in the same way that "we" do. This reinforcement not only makes it easier for the characters to treat Josie with less respect, but encourages the belief that she does not expect better, and even suggests that she deserves their mistreatment. The ellipses in Josie's confession are legible to Western viewers familiar with the practice of poor families in China selling their daughters. Because it is assumed that she is speaking about her own situation, she does not need to personalize her story, but uses the second person "you" and the third person "they." The effect of the narration is to generate affect that does not require links to other historical or social information. This story of a poor girl who may have been forced into prostitution and who is rescued from the streets resonates with other melodramatic story lines, though not with other plots that take place in Twin Peaks. The different, unique touch—that her family sold her—is a small but explosive reminder of racial, class, and cultural differences. The circumstances of producing this confession without providing context not only champions but ensures Western feelings of superiority over an "uncivilized" practice.

 Anxiety over consumption in *Twin Peaks* is intimately linked with anxiety over the consumption habits of Asians. Edward Said's critique of Orientalism points out that the "Oriental" in the United States is equated with the feminine and the passive. To argue a link between consumption and feminization, Lynn Joyrich writes: "Not only are women presumed to be the best of consumers, but all consumers are figured as feminized—a situation yielding tension in a culture desperately trying to shore up traditional distinctions even as its simulations continue to destabilize such attempts."[16] Although Joyrich's article does not discuss race as a sort of "traditional distinction," her argument suggests a new reading of the scenes of consumption in *Twin Peaks*. It is not simply Josie's status as a woman that codes her as a consumer, but her status as Asian. U.S. television programs have a tradition of representing Asians as feminine/effeminate; recent images of Asians mobilize the role of ultimate consumer, and as a result, consumption by Asians, whether women or men, is feminine behavior intensified.[17] *Twin Peaks*'s attempts at producing "traditional distinctions" compound the issue of gender that Joyrich addresses with national and racial concerns. If in contemporary times Asians are seen as particularly aggressive consumers of goods owned traditionally by the United States (in this case, prime forest land), it might be easier to stomach if this activity is emasculated. In other words, rather than a masculine conquest of so-called virgin territory, the activity is coded as feminine consumption, which is suspect, selfish, and destructive.

Twin Peaks produces and consumes "Asia" through the figure of Josie Packard in ways that absorb her body into the social economy of the Pacific Rim. Josie's performance as an avid shopper manipulates the traditionally assigned female role of consumer. In the second season premiere Harry is alarmed because he cannot find Josie, who has disappeared during a fire.[18] (The first season ends with a fire, arranged by Josie, which burns down Packard Saw Mill and supposedly kills Catherine but actually does not. The "cliff-hanger" scene shows Dale Cooper being shot in the stomach; months into the second season viewers learn that the assailant is Josie.)[19] Pete Martell, Catherine's husband, reassures Harry it is common for Josie to travel to Seattle, saying mysteriously, "Want my opinion, I think she goes to indulge a secret vice." The "secret vices" of characters so far include cocaine use and trafficking, wife-beating, working as a prostitute, soliciting sex workers, insurance fraud, arson, attempted murder, and murder. What is Josie's "secret vice"? The answer is reassuring, "Shopping!" As far as Pete and Harry are concerned, the seemingly innocuous purpose of her trip throws suspicion off of her. However, for Josie, the purpose of her trip is precisely to throw off suspicion. By posing "shopping" specifically as an alibi, as proof of innocence, when the series has already shown Josie to be guilty, the show casts suspicion on this mode of consumption. Having neither husband nor children, it seems that she does not consume for her family but solely for herself. (It is only several episodes later, when Josie is forced to be a maid by and for Catherine that her consumption habits are curtailed. Catherine asks Pete whether Josie has gone shopping in order to find out whether, having curtailed Josie's mobility by limiting her to prescribed errands, she is gone from the house.[20] Put in her place, Josie is now shopping for the household, rather than for herself. Josie is absorbed into a fantasy of a master-servant economy.) This character is represented as an insatiable consumer; after all she is from Hong Kong, a city which touts itself as an international site of shopping for tourists (much more so than the city of Seattle). Her return to Twin Peaks is signaled by a close-up on a door being opened with difficulty because her arms (in a black sable coat) are full of boxes and bags.[21] Josie successfully uses her purchases to seduce Harry, who attempts to question her about the mill fire, insurance fraud, and Catherine's disappearance. Since her purchases take the form of clothing which she models for Harry's approval, the scene recuperates a critique of the accepted forms of female consumption. While twirling around in a long black nightgown with a lace jacket, Josie proudly notes that she paid too much for it. She also relays what the clerks said about her, that the only reason their business survives is because "Josie Packard still buys retail." Josie's status as a consumer is one that is highly prized, not only by her, but by the Seattle stores. Harry asks Josie where she was on the night of the arson but does not investigate her alibi. Instead, he permits himself to be seduced. The scene ends when she tells Harry (twice) "I want you to take me," and then (twice) "tear it." Harry complies, naively willing to be manipulated, overwhelmed not merely by Josie's purchases, but by her active desire to be "taken" by him. By the end of the scene, Josie's consumption habit takes on dangerous meaning: she adeptly uses her purchases to manipulate a man of the law.

Mr. Tajimura (Piper Laurie) is another voracious consumer whose ambiguous relationship to gender is recuperated by the show. Catherine escapes the fiery death Josie and land developer Ben Horne (Richard Beymer) planned for her and returns in gender and racial drag as Mr. Tajimura. Catherine's choice to perform as a Japanese man, a wealthy investor interested in land acquisition, speaks to a town sensibility where such investors are increasingly familiar. Mr. Tajimura gruffly explains, "I represent Japanese investment firm," as if that national descriptor were enough and offers Ben Horne a check for $5 million in order to buy the (nonexistent) Ghostwood Development, which includes land owned by the Packard Saw Mill. By performing as a Japanese investor (and passing even with her husband Pete and lover Ben Horne), Catherine's character perversely replaces white female and Asian male consumers.[22] In the context of the local forest acquisition deal, Catherine's drag performance as Mr. Tajimura is also an emasculating tactic since Mr. Tajimura does not actually succeed in buying the land, Catherine does. Aside from Catherine's Mr. Tajimura, the only other Asian male character, Jonathan Kumugai, appears only briefly and is killed off-screen by Josie. Jonathan is not his own agent but works for Thomas Eckhardt. Physically rather than economically, Jonathan overpowers other characters, including Josie. In a scene that begins immediately after he rapes Josie, Jonathan passes along Thomas Eckhardt's orders that she return to Hong Kong.[23] Josie notes that she had "an arrangement" and that she needs just one more day to consolidate her resources, collect the insurance money, and then sell the sawmill. Jonathan retorts that Josie must leave now, and she has done well enough for herself, having collected "sapphire rings, Parisian perfumes, cashmere sweaters." The painstaking work that Josie has done over the past six years in Twin Peaks is reduced to the suitcases she can carry with her. Josie's consumption habits and affection for luxury goods are ultimately ineffectual tools for surviving in the town of Twin Peaks.

Fluidity

For lack of a more precise term, "passing" resonates throughout the originary narrative on which *Twin Peaks* is grounded: the murder of a young white woman of seemingly impeccable background and how the town inhabitants did or did not know her secrets.[24] Laura's ability to pass depends on her privileged class status and national identity as well as her race. Laura passes as the only child of securely middle-class parents, blond-haired, seventeen-year-old homecoming queen of her high school. But she is also a sex worker at the locally owned brothel and participates in cocaine use and trafficking across the Canadian border.

"Passing" and my term "fluidity" are not synonymous. Josie seems to pass, she seems to be an agent, but she acts out what other people want her to be and to do. Fluidity is not something she does, it is something she is, a quality that other characters assume she possesses. Fluidity describes the ease with which she is absorbed into a discourse of stereotypes. Drawing on Frantz Fanon and Edward Said, Homi K. Bhabha argues that identifying and creating a discourse of racial and sexual differences is the means for constructing a discourse on the colonial subject and thereby wielding colonial power.[25] Moving away from judging images as positive or negative, Bhabha argues for readings of the ways stereotypes enable what he calls "processes of subjectification." Bhabha asserts that the body occupies a space in two economies, that of "pleasure and desire," and that of "discourse, domination, and power." According to Bhabha, stereotypes simplify not by falsely representing any reality, but by fixing and fixating on a specific representation. Arresting the space and play of difference, stereotypes then become obstacles for the subject. For Bhabha, the stereotype is a fetish that disavows difference. Josie is fixed with the attribute of fluidity, which offers only the illusion of space and power. As a Chinese American woman whose wealth derives from her marriage to the town patriarch, Josie manipulates and uses her fluidity to convince some of the white townspeople that she is an immigrant wife without designs on her husband's property, without even a command of the English language. Her malapropisms, foreign accent, and manner of speech serve to point up the foreignness of her language and to disarm those around her. Josie moves from one role to another. She was a dutiful wife to her late husband Andrew Packard. When the series begins, she is a rich young widow, heir to and owner of the town's most prominent legal means of livelihood. In a secret affair, Sheriff Harry Truman views her as a naive damsel-in-distress. Describing the women characters of the series, Richard Dienst notes that Josie's character depends on the reversal of all the information the show first presents about her.[26] But it is not so much reversal the character depends on as the traits which are already in play: she is always already mysterious, exotic, orientalized, someone whose secrets need to be exposed. Arguing that Josie is fluid, not fixed, shiftless (and that her shiftlessness constitutes her), various characters attempt to contain and control her fluidity by impugning her loyalty to the white townspeople, specifically, to the brother and sister Andrew Packard and Catherine Packard Martell. At the same time, the Packards mobilize Josie's fluidity to explain her as untrustworthy. No one condemns Laura Palmer's ability to pass, no one questions Laura's loyalties. The town knows Josie as an immigrant who used to take lessons in English conversation from Laura: this is the reason FBI special agent Dale Cooper gives for wanting to talk with Josie. While the relationship between Laura as teacher and Josie as student was publicly predicated on English language learning, as a former sex worker Josie could teach Laura some lessons too.

Josie participates in what I think of as white triangles, a variant of the homosocial triangle in which a woman is the means and connecting link for a relationship between men.[27] One of the more overt homosocial triangles in the program involves Josie Packard, Andrew Packard, and Thomas Eckhardt. In Andrew Packard's words, he began a partnership with Thomas because "I knew lumber, he knew Hong Kong. We made a lot of money, had some fun."[28] *Twin Peaks* establishes "proper" masculinity through the consumption of women, women's sexuality, and U.S. territory and resources. The elderly white patriarch of Twin Peaks, Andrew Packard, ships lumber to Hong Kong and brings back a wife, Josie. The character Thomas complicates the notion that a typical Hong Kong resident must be of Asian descent. At the same time, however, the program implies that men of Asian descent do not control business in Hong Kong; instead, business is controlled by white men of European descent. Using Josie as the veritable center, the show sublimates the U.S. fear of the Asian Pacific Rim countries. Josie is caught in the white triangle composed of Catherine Martell and Thomas Eckhardt (David Warner), who negotiate with each other for Josie's services. Catherine blackmails and strikes a bargain with Josie. She demands complete servility from Josie as her personal maid, and in return, promises to protect Josie from Thomas, a false promise as it turns out. Both Catherine and Thomas gain status through their subjectification of Josie. In one scene, as Catherine and Thomas politely but antagonistically negotiate ownership over Josie, Josie is forced to be the witness to her own domestication by waiting on them at the dinner table, dressed in her maid's uniform.[29] Their conversation is predicated on Josie's silent presence and role as servant. Catherine depicts Josie as treacherous, lying to Thomas that Josie confided in her. The confidence with which both Catherine and Thomas discuss Josie's ultimate fate points to the power that the white privileged woman has over the domestic servant. The manner in which Catherine orders and treats Josie as a maid demonstrates that she finds something pleasurable about Josie's domestication, about her submission and her silence. The "owner" of Josie possesses power over his or her opponent. Catherine asks Thomas, "I wonder what shall we do about [Josie]. It would be a shame if you left empty-handed," and offers, "If I give her to you, what will you give me in return?" Though enemies, Catherine and Thomas cooperate in their performance of domination over Josie. Though he protests that he finds it difficult to "place a value on something so very precious," Thomas agrees to try. Catherine has become Josie's madam.

The Packard brother and sister beat Josie at her own game, which, in the end, turns out to have been Andrew Packard's game all along; Josie kills Thomas, as Andrew and Catherine had planned from the beginning, then dies herself. The wily U.S. family-owned business conquers Hong Kong: by engineering the deaths of Josie and Thomas Eckhardt, Catherine and Andrew survive. Hong Kong operators are not allowed to share resources or to survive with U.S. business partners. The program shows that Josie's actions are largely ineffectual. Although Andrew functions as a route for Josie to escape a relationship with Hong Kong and her "father, master, lover," Josie provides for Andrew a means of maintaining a relationship with Thomas and Hong Kong. When Josie arranges a boating accident to kill her husband Andrew and the fire to kill Catherine, she is a conduit for Thomas Eckhardt. When she herself shoots Cooper in the stomach and wounds him and shoots and kills Thomas and his assistant Jonathan, the police trace the bullets to her. The Packards are only concerned with engineering Josie's downfall as a means to bring down Eckhardt, who, it seems, is the more important Hong Kong operator; Josie was and always is merely the mediator in the white triangles.

Reconfiguring Josie's Fluid Body

Structurally, Josie's death is crucial to the series and provides spectacle, fantasy, and even a kind of closure.[30] After the broadcast of the episode that ended with her death, ABC announced that *Twin Peaks* was on "indefinite hiatus," an interruption which signaled imminent cancellation.[31] Although ABC continued broadcasting after a break, Josie's death can be read as one end of the series. With a warrant for her arrest for the killing of Jonathan, the police search for Josie and learn from Catherine where she is. Taking great pains to create a highly volatile situation, Catherine and Andrew leave Josie no choice but to seek out Thomas, who may be able to smuggle her out of the country. In the Great Northern Hotel corridor Cooper hears Josie and Thomas arguing and then a gunshot. Cooper forces open the door to find Josie has shot Thomas. Kneeling on the bed and aiming her gun at him, Josie tells Cooper, "I'm not going to jail. I can't." She refuses to lower her gun and Harry suddenly appears in the hotel room doorway also wielding his gun, yelling and threatening her. Josie begins to tremble. She clutches the gun to her chest, convulses silently, and then collapses across the bed. Harry rushes to her. After Harry says that she is dead, Cooper has one of his visions. A spotlight shines on the bed where Harry is cradling Josie's corpse in his arms. As Harry and Josie fade, the character BOB appears. An evil spirit and alternate identity of Leland Palmer, BOB crawls onto the bed asking, "Coop, what happened to Josie?" He too fades, and the man in the red suit (Michael Anderson), a dwarf known as the Man From Another Place, dances on Josie's bed. Following the disappearance of the red-suited man, which is the end of Cooper's vision, Harry reappears, still crying over Josie, calling her name. In this scene at least, it is difficult to ignore the phallic connotations of a red-suited man dancing on Josie's deathbed.[32] The dancing man is a visible display of sexual thrill over a woman's corpse.

Who or what consumes Josie is a mystery the characters never solve. The audience is treated to a view of Josie's face in a wooden knob, presumably a fixture on the table by the hotel bed. At first, her face is superimposed on the wood and she peers around, as if examining the new boundary. This image recalls the opening scene at the mirror in the pilot episode, but with a difference. This time Josie is not presented as looking at herself—as consuming her own consumption—but as looking at her boundaries. As she pushes her face against the surface in an attempt to escape, her face becomes part of the wood grain. The contours of her face stretch the wood. The image is accompanied by her cries and what sounds like squeaking wood. The image of Josie's head in the wooden knob accumulates an extensive history of visual representations of orientalized women who are objects of male desire. *Twin Peaks* traps the Asian woman in a site that resonates with domesticity and sexuality. The colonialist overtones that pervade the program fix Josie's fluid body at last, demonstrating that the fluidity offered to her can be contained within specific culturally imposed and colonialist boundaries. This wooden knob is ironically appropriate for the final resting place of the former owner of the town's sawmill. The series draws on the fairy-tale notion of a genie imprisoned in a lamp. The regional concerns of Orientalism in *Twin Peaks* are apparent: the episode uses wood, rather than the traditionally prescribed brass or silver, as the prison. Josie is a genie in that she must respond to the master, and moreover, must fulfill the master's desires. With her mobility severely curtailed, the genie is completely dependent on the master for release. Absorbed into the wood Josie is completely trapped. The series represents Josie as a nominal agent only when she was alive to be reflected on surfaces. Josie's entrapment is a metonym for the town's trade; she is literally made into an extension of the town's business and punished for her part in it.

Characters contemplate Josie after her death and find that Josie reflected their desires. Blatantly disregarding the fear that Josie expressed for Catherine and their obvious master-servant relationship, Harry nonetheless approaches Catherine with a plea. He wants any information she can tell him that will help him to understand "what made [Josie] do the things she did, what was she after."

Catherine replies, "I think that early in her life she must have learned the lesson that she could survive by being what other people wanted to see, by showing them that. Now whatever was left of her private self she may never have shown to anyone." When Catherine speculates that Josie probably did not think she was telling lies, she explains Josie in terms of a colonial subject whose discriminatory powers are negligible. According to Catherine's comments, Josie cannot tell the difference between lies and truth. Josie is different from the investigators of Laura's murder, Jonathan's murder, Thomas's murder, and the attempts on Catherine's life and Cooper's life. She cannot tell the difference between wrong and right. Catherine's disavowal of hatred for Josie may be understood as knowledge of Josie's status as fetish, as an object of male desire. This is apparent in her somewhat smug, silent response to Harry's unsurprising reply. Harry notes how difficult it would be for anyone to hate Josie, "Well, she was, she was so very beautiful." So it is that Catherine, her nemesis, and Harry, her lover, can ponder what made Josie tick after her death. They assert their mastery through this attempt at explaining her. Catherine even speculates that Josie was pure performance, pure reflection of other people's desires. Because she is fixed as the object of desire rather than the subject who desires, Josie cannot see that she will be the agent of Thomas's death for the ultimate benefit of Catherine and Andrew. Because *Twin Peaks* fixes her in an imaginary, bounded space as daughter, lover, and servant, Josie does not seriously undermine the dominant balance of power.

Assigning an individual the task of representing her origin is another means of fixing by stereotyping. Not only does Hong Kong represent China in *Twin Peaks*, but Josie represents China. In the episode following Josie's death, a very drunk Harry confesses to Cooper, "Something else I've never done, I've never crossed the ocean. Never got to China. She came to me and she made everything better, everything so much better." The conflation of the character Josie with the broadly named China reveals Harry's mode of representing Josie and a regional desire to cross the Pacific and get to China. This desire to fix an individual to an exoticized national and racial origin is the first step in wielding colonial power. The series suggests that once China has crossed the ocean to the United States it cannot expect to return alive. Through his assistant Jones, Thomas had arranged for a double burial, himself and Josie side by side, in Hong Kong. Josie's Twin Peaks family makes no objections, and Harry has no acknowledged claims on Josie. That Josie did not want to return to Hong Kong and so killed Jonathan, that she feared Thomas and killed him are points disregarded. Overstepping the bounds of personal responsibility, Harry blames himself for Josie's death and implies that she was not as mobile an agent as he is, "I should have taken her away from here.... She didn't have to die." Where would he "take" her? "China" cannot live in this region of the United States. There are too many forces harassing her at every turn, forces of which Harry has not the slightest inkling. Ultimately, *Twin Peaks* argues it is not social, political, and economic forces that prevent Josie from living in this region, but her own essential nature. She cannot live in Twin Peaks and is herself at fault. The specific cause is, in Cooper's reading, fear, her own fear.

The show enacts the U.S. fear of Asians and displaces this onto fear of Asians, that is to say, Asians' own fears. Cooper speculates on "the mysterious circumstances of Josie's death," saying to Harry, "When she died ... she was trembling with fear. I would go so far as to say quaking like an animal. I might venture a guess to say that it was the fear that killed her."[33] Cooper's reading is very suggestive for what it reveals about his perceptions of Josie. Cooper finds that being shot in the belly (by Josie, we later learn) is not so bad, so long as he can keep the fear at bay, and continues, "That's pretty much what life is like. Okay, as long as you can keep the fear from your mind." Unlike Cooper, Josie dies of her fear. In Cooper's discourse, fear is internal rather than external, that is to say, it is the individual's problem. Cooper's assignment of nonhuman qualities—"quaking like an animal"—further differentiates Josie from himself. She cannot control her body like a human being. Josie consumes herself in an orgiastic display, trembling, pointing her gun at Cooper and then at Harry. Her sudden collapse is a release of tension for the men too, who lower their guns. Josie's death problematizes agency: her death has no agent except for herself, and it is a form of agency that is foreign to *Twin Peaks* but absolutely familiar to the character of Josie—her fluidity—what characters already know about her. Even her death does not seem to be something she does, it is something she is that causes her death: she is fearful. *Twin Peaks* locates the problem in her, not in her connections to Hong Kong, not in her situation in the Packard household, not in the region, not in the politics of the Pacific Rim, but in her inability to keep her fear from her mind. Josie's body is viewed as a threat by characters who attempt to contain her, and the manner of her death confirms their suspicions that her body is uncontrollable. In her demise *Twin Peaks* represents Josie's body as one without integrity, as uncontainable: her corpse lies on the bed, but her head appears in the wooden knob.

Josie's sudden death, without visible cause, may seem to be very much unlike deaths caused by AIDS or AIDS-related complications, however, both location and manner enable a reading of her death as an allegory of AIDS.[34] Dying in a rented bed in a hotel recalls hospital rooms, which are similarly transitory and transitional spaces. Unlike a television bullet wound, AIDS is a slower process of decline, and people with AIDS spend time moving in and out of the hospital. Perhaps most stunning is the information which is precisely not visible to the spectator and is instead spoken, that she weighed 65 pounds at death and the cause of her death cannot be medically determined. This information is particularly evocative of representations of AIDS as a disease that manifests itself in wasted bodies. Bodies that are wasted signify bodies that are not properly (re)productive. The "appearance" of a mysterious illness in a group of previously healthy people, one that could be homogenized under the rubric of "gay white male," was one of the earliest modes of recognizing and diagnosing AIDS.[35] Claims that the earliest people diagnosed with AIDS had been overzealous consumers of sexual pleasure and were now paying for it operate in a discourse of economics and sex. *Twin Peaks* mobilizes the stigma attached to AIDS, sex workers, and homosexuality, categorizing Josie as a nonreproductive body. Cooper mobilizes Josie's past as a sex worker to discount her death. His reminder to Harry that she was a "hardened criminal" charged with prostitution in Hong Kong pathologizes sex workers. *Twin*

Peaks mobilizes and conflates Josie's perverse consumption practices, from economic consumption to bodily consumption, as she wastes away before the viewers' eyes to 65 pounds. *Twin Peaks* does not permit her to take up much space. Josie's sudden wasting away suggests that she consumed too much, and perhaps she consumed herself too much. Her astonishing weight at death also refers to photographic displays of wasted bodies of nineteenth-century opium addicts. One does not need to look far to see where the opium eater comes from; previously, Joan Chen performed the role of the opium-addicted empress Wan Jung in Bernardo Bertolucci's *The Last Emperor*. Through the death of this representative of Harry's "China," *Twin Peaks* links perverse desires, AIDS, and opium, a harsh reminder of China's defeat by the British during the Opium Wars and the subsequent lease of Hong Kong, and displaces sexual epidemics onto Asian bodies. The epidemic is contained: Josie wipes out the people from Hong Kong, killing Jonathan and Thomas. Her own death prevents further transmission of perverse consumption habits. In the end, Josie is rejected by Twin Peaks, and her corpse is returned "home" to Hong Kong.

In spite of, or perhaps because of, their familiarity with the consuming power of businesses from Hong Kong and Japan, Twin Peaks ejects these foreign presences. This program relies on interpersonal, inter- and intrafamilial relations to such a degree that it repudiates relations to larger communities. Josie's former status as a sex worker in Hong Kong is reinscribed through a struggle between men: either her former lover/pimp Thomas Eckhardt or his business partner and her late husband Andrew Packard will control her. At no point does *Twin Peaks* problematize the socioeconomic and political implications of Josie's "rescue" from the streets of Hong Kong and then from the city of Hong Kong. The program avoids discussing Josie's migration to Twin Peaks in terms of white U.S. importation of domestic workers from Asia but demotes Josie from owner of the Packard Saw Mill to Catherine Packard Martell's maid in the context of a private family struggle for power. Presenting Josie as a mystery, the show rejects any single authority's attempts to explain the character; not even her own words of explanation are trustworthy. Brandishing her file from Interpol, the international policing organization, Cooper offers Harry information on Josie's criminal activities—she is wanted for several (unspecified) felonies—as proof that she was a "hardened criminal," who therefore does not deserve Harry's emotional expenditures. (Luckily, Laura was never picked up for prostitution.) The final word on Josie comes from Cooper, who overlooks the similarities between Josie and Laura: whereas the town native deserves sympathy, the immigrant gets what she deserves—death.

This television series calls on other demonstrations of anxiety over Asians' increasingly visible socioeconomic presence in the U.S. media and recognition of their importance to the United States. In the circumstances of Josie's immigration as a figure of exchange between men, *Twin Peaks* mobilizes an extremely specialized illustration of Asian women in mail-order bride catalogs. The catalogs list women from Asian countries (Hong Kong, Korea, the Philippines, Taiwan, and Thailand, among others) who wish to correspond with men in the United States, Canada, Australia, and Europe. Some businesses provide package tours, including airfare, hotel, and even a minister waiting at the hotel for immediate marriage after the client has made his choice. These catalogs participate in a discourse that presents Asian women as sexual beings who are safely domesticated and submissive, and is predicated on replacing Asian men with U.S. men as prime consumers of Asian femininity. The catalogs sanction a desire for and then provide domesticity to First World men. Sold by companies with names such as U.S.-Asian connection, Cherry Blossom, Sunshine Girls, Thai Ladies, The Asian Experience, The Pacific Century Club, the catalogs serve as the mediators for the male clients and the women. By creating an aura of the attainable exotic, the catalogs have prompted thousands of marriages whereby primarily white men "deliver" their brides from their situations in Asian countries and install them into U.S. homes as "wife, mother, and best friend" (in the words of one customer).

The women listed are not so strange as to be completely unfamiliar, in fact, the catalogs rely on a familiar portrayal of Asian women, notably the "Lotus Blossom," the geisha, the exotic, submissive, feminine woman. Unlike personal advertisements, the company rather than the individual chooses the wording or excerpts from letters written by the women, often leaving grammatical errors intact. The most orientalizing move might be that the women are not listed in any sort of expected order, not by age, height, weight, profession, education, hobbies, religious practices, ethnicity, or nationality. In these representations, the women are not differentiated. Family names are not included. The effect of "disorder" in these catalogs accentuates the photograph as the ultimate selling point, for it, more than words, catches the eye and the imagination, confirming the fantasy that the Other exists in multitudes. The photographic representation fixes the Other in place while the text of the catalogs solicits potential clients as (future) connoisseurs.

In *Twin Peaks*, characters generally produce their own or someone else's secrets only to the viewer or to one another. Even if Josie's death cannot be explained, it is through Josie that viewers possess knowledge that none of the other characters have. Through Josie, *Twin Peaks* offers audiences an opportunity to displace their frustrations about the convoluted story lines. Bhabha argues that the gaze is a means of controlling what is frightening, a way of controlling that is afraid of losing control.[36] Josie's death and the non-integrity of her corpse and her trapped face fit into the epistemological framework of *Twin Peaks*. *Twin Peaks* encourages audiences to participate in controlling Josie and to be afraid of her rather than to identify with her. Josie's narcissism discourages audience identification; in her incomprehensible death she is represented as a victim with whom viewers need not sympathize. Instead of identifying with Josie, viewers are encouraged to identify with the detective process of trying to figure out Josie. While Laura's interiority is the object of much fascination, *Twin Peaks* treats Josie as if her interiority is incomprehensible. With her death, *Twin Peaks* displays Josie's fluid body as always having been a mystery to the characters and to viewers. Unlike the other murders of this series, this death does not need to be reconstructed; viewers see it happening, see her face imprisoned in the wood, and yet it is still a mystery. *Twin Peaks* tenders its best-kept secret, that is, the mystery of Josie, at the site of her death, fixed in place at last and again.

As a commodity of the early 1990s, *Twin Peaks* operates as a highly specialized venue that privileges knowledge and knowers. The phenomenon of the series included much discussion about characters, plot, and story on the part of the audience, and speculations about Lynch's other film works.[37] *Twin Peaks* requires viewers to decipher the series in a manner reminiscent of Said's Orientalism, specifically, the manner in which practitioners of Orientalism know, rely on, and recognize previous texts about the Orient produced by other Orientalists.[38] In this way, the art of viewing and dissecting *Twin Peaks* that the series generated is reminiscent of Orientalism. An exceedingly self-referential field, eighteenth- and nineteenth-century Orientalism provides students with excerpts of texts and commentary provided by other scholars. In episodes and commercials, *Twin Peaks* refers not only to itself, tongue in cheek, but also to other Lynch productions. To avoid frustration and to take pleasure in the series it helped to be conversant with Lynch's film works, to discuss the episodes with other devout viewers, and to watch videotaped episodes repeatedly in order to decipher the minute clues to what was happening. The series determinedly displayed its project of providing viewers with enough revelations and tried to ensure its cult status through recognizably Lynchian touches such as comically banal dialogue, quirky characters, the use of actors from his previous work, and extreme close-ups. Said described the process of Orientalism as one where readers in the West relied on experts, the Orientalists, to decipher the essential Orient.[39] As a mystery series, one of the pleasures the series delivers to viewers is the opportunity to detect meaning. *Twin Peaks* offers Josie Packard as a site of fantasy and, more important, as an embodiment of perpetual discovery and mystery for consumption by the connoisseur.

Part Three

Science, Modernity, Aesthetics

Chapter 7

Travel and Translation: An Aspect of China's Cultural Modernity, 1862–1926

JOHN YU ZOU

The years between the inception of the *yangwu* policies and the conclusion of the May Fourth "literary revolution" are often considered a crucial phase in the development of modernity in China.¹ But until recently, scholarly interest in this period has been largely focused on its social and political implications. The appearance of a properly cultural modernity has been only too frequently credited to the mutations of intellectual life in the May Fourth era. The objective of this essay is to suggest a way to supplement this lack of attention to the significance of cultural practices between the 1860s and 1920s, so that on the one hand, a more complete picture of the rising modernities in the period can be rendered; and on the other hand, the May Fourth movement may be perceived within a better mediated historical context and not viewed as primarily a moment of radical discontinuity.

The subject matter I discuss in the following pages pertains to two cultural behaviors that informed virtually all modernizing schemes in China since the beginning of the 1860s: travel in the West and the translation of works from Western languages. One distinctive attribute characterized these cross-cultural practices: since Chinese modernizers in the period had to negotiate their positions between their knowledge of the West and the circumstances in their home country, it may be no exaggeration to claim that they were all cultural crossbreeds to a certain extent.² Yet, as a result of the disastrous events of the so-called Arrow War, self-strengthening initiatives under official and semi-official sponsorship represented a particular form of cultural hybridity. Determined by the unequal balance of power between China and the West, they did not partake in an innocent interest in the exotics of the other, but rather constituted projects that fulfilled an urgent purpose: the acquisition of powers from the West. Positioned against the overwhelming shadow of Western imperialist hegemony, travel and translation were meant to remedy deficiencies. This essay briefly analyzes the discursive configurations of the political, social, and ultimately cultural deficiencies in order to present a new perspective on the often-discussed aspect of modernity in China: the positioning of subjectivity between China and the West. I begin with a general analysis of the significance of travel and translation in relation to the formation of the discourse on modernity and then proceed to present three case studies to illustrate their formal characteristics under changing historical circumstances.

Travel and Translation

No doubt, neither travel beyond the bounds of the Chinese empire nor translation of works from foreign languages originated with the problematic of self-strengthening in the 1860s. But the Qing policies in the Tongzhi period (1862–74) certainly provided such travel and translation with a unique institutional basis and ideological impetus, so that they were distinguished from earlier literati efforts and contemporaneous missionary enterprises.[3] Under the auspices of the newly founded *Zongli Yamen*, or Council of Foreign Affairs (1861), as well as the powerful anti-*Taiping* regional administrators, two radical changes of attitude toward the West were effected between 1862 and 1872.[4] First, the study of Western languages came to be recognized as a matter of strategic importance. Schools were set up in the capital and key treaty port cities to provide interpreters with necessary training in European languages and fragments of Western modern education, such as mathematics and geography.[5] Concurrent with the appearance of such language schools, the translation of Western texts, a standard practice among the missionaries, was also absorbed as part of a concerted program in collecting information about the West. For instance, after the inauguration of the famous Jiangnan Arsenal in Shanghai in 1865, a translation bureau was created as its subdivision in 1867.[6] Second, first-hand experience in the West also took on unprecedented value. Diplomats were sent to Europe and America under diverse circumstances.[7] Gifted teenagers were dispatched in packs to be students in various disciplines.[8] The combined result of these activities went far beyond the provision of sources on the West and the staffing of the earliest self-strengthening projects. Indeed, in the course of the following decades, experience in the West and access to texts in Western languages not only created a code of cultural behavior but also formed a renewable intellectual and political legacy.

Travel and translation are certainly loose terms that cover a wide range of experiences. For one thing, the types of travel in the West varied significantly. Some were indeed itinerant visits that consisted of constant movement and occasional stops. Others involved extended sojourns.[9] In terms of the worth of actual communication and interaction, some travelers were fluent in the language of the host country; others always had to depend on interpreters or nonparticipatory observations.[10] The amount of social exposure was by no means uniform either. There were those who married into the local families or went through degree programs and those who were confined by the written and unwritten rules of official protocol.[11] In addition, exactly what constituted "the West" also appeared to be rather unstable. The emergence of Japan as a major imperialist power in East Asia projected an unexpected and disorientating version of the modern and was responsible for the flood of Chinese youths studying in that country after the 1895 Sino-Japanese war. As for the translation of Western texts, a universally accepted norm was likewise unavailable. Although the translation of Buddhist texts from Sanskrit had existed for almost two millennia, the idea of a neutral and complete rendition based on adequate bilingualism was yet to develop into a rigorous notion. For the linguistically uninitiated, haphazard transliteration was common. Direct and indirect access to texts in Western languages provided occasions for commentaries, introductions, moderated quotations, casual references, and fantastic hearsay.[12] Among what claimed to be serious works of translation, some were no doubt complete and even annotated; some were abridged; some were digests.[13] Liberal adaptations and speculative elaborations were by no means the exception.[14] Meanwhile, because of the shortage of necessary expertise, relayed translation was popular. Russian works were sometimes rendered via German, and German texts were translated through Japanese.[15]

The most respected textual products generated in these processes were the eyewitness accounts about encounters in the West and the texts that claimed to be renditions of Western originals. The circulation of these texts in the reading public had several far-reaching consequences. At the most basic level, they helped convey a sense of the hard reality of the world beyond China and its neighboring states. Fables and fantastic fictions gradually appeared to be much less compelling under their influence. The West began to assume a tangibility that had to be reckoned with both discursively and institutionally. A new language about the outside world was developed.[16] Also, the consolidation of experiences of the West in textual forms testified to the awakening of a passionate gaze. The more these experiences were rendered in detail, the more they were transformed into a cluster of surfaces that baffled sweeping generalizations and demanded sustained attention to their specific shapes, colors, and texture. The West was neither a simple geographic reference nor a speculative construct subjected to penetrating insights. It no longer possessed a content to be toyed with as fantasy or dismissed as nonsense. Furthermore, when travel and translation became regular practices recognized by the state, border-crossing between languages and cultural geographies began to claim a value of its own. Because of the unprecedented narrative conventions and possibilities they entailed, the travelogues and translated texts represented something that was neither specifically Chinese nor Western. Rather, they inserted a discursive territory between China and the West. Accordingly, the producers of these texts constituted a new species of cultural subject.

Finally, related to these factors, the representation of experiences in the West and of Western texts left an indelible imprint upon the conception of modernity in China. Travelers and translators crossed not only diverse geographies but also different time zones. In their textual renditions, the West possessed not just what China did not possess at the time but also what China would endeavor to possess at a later point. In other words, they configured a West that held at least part of China's future. Accordingly, knowledge about such a threatening other was no longer in answer to a contingent and strategic interest, as reflected in the compilations around the 1840s.[17] Rather, it took on intrinsic values and became an indispensable form of cultural self-understanding. It was recognized as the key to locating, measuring, and analyzing the present state of China and the Chinese against a visible alien reality that would be China's future. The implications of this recognition are the following. First, the generation of knowledge and discourse about the West became a legitimate Chinese cultural behavior. To know and to speak about the West constituted an indispensable condition for knowing and speaking about China's present and future, if not its past.[18] In other words, the discourse on modernity in China was always informed at least partially by a discourse about the West. It was established in a position of constant negotiation between two different cultural legacies. Second, since China's future was understood to be the duplication or reproduction of—at least certain elements in—the Western present, there emerged a unique time-consciousness: the trajectory to the future was configured as a closed circuit within the present, consisting of a preconceived program rather than an open-ended adventure. As duplication, modernity in China could not be considered a creative achievement. It did not embody novelty in an original sense. Third, because the realization of modernity in China consisted in a spatial and linguistic transfer, the attributes of the modern had to be imagined primordially in terms of neutrality and universal relevance. In other words, modernity as such was thought to transcend the differences of culture and history.

The Discourse of Deficit

Knowledge of the West through eyewitness accounts and translated texts first established itself as respectable because of an awareness of the superior Western powers. The special discourse created to map and address the particular strengths of the West was the very result of this canonization. What often remains to be clarified, however, is the fact that the interest in the West was not an innocent curiosity about facts and details. Rather, because it was motivated by an obsessive curiosity about the drastic inequality of power, the primary concern was with the relational or contrastive aspect in the making of knowledge about the West. Implicit in the characterization of those peculiar features of the West for emulation, there was therefore a discursive countermove that correspondingly documented the particular deficiencies of China.[19] In other words, travel and translation as power-seeking measures not only rhetorically created a West of numerous wonders but also constructed in the same fashion a China of many ills. The canonization of knowledge about the particular strengths of the West thus always stood for the canonization of another type of knowledge—the knowledge about China's deficits in analogous areas of discursive representation. The more Western strengths were brought forth to be recognized, the more Chinese weaknesses and insufficiencies were exposed to intellectual attention. Animated by a radical imbalance of power between China and the West, travel and translation were thus inclined to further confirm discursively such an imbalance.

In the meantime, although the discourse of deficit consisted chiefly in marginal or implicit references and was often concealed as a subtext in the discourse about the West, its impact upon the Chinese conception of the modern cannot be overestimated. In practical terms, the characterization of the differences between the two discursive entities of China and the West could not cease at simply conveying contrast. In general, the subtextual representation of the contrast had to come to terms with the kind, degree, and extent of the insufficiencies of China on a detailed comparative basis. From the perspective of the transfer of modernity, such a discourse not only helped earmark the particular areas in need of modernization, but also was responsible for an assessment of the type, amount, and urgency of modernization thus required.[20] In other words, the discursive configuration of deficit was endowed with a capacity to simultaneously justify in the metalinguistic sense the process of modernization as an extraction from without, and constitute a working agenda which ordered the priorities with pragmatic precision. It both legitimized and distributed the flow of words and things from the West to China. I call such a flow of substances a process of cultural trafficking, since it created a new route of exchange and a new economy with its own system of supply and demand.

For such a transfer of words and things, there existed two different uses of the words and things from the West. Just as the reference to a Western "wonder" was intrinsically connected to a designation of a Chinese deficiency, the supply of modernity in the representation of experiences in the West and of Western texts could not be disjoined from the demand for modern powers implicitly figured in China's "wonder"lessness. More important, although the demand reflected in the various modes of insufficiency always had a regulating effect on the supply of necessary instruments for empowerment, the supply could always be programmed in such a way as to stimulate the demand.[21] On the supply side, the discursive representation of the Western powers provided an occasion for the travelers and translators virtually to speak for the West. Because of their privileged physical and linguistic access, they possessed the ultimate authority in configuring the West for the Chinese readership and therefore occupied a key position in the imagination of modernity. But to accomplish their authentic representation, they had to first commit themselves to the endeavor of mimesis. In other words, their representation could achieve authenticity only if it claimed to perform a faithful rendition of the West. Mimesis in the context had two related meanings. For one thing, a prerequisite for the travelers and translators to speak for the West was their ability to convey "accurately" the various features of the West in their discourse. One effective method along this line was that the narrators of the eyewitness accounts and translated texts systematically manipulated their specifically positioned participation in the production of texts so that representation appeared as reality and the perspective upon the West was confused with the "West" itself. In addition, the mimicking interest in the imaginary discourse on modernity also aimed at the discursive imitation of Western style, viewpoint, and voice, for it was understood that only by looking, thinking, and speaking like a Westerner could one display the West in its true forms.

On the demand side, the implicit, often subtextual, references to China produced a scenario in which the assortment of insufficiencies asked for articulation. Because of their extended horizons and privileged experiences, travelers and translators often constituted the class of persons who could claim to be best equipped to assess China's weaknesses and to make adequate suggestions for its achievement of political, cultural, and social well-being. They attained prestige by placing themselves in the vanguard of social change and national salvation. In the context where the Western modern was understood to be the future of China, their often pragmatic and haphazard knowledge about the West had the extraordinary resonance of a sublime vision, and any of their equally unsystematic and contingent critiques of China's present circumstances could sound singularly pointed and profound. In this sense, travelers and translators functioned as prophets, whose existence, authority, and intervention were first and foremost sanctioned by an exacerbated deficit of power and who therefore had a consistent interest to engage in an elaboration on the state of powerlessness and in discursively sabotaging the configurations of independent native values and contextually determined traditions.

The difference between these two modes of cultural trafficking, namely, the interest in mimesis and discursive sabotage, is obvious. In the representation of the West, the cherished assets were accuracy, faithfulness, neutrality, and so on. The simulation of Western realities required that the specific historical perspective incurred in the transfer of modernity be excluded from consideration. And the mimicking of the Western views strove to facilitate the moment of passing. For such a form of representation, the Chinese versions of the modern scientist figured prominently for his embodiment of a set of neutral values and truths in spite of cultural and historical differences. As scientists, travelers and translators not only rendered a portion of the West, namely, the discipline and institution of science, with specious faithfulness but also projected themselves as behaviorally akin to their Western counterparts. The representation of China, on the other hand, was effectively served with a different class of attributes, such as passion, irony, and so on. The rendition of the present circumstances in China was for the purpose of pointing toward some as yet undeveloped potential and ultimately toward a radically different future. The best exemplar in this category was the dedicated and engaged reformer, whose ultimate interest was not in expounding on the nature of modern values but rather in specifying how to achieve such values in his native context. From the perspective of the reformer, the system of power insufficiencies had to be extensively and urgently criticized before a well-formed modernity, such as that in the West, could be realized. As reformers, travelers and translators designated the accomplishment of modernity as the result of radical mutations and of a rite of passage.

In the rest of the essay, I analyze the tension between these two aspects of the discourse on modernity to argue the continuity of cultural reflections upon modernity from the 1860s to the 1920s. Conventionally, the history of modernization in China is divided in three large periods: the self-strengthening (1860s–90s), reform and revolution (1890s–1910s), and the May Fourth literary revolution (1910s–20s). These periods are often said to correspond to three different projects of modernization: the introduction of diplomacy and the fortification of national defense, the institutional changes, and the revaluation of cultural traditions. The first project was a political one, since it was fundamentally informed by an agenda to make China better able to resist Western encroachment. The second project emphasized social modernization by prioritizing the necessity of institutional change. The third project addressed the articulation of new subjectivities in relation to cultural values and contributed to the discursive formation of cultural modernity.

For the emergence of figures of modernity in the period of self-strengthening, I concentrate on an important member of the powerful Hunan clique in the mid-nineteenth century. Guo Songtao was a sworn brother of Zeng Guofan's and served as the first Chinese ambassador in the West between 1876 and 1878.[22] What distinguished him from the more systematic spokespersons for the self-strengthening program, such as Feng Guifen and Zheng Guanying, was the fact that during his tenure in London he produced a meticulously detailed eyewitness account of the West which vividly registered the initial tensions in the representation of powerful modern forces and China's deficits of power. In the reform and revolution period, I focus on Wang Guowei rather than the more influential Yan Fu, Kang Youwei, or Zhang Binglin, for the reason that Wang was the among the very few men of the time who briefly lingered on the phenomenon of linguistic discrepancy between the translator's two languages in the widespread practice of translation. A leading historian in the Chinese academy, Wang was an avid reader of Western philosophy and a passionate advocate for educational reform. My reading of his configuration of the gap between China and the modern West seeks to illuminate the dimensions of power within the course of the negotiation of cultural subjectivity across languages. In the May Fourth period, I focus on Lu Xun, one of the eminent spokespersons of the New Culture movement. He was among those who pointed toward an end of the innocent discursive relationship between the characterization of the Western modern and the conception of a blueprint for China's modernization. In such works as "Preface to *Outcry*" and the later memoir "Mr. Fujino," he made a case for the uncoupling of the configurations of Western power and Chinese deficits.

An Aesthetics of Terror

In 1876, Guo Songtao, seasoned bureaucrat and renowned expert on Western affairs, was appointed the representative of imperial China to visit Europe. The ostensible reason for his trip was to respond to the demand from the

British ambassador Thomas Wade that the court dispatch a senior member to formally apologize to his government for the killing of a staff member of the British embassy in southwest China earlier in the year, so that another military engagement would not be precipitated.[23] But of equal importance was the court's own interest to learn about the Westerner's ways. Beside his capacity as conveyor of apology and good will, Guo was instructed by the dowager empresses, then *de facto* heads of the state, to "comprehensively study and exhaustively interrogate (things) once arriving in Britain."[24]

The irony of such an instruction was that Guo discovered many things worthy of study and interrogation long before reaching the British Isles. Once he was outside the boundaries of China proper, the language of his diary took a drastic turn. The meager narrative gives way to luxurious description. Suddenly, details become worthy of comment; conversations are recorded word-for-word, and visual experiences are rendered into minutely arranged verbal descriptions. It is as if his attention was awakened to a multitude of incoherent details. He mobilizes a new language to counter his bewilderment, a language that lingers over surfaces, giving them pattern, a language that registers a lack of transparency and his own semantic poverty. On December 5, five days after departing Shanghai, as his ship drew near the port of Shantou in Guangdong province, the elderly man at one point caught sight of a great armored vessel approaching quickly from astern.[25] He was informed that it was commanded by Admiral Ryde. But the consequent hustle and bustle on the two ships later prompted the following curious dialogue between the diplomat and his British captain:

—Why did we hoist the flag? I asked.
—To inform them [about the state of our ship], said he.
—But why did they also hoist the flag?
—To respond. As if to say, we now respectfully recognize that the ambassador is on board.
—Then, why did we again lower the flag?
—Having so communicated with them, we may lower the flag.
—And why did those men of that ship climb and stand on the masts?
—To show respect, just as forming a file. They stand on the masts, so that they may be viewed from afar. As for the music, the reason to play military music was to give rhythm to the formation of files.
—Why did that ship then quickly pass our prow?
—To speed forward to greet us. We stopped our engine, so as to show modesty.
   Alas, with such balanced civility and spontaneity were the rituals maintained. China is indeed trailing far behind.[26]

The terse wording in Chinese lends unique stylistic elegance to the recorded conversation, which vaguely evokes some pre-Qin historical writing. An accomplished man of letters, Guo Songtao certainly did not let the occasion pass without a good exercise of his pen.[27] But the encounter comes across as sinicized. Apparently he saw nothing absurd about the idea of two modern seafaring vessels observing the communal rituals of China's distant past. In his fascination about the ritualistic accuracy of the Western seamen, the presence of the Western power, as manifested in the great warship, loses its strange menace. As long as ritual and ceremony were dogmatically identified as China's forte, the strength of the West was recognized as somehow akin to the type of power conventionally accessible to the literati. He could indeed recover a thankful sense of security since the invincible Westerners only appeared to be more ritualistic, and therefore, more Chinese than the Chinese. In other words, the difference was in degree rather than kind. And yet, it was still an extraordinary occasion. A deep-seated puzzlement could hardly be suppressed. In terms of content, the rituals among these Western men was a closed book to him. For a coherent reading, the ambassador had to reconstruct consistent and complaisant explanations from the words of the captain, possibly via an unmentioned interpreter.[28] The meaning of the interaction only began to emerge after relentless inquiries. For all his willingness and effort to appropriate the unknown, the savvy literatus had to overcome the critical moment of incomprehension and the loss of meaning. The reconstructed explanations and the sinicizing interest were thus nothing but counteractive measures against the fundamental experience of bewilderment and wonder, as mandated by an awareness of his insufficiency of knowledge and lack of immediate linguistic access. But such deficits did not remain personal. Ultimately, the impact of wonder was not directed toward the individual but rather toward a culture in its entirety. The very reason that the Western rituals could be bewildering was because of a fundamental cultural gap: the Westerners now exceeded the Chinese in the observation of courtesy and ceremony to such an extent that their excellence reached beyond the interpretive horizon of the lesser Chinese and had to be explained in detail for the latter's comprehension. The insufficiency in the individual was thus inscribed as a collective insufficiency.

Such defensive rationalization, however, was at his disposal only for a brief time. The radical otherness of the British colonial empire soon began to work its mesmerizing power on him. Once relentless and menacing as in the figure of a dyspeptic Wade, now the West revealed itself via the efficient and sanitary prisons in Hong Kong, the strange animal known as a kangaroo in a zoo in Singapore, and so on. Crossing the Indian Ocean by Christmas, a white woman's music and singing pleasured him deeply. And there was the glorious seascape, the exotic, bustling harbors and coastal towns, and the majestic engineering projects such as the Suez canal. But true to the instruction of the imperial matrons, it was always the establishment at such strategic sites as Aden, Malta, and Gibraltar, where the military puissance of the British was on full display, that provoked his fascinated gaze. The following is excerpted from his January 12, 1877, diary entry, which concerns the day he spent on Malta:

> The island is shaped like a mortar. In the middle there is a mountain, to which the rest of the island rises. It is 45 *li* in width, and 30 in length. Its extended branch makes four or five partitioned havens. There is an arsenal on the island, around which stand eleven fortresses. Such is Britain's foremost military base in the Mediterranean.... The governor sent carriages to receive us.... We reached the governor's residence after passing two fortresses. The vista is grand and open, the streets orderly and clean. The houses may reach five to six floors, poised against one another in rows....
>
> After lunch, [we were] accompanied on a tour of a nearby fort, which was equipped with a total of a hundred and twenty guns. Six of them weigh 18 tons. (Each ton accounts for one thousand and eight hundred *jin*. Thus they are thirty-two thousand and four hundred *jin* in weight.) Their circumference is in the vicinity of one *zhang*.[29] There is still a high fort that sits atop of the hill, which holds three massive cannons we did not have time to see. (One weighs 36 tons, two others 25 each.) For each gun, there are hundreds of shells piled up front, as if to engage in imminent battle. There are 6,000 troops and three armored battleships....
>
> The size of the governor's residence is unsurpassable. There are two chambers for conference.... An additional hallway stores ancient weapons.... In the middle lay five glass covers, (respectively holding) an ax Arabian Muslims won from the Maltan barbarians when they first came to be a powerful people; a Saracen trumpet of the winding kind; a scripture recited by priests seven hundred years ago; the seal and ribbon of the king of Malta and a document that confers upon him the title.[30]

By now a rather experienced traveler, Guo had regained much of his ease and aplomb. As a guest of the governor, Guo secretly scanned the island for critical information, counting its features as part of an inventory, translating the measures into the Chinese system. A pause was effected, in both his voyage and narrative. Here is a moment to leave aside speculative observations and concentrate on facts. Malta is taken out of the narrative flow. It is not connected to what happens before and after, such as the arrival and departure of the entourage. It consists of a string of descriptive notations, a narrative element that in Roland Barthes's terms, achieves the reality effect.[31] Malta stops the reader, tears him away from the narrative, it is presented as reality, heavily metal, highly explosive, but orderly, grand, mastered by the British military, congealed as a map. Reality is simulated when the additive structure of textual details successfully bears sustained attention to the surface of the referent. The guns at the fort and holdings in the hallway do precisely that. They are there to meet the reader's gaze with a palpable density.

And yet, what sort of reality? Barthes suggests that such deployment of descriptive notations, detachable from context, counteracting the forces of narrative progress which are tirelessly predictive, incurs the aesthetic. In Guo's discourse, the aesthetic is incurred in a standstill, when the ambassador was transfixed, literally and verbally. The hand that counted the inventory passed sensually from one object to the next. The objects added up. But the count was not complete. The three colossal guns were hidden from view. There was no separate mention of the contents under the fifth glass cover. Was he again in such haste when passing through the hallway that he missed them? For at the end of that day's entry, he regretted that he could not linger a few more days to visit other remains of old Malta. Did this armored citadel finally awaken the genuine interest of this accomplished man of letters to its cultural aspects? Did old Malta, with its layers of history, speak to him, as through the cased seal and ribbons of a remote king? And if so, how? as a resigned stranger? a member of an alien and discontinued culture? a hapless victim crushed under Britain's insuperable metal forces? Or were the remains of old Malta a mere pretext to visit the hilltop fort with those massive guns, so that he might satisfy his secret curiosity in relishing the panorama from the angle of those immense barrels? And what, indeed, was the nature of this curiosity? Was there some untold attachment to the sight of those colossal pieces of artillery, apart from a bureaucrat's interest in the numerical count of their sizes? Struck by such a sublime sight, even though in imagination, was he, shall we say, moved?

Embarrassment

The aesthetics of terror resulting from contact with an overpowering West, of course, had to be suppressed, just as the fact that the politics of self-strengthening were fundamentally informed by a dynamism of fear. Guo's application of self-censorship was rigorous enough for him to produce an official version of his travelogue for his colleagues at the *Zongli yamen*, a version cleansed of terms and references that he thought might offend their sensibilities. Even so, his report sparked outrage. It was thought to contain such effusive compliments to British prowess that the court had to issue an edict banning its circulation and ordering the destruction of all printing blocks. In less than a year, Guo found his name as a traitor firmly made throughout Chinese officialdom. He asked for leave, upon which he was recalled from service and dismissed from the court when he arrived home.

The clandestine fascination with the hostile power of the West was only transformed into something tantamount to a joyous affirmation of Western superiority as the self-strengthening episode drew to an end in the 1894–95 Sino-Japanese war. In one of his acute essays, Wang Guowei, a peripheral figure in the postwar reform movement, registered the discrepancy between the languages of China and the West and sought to justify the practice of translation on the ground of their complementarity.[32] "On the Introduction of Neologisms" was mainly a response to the anxiety over the post-1895 influx of the *kanji* renditions of Western terms from Japan. In the essay, Wang argued against Yan Fu's obsession with the elegance of native speech, defending the adoption of the ready-made and plain Japanese phraseology. To highlight the futility of attempts to sinicize the radically un-Chinese wordings of the West, he formulated the following contrast:

> The men of the Western ocean are speculative and scientific in character. They excel at abstraction and are sophisticated in analysis. To any object of the world, be it visible or invisible, they consistently apply the two methods of generalization and specification. Thus it is only natural that [they have] a larger vocabulary. The forte of the Chinese is rather in the sphere of practice. In terms of theory, we are satisfied with specific knowledge. As for classification, unless we are pressed we would prefer not to exhaust the possibilities.... Therefore, in China there is argumentation but no logic. There is literacy and learning but no grammar. Suffice it to say that abstraction and classification are not our strong faculties, and that the scholarship of our country has yet to reach self-consciousness.[33]

Yan Fu's fault, in other words, was that in relentlessly sinicizing the Western terms, he broke down the fundamental difference between Western and Chinese thought. By concealing the Western substance behind a Chinese façade, he denied the radical, uncompromising novelty of Western learning.[34] According to Wang, since the difference between China and the West was ultimately manifested in the difference of vocabulary, the acquisition of Western learning required the acquisition of the Western system of words. Such an acquisition had to take the form of absorbing the different rather than reasserting the same. It consisted in obtaining the Westerner's verbal abundance, rather than repeating the impoverished vocabulary of China. Reiterating the scholastic thesis that in the sphere of conception, the existence of things depends on the existence of names and that that which does not have a name cannot be thought, Wang conceived the Westerner's language as a dramatic force that could shake the Chinese speaker out of a certain unthinking stupor, in which confused translators such as Yan Fu still chose to hide. Translation, which provided the context for the introduction of neologism, was thus understood by Wang as a quest not only for new words but also for new meanings, new relations, and new forms of life. Through translation, things materialized out of invisibility. Thus, despite the drastic differences between Chinese and Western languages, Wang did imagine that they shared a certain deep structure, for only thus could he posit that an influx of neologisms ultimately originating in the West could fill the linguistic voids in Chinese. The discursive insertion of these neologisms in Chinese constituted a developmental stage for the translator and an evolutionary phase for the reading public and the entire cultural establishment. It meant an expansion of capacity, an instance of enlightenment, a higher degree of reflexivity, and a broadened horizon.

In the meantime, the interpretive mediation between the fundamentally different learnings of China and the West also projected a crucial discursive condition that those bent upon the enterprise of sinicization often passed over without noticing. That is, translation demanded that the power-seeking subject pass for a Westerner by mimicking his vocabulary, style, and point of view. According to Wang, the neologisms spoken by the translator not only enabled him to simulate the author and serve as the latter's representative and impersonator in a different speech community, but also allowed him to escape his native language, to be distinguished from an ordinary speaker of Chinese, or in his own words, to reach the state of self-consciousness. Furthermore, even Yan Fu, who insisted on imposing elegant Chinese phrases upon Western vocabulary, was in no way to be confused with an authentic classical stylist. As a translator, he had made the initial commitment to represent the other and the extraordinary, that is, to reproduce in his own impoverished tongue the happy and abundant language of the Westerner.

This being said, however, translation was not exactly an equivalent of speaking the European language. Nor was there any possibility that the translator would be confused with the author. Regardless of how close the translation might get to the original, it was never close enough to be mistaken for it. Between translation and original text, as between translator and author, the linguistic boundary was often crossed but never totally abolished. The translated Western speech was thus always embodied in a different, and therefore often contrastive, language. For the translator, the author was never dead, since he was always the subject of emulation. It may thus be said that while working in two different languages, the translator in fact occupied neither.

Subsequently, in the translator there was always a disunity of the self. On the one hand, under the intoxicating influence of the wonderful words of the West, the impersonator was equipped with courage and charisma, ready to charm, announcing himself as a prophetic "I" who envisioned a future of fulfillment beyond the present deficits and poverty. On the other hand, he was part of China's lack of words and wonders. He spoke in the monotonous voice of seduced passivity, of a humble assimilated intellectual. He was the mere observing "I," haplessly sober and disoriented, eager for sensation. Between these two positions of subjectivity, then, there was a space which at once separated these two "I's" and kept them integrated. The space consisted of a dark area of embarrassment, in which the speaking "I's" mode of existence was such that he always acted below his own standards. It was almost a compulsive mania that he underperformed himself, constantly mocking his own words, positioning himself between excessive reflexiveness and uncontrollable naïveté.

Such a space of embarrassment categorically fell outside the scope of intellectual experience that informed Yan Fu's program of knowledge assimilation. It was largely connected with a fascination with the wonderful language of the West rather than with a predominant interest in recycling the linguistic assets of classical Chinese. In other words, the translator felt embarrassed primarily because of the tension between, on the one hand, the full acknowledgment of wonder which elicits a willingness to surrender to the cathartic experience of union and consummation, and on the other, a sober awareness of the absolute impossibility of such a union, on account of the fundamental linguistic difference that situated him in an intermediate space. To a certain extent, the translator thus configured by Wang was not much different from Ambassador Guo, the sentimental captive of the Westerner's power. Like the latter, he came across as a worshiper, imprisoned by his gaze, by his rudimentary knowledge of the Westerner as an intriguing anthropological presence. But at the same time, the repugnance of such connoisseurship was also evident. The appreciation of the West no longer took the form of some private and tender pleasure subjected to blunt censorship. It became itself a painful experience. It represented a different mode of immobility vis-à-vis Barthesian aesthetics.

Besides the essay on neologism, Wang argued against neglecting the fine distinctions between Chinese and Western thought on several other occasions. According to Wang, both Yan's sinicization of Western learning and Kang Youwei's christening of the Confucian orthodoxy seemed to indulge in a naive approach that took mediation for granted and were quite unaware and unashamed of the awkward, self-defeating position they were in.[35] As a remedy, Wang looked toward a master discourse he called philosophy, which would help restore a degree of sameness between the cultures without the hastiness of Yan and Kang. His readings of Kant and Schopenhauer yielded terms such as *chaoyue* (transcendence) and *xiner shangxue* (metaphysics) that allowed him to imagine a certain fundamental affinity between Chinese and Western thought in spite of the empirical differences. But it did not take him long to realize that such figures of sameness always presupposed the distance between the Western language of sophisticated abstraction and the Chinese language characterized by vagueness and absence of reflection. In other words, even in terms of the master discourse, translation was still inevitable. And to further dwell upon the task of translation was not only to represent but also to generate such voids between languages. By 1910, Wang relinquished Western learning once and for all.[36] He became even more sinicized than Yan Fu. But clearly he did not need to fear repeating Yan Fu's mistakes, since as a classical scholar, he had left translation behind.

Hypochondria

Besides the immobilizing gaze and embarrassment, there were of course other expressions of the experience with the West as manifested in the practices of travel and translation. In the May Fourth period, Lu Xun's biographic accounts of his experience as a student of medicine in Japan, such as "Mr. Fujino" and the preface to *Outcry*, give ample treatment to a quite different bottleneck in cultural trafficking.[37] Instead of being troubled by the pleasure in experiencing Western words and things, Lu Xun's quest for power in Japan was informed by a mixture of instrumental interest and moral passion. As stated in the preface of his first collection of short stories, *Outcry*, his personal commitment to the quest for knowledge in Japan was prompted by his father's death at the hands of the ridiculous charlatans of premodern China. He came to the mediating site of the modern sciences in pursuit of that specific wonder that China lacked: scientific medicine. He wished one day he could use the wonderful art to cure all those who suffered like his father. Unlike Guo and Wang, who were troubled by the very medium of their experience with the West, Lu Xun was able to provide a quite mundane and practical justification for such a pursuit from the very beginning. In other words, for Lu Xun, the experience with the West did not cease nor even linger at the sensual level. Whereas visual and verbal impressions were crucially important in the cases of Guo and Wang, they did not figure prominently in Lu Xun's narrative about his contact with the West. He seemed to bypass such subtle moments with remarkable concentration on his mission as a student. In fact, he never gave full rein to his admiration of Japan. Approaching the subject of his study with professional dedication, he even poked fun at those who were susceptible to the superficial charms of Japan.

The story "Mr. Fujino," which forms a part of the collection of his reminiscences called *Morning Blossoms Gleaned at Dusk*, opens with facetious images of failure to "pass" in Tokyo: under the beautiful cherry blossoms, the awkward pigtails of the frolicking Chinese students betray their origins despite the modern Japanese school uniforms; and their ridiculous passion for extracurricular trivialities such as dancing show their inability to conform to the styles of Japanese student life.[38] Obviously, for Lu Xun, passing was a much more serious matter. It did not primarily consist in resemblance in attire and gait, but rather had to do with the acquisition of a toehold in Japan's rapidly growing modern sciences. Therefore, to keep a distance from the frivolous pursuits of the Chinese, he left the metropolis for a small medical college in the country, where he found himself the only foreign student. But things were not much easier. His progress in academic studies was still impeded, this time by the Japanese students rather than his Chinese colleagues. Although his professor, Mr. Fujino, took him under his wing, he was blocked at every turn by chauvinistic Japanese students.

He tried to dismiss such hostility by simply ignoring it, until a traumatic event shattered his entire plan to transplant Western medicine to China. In the microbiology class, slides were usually employed as a teaching aid. Pictures of landscapes and current events were occasionally shown to use up unfilled class time. As the Russo-Japanese war was going on, the students mostly watched wartime reports on those occasions. But in one of the pictures Lu Xun saw the execution of a Chinese spy in the Russian employ. Amidst the cheers of the class, he also caught sight of the nonchalant spectators of the terror who surrounded the victim in the picture. They were his compatriots.

He gave up his medical studies at the end of the semester. Obviously, he found himself not Japanese enough to share such euphoria over the terror directed toward his countrymen. That particular surge of collective euphoria alienated him not only from the microbiology class but also from modern science per se, since while he placed himself among the Japanese, he came to realize that the Chinese were positioned as the "other" by modern powers. After such an incident, he could certainly still introduce modern medicine to China, but only with a bad conscience, given his understanding of the science's hatred, exclusiveness, and violence. For a moment, the personal and sensory dimension of his experience resurfaced.

Lu Xun's position in Sendai was remarkably similar to that of Ambassador Guo on Malta. Like Guo's gaze upon the objects of the island, Lu Xun's attention was fixated on the screen in the classroom.

> Once I even encountered in the pictures numerous Chinese whom I had not seen for some time. One of them was tied up in the middle. Many stood around. All had robust bodies but dull expressions. According to the subtitle, the man worked for the Russians as a military agent and was about to be decapitated by the Japanese soldiers as a warning. And the crowd were those who gathered to relish the spectacle.[39]

In the place of the cased symbols of the Maltan King, what appeared before Lu Xun's eyes was the framed image of the Chinese captive. Whereas the Maltan regalia occupied a unique position in the governor's mansion as a symbol of the invincibility of British colonial power, the hapless Chinese spy was featured during the microbiology class, just as casually and coincidentally, to reinforce the fierce nationalism and imperialism of a Japanese scientific institution. What ultimately distinguished the two cases was the fact that while for Guo it was still possible to empathize with the British and to assume for a moment his sublime view while maintaining sympathy with the crushed old Malta, in Lu Xun's case, the viewer was born between the executioner and the victim, since although he deeply admired the modern science associated with the former, he had to identify with his countryman.

Similarly, between the triumphant Japanese and the humbly animated Chinese spectators, the images on the screen also induced a profound experience of embarrassment. If Wang Guowei's discussion of neologism ultimately reached a point where the distinction between the Chinese and Western languages no longer justified their complementarity, the radical contrast between the Japanese and Chinese also made Lu Xun wonder about the validity of his initial plans to mediate between modernity and China.

> I was back in Tokyo before the end of the academic year. Since that incident, I had begun to see that medicine was not an urgent concern. As to the people of a benighted and weak country, regardless of how healthy their bodies were, they could do nothing but serve as spectators of the absurd public warning. One need not consider it a misfortune, no matter in what numbers they perish.[40]

Whereas Wang believed that the speaker of the impoverished Chinese language was trapped in an unthinking stupor brought about by his limited linguistic experience, Lu Xun was convinced that the life conditions of the Chinese were such that they were living in cultural poverty and intellectual stupor. The Chinese certainly were far from achieving self-consciousness. Like Wang's translator, who defined himself by his position between languages, Lu Xun's medical student occupied the awkward space between well-defined positions of cultural and political geographies, between the scientific Japan and a benighted China.

Because of his realization of the futility of his work on medicine, he decided to move beyond his concern with the bodies of his compatriots. He now recognized that priority had to be given to changing the condition of their minds. He decided at that moment on a literary career. And yet, although he discontinued the negotiation between the wonderful sciences of the West and the ignorance of China, Lu Xun did not close the book on his experience with the West as had Wang. In his later works, he kept revisiting the site of his embarrassment. As indicated in his famed preface to *Outcry*, he regarded his troubling experience as a medical student in Japan as the ultimate impetus for him to embark on his successful literary career. In other words, embarrassment became a useful lesson about the politicized origin of his own self-consciousness, about the critical moment that yielded reflections upon the wonders of the West such as modernity and science.

But while his discourse about the West still served as the springboard for his discourse about China, he had changed his position fundamentally. He no longer defined China's weaknesses in terms of corresponding wonders in the West. As in the case of medicine, even with Japanese excellence and Chinese insufficiency, the complementarity could not be taken for granted. In fact, the transfer to China of this particular mode of modernity was by no means an easy matter, given the Chinese student's tension-ridden process in role initiation and knowledge acquisition.

And because of the uneasy relationship between the supply and demand of the modern, now it became possible to suspect that Western wonders and Chinese deficits were not meant to work together as parts of a larger economy. Insofar as Western wonders were not necessarily duplicable under Chinese circumstances, the deficits of power in China might not always be relieved by the wonderful remedies of Western modernity.

Chapter 8

Baoyu in Wonderland: Technological Utopia in the Early Modern Chinese Science Fiction Novel

FENG-YING MING

Since technological developments, as temporally specific events, may compel drastic change, they are a fruitful source for historical interpretation. Introduced into China at the end of the nineteenth century, innovations spawned by Western science had a tremendous impact upon the lives of the people. In the West, from around 1880 to the outbreak of World War I, a series of sweeping changes in technology and culture created distinctive new modes of thought about the experience of daily life. Products of technology such as the telephone, wireless telegraph, x-ray, cinema, bicycle, automobile, and airplane established the material foundation for this reorientation; parallel cultural developments such as the stream-of-consciousness novel, psychoanalysis, and cubism and the new scientific theories of relativity and evolution further shaped modern consciousness. As news of these cultural innovations and technological inventions seeped into China, conceptual modes that had been evolving and persisting for thousands of years were challenged. While the transformations in Western thought had been anticipated in the science fiction of such writers as Jules Verne, in China, the late Qing "science fiction" novel (*kexue xiaoshuo*) appeared to mark the advent of streams of thought flowing from sources in early antiquity into the modern era, exemplifying a confrontation between China and the West.[1]

To avoid the gross simplifications of a monocausal determinism, we should analyze technological and cultural interactions in their specific historical contexts. In the case of late-nineteenth-century China, such interactions were tempered by the urgent need of the Chinese to rebuild a strong nation and to defend it against foreign political and military invasion. In this specific context, the emergence of the "science fiction" novel in China is inseparable from social and political issues engendered by the dominant discourse of Western imperialism. Written by late Qing literati and published in pictorial or popular magazines, these stories not only exemplify a process in which old and new, native and foreign, came together in a distinctly protomodern hybrid narrative form, they also illustrate the complex process whereby the discourses of Western science and technology mingled with, and were complicated by, the discourses of nationalism, exoticism, and ancient Chinese narrative.

The late-nineteenth- and early twentieth-century Chinese writers wrote their fiction at a historical juncture when the traditional narrative modes were not sufficient to reflect a new vision of China. As intellectuals and literati desperately sought the way to rebuild a strong country, the question of how to read and write about China ranked high on their agendas. Their search for a new narrative paradigm was never merely a literary game. It was a crucial part of their cultural-intellectual approach to crises, centered on a pervasive anxiety about the reception of and resistance to Western knowledge.[2] Both rhetorically and conceptually, a renovated narrative paradigm was regarded as the prerequisite for reflecting and rectifying current reality.[3] This mode of thinking is exemplified by Liang Qichao's promotion of the "new novel" (*xin xiaoshuo*) as the powerful vehicle to transform Chinese mentality in the late Qing period.[4]

The series of sweeping changes in politics and culture that forced China into closer contact with Europe and America was a product of technology. British gunboats in the 1840s proved decisive in battle, highlighting China's military inadequacy; the latter's musketeers, mounted archers, and banner-decked war junks came to be seen as symptomatic of a cultural backwardness.[5] Following the successive shocks of the defeat by Japan in 1895, the crushing of the 1898 reforms, and the Boxer uprising, a progressive elite looked outward with great urgency for ways to save China. Against this historical background, a series of political and cultural negotiations between China and the West took place.

This essay analyzes turn-of-the-century fiction, which provides us with a "window" to look into how the Chinese people integrated science and technology into their worldview and experienced their effects. By 1898, following the so-called Foreign Affairs Movement (*yangwu yundong*, 1862–95), there was a prevailing recognition that China would have to incorporate the repertoire of new Western knowledge into its nation-building project.[6] But what was the relationship between Western knowledge and indigenous modes of thinking? On what cultural bases and intellectual assumptions could the two diverse bodies of knowledge be integrated and a utopian China be constructed?

This essay argues that late Qing science fiction reflects the narrative instability and paradox generated by the attempts by Chinese intellectuals to reconcile Western scientific knowledge with Chinese ideas. The incorporation of Western learning with indigenous Chinese conceptual modes became a recurrent theme in late Qing narrative, with overtones reaching throughout the twentieth century. However, despite attempts by late Qing writers to "imagine," in literary terms, a well-resolved reception of the West, they were not able to find a conceptual equilibrium between the need to import foreign ideas and the need to insist upon the value of domestic ones.[7]

How to construct a literary "utopia" by accommodating Western scientific advances thus became a revealing indication of the overall problems of the time. Related issues included the following: How was Western learning to be integrated into the narrative discourse of the late Qing people? How were the old convictions to be remapped onto a changed social context? How did this changed social context affect the Chinese views of nation and life? How did late Qing writers position themselves in this literary engagement? How did their rhetorical struggles affect the formation of the so-called modern "subject"? With these questions in mind, I suggest further that the late Qing science fiction novel reveals a rhetorical detachment and an anxiety that eventually evolved into a pervasive intellectual instability within modern Chinese cultural and literary discourse.

Understanding that science fiction implied a capacity for literary representation that Chinese critics saw as unprecedented in Chinese letters should help to clarify the vast appeal of science fiction to late Qing writers and reformers. While science fiction novels were assumed to be efficient in transmitting Western knowledge and were set in the context of traditional productive writing ideas, it is clear that their appeal is closely related to social practice.

Since Western science and technology were regarded as having the power to create things that were truly invisible before they were written into existence (like science fiction), Chinese writers thus adapted science fiction as a profound and utopian source of liberation from the Chinese past. The question of whether a literary ideal could be transplanted onto Chinese soil did become a perpetual concern, but Chinese writers worried primarily about whether they could sufficiently transcend their habitual modes of thinking to be effective in incorporating the Western for their immediate use.

The anxiety about Western knowledge and the influence of Western science fiction are clearly visible in *The New Story of the Stone (Xin shitouji)*, a 1905 rewrite of the well-known Chinese romance *Dream of the Red Chamber*

(*Hongloumeng*).⁸ The *New Stone's* author, Wu Woyao (1866–1910), was a prolific but uneven writer who took advantage of Western printing facilities to develop multiple enterprises related to the writing craft. While one strain of Chinese science fiction developed as rewrites of Japanese translations of Western science fiction, another originated from the highly conventionalized practice of recasting and parodying a mixture of indigenous and Western science fiction, oscillating back and forth between the exotic and foreign and the familiar and native. *The New Stone* clearly manifests the latter practice. However, all of these fictional works are earmarked by processes of cross-fertilization which gave rise to a literary subgenre, the "Polygeneric Novel" (*zati xiaoshuo*).⁹ The function of the Polygeneric Novel was to serve as a creative imaginary space where literati, under the influence of native narrative modes and translated foreign novels, could juxtapose and interweave various hybrids of the conventional narrative genres and fuse these with modern Western ideas in order to produce literary solutions to China's real-world social crisis.

What distinguishes the Chinese science fiction novels based on Western science fiction from the novels related to science but derived from traditional narrative is that the former focus on the utilitarian and educational function, while the latter are more concerned with life's quotidian details. Under the influence of the former group, the latter exemplifies the process whereby Western knowledge is both appropriated and challenged by the Chinese mind. *The New Stone*, a narrative derivation, will be the primary focus of this essay, for it reveals how Western science and technology were resisted and reformulated, through popular narrative, into the lifestyle and the modes of thinking of the late Qing populace. I will analyze the paradoxical oscillation revealed in this process by using other science fiction novels, such as those of Lu Xun, as a reference to show how this paradox was extended and related to modern literary discourse.

Lu Xun "translated" two of Jules Verne's science fiction works—*Yuejie lüxing* (Traveling to the moon, 1902), adapted from *From the Earth to the Moon* (1865), and *Didi shijie* (The world underneath the ground, 1903), adapted from *A Journey to the Center of the Earth* (1864).¹⁰ In his preface to *Traveling to the Moon*, entitled "Defending Words" (Bianyan), Lu Xun summarized the characteristics of the early modern Chinese "science fiction novel," suggesting that its purpose, in general, was to convey scientific knowledge through stories firmly embedded in Chinese social and moral conventions. As an unknown Chinese student in Japan, Lu Xun developed the concept of adapting science fiction as a means to "lead the Chinese forward" (*dao Zhongguo renqun yi jinxing*). His concept parallels that of Liang Qichao, the late Qing reformer who propagated ideas for a "New Novel." While Liang Qichao's idea of using the New Novel as a vehicle to inspire the Chinese people to revitalize China constituted the ideological basis for much of late Qing and May Fourth literature, Lu Xun's statement reveals a more complex assessment. Viewing the science fiction novel as having multiple purposes, he summarized its essence as follows:

> [The science fiction novel] foresees the progress of the world and constructs the future. It is based on scientific knowledge as well as literary imagination. More important, it is rooted in human sentiment and plumbs humanistic depths. The sorrow of departing, the happiness of reunion, factual history, and legendary adventure should all be sources for science fiction. Coupled with satire and irony, science fiction can lead to effective social commentary.[11]

The basic elements of the science fiction novel entail, then, the following agenda: (1) to envision the future, (2) to assert imagination without betraying social reality and human sentiment, (3) to emphasize humanistic depth, and (4) to make social commentaries in a playful and ironic way.[12] At issue is how to integrate the new Western technological knowledge and render it compatible with the perennial, deep-seated Confucian concern with morality and social obligation. In brief, turn-of-the-century Chinese science fiction has one primary purpose: to bridge the gap between old and new.

The New Stone is an exemplary work in that it embodies much of the ideology noted above. The first part of the story is basically an ironic recontextualization of the original novel, while the second part is devoted to a survey of current technologies and an inventory of possible ways to incorporate them into the Chinese cultural context. In *The New Stone*, the traditional romantic hero Baoyu may best be characterized as a kind of Chinese "Rip van Winkle" who awakens after a long sleep to find that the world around him has totally changed. The reader is therefore invited to view this strange new world through the eyes of a hero whose mind-set belongs to an earlier era. Baoyu, as mediator between the native and the foreign, the mythical and the "real," shows us how the late Qing intelligentsia adapted to the intrusion of Western knowledge in the form of science and technology.

After having discarded his colorful life in the GrandView Garden (Daguanyuan) and lived the life of an aesthete for several decades, Baoyu decides to revisit the world he has abandoned to fulfill his "vow/desire" (*yuan*) to "patch up the sky." There are, of course, multiple references embedded in this "vow." It recalls the circumstance of the original Baoyu's descent into the "red dust" (*hongchen*), the mythological creation story of Nüwa and the frame story of *Dream of the Red Chamber*.[13] For the purpose of the later version, the reference to this original "desire" takes up again the idea of a cosmological crisis, the need to repair a damaged world and recreate its original harmony. Baoyu reappears in Shanghai in 1904, a decade after the first Sino-Japanese war. His role is to mediate between the life of the classical protagonist of the original novel, and that of the "new" Baoyu who finds himself in a "new" world, invested with all manner of "foreign" things and ideas. This reinvented Baoyu becomes a focal point of interest by pointing up what values the late Qing intellectual assigned to the new foreign objects in his environment and how he proposed to incorporate them into his world.

When Baoyu first arrives in Shanghai, he finds that the original novel, *Dream of the Red Chamber*, has been widely circulated and that he himself has become a "cultural product," a commodity. In service to the now very public nature of this once privately shared and understood novel, the names of the twelve fairy maidens who peopled the dream sequence in the "Land of Great Disillusionment" (Taixu huanjing), including the names of the cousins who inhabited the Grand View Garden, are now names commonly given to prostitutes. Beyond the simple juxtaposition of the private and the public selves, we see also the transformation of sociocultural beliefs in the wake of the scientific impact upon the print media and writer-reader reciprocity in this technologically transformed world.

In the first part of *The New Stone*, Baoyu roams about Shanghai in the company of the infamous Xue Pan. This extrapolation, like the suggestion of fairy maidens becoming prostitutes, cannot fail to cast a negative moral judgment on the "new learning" (*xinxue*). Xue Pan, now a Shanghai merchant, is familiar with all the secular and trendy fashions emerging in this new society. He is the agent who leads Baoyu to perceive the world and foresee the future. He moves in the gap between Baoyu's Grand View Garden and contemporary events.

A significant portion of Baoyu's experience in Shanghai is composed of minute observations of the latest trends. Modern steamboats are an object of his attention, as are manufacturing processes for weapons and artillery. He is fascinated by boat sirens and electric lights. He has the opportunity to observe Westerners in the course of dining, a type of cuisine he himself samples. In one episode, he is observed dining in a Western-style restaurant, which occasions precise descriptions of such things as knives, forks, and matches. In this scene, the reader witnesses Baoyu's fascination with certain small sparkling white cubes heaped on a dish on the table. In order for Baoyu to recognize these strange items as sugar cubes, the waiter puts one in his cup of tea.

Sugar cubes, Western dining utensils, housewares, electric utilities, telephones, fire and travel insurance, and so on—almost every Western product that has attracted Baoyu's attention in *The New Stone* can be founded in the commercial section of the late Qing newspapers, such as *Shen bao*. Like most of the late Qing literati-writers who had amazingly gigantic appetites for incorporating a wide range of materials into their literary works, Wu Woyao has inserted into his popular novel lengthy excerpts from different writings, focusing on exotic foreign genres.

It is likely that the detailed descriptions of exotica had their origin in travelogues, reports by late Qing travelers to the West which were widely read and greatly influenced the literary works produced at the time. Travelogues began to appear in the 1860s after the first official embassy had been sent to the West, although there were some precursors like *Hailu* (Record of the sea, 1820) written by a seaman and *Xihai jiyou cao* (The travel of western sea, 1847–49) by an interpreter who had traveled to the United States.[14] While many of these memoirs and travelogues were dated considerably earlier, it was only with the full-scale introduction of Western ideas in the late nineteenth century that they began to attract readers nationwide. As a consequence, a great number of them were reprinted in the 1890s, including the well-known *Xiaofanghuzhai yudi congchao* (Little studio collected travelogue) and *Youji huibian* (Collected travelogues).[15]

Many of the descriptions from these travelogues were written into novels such as *The New Stone*. In the story, since Shanghai was the earliest site for the proliferation of commercial institutions, media enterprises, and military and missionary schools, Baoyu visits each of these venues in turn. The missionary presence had long been instrumental in encouraging the reception of new ideas. Jesuit missionaries had, as early as the sixteenth century, been engaged in the translation into Chinese of foreign works, particularly treatises on science and technology. This work continued unabated down to the nineteenth century, when the chaos engendered by the Opium Wars and ensuing civil unrest allowed for considerable relaxation of the traditional controls maintained by the imperial government over such enterprises. Toward the end of the nineteenth century, there was a media explosion, and all manner of commercial, printing, and educational institutions sprang up as new media for the appropriation and dissemination of new sources of knowledge and information.

In contrast to Xue Pan, a bellwether of the future, Baoyu's other companion from the original novel, Peiming, the page who carried his books and papers to and from school, is a reminder of the past. He reunites with the new Baoyu at a local Shanghai temple, where he is worshiped by the local populace as a little Buddha but "re-incarnates" into the brave new world in order to become Baoyu's attendant once again. Peiming, like Xue Pan, is a bridge who links past and present, the Grand View Garden and Shanghai. Situated at the crossroads between past and future, the new Baoyu is very much a symbolic embodiment of the predicament of Chinese intellectuals at the turn of the twentieth century. They foresaw the future while looking back on the past. They were nostalgic about the old China but were at the same time realistic enough to know that their task was to envision a new China.

During the course of Baoyu's travel, one of his concerns is to hold up to critical scrutiny the weaknesses and strengths of Western technology and set it in contrast to Chinese ideas, thereby reopening the contested ground that the earlier "Foreign Affairs" reformers had struggled to come to terms with.[16] While Baoyu insists upon making radical distinctions, he also articulates a parallel urge to seek an underlying identity between China and the West. The oscillation between these two antithetical modes of perception—seeing China and the West as completely distinct on the one hand, but sharing an ultimately similar identity on the other—creates a tension in *The New Stone*, which can be described as paradoxical commitment to or a partial understanding of the values of the new ideas the late Qing scholars were introducing from the West.[17]

Baoyu is the embodiment of the experimental path laid down by the late Qing literati toward an ambiguous future. From the position of classical/mythical hero in the narrative mode of *caizi jiaren* (scholar-meets-beauty) to tentative modern "national" hero, the trajectory Baoyu follows is one that does not follow the norm of "linear progress" as preferred in the West, but rather is a path which is, in some sense, static. Significantly, Baoyu's "transformation," if it can be so termed, is performed for the most part on an interior stage, the "subjective" experience of the hero who attempts to incorporate the hard, rational "facts" of twentieth-century realism into a psyche tempered in a "mythopoeic" environment.

As Baoyu tries to make a place for the new material world in the transformed Shanghai landscape, he embodies a set of qualities intended to depict a spectrum of acceptable responses to the experience of modernity. In a word, he is a cultural hero in the service of didacticism. In the same vein, the experiences he encounters are depicted as a spectrum of possible solutions. As we shall see, Freedom Village and the Domain of Civilization (Wenming jingjie) stand at the two extremes of the spectrum.

Increasingly disillusioned by the state of affairs he has witnessed in Shanghai, Baoyu follows Xue Pan, who has escaped to Freedom Village in the aftermath of the Boxer Rebellion and his ill-fated participation in that movement. In a word, Freedom Village is a haven for radicals and sociocultural dropouts. With Peiming in tow Baoyu departs Shanghai for Freedom Village, but on the way Peiming is shot and turned into a wooden statue. Peiming's demise is a cue to the wrong-headedness of this decision. Shortly thereafter, Baoyu links up with his alter ego, Zhen Baoyu, who dissuades him from his journey, describing the populace of Freedom Village as a motley crowd of uncultured idealists lacking sound moral grounding. To make his point, Zhen Baoyu encourages Jia Baoyu to change course and go to the Domain of Civilization.

The ensuing journey through the Domain of Civilization offers the reader a panoramic display of alternative strategies for coping with the problems engendered by Western science and Western learning. The novel ventures at this point into an area familiar to traditional Chinese readers—the utopian vision. The utopian novel was very much in vogue in the late Qing period, the most prominent example being *Wutuobang you ji* (Journey to utopia, 1905).[18] The essence of these tales involved the search for distant lands where the necessary conditions to ground a more viable society could be found. Destinations included Europe, paradisiacal islands, and even the moon. In *The New Stone*, the utopian strand of thinking becomes most obvious after chapter 23, when the hero enters the Domain of Civilization, an idealized realm somewhere outside the Chinese heartland.[19] As is well known, the most famous literary representation of Chinese utopia is "Peach Blossom Spring" (Taohua yuan). Tao Yuanming's fourth century masterpiece features, however, an agriculturally based, static realm, whereas the Domain of Civilization is a progressive technocracy.

In *The New Stone*, once entering the Domain of Civilization, Baoyu, the archetypal sentimental hero who has an acute literary sensibility and is talented in the composition of classical Chinese poetry, reemerges as a pragmatic dilettante who is interested in everything in the outside world. He is eager to learn from the West, but is reflexive in his constant urge to compare and distinguish between China and the West. It is noteworthy that his classical Chinese erudition is not lost but merely expanded. In the Domain of Civilization, those characteristics that distinguish the "Polygeneric Novel" are fully demonstrated. A melange of traditional roles, such as the Chinese knight-errant, the Confucian scholar, the Taoist alchemist, and the powerful general featured in historical novels, are joined to a repertoire of novel exploits to which the hero is exposed, including those of an inventor whose wild flights of fancy are fueled by images of new military weapons, national defense projects, and pseudo-scientific discoveries. Baoyu rides a space shuttle, travels in a "flying auto" (*feiche*), and is seen traversing the high seas in a high-tech submarine to exotic places such as the South Pole and Africa, where he conducts a mission to find rare animals. While engaged in these explorations, he variously exchanges the prototypical role of romantic scholar for that of lab director, and occasionally masquerades as an efficiency expert, proficient in the management of the new technology. Baoyu's outrageousness endears him to readers, while at the same time he serves as a cultural translator introducing a new and exciting lifestyle with the potential to displace the traditional worldview. As a transformed "scholar," his aim is to "invent the new and useful and make it available to the public." It is this combination of efficiency and proficiency grafted on the mythopoeic figure that marks him as a suitable hero for the new China.

What distinguishes *The New Stone* as an early modern version of Chinese science fiction adapted from the traditional literary subgenre of the *zhiguai* (fantastic), which features supernatural magic and the overthrow of Evil by Good, is that in *The New Stone*, emphasis is on detailed descriptions of the scientific and technological aspects of the fantasy. These tend to form a superficial overlay on a deeper base of traditional literary wares. When, for example, Baoyu visits a military institution and army exhibition in the Domain of Civilization, familiar scenes from classical fantastic narrative predominate, scenes such as "fighting in the clouds" (*yunduan dazhan*), "flying knife and the magic rope" (*moshen feidao*), "riding on the mist" (*tengyun jiawu*), and so on. Moreover, the technological elements are diffused throughout the rubric of traditional moral and political ideologies. In other words, the utopian vision of the late Qing intellectual is based less on scientific and technological mastery than on humanistic and moral issues. Baoyu does not fail to exhibit this moral, or one might say, "interior," dimension. In fact, it should be emphasized that it is this dimension which forms the deep structure of the future ideal, whereas the external material construct is but a superficial crust.

Baoyu digresses at length on the differences between various ideas, civilized versus enlightened, or progressive versus evolutionary. China, he tells us, is a country that "became civilized early in the age of the Three Emperors and the Five Kings." But "China has been unable to make progress" because of its attempts simply to maintain stability and solidarity. Western countries, on the other hand, are countries that became civilized very late, but made rapid material and technological progress.[20] In Baoyu's estimation, those countries which achieved a late enlightenment and rapid material progress had to function with moral values imposed upon them. The inference here is a negative judgment upon the institutionalized legal system necessary to the operation of the free, democratic state. In contrast, in Baoyu's utopia, the Confucian system of virtues, including tolerance, generosity, humility, and responsibility, is sufficient. "When it comes to an age of both spiritual and material progress," Baoyu is convinced that "all human beings will act according to their acculturated notion of ethics and morality," obviating the necessity of imposing a legal system based on the Western pattern. Of course, it is understood that this presumed "natural" system of ethics will function as a result of the solid inculcation of classical Confucian values.[21]

Given the rhetoric of the last part of the story, with its manifest intent to validate what he seeks to define as "Chinese" qualities, Wu Woyao makes a forceful attempt to reassert Chinese superiority within a newly constructed technological utopia in which he had just assigned all the positive instrumental values to the West. It is an assertion of superiority without real conviction to it. Moreover, his sudden emphasis on what seems to be a mixture of national and utopian sentiment further complicates the ideological imperative of the Chinese system of ethics. Although Wu Woyao seems to have harmoniously framed the mixture, this mixture remains, in fact, a fantasy devoid of any realistic assessment.

It is well for us to keep in mind the point Baoyu makes here: his instrumental need to prescribe the gospel of wealth and power does not necessarily mean that it must supplant all other notions of morality or visions of how to order the world. Baoyu seems to remain committed in some part to the worldview, common to both Confucianism and Taoism, of a non-contentious social structure uninfected by schemes of personal gain. He seems, in other words, uncomfortable with positions in both extremes, but cannot appear to find any way to mediate between them.

At the end of the story, after serving as a modern hero in the Domain of Civilization and witnessing the operation of the technological utopia completed by Chinese morality, Baoyu willingly relinquishes the project of nation-building to his alter ego Zhen Baoyu and withdraws from the "red-dust" world once again. The story ends with a seemingly well-resolved incorporation between China and the West, in which the strength of Western science and technology is judiciously adapted and complemented by Chinese ethics.

Nevertheless, because of his apparent inability either to imagine a situation in which the Western ideas he is so eager to introduce can be integrated smoothly with the indigenous ideas, or to accept the premise that the ideas are indeed similar, Baoyu in effect becomes the first enunciator of a new discourse of anxiety that was to become widespread in the twentieth century. The dominant theme in this discourse has been that certain key Western ideas were superior and that China could not do without importing them, but there has been an equally steady undercurrent resisting it.

It is significant to trace the dynamics of how this issue of conflicting ideological traditions was worked out in other late Qing literary works. The translations of Jules Verne's *Twenty Thousand Leagues Under the Sea* (1869) and *A Journey to the Center of the Earth* exemplify such a bearing.

Adapted from Jules Verne's *Twenty Thousand Leagues Under the Sea* and serialized in *The New Novel* (Xin xiaoshuo), Hong Xisheng's *Haidi liixing* (Journey to the bottom of the sea, 1902)[22] explores these anxieties through the setting of an unusual, exotic place. The story recasts the original story into a Chinese setting and transforms the original characters into prototypical Chinese heroes reminiscent of the erratic and romantic scholars, the fierce and righteous warriors, and the loyal servants featured in classical Chinese narratives.[23] It features an enchanting world beneath the ocean, highly equipped with transplanted Western scientific and technological inventions—in a submarine. In the story, an oceanographer is involved in a worldwide undersea adventure, capturing a mysterious animal hiding in the ocean. Described as "sharp in head and tail, as huge as an island, as fast as an arrow, and as bright as phosphorus,"[24] the mysterious creature threatens humanity and becomes a worldwide concern. In close combat with this menacing sea monster, the oceanographer and his servants fall into the ocean. After a dramatic submarine rescue, they realize that the very vehicle that rescued them and the "mysterious being" they have been trying to capture are one and the same.

Now a hostage of the submarine by necessity, the oceanographer soon befriends its mysterious captain and inventor, now named Li Meng, a typical name for a Chinese romantic hero or recluse, rather than Captain Nemo, and becomes an observer and analyst of this high-tech fantasy land. He takes notice of the mechanical and engineering principles involved in the submarine's construction, what we now call electronic engineering, aerodynamics, thermodynamics, mechanics, magnetism, acoustics (*shengxue*), photography, and optometry (*guangxue*). The details of this technologically oriented and self-enclosed world, including abundant foreign products, machines, electrified tools, jewelry, art works, books, Chinese porcelain, extravagant decor, gourmet food, and rare collections, form an exotic landscape for Chinese readers. While the story is filled with Western technological terms and information that bewilder modern readers, its enthusiastic adaptation of the foreign setting and undertone sometimes makes the story read like a catalog of Western products.

By converting the ocean into a material and technological utopia, the mysterious Li Meng claims that he has acquired complete "freedom" and "independence" (fashionable ideas borrowed from the West) devoid of any national or political problems, which he could never obtain on land. As owner of this oceanic utopia, he is characterized as a pragmatic scientist interested in everything scientific and technological. He captains the submarine, dives to the bottom of the ocean, and traverses the high seas to exotic places, where he conducts various missions to hunt rare sea animals. While engaged in these explorations, he fluctuates between the prototypical hero role of an emotional cynic and an oceanic engineer, and occasionally masquerades as an efficiency expert, proficient in managing his utopian land. It is this combination of vulnerability, erudition, efficiency, and proficiency grafted on the enigmatic figure that marks him as a new type of hero for Chinese readers.

However, echoing the story of Captain Nemo in *Twenty Thousand Leagues Under the Sea*, there is always a hidden mystery attached to this technological wizard. In the eyes of his hostages, Li Meng is a riddle—a mixture of the traditional Chinese and Western heroes, exemplifying conflicting qualities such as kindness, manliness, vulnerability, puzzling background, and perplexing personality. Other than being portrayed as a knowledgeable scientist, Li Meng also embodies the quality of a traditional Chinese exile. He is a misanthropic person, full of intertwined love and cynical anger for the human world. He has intentionally departed the "human realm" (*renjie*) to escape "the annoying worldly matters and ostentatious social trivialities" and the pretentious man-made legal regulations found on land. In the character's own words, "I have abandoned the human world for a long time. . . . The worldly standard irritates me" (p. 34).

Moreover, the technological elements in this story are diffused throughout the rubric of traditional moral and political ideologies. In other words, the utopian vision of the late Qing intellectual is based less on scientific and technological mastery than it is on humanistic and moral issues. Like Baoyu in *The New Stone*, the oceanic utopian hero does not fail to exhibit this moral dimension.

Just as the submarine captain is used to portray a new type of Chinese hero and the reception of Western learning, the hostages in the story have their own role. As the notions of "Western" and "modern" became the fashionable conceptual modes and languages for writers and reformers in late Qing society, so the submarine captain promises the hostages the "right of freedom" and allows them to walk freely in the submarine. But once in a while the hostages are told to return to their room and are not allowed to see anything until they are released. The reason why not only bothers the hostages but also creates a narrative tension. This mystery seems to be related to part of the utopian hero's personal history; it is indicative of the emotional or personal life that has been segregated from the utopian land.

The mysterious submarine captain seems to have forcefully and purposely replaced his need for human companionship with science and technology and thus can be interpreted as an emblem of the paradoxical spirit of the time. Rather than seek emotional fulfillment and satisfaction, he turns away from the human world to the world under the sea. His reasoning is multi-faceted: first, the ocean is large and full of resources; second, the air is clean; third, numerous kinds of sea animals can keep you from being lonely; fourth, one can get away from political and military threats. He claims that in this way he has obtained "the right of freedom and independence" and created a land "that can never be found on the earth."[25]

In addition to the detailed descriptions of the technology, the story is interspersed with comments on human nature, humanistic issues, and moral concerns. The story goes to great lengths to discuss the "content life," or "utopian lifestyle." The oceanographer comes to the realization that the notion of "content" (*xinman yizu*) is a subtle one: "The proverb goes, 'The human heart is hard to satisfy. Once it obtains one thing, it will be looking for another' (*renxin buzu, de long wangshu*)."[26] After a series of experiences or conversations exploring the details of material extravagance and literary fantasy and of scientific and technological information, the three hostages finally decide that in spite of their pleasant utopian living quarters, they would rather live in a world of complex relationships, secular trivialities, and the details of daily life. They long for home and decide to seek ways to escape. While the hostages are eagerly seeking chances to escape, the oceanographer himself seems to waver between the material utopia and his subjective sentiment for the real, mundane world. The reader will never know his final decision because the story is left unfinished (the magazine in which it was serialized ceased publication). But like most of the late Qing novels, the last part of the story seems to be wandering in a situation—as if it does not know quite where to go.

Given the language, setting, and actions of the last part of the story, with its earlier intent to assign all positive instrumental value to Western science and technology, the author makes a forceful attempt to search for an outlet from this newly constructed utopian land. His emphasis on what seems to be a mixture of moral and national sentiment further complicates the story's ideological imperative of the superiority of science and technology.

The oceanographer seems to remain attached to some part of the traditional morality and sentiments and wavers between the utopian land constructed by science and technology and an old China conditioned by more humanistic concerns. He seems, in other words, uncomfortable and unsatisfied with both positions, but cannot appear to find any way to integrate them. If we understand this, it may not be hard for us to understand the reason why the story was never finished and, in fact, why the reformers' call for a "New Novel" was never realized.

Like *Journey to the Bottom of the Sea* and *The New Stone*, Lu Xun's science fiction novels also echo such a seemingly resolved, yet paradoxical and unsettled incorporation with the West. In *Didi Shijie*, his translation of Jules Verne's *Journey to the Center of the Earth*, this paradoxical conflict was developed into a critical examination of the transforming intellectual subject in a specific moment of late Qing history. This is an example of what I have termed "rewriting in the name of translation," since few readers of the original would recognize the story. It is recast in a manner common among literati, namely, into a paradigmatic representation of the traditional scholar/student relationship. The variations in this version are the characterization of Yalishi, an old scholar who is addicted to new knowledge, and Leiman, a young student who bears a strong resemblance to Baoyu in that he resists learning and is romantically inclined. In its Chinese setting, the trip to the earth's center is loaded with moral significance. Yalishi, the old German scientist, is portrayed as an outrageous genius, obsessed by the sciences, particularly geography. He is an addictive consumer of the "wonder books" (*qishu*), which, as we shall see, were advertised in all the newspapers and other popular magazines. His pursuit of scientific knowledge mimics the drive of the traditional Chinese scholar intent upon succeeding in the civil service examinations, a traditional endeavor parodied in the well-known novel *Rulin waishi* (The scholars). In Lu Xun's characterization, Yalishi appears to be monomaniacal in his pursuit of science and his response to the latest scientific innovations. However, his inquisitiveness and adventurous spirit differentiate him from the traditional scholar, whose character is more fully appropriated by Leiman (in some respects a clone of Baoyu). As a favorite cultural hero, Leiman's indeterminate response to new knowledge and his pronounced lack of diligence are noteworthy. He tends to withdraw. For example, when the two characters are about to step into a volcano that has just ceased erupting, Yalishi surges forward with no inhibitions, while Leiman hangs back, hesitant and fearful. By using Yalishi to satirize Leiman's "intention of devoting himself to the pursuit of knowledge" (*xianshen weixueshude xisheng zhi zhi*), and by having the two scholars engaged in constant quarrel, Lu Xun is clearly presenting a cultural critique of the value of scholarly pursuits associated with traditional knowledge.

Another important element in the story involves the romance between Leiman and a young woman who is the source of Leiman's motivation, albeit tentative, to pursue the new knowledge. In order to please his sweetheart, Leiman sets out on this adventure to the center of the earth, all the while suffering the pangs of separation. Sentiment, it will be remembered, is a necessary ingredient in Lu Xun's appraisal of the value of the science fiction novel. The two basic elements that form the Chinese worldview are *qing* (sentiments), the primary guideline in the Chinese moral vision, and *li* (reason), which was not developed to lead China into material advances. Lu Xun felt it was necessary for Chinese to import the Western version of *li*. Thus he conflates the scientific issue with the moral one and attempts to contextualize a materially oriented value system within an ethical one.

Lu Xun's story is a cross-fertilization of different traditional models. By reworking traditional motifs, he presents the scholar in a new role of the powerful "other" whose mission is to motivate the typically weak Chinese scholar to explore the dangerous "underground." Yalishi is the alter ego of the Chinese hero, whom he looks upon as cowardly: "a born servant, having graduated from Chinese school knowing how to get by only by bowing and offering cigarettes."[27] Because it is the lover's encouragement and inspiration, rather than Yalishi's condescending criticisms, which drive Leiman finally to overcome his scruples, the pursuit of knowledge acquires moral significance. As Yalishi's critique reaches to the heart of Leiman's character, the seat of all morality, the story can be read as a sermon preaching morality, righteousness, and commitment (*daoyi*). By depicting the pursuit of knowledge in such terms, Lu Xun presents the acquisition of Western science and technology as a moral imperative, a matter of *yili*. In this context, traveling to the center of the earth is also a moral imperative, which will both enlighten the people and save the nation.

Serialized in *Zhejiangchao* (Zhejiang tide, 1902–3), an overseas Chinese student journal published in Japan, *Didi shijie* is presented as but one among many different types of media productions promoting Western culture and civilization to Chinese readers. These literary magazines routinely featured columns with headings such as "Science" (*Kexue*), "Glossary of New Terminology" (*Xinmingci shiyi*), "Academic Learning" (*Xueshu*), "Talks on Strange Foreign Topics" (*Taixi yitan*), and "Western New Learning" (*Taixi xinzhi*). Among the features were reports on items of interest ranging from the latest chemistry books to foreign policy to housekeeping tips. Lu Xun's text may be envisioned as a small item within a larger text, the whole of which is designed to transmit Western science and technology to the reader in the most efficient way. It is not uncommon to find excerpts from science textbooks inserted directly into the science fiction written at this time, and Lu Xun's *Didi shijie* was no exception. Advertisements, such as the following for *The New History of the West* (*Taixi xinshi*), were common in magazines and published stories:

The MUST-HAVE book for the fields of examinations and current affairs. The change in current affairs and our national situation is the crucial matter over the last one hundred years. Summarizing the essence of hundreds of Western books, the Englishman Mackenzie (Maikenxi) edited and compiled *The New History of the West*. If you have this book handy, you will definitely beat all your rivals.²⁸

Of particular interest in the following advertisement for *Shiyin huaxue zhinan* (The guide to chemistry in lithography) is the portrayal of Mr. Biligan, a man whose moral qualities confirm the value of this book, doubtless a prototype of the wonder books which fueled Yalishi's obsession:

> In recent years, we Chinese have come to realize the importance of chemistry. But we find that books dealing with such knowledge are like flickering lights and flying feathers; it is very difficult for us to get into them. The most comprehensive among them is *The Guide to Chemistry in Lithography* by Mr. Biligan. Mr. Biligan is a very knowledgeable scholar. He is a member of the principal teaching faculty in the College of Foreign Languages (Tongwen guan) and has used his spare time to translate and write this book. The book covers everything from military weapons and electrical equipment to the accessories of daily life. It tells us everything about chemistry, such as the nature of useful materials, their formation, constituents, weight, and ways to reproduce them. It is written in the form of questions and answers, and divided into categories for easy reference. To make it even more convenient for readers, there are two English-Chinese glossaries appended to the book. Says Mr. Biligan, "This is a book, not only for the students of Tongwen Guan, but also for general readers who are devoted to learning." It is clear from these remarks that Mr. Biligan is a moral man. How then can we Chinese people not share this book with our friends who have the same interest?²⁹

Lu Xun's *Didi shijie* opens, in fact, with what would seem to be direct scientific reportage, a disguised authorial voice which thus informs readers:

> [In Europe] there was a scholar named Shigonglizi who said that the center of the earth is composed of nothing more than liquid. His theory was accepted unanimously by scholars. Later on, someone surnamed Polin challenged this theory and contended that the rotation of liquid can generate heat and powerful energy, thus causing eruptions of the earth's crust. But the fact that the earth remains in good shape suggests that Shigonglizi's theory is not sustained. This theoretical issue has never been pinned down, and as our reasoning must be based on solid factual ground, nothing is more important than investigating ourselves. By means of the electric light, we can now explore

the mystery of the center of the earth. This is an opportunity and obligation we cannot evade.[30]

The Chinese practice of integrating new knowledge into daily life by airing it first in fictional narrative was not unknown in other countries. Studies of literacy during the Industrial Revolution in England have revealed that one of the functions of early popular periodical literature was to orient readers to a changing environment. Common readers in London and Manchester found in popular science magazines their best guide to interpreting the Industrial Revolution. In Meiji Japan, where similar changes arrived much more rapidly, urban youth were infatuated with the "self-help" ethics expressed in numerous translations of Samuel Smiles. The same phenomenon is clearly present in the early journals promoting political reform in China, which presented the readers with the knowledge they needed to thrive in a rapidly "modernizing" environment: principles of household electricity, the workings of a modern bank, behavior expected on streetcars, foreign language lessons, and so on.[31]

The exponential increase in knowledge and the explosion in media production and other technologies that occurred in late-nineteenth-century China engendered the science fiction novel and other innovative forms of fictional narrative. The major concern of many fiction writers at the time was to reinvigorate the populace in order to save the nation. For this purpose, they discerned the possibilities inherent in new technologies of publishing and quickly employed them as a vehicle for transmitting new ideologies. The earlier practice of circulating manuscripts among friends and friends of friends was replaced by the commercial offering of printed texts. The late Qing readers and writers quickly came to appreciate the multifunctional capabilities of new printing technologies. Fictional texts, in addition to their traditional functions as sources of entertainment and diversion, became valuable sources of new and foreign ideas, and they were also in demand as general guides to living.

Because Western science and technology formed the essential nucleus of the new knowledge, science fiction novels became a locus for the integration of old and new, native and foreign, and an experimental ground for every imaginative adaptation. As we have seen, these fictional narratives bridging the old and the new had a primarily didactic function, and it is this that makes them appear embarrassingly naive and even silly to more sophisticated readers. But the fact that they were read alongside serious academic texts and highly crafted fiction—Lu Xun himself was a very accomplished writer—attests to the critical demand for the messages they contained.

The immediate purpose of "enlightening the people" (*qimeng*) seems to have set the agenda for, and endorsed the creation of, these science fiction novels.³² However, the functions of didacticism and enlightenment of these groups of novels were very soon taken up by more institutionalized literati and intellectual organizations in the era of the early Republic. Printing entrepreneurs and intellectuals engaged in publishing, such as the Commercial Press group, soon adapted to a self-appointed role as educators and took charge of the project of "enlightenment education" (*qimeng jiaoyu*) in China.³³ The magazine *The Eastern Miscellany* (Dongfang zazhi, 1906–27), for example, made a concerted effort to accomplish this self-assigned task. A series entitled *The Textbooks of the Republic* (Gongheguo jiaokeshu) was published by the Commercial Press in 1912. One advertisement in *The Eastern Miscellany* was headed by the following announcement: "With the founding of the Republic, the political structure has been changed to that of a Republic. . . . All the necessary knowledge that a citizen of the Republic should possess, as well as the origins of this Revolution, have been narrated in detail in them [publications], so as to cultivate the complete Republican citizen."³⁴ The institutionalized publication of science superseded the science fiction novel as a vehicle to promote Western science. Therefore, it is easy to understand why the science fiction novel disappeared in early twentieth-century China.

The relationship between domestic value systems and foreign learning, the major factor that conditioned the oscillating tension in the science fiction novels of Wu Woyao, Hong Xisheng, and Lu Xun, has been an enduring issue in modern China.³⁵ It is important to realize the extent to which this tension sums up the problems involved in the collision between the foreign and the native in China. In contrast to this period of the late Qing endeavor to justify intellectually Western material advances in China, what the later Chinese revolutionists wanted, however, was an idea that would provide leverage for change, a change radical enough to enable China to transform itself sufficiently to hold off ever more exigent Western incursions. The late Qing effort came to a halt with the founding of the Republic of China, which brought back the traditional values and lifestyle in full force. After nearly a decade of frustration with the Republican regime, the intellectual community launched a radical political and cultural revolution, the May Fourth movement, in 1919. Actively participating in this new cultural movement, progressive writers like Lu Xun, Yu Dafu, and Mao Dun tried to bring home to their contemporary readers a critical sense of the unrest and bewilderment they felt as part of their contemporary experience.

Lu Xun, for one, provides us with a perfect case in which the intellectual contradictions of the modern Chinese were multiplied, rather than simply resolved, in the literary text. As the leading writer of his time, Lu Xun's strong concern for the status of Chinese modernization was in line with his ruthless criticism of the repressive practices of traditionalism as a whole. Yet despite his persistent commitment to help cure what he termed "the disease of the Chinese mind," Lu Xun, like the earlier Foreign Affairs reformers, was caught up in his own struggle between the commitment to bring about social changes and an intellectual distrust of the value of such an endeavor. It is exactly the same conflict that constituted the conceptual crisis for the majority of the May Fourth intellectuals—namely, could China ever succeed in its "appropriationism" (*nalai zhuyi*) while retaining its cultural identity? It was this crisis of split consciousness, of phantom reality, that caught the Chinese writer—as a socially committed individual—between the will to hope and the retreat in despair. Thus it is easy to comprehend why, after publishing some prominent works of realist fiction in modern China, Lu Xun chose to end his career by publishing a unique volume of prose poems, *Yecao* (Wild grass), which resonates with moments of his intense despair.

Wu Woyao's rewriting of Baoyu and Hong Xisheng's appropriation of Captain Nemo both magnified the equivalent of Lu Xun's split consciousness in its attempt to recast a traditional Chinese fantasy in Western mode. In a significant way, their works were the forerunners in the use of traditional Chinese narrative for the purpose of envisioning China as a new utopia, only to end, on another level, in their failures to find a positive way to realize this utopian dream. On the other hand, we all see that they crossed the threshold of Western science fiction while retaining a foothold in traditional Chinese systems of the fantastic and the supernatural. In many other novels of the period, writers mixed their knowledge of Western science and technology with their residual superstitions, their desire for utopia with their realistic anxieties, in such a way as to form a highly provocative perspective from which to look at and imagine China's past and future. From them, we see the remapping of canonical Chinese virtues onto a changed social context.

Even at the very beginning of the integration of Western knowledge into Chinese literature, these writers entertained a paradox that called into question the essential "China" while at the same time re-essentializing "China." Their endeavors echoed the Foreign Affairs movement and challenged what had been regarded as sacred and immanent cultural-political institutions. Both groups' efforts were inconclusive, and the replacement that they nervously prescribed merely cultivated the old yearnings for a new China. However, the technological utopia constructed in their science fiction novels suggests a sustaining intellectual tension that was carried into the modern phase of Chinese history. Lu Xun's works, for example, exemplify the process that this tension carried and developed into the discourse of the post–May Fourth narrative. In this sense, the tragic scenario that the late Qing science fiction novels reflect does provide us a window to look into an important part of the Chinese experience of modernity.

Chapter 9

The Texture of the Metropolis: Modernist Inscriptions of Shanghai in the 1930s

YINGJIN ZHANG

In the field of modern Chinese literature, the city has not received much serious, sustained critical study for a long time. A few canonical works of city literature, such as Mao Dun's *Ziye* (Midnight, 1933) and Lao She's *Luotuo Xiangzi* (Camel Xiangzi, 1936), were generally discussed under the rubric of realist fiction, which often emphasizes sociopolitical issues (e.g., class struggle) and narrative convention (e.g., typical character). As a result, the city in literature hardly constituted an aesthetic object in its own right. However, literary scholarship in the past decade has begun to uncover a variety of urban texts (such as the "Beijing school of fiction" [*Jingpai xiaoshuo*] and the Shanghai "New Perceptionists" [*Xin ganjue pai*]), and has demonstrated that the city actually assumed multiple forms in modern Chinese literature.[1] As I have demonstrated elsewhere, images of the city cut across a wide spectrum of cultural imagination in modern China, ranging from a provincial city to the ancient capital and the modern metropolis.[2]

In this essay I focus on the modern city of Shanghai and study the texture of the metropolis as inscribed by modernist writings in the 1930s. For this purpose I do not question how authentic or realistic the representation of the city may be in a given text,[3] but rather examine how the city is "produced" through imaginative writings and narrative devices. To be sure, the "production" in question is not "industrial"—as in the sense of constructing a building or a factory, but "semiotic"—as in the sense of representing the city as a sign system whose multiple layers of meaning need to be decoded and deciphered. Focusing more on the process of production than on its end result—the city as text (or the city-text), I contend that the textual production of the modern city might in fact be a particular type of experience of modernity in early twentieth-century urban China, namely, the production of a new perception and a new knowledge of the modern city.

In the main body of this essay I analyze a modernist piece of writing on Shanghai from the mid-1930s in order to reveal how specifically a new perception of the city is reflected in textual production. The new perception, once identified in the written text, is further secured in a group of visual texts which seek to approximate the experience of the metropolitan phantasmagoria. But before proceeding with the textual analysis, a general survey of different modes of city narratives will help us map out the field of research on the city and literature.

Modes of City Narratives

According to the German critic Klaus Scherpe, city narratives fall into the following four modes. "The first mode would derive from that traumatic opposition in German eighteenth- and nineteenth-century novels between a 'rural utopia' and an 'urban nightmare.' In this example an earlier, allegedly peaceful subjective identity is threatened by advancing industrial civilization."[4] In the second mode, which is exemplified by "the socially critical, naturalistic novel of the nineteenth century, the country-city opposition gives way to class conflict.... Urban life and experience are reduced here to an opposition between the individual and the masses."[5] The third mode is found in the modernist writing, where "the contemplative gesture of the Parisian flâneur" points to "the imaginative potential of urban experience," and where "an aesthetic subject ... apprehends objects spontaneously, fixing and securing them in its gaze."[6] The fourth mode is "functional and structural narration," by means of which the city "is newly constructed as a 'second nature' in terms of the dynamic flow of its commodities and human movements, which appear to take place according to self-sufficient and complementary patterns in space and time";[7] in other words, the city now takes up the role of agency and narrates (i.e., unfolds) itself discursively in the text.

In spite of its apparent neatness, Scherpe's classification can be subjected to critical interrogation, especially his distinction between the third and the fourth modes, both bearing a trademark of modernism. Taking his examples exclusively from modern European literature and film, Scherpe implies a historical development of city narratives from the pastoral (e.g., the rural-urban opposition) through the realist (e.g., class conflict) to the modernist (e.g., aesthetic contemplation), a development that occurred largely in response to the sociohistorical developments in the West since the eighteenth century. Given its Western grounding, we have to exercise caution when using Scherpe's model to approach a non-Western literature.

In modern Chinese literature, we do not find any linear development of city narratives; instead, the pastoral, the realist, and the modernist modes *coexisted*, and indeed competed with one another, in the early twentieth century. The competition was especially intense in the 1930s. Critically acclaimed as a first major realistic novel upon its publication in 1933, Mao Dun's *Midnight* was intended to picture the metropolis of Shanghai as the nucleus of uncontrollable economic and political energy in modern China. A year later, annoyed with all types of urban politics (including the accompanying literary polemics) in Shanghai, Shen Congwen published *Biancheng* (Border town) and offered a pastoral tale of rural virtues in remote West Hunan as a "medicine" for the "diseased mind" of his urban readers.[8] Also in the early 1930s, a group of Shanghai writers became well known for their modernist fiction, which sought to represent the city selectively through the intensity of perception of the aesthetic subject. The images of the city to emerge from the Chinese literary production in the 1930s are, therefore, both numerous and variegated, leaving no clear indication as to which mode of city narrative actually dominated the literary scene.

Of these modes mentioned above, the pastoral and the realist—with their dramatization of opposition—have been substantially studied in the field of modern Chinese literature.[9] From C. T. Hsia's history of modern Chinese fiction completed in the early 1960s to recent critical studies by Marston Anderson and David Der-wei Wang, realism has been consistently singled out as the most important mode, whereas the pastoral—associated with lyricism and nostalgia—is seen more or less as a subgenre, a theme subsumed under realism.[10] Given this sustained critical engagement with realism, it is understandable why early Chinese modernist writings are scarcely studied. They surfaced from the late 1920s to the mid-1930s and then vanished entirely from Chinese literary history until the 1980s.[11] However, since they present a vision of the city drastically different from the realist and the pastoral modes, these early modernist writings deserve much research and methodological analysis. What follows is my attempt in this direction.

The City as Text

Liu Na'ou and Shi Zhicun began publishing stories and editing literary journals in the late 1920s. They did not receive much critical attention until they turned to modernist techniques, such as fragmentary images, isolated perceptions, and interior monologues. In a review of Shi Zhicun's two psychoanalytic stories, "Zai Bali daxiyuan" (At the Paris theater) and "Modao" (Sorcery), both published in *Xiaoshuo yuebao* (Short story monthly) in 1931, the leftist critic Lou Shiyi used the label "xin ganjue pai" (New perceptionism) and traced the influences of French surrealism and Japanese new perceptionism.[12] According to Su Xuelin,[13] it is the French writer Paul Morand who influenced the Japanese new perceptionists in the first place and who should therefore be regarded as the forerunner of the movement. In addition, new perceptionism in Japan might have borrowed from futurism, which idolized the machine, celebrated material culture, and embraced the chaos, speed, conflict, disturbance, and fanaticism that are characteristic of the modern metropolis. Like their foreign counterparts, the Chinese new perceptionist writings, especially those by Mu Shiying, sought to inscribe all metropolitan glamour, phantasmagoria, eroticism, decadence, and complexity. From this perspective, Su Xuelin concludes that "Chinese city literature was legitimately established" with the appearance of Mu Shiying in the early 1930s.[14]

Whether or not Chinese city literature was established with Mu Shiying or with a writer of more literary status (e.g., Mao Dun or Lao She), there is no question that the new perceptionists introduced a totally new perspective on the city and urban experience in modern Chinese literature. As a matter of fact, after the establishment of the literary journal *Xiandai* (Les contemporains) in May 1932, initially edited by Shi Zhicun and later coedited with Du Heng, this Shanghai modernist group gained increasing prominence in Chinese literary circles. As a major nonpartisan journal founded shortly after the Japanese attack on Shanghai in January 1932, which had virtually shut down its literary establishment, *Les Contemporains* published writings by the leftists, the liberals, and the Nationalists alike, including Lu Xun, Mao Dun, Liang Shiqiu, Hu Qiuyuan, and many others.[15] With the prestige of *Les Contemporains* and the influence of their writings, the new perceptionists set a brief modernist trend in the early 1930s, which was to attract a number of young urban writers.[16]

One of the writers attracted by the new perceptionists was Hei Ying (pen name of Zhang Bingwen). Originally from Sumatra, Hei Ying came to Shanghai for his college education in the early 1930s and became a close friend of Mu Shiying, with whom he frequented exotic cafes and dance halls.[17] In April 1934, he published a short story, "Dang chuntian laidao de shihou" (When spring arrives), in *Liangyou* (The young companion), a Shanghai-based pictorial popular from 1926 to 1945.[18] The story is printed in an attractive two-page layout (about 11-by-17 inches each page) and visually enhanced by twelve photographs of city scenes.

"When Spring Arrives" tells of a young man's romance with a modern girl. Here is how the story begins:

> "When spring arrives"—
> This warm season is the best time for walking outside. Reciting the first line of my poem, I walked briskly on the dusky street. A ray of sunlight, with lingering love, kissed the top of a twenty-two-story skyscraper; night fog was already slowly spreading throughout the city.[19]

From the skyscraper the male narrator's gaze falls on the streetlights and the shop windows.[20] Then, all of a sudden, a slender figure emerges from behind a glass exhibit case of chocolate. "Hello!"—she is cloaked in a black wool coat, standing on the sidewalk of a street where cars line up like a long snake and where a traveler from California is smoking a cigar while dreaming of gold and women. Metaphorically "taking" the girl along as a "walking stick," the narrator recites two more lines of his poem:

> Coming with the melancholy of lilacs,
> It is a nineteen-year-old girl, Suzie.

The next day is the Chinese New Year. It starts to rain before dinner time, and the narrator feels lonely. He telephones Suzie and invites her to a dance party at the Bailemen (Paramount).[21] She declines his invitation, because her father is telling her a story from "A Thousand and One Nights" and she is enjoying it. The narrator turns to the poetry of Dai Wangshu and Xu Zhimo, but it does not make him feel better. Stricken by homesickness, he writes a letter to his mother, then walks out of his apartment and drops the letter into a letter box, which stands alone in a quiet street. A newspaper boy comes by. The narrator gives him four coins for an evening newspaper. He is startled to read a bold-type headline: "Ai Xia Commits Suicide," and his vision is blurred by thousands of exclamation marks crawling like ants—"!!!!!!!!!"[22]

The narrator rushes to the girl's house and shows her the newspaper, but she does not believe the news since she had just met the film actress Ai Xia two weeks ago. "Suicide"—how could it possibly be? and on the lunar new year's day when everyone is cheerful? On the bus on his way back, the narrator watches the urban night scenes—a nightclub with revolving doors, melodious jazz, and elegant dancers; the tramps shivering outside the closed shops, waiting for the donation of a coin or two. Spring is vanishing, and the narrator recites the rest of his poem:

> She has knowing eyes,
> She has a glib tongue;
> When she cries, I know.
> She also has a melancholy heart.[23]

The next day, the narrator tries to ease the girl's sorrow by bringing her to Xiafei lu (Avenue de Joffre), where the Paris Theater is showing a Chaplin film, the Guotai (Cathay) Theater is showing Lloyd Bacon's *Foot-Light Parade* (1933, the title is printed in English), and refugees from the old Russian empire wander aimlessly.[24] The narrator then leaves the melancholic girl to the care of her father. Two weeks later, he returns from a trip to Hangzhou. He notices that a long chimney towering over the roof of a factory is spitting out black smoke, and finds this scene to be a sharp contrast to his memory of boating on the West Lake.[25] Even the bus now looks like a giant frog (illustrated in a photograph). In a street as quiet as a convent in the afternoon, when the *huiliqiu* courts are taking a nap before the crazy evening programs,[26] the girl declares to the narrator that she is no longer to be fooled by his love but she will never commit suicide. She will visit the cemetery tomorrow rather than go with him to see a movie.

The final two paragraphs of the story repeat the beginning, but palindromically. The sentences of the first two paragraphs are repeated in reverse order (with only a deletion of the phrase "dusky"):

> Night fog was already slowly spreading throughout the city. A ray of sunlight, with lingering love, kissed the top of a twenty-two story skyscraper. Walked briskly on the street, I recited the first line of my poem. This warm season is the best time for walking outside:
> "When spring arrives—"[27]

Textual Production, I: Walking on the Street

The reader sees in Hei Ying's story none of the chaotic scenes of urban struggle described in Mao Dun's *Midnight*, such as stock market conspiracies, suppression of a workers' strike, and a violent political demonstration. Nor does the evocation of the natural beauty of the West Lake suffice to counter metropolitan phantasmagoria (captured in the photographs of flashing neon lights and the exotic Avenue de Joffre). Obviously, Hei Ying's interest lies elsewhere. Instead of focusing on the operation of economic and political forces in the metropolis, he chooses to stay in the ephemeral zone of isolated individual perceptions. He does so by adopting a particular narrative strategy, which is to follow a male adventurer *walking on the street*.

Indeed, "walking on the street" has been theorized as a significant form of spatial practice in the city. For instance, Michel de Certeau sets in diametrical opposition the street-level view and the panoramic (or bird's-eye) view. Once elevated to the 107th floor of the World Trade Center in Manhattan, the viewer may be struck with awe: "The panorama transforms the spectator into a celestial eye.... It transforms the city's complexity into readability.... The city-panorama is ... a picture, of which the preconditions for feasibility are forgetfulness and a misunderstanding of processes."[28] In other words, what one tends to forget on top of the Manhattan skyscraper is that real life begins down on the streets, where the city-dwellers walk in countless numbers.

Walking on the street, therefore, is posited as an indispensable way to perceive and know the city. Perception is here linked to creation—not just the creation of the city as a text, but the creation of knowledge about the city as well. In Hei Ying's story, the unnamed narrator—unnamed because he is only one among countless—acquires his knowledge of the city by walking the streets. He walks at a leisurely pace, as if undisturbed by any mundane business. In this way he is able to select for his "aesthetic" appreciation a number of urban images and icons that produce new ways of perceiving the modern metropolis: a low-angle view of the towering skyscraper, a voyeuristic gaze at the female body, and an imaginative processing of urban figures (e.g., a frog-like bus and a lilac-like girl).[29] Such acts of aesthetic appreciation not only transform the narrator into an aesthetic subject but also mark Hei Ying's text with a distinct *modernist* imprint.[30]

In spite of this, Hei Ying's story does not feature a perfect nineteenth-century Parisian *flâneur*, "the passionate spectator" who roamed about the city streets and who enjoyed every moment of his anonymity amid the urban crowds.[31] It is true that Hei Ying's male protagonist is as passionate a spectator of the city as his Parisian counterpart, but unlike a typical *flâneur*, he does not remain completely *incognito*. Instead, he prefers to be known, to enjoy private moments with the city girl Suzie. To the extent that he avoids the urban crowd, he eschews a typical metropolitan experience—"The delight of the city-dweller is not so much love at first sight as love at last sight."[32] It is precisely this "love at last sight"—the feeling the city-dweller has when he loses his object of desire, oftentimes an unknown woman on the street—that constitutes the erotics in a crowd and makes life in the metropolis a never-ending adventure.

If the erotics in a crowd is not alluded to in Hei Ying's story, the erotic nature of urban imagination is nonetheless inscribed in another form, namely, the reading of woman as a text, which parallels the reading of the city as a text. At the beginning of the story, urban voyeurism is set in motion verbally as well as visually. The female body is described and displayed in fragments, and value judgments are made accordingly: the "slim figure" (photographed as a headless girl in a fashionable overcoat and high-heel shoes), the "knowing eyes" (photographed as more alluring, I would say, than knowing), and the "glib tongue" (photographed as two tightly closed lips with thick lipstick). Obviously, suggestive female body parts such as these are not randomly selected urban sights for anyone to enjoy. Rather, to display these evocative images is not only to present them as distinctively urban icons but also to enhance their "aesthetic" values for the voyeur.

Indeed, value judgments attached to a woman's body parts are found as early as 1928 in another popular urban pictorial, *Beiyang huabao* (The peiyang pictorial news). In a display originally titled "The Fifteen Beauty Points of a Woman," these enticing parts of a woman's body are each inscribed in a photograph and accompanied by a caption: hair, eyebrows, eyes, nose, teeth, lips, ears, neck, shoulders, arms, hands, thighs, feet, waist, and breasts.[33] Many of these captions contain poetic lines: for the eyes, "An intense gaze yielded to a smile of profound meaning"; for the nose, "A piece of jade flanked by two autumn pools"; for the lips, "A taste of cherry, a bite of red velvet"; for the ears, "A soft whisper delivered to the depth of night"; for the hands, "Gently massage the tender heart in spring sickness"; and so on. This kind of poetic language reminds the reader of an aesthetic tradition in Chinese literature, whereby a literatus would write poems exalting a courtesan's physical beauty and her extraordinary talents. Read against this specific Chinese cultural tradition of fetishizing the female body, Hei Ying's text, together with the inserted photographs, points to a conscious effort in the city narrative to highlight the male urban adventure as a fundamentally sexual experience.

To better illustrate the sexual experience implied in urban adventures, we may turn to a two-page spread in the February 1934 issue of *The Young Companion* (see figures 2 and 3). The theme is "Intoxicated Shanghai" (printed in English), with the Chinese title "Duhui de ciji" (Stimulation in the metropolis). As the reader can easily tell from the photographs, the stimulation in question is predominantly sexual or erotic, and the experience captured there is that of male adventurers. Apart from such expected urban attractions as skyscrapers (one of them resembling the skyscraper in Hei Ying's text) and sports facilities (the race clubs and the *huiliqiu* courts), what is graphically highlighted in the theme pages are female bodies, displayed on a glamorous stage or in the latest fashions, and juxtaposed with beer, liquor, jazz, and a giant poster of Merian Cooper and Ernest Schoedsack's *King Kong* (1933)—its Chinese caption reads: "The terrifying uproar in the horror, the detective, or the adventure films." In lines of small print near the center, the reader is told that these photographs are included to stimulate, or indeed simulate, the experience of "the dancing flesh and sexual arousal."[34] Experience and perception of the modern city are visually linked to, if not conceptually defined by, images of modern women.

Voyeurism thus comes to be an important "modern" way of knowing the city, and the process of knowing the city is parallel to that of knowing a woman. As in many new perceptionist texts, a consistent male gaze dominates in Hei Ying's story, though the female "object" in this case is a melancholic girl rather than a seductive *femme fatale*. Regardless of whether they feature a *femme fatale* or a melancholic girl, what happens in many Shanghai modernist writings is that the male narrator ultimately fails to understand or capture the woman in the city. In Liu Na'ou's "Liangge shijian de buganzheng zhe" (Two men who were impervious to time, 1929), the male characters, named H and T, cannot keep up with an erotic modern *femme fatale* who embodies the fluid time in the metropolis.[35] Similarly, in Hei Ying's story, the male narrator cannot figure out why the girl suddenly changes her mind and rejects his "love." The end of the story thus creates a narrative situation reminiscent of Teresa de Lauretis's statement, "The city is a text which tells the story of male desire by ... producing woman as text."[36] In both Hei Ying's and Liu Na'ou's stories, the reader comes to learn more about the male desire to penetrate (i.e., to see through) the city woman than about the woman herself, who is objectified as an enigmatic semiotic text. It is true that in the love poem composed by Hei Ying's narrator, the city girl Suzie appears all the more "lovable" with her "knowing eyes" and her "melancholy heart." However, in spite of her "textualization" as a love poem, Suzie as a character in the story refuses to be kept simply as a text: she resolutely parts with the male narrator and warns him that she may not recognize him the next time they meet.

To return to the question of walking on the street, the function of Hei Ying's male narrator may be better understood in light of Certeau's reasoning: "*To walk is to lack a site. It is the indeterminate process of being both absent and in search of the proper, of one's own.*"[37] In the process of knowing the city and the woman (both distanced in the text as the "other," the unknown), the narrator is at the same time searching for the "self," for his own identity, and for the meaning of his existence in the metropolis. The urban sense of alienation and deracination seems to be best expressed in the metaphor of walking on the street, which has remained an effective strategy in city narratives up to the 1990s, most noticeable in narrative films.[38] In this connection, Raymond

Figure 2. "Intoxicated Shanghai": Fashion, jazz, and the horse race. From *Liangyou*, February 1934.

Figure 3. "Intoxicated Shanghai": Beer and women. From *Liangyou*, February 1934.

Williams's assertion appears an apt comment on Chinese literature as well: "Perception of the new qualities of the modern city had been associated, from the beginning, with a man walking, as if alone, in its streets."[39]

Textual Production, II: Intertextuality

Brief as it is, Hei Ying's story produces a thick layer of intertextuality, with rich resonances to contemporary historical events as well as allusions to other fictional narratives of the time. The reference to Ai Xia's suicide, for instance, is extremely evocative. A well-known film actress and script writer, Ai Xia obviously captured the urban imagination when she committed suicide in early 1934. In the same year that Hei Ying published "When Spring Arrives," *Xin nüxing* (New women, 1934), a film based on Ai Xia's life, was produced by the Lianhua Film Studio in Shanghai. Directed by Cai Chusheng, who had known Ai Xia personally, the film featured Ruan Lingyu, a star whose fame at the time was perhaps second only to that of Hu Die. And one month after the film's release in February 1935, Ruan Lingyu herself committed suicide. Ruan's widely publicized suicide reached a sensational climax at her funeral, which was attended by ten thousand people in Shanghai and was reported even in the *New York Times*. According to one source, at least three young girls committed suicide on the day of Ruan's funeral.[40] The public's fascination with Ruan's suicide was manifest fifty-seven years later, when Stanley Kwan's (Guan Jinpeng) new film, *Ruan Lingyu* (Center stage, produced by Golden Harvest, Hong Kong), was released in 1992. The film proved successful even outside the Chinese community; indeed, Maggie Cheung (Zhang Manyu), who stars as Ruan Lingyu, won the Best Actress award at the Berlin Film Festival in the same year.

What is significant in all these instances is that suicide is represented again and again as an act of profound symbolic meaning: Ai Xia's suicide was represented in the film *New Women*, which seemed to predict if not predestine Ruan Lingyu's suicide, which in turn was represented in contemporary news media and in a Hong Kong film half a century later. One may wonder if, at least in these two filmic representations, suicide has not been transformed from an act of resignation to an act of "heroic passion," a passion which triumphs in—and perhaps only in—the symbolic realm in the modern era.[41] To be sure, suicide itself is by no means a modern phenomenon, but its media coverage—oftentimes carried to the point of sensationalism, as in Ruan Lingyu's case—bears an unmistakable sign of the modern.

Other historical figures evoked by Hei Ying are Dai Wangshu and Xu Zhimo, two modern poets noted for their romantic subject matter and sensuous imagery. Dai Wangshu, who succeeded Xu Zhimo as the most gifted love poet, had often been referred to as "the poet of the rainy alley" since he published the poem "Yuxiang" (The alley in the rain, 1928) at the age of twenty-three.[42] The poem's popularity was such that it was referred to in Mu Shiying's "Gongmu" (The cemetery, 1932) and in Hei Ying's story under discussion, both presenting a girl with "lilac-like melancholy" in the urban setting.[43]

Yet Hei Ying's story contains even more textual references to Liu Na'ou and Mu Shiying, the two new perceptionists who apparently appealed to him the most. The metaphor of taking the girl as a "walking stick," for example, is taken from Liu Na'ou's "Two Men Who Were Impervious to Time," where the male protagonist asserts that taking a walk on the street with one's girlfriend is an essential ingredient in modern romance.[44] Moreover, the graphic use of exclamation marks "! ! ! ! ! ! ! ! !" as a means of expressing the experience of shock is Hei Ying's creative transformation of a similar technique Mu Shiying uses in "Hei mudan" (Black peony, 1933), where an exhausted urban adventurer sees his trivial life as an endless procession of tiny ants steadily crawling toward him from all directions: "3 3 3 3 3 3 3 3 3 3 3 3 ..."[45]

In cases like these, Hei Ying tried to join the new perceptionists in creating new ways of perceiving the city and of describing the urban experience. One more example from Hei Ying may illustrate the extent to which the modernist writers went in their production of urban perception. While introducing the new perceptionists to his readers in the mid-1980s, Leo Ou-fan Lee noticed a rare case in Mu Shiying's "Shanghai de hubuwu" (Shanghai foxtrot, 1933), where an entire paragraph is repeated, but with the sequence of the (slightly modified) sentences reversed.[46] The resulting sense of "circularity" in Mu's story, I would suggest, best captures the circular nature of male urban adventures, which proceed in the motion of a waltz but do not lead one anywhere.[47] The same reading applies to Hei Ying's text, where two similar, but rearranged passages frame the story. Through this device, the author presents the male narrator's urban exploration as symbolically futile from start to finish: what changes in between is not the substance but rather the pattern of urban experience. Indeed, the patterning of urban experience became such a strong desire in Hei Ying that he published a similar two-page story in *Qingqing dianying* (The chin-chin screen), a Shanghai fan magazine, in June 1934. Titled "Chun" (Spring), this new piece closely resembles his story in *The Young Companion*: it tells of the love between a young man and a girl in Shanghai, both unnamed, and their romance is framed by the same device—a beginning and an ending composed of basically the same sentences.[48] In cases like this, intertextuality is made almost self-referential, and this self-referentiality further reveals the narcissistic nature of much of Shanghai modernist writing in the 1930s.[49]

I want to suggest that intertextuality as an aesthetic pattern enacts a structure of perceptions and emotions in the city-text. Not only does Hei Ying's verbal description of urban perceptions function as an effective intertext to the inserted photographs (which further fix perceptions in the text), but all these verbal and visual inscriptions also combine to evoke certain emotions and feelings (e.g., nostalgia and phantasm) in the urban reader. Through intertextuality, Hei Ying has succeeded in weaving an unusually rich texture of the modern metropolis.

Modernity and the City

I suggested at the outset of this essay that the production of new perceptions of the modern city might be related to a particular type of experience of "modernity" in early twentieth-century China. Here I would like to consider some specific issues regarding modernity and the city. Critics have distinguished two types of modernity in the history of Western civilization: the first is "bourgeois modernity," "a product of scientific and technological progress, of the industrial revolution, of the sweeping economic and social changes brought about by capitalism"; the other, an "aesthetic modernity" or "cultural modernity," "was from its romantic beginning inclined toward radical antibourgeois attitudes."[50] These two types of modernity are conceived of as opposed to each other in this schema.

In the context of modern China, the new perceptionists were among the first groups of urban writers who conscientiously sought to represent "aesthetic modernity"—a modernity experienced through "the personal, subjective, imaginative *durée*, the private time created by the unfolding of the 'self.'"[51] In their writings, this private "self," often undefined by any urban trade or occupation (such as the capitalists or financiers in Mao Dun's *Midnight*), is figured prominently as an aesthetic subject, a sensitive male urban adventurer, through whose perception the modern city and its enigmatic women are presented voyeuristically to the reader. Although new perceptionist writings may contain many of what Matei Calinescu describes as the self-conscious values associated with the idea of artistic modernity, such as change, newness, unpredictability, adventure, uniqueness, yet as far as its attitude toward capitalist civilization is concerned, new perceptionists are never entirely antibourgeois.[52] To the extent that they idolize the machine and celebrate material culture, new perceptionist writings endorse fundamentally bourgeois values. Images of bourgeois lifestyles are found everywhere in their stories: gambling at the race club in Liu Na'ou's "Two Men Who Were Impervious to Time," watching a German film in Shi Zhicun's "At the Paris Theater," dancing in a nightclub in Mu Shiying's "Shanghai Fox-trot," and taking a leisurely walk along the Avenue de Joffre in Hei Ying's "When Spring Arrives." Perhaps it is due more to their ideological orientation than to their modernist technique that the new perceptionist group has been marginalized in modern Chinese literary history since the mid-1930s. It is not until the 1980s, when a new modernist trend emerged to claim critical attention in mainland China, that the new perceptionist writings were excavated from the literary archives.

The new perceptionists made a number of original contributions to the development of modern Chinese literature. Yan Jiayan, who drew our attention to the Shanghai modernist group in the early 1980s, enumerates the following: a fast-paced rhythm to render metropolitan life, a relentless pursuit of subjective impressions and of stylistic innovations, an exploration of the subconscious and the unconscious, and the establishment of psychoanalytic fiction in China.⁵³ On the one hand, it is obvious that the metropolis of Shanghai furnished the new perceptionists with a perfect site for exploring different experiences of modernity; on the other hand, it might be contended that through their modernist writings they "produced" new ways of perceiving and of conceptualizing the modern city.

In many ways, the writings of the new perceptionists established new configurations of time and space in modern Chinese literature. In Hei Ying's story, for instance, time is not conceived as teleological, forever rushing forward to a given end; rather, it is rendered almost circular, made significant only with each and every round of the narrator's walking in the city. Moreover, the image of Shanghai in Hei Ying's text is characterized not only by a sense of dispersed space crisscrossed by urban forces of various kinds (e.g., economic and erotic), but also by rich layers of intertextuality accumulated through a juxtaposition of urban texts of different genres and media (e.g., history, journalism, poetry, fiction, film, and photography). It is not surprising, therefore, that a lack of historical depth in Hei Ying's configuration of Shanghai is compensated for by a variety of textual references to history (e.g., the Russian refugees), journalism (e.g., Ai Xia's suicide), poetry (e.g., Dai Wangshu and Xu Zhimo), and fiction (e.g., Liu Na'ou and Mu Shiying). With its juxtaposition of a printed text and photographs in a two-page layout, Hei Ying's modernist work not only provided a reader in the 1930s with immediately recognizable signs of the city (such as the fashionably dressed girl, the frog-like bus, and the exotic Avenue de Joffre where the latest Hollywood films were shown) through the inserted photographs, but it also enabled a reader in the 1990s to perceive anew, through the eye of the unnamed male narrator, what it was like to stroll down the streets in Shanghai, then the foremost modern metropolis in East Asia.

Chapter 10

The Cult of Poetry in Contemporary China

MICHELLE YEH

> We are poets, which has the sound of outcast.
> Nevertheless, we step out from our shores.
> We dare contend for godhead, with goddesses,
> And for the Virgin with the gods themselves.
> —Marina Tsvetayeva, "The Poet"

A renaissance in literature and art took place in the People's Republic of China from the late 1970s through the 1980s. In poetry, the outburst of vitality first showed itself in 1978–80 in the underground *Jintian* (Today) group, which included cofounders and editors Bei Dao and Mang Ke, and such contributors as Jiang He, Shu Ting, Gu Cheng, and Yang Lian, to name only a few of the best-known in the West. *Today* lent momentum to the flourish of *menglongshi*, commonly translated as "Obscure Poetry" or "Misty Poetry," in the early 1980s and became the major source of inspiration—no less than the target of criticism and revolt—to post-*menglong* poetry in the second half of the decade. Like *menglongshi*, "post-*menglong* poetry" is a term of inevitable, even misleading, simplification, since it refers to a wide range of varying styles and modes of writing. Rather than being unified by a set of formal and stylistic characteristics, it is marked by a radical openness to experimentation. The multiplicity of experiments in poetry since the mid-1980s may be more broadly and appropriately referred to as avant-garde or experimental.[1] This essay focuses on an interesting—and unique in today's world—phenomenon that I call the "cult of poetry." I first examine the "cult" by defining its salient features and then present a critical analysis of the diverse historical and psychological forces that helped bring it into being.

As a prefatory note, I would like to point out that there exist two "poetry scenes" in post-Mao China: one official, the other unofficial.[2] The official poetry scene exists in the newspapers, literary journals, poetry magazines, and books of poetry funded, edited, and published by the state at various administrative levels (e.g., central, provincial, city). Official periodicals tend to be long-running, and those with nationwide distribution, such as *Shikan* (Poetry monthly) in Beijing, have an immense circulation. In contrast, the unofficial poetry scene exists in a fairly large number of poetry periodicals sponsored by the private sector. Unlike their official counterparts, unofficial poetry magazines tend to have a highly irregular publication schedule and a short life span, mainly for political and financial reasons. The unofficial status of these publications subjects their editors to occasional harassment and repression, a point to be elaborated on later. The other equally formidable stumbling block is financial. These publications rely on a coterie of poets for financing, a less stable source, which accounts not only for their irregularity of publication but also for their use of primitive printing technology. (Before the 1990s copies were mostly mimeographed, and occasionally even handwritten.) Compared with that of official publications, their volume of production varies from small to minuscule, and they are usually available only through the poets' networks, which can be nationwide or locally based.[3]

Despite their relatively low production numbers, the importance of unofficial poetry publications should not be underestimated. Arguably, from the beginnings of *Today*, the first underground literary journal in the history of the People's Republic, to the present, it is unofficial poetry that has spearheaded experiments in avant-garde literature in post-Mao China and has won international recognition as the main representative of contemporary Chinese poetry. The poets range in age from their twenties to their forties; they are predominantly male, although a handful of women poets has achieved distinction. Unofficial publications circulate fast and wide among poets within China, mainly because the literary world is small and well connected. Although at the mercy of the changing political climate, avant-garde poetry is occasionally published through official outlets, especially when the editorial board of a journal consists of liberal-minded poets. In general, however, it can be read only in unofficial publications. It is from these sources that most of the data used in this essay are drawn.

Some scholars have used the term "underground" or "samizdat" to describe unofficial poetry in contemporary China, a term I do not use for the reason that in recent years the control of private publications has relaxed considerably and there has been more tolerance on the part of the political establishment. Consequently, some of the unofficial poetry periodicals are registered with the state, i.e., they have a permit for publication (*zhun yin zheng*) and, therefore, are not, strictly speaking, illegal. Thus, in China they are referred to as "people-run" or civilian publications (*minban kanwu*) as opposed to "official" or state-run publications.

The Cult of Poetry: Constructing a Discourse

By "cult of poetry," I am referring to the phenomenon and the concomitant discourse in the 1980s and the 1990s that bestows on poetry a religious significance and cultivates the image of the poet as the high priest of poetry. The word *cult* has no exact equivalent in Chinese and is used here as an approximate translation for "worship" (*chongbai*) with strong religious connotations. The "cult of poetry" thus denotes a religious poetic that is based on the worship of poetry and that inspires a religious-like devotion among poets. Such worship in turn generates, and is demonstrated by, a discourse often couched in a religious vocabulary and imagery. In a society where freedom of religion has been denied for nearly four decades, the reemergence of a religious discourse and the equation of poetry with religion is itself worth study.

The term "discourse" is understood here as "a dynamic field of interests, engagements, tensions, conflicts and contradictions."[4] The discourse I analyze in this essay refers specifically to an extensive body of writing by Chinese avant-garde poets and critics, including critical essays, biographical or autobiographical prose, and interviews, as well as poetry. In addition, graphic art (e.g., drawings and illustrations) in unofficial poetry publications is an integral part of the discourse and is used below to illuminate the poetry and the prose. As pointed out earlier, this body of writing is predominantly "unofficial" and is circulated among the poets privately but widely. The following discussion of the nature and characteristics of the "cult" is followed by an analysis of the tensions, conflicts, and contradictions embedded in the discourse, especially as they relate to the ideological and cultural matrices of contemporary China.

As to the constituency of the cult, I do not claim that all avant-garde poets in China participate in it. In fact, the poets discussed here may not be aware of the "cultist" element in their theory and practice and would not see themselves as creating or contributing to a cult. The term "cult of poetry" is constructed based on my interpretative analysis of the unofficial poetry and prose that have come out of China in the 1980s and the 1990s. Granted, it is impossible to provide statistical information or a complete bibliography, but the large numbers of poets and texts cited and discussed throughout this essay attest to the fact that this is not an isolated phenomenon. Moreover, the continuity of the theme for over a decade is a telling indication of the significant presence and extensive influence of the cult of poetry. The poets involved come from various parts of China, mostly urban centers (e.g., Beijing, Shanghai, Nanjing, Chengdu, Hangzhou, Tianjin) as well as smaller provincial cities. Although they often differ in poetic beliefs and styles, they all tend to define poetry in religious terms, and their poetry and prose share certain religious overtones.

To elaborate on the cult of poetry, I examine the four major aspects of the discourse of a religious poetics: first, the elevation and deification of poetry; second, the sense of crisis accompanying poetry as a religion; third, images of the poet; and fourth, the construction of a genealogy of poets.

Poetry as Religion

For many avant-garde poets in China today, poetry is not just a private and personal endeavor of a creative and spiritual nature; rather, it is the supreme ideal in life and a religious faith. On the frontispiece of *Bashu xiandai shiqun* (The modernist poetry group of Sichuan) published in 1987, we see four ink sketches by A Xia: "Prophet," "Eternity," "Prayer," and "Religion." The preface to the first issue of *Qingxiang* (Tendency) quotes from the New Testament to link poetry with religion:

> The poets of *Tendency* will probably accept these words from the Gospel of Luke: "You shall try to go through the narrow gate." For the effort to discover and to have discovered is the effort to go through the narrow gate and to have gone through it. *Tendency* sincerely hopes that its tendency will become the general direction of Chinese poetry from now on, but at the same time it holds a skeptical attitude toward this possibility "because narrow is the gate and difficult is the way which leads to life, and there are few who find it" [Matthew 7:14].[5]

Religious overtones can be traced back to 1982, when an unofficial poetry collection entitled *Cishenglin* (Second-growth forest) was published in Chengdu, Sichuan. One of the illustrations in the volume shows a human being shaped like a cross, thus associating the poet with Jesus Christ.

In fact, Christian symbolism dominates in the discourse of the cult of poetry. The following poem by the Shanghai poet Cheng Maochao presents poetry as the sole remaining light in a cold, bleak world and the poet as the only believer:

Bell chime begins
Sinking into the heavy day

> Striking
> Wet boughs
> A psalm trembles on the silver-gray candle stand
> Holding back the suffering tears of Jesus Christ
>
> There is only one believer
> Only one believer there is.[6]

The identification between the poet and Christ is also evoked on the cover of the 1991 poetry journal *Babieta* (Tower of Babel), depicting an inverted pyramid thrusting through the sky overlooking some drifting clouds. At the top of the pyramid is the Crucifixion. Again, the poet is portrayed as a Christ figure who sacrifices his life for the redemption of humankind, a point to which we will return. By the same token, the illustration of a poem called "Tuwei" (Breaking through the encirclement) in *Fengren* (Knife's edge) published in 1994, depicts a broken cross entangled with a disembodied human body.

Two more examples may be cited. The preface to the 1993 issue of *Beihuiguixian* (The Tropic of Cancer) proclaims: "In this world poetry is the only holy temple worthy of our genuflection and worship. Nothing else is worth expending one bit of our energy and feeling!"[7] And the preface to the 1992 issue of *Guodu* (Transition) raises this question: "Who . . . is the favorite son of the gods on Parnassus, who has the same head and torso as the gods?"[8] Whether drawing on the Christian or ancient Greek religion, these examples suggest that religion is used not only metaphorically to signify poetry but the two are virtually equated. To these poets, poetry is not like a religion—it is a religion!

Discussing the recent development of contemporary poetry, Chen Zhongyi identifies its tendency to become "more pure, mysterious, supra-experiential, and divine [*shenxing*]."[9] "Divine" also appears in the poet Yu Xinjiao's autobiographical essay "Yingxiong zhuyi he Zhongguo wenyi fuxing" (Heroism and the Chinese renaissance), where he describes how he has used different literary genres to "express the poetic and the divine."[10] Other words such as "sublime" (*chonggao*), "immortal" (*buxiu*), and "great" (*weida*) recur over and over again in discussions on poetry in unofficial publications.

The Sense of Crisis

The religious discourse in poetry reflects a profound sense of crisis. An anonymous poem published in 1985 is attributed to a fifteen-year-old girl in Guangzhou. The poem ends with these lines:

> No one else understands; only we know the coldness and the tears
> Only we only you and I
> My rose-colored dream my fire of infatuation my pure austere god of
>   poetry.[11]

"Infatuation" with the god of poetry is juxtaposed with the poet's suffering in a "cold," indifferent society. The poet engaged in the sacred pursuit of poetry is at odds with the mundane world, which she rejects. Such rejection also looms large in all the passages that have been quoted earlier, with their strong visual images of suffering and their hyperbolic tone. For example, in the 1993 preface to *The Tropic of Cancer*, the editors' elevation of poetry is preceded by a lament over "the tragedy of our time, the pitifulness of humankind."[12] The epigraph on the frontispiece of every issue of *Tendency* quotes the poet Rainer Maria Rilke: "What victory is there to speak of? The only thing that matters is survival." Endurance and perseverance is a recurrent theme in avant-garde poetry, which Yang Yuanhong describes as resistance and "a great spiritual exodus."[13]

The sense of crisis is a salient feature of avant-garde poetry throughout the post-Mao period. Its presence may or may not be understood as a response to specific political movements (e.g., the Anti-Spiritual Pollution Campaign of 1983–84, the Anti-Bourgeois Liberalization Campaign of 1987, and the Tiananmen Square Massacre of 1989), although there is no denying that many of the avant-garde poets experienced the Cultural Revolution as youngsters and have been involved, even as targets of criticism, in post-Mao political movements. In other words, while I am fully aware of the inevitable repercussions of any major political event in every sphere of life in China, especially when we are speaking of something as momentous and tragic as the Tiananmen Square crackdown, I am skeptical about any simple, direct correlation between politics and literary expression. I would argue, instead, that the sense of crisis among the avant-garde poets is derived from deeper sources of repression and alienation that are not only political, traceable at least to the Cultural Revolution, but also economic and cultural.

Although the relatively open sociopolitical atmosphere in post-Mao China allows far more freedom for writers and artists than before, the repressive nature of the communist system is poignantly felt by the artist. To give a few examples, periodicals of avant-garde poetry still cannot be sold openly in bookstores and are considered illegal publications. To protect themselves, poets often put the words *For Internal Circulation* (*neibu jiaoliu*) in their journals as a strategy to circumvent harassment and potential risk. Nor can unofficial publications be sent out of the country by mail or any other means. When discovered at customs, they are inevitably confiscated. In the aftermath of the Tiananmen Square crackdown of June 1989, a number of avant-garde poets were arrested and detained; at least six were sentenced to jail terms, including Liao Yiwu, Zhou Lunyou, and Li Yawei in Sichuan.[14] In the latter cases, their literary work was used against them in the trial.

The repressive political environment is sharply and ironically contrasted to China's liberal economic policy since the early 1980s. The acceleration of commercialization has dramatically widened the gap between the rich and the poor and changed the social dynamics significantly. There is no lack of anecdotes about how the *nouveaux riches* flaunt their wealth in such big metropolises as Shenzhen, Guangzhou, Shanghai, and Beijing. Most of the avant-garde poets who choose to continue to write, however, tend to be in the lower echelon of the current economic structure, holding low-paying state-assigned jobs or no jobs at all.[15] Their situation is diametrically opposed to that of the establishment poets, who as members of the Writers' League draw a relatively handsome salary plus other benefits from the state (e.g., overseas travel, easy access to publication channels). They are also unlike their counterparts in the United States and Western Europe, where many hold teaching positions at colleges and universities and enjoy a good income and respectable social status.

The economic pressure on the Chinese avant-garde is succinctly captured in these lines by Zhou Lunyou. A cofounder and editor of the long-running Sichuan-based poetry journal, *Feifei*, Zhou spent seven months in a prison in Xi Chang before he was sentenced to three years in a labor-reform camp on Mount Emei for "counterrevolutionary incitement" (*shandong fan'geming*).

> To prove through my writing: to be alive is important.
> What is food? What is Sartre?
> The blows of commodities are more gentle, more direct than violence,
> More cruel too, pushing the spirit toward total collapse.[16]

Written after his release from prison, Zhou's poem reflects on the dilemma of the artist in China today. In view of his personal tragedy, the humorous juxtaposition between food and the French Existentialist philosopher Jean-Paul Sartre takes on a note of poignancy. How does the poet persist in a spiritual pursuit when his spirit itself is on the brink of collapse? "Commodities" (*shangpin*) in line 3 evokes "commodity economy" (*shangpin jingji*), a term often used in China these days; it is seen as more threatening than physical violence. The latter could be a reference to the harsh treatment that he received (or prisoners in general receive) during incarceration. In comparison, economic disenfranchisement is even more unbearable than physical abuse because, although less tangible, it is more destructive to the spirit. By linking food and spirit, the poem thus touches on not only the difficulty of survival for some poets but also the crisis of rampant commodification as a result of the commodity economy.

To borrow Zhou's oxymoron, the "gentle cruelty" of commodity economy is not limited to the economic sphere, but even more significantly it is changing the cultural landscape too. The rise of a highly commercialized popular culture has resulted in the shrinking of readership for serious literature in recent years. A quick tour of bookstores in any major city in China these days easily reveals a marked decline in scholarly works and serious literature; the impression is confirmed by scholars themselves. Although poetry anthologies continue to be published and occasionally some even sell well, avant-garde poetry is increasingly read only by a small audience, including poets themselves, aspiring poets (often college students), and a select group of sinologists and China watchers. If this situation is not much different from that in any highly industrialized society in the world today, we must remember that, as noted earlier, for the Chinese avant-garde poet the sense of marginalization is compounded by both a repressive political system and economic disenfranchisement, which do not exist, for the most part, for their counterparts elsewhere.

The sense of crisis experienced by many avant-garde poets is not always expressed explicitly, the way it is in Zhou's poem. I would like to take a close look at a poem entitled "Yidali zhi xia" (Italian summer), whose critique of consumer culture takes a more subtle form. Written in July 1990 by Yi Chuan, a young poet in Beijing, it belongs to a sequence of poems under the general title "Geren shenghuo de shunjian" (Moments from an individual life).

> This summer soccer is the most erotic
> crowded sounds in the dust
> feverish eyes opening and shutting
> like dripping glass drying on the balcony
> A soccer ball is watermelon skin
> abandoned on a moonless night—
> all slip and fall
> Soccer is the only way to unite the people
> this season
>
> The World Cup and the mascot on my T-shirt
> I am an advertising billboard
> floating here and there in the surge of fashion

> I want to tell the people I am commercials
> I am propaganda phrases and slogans
> I am guiding the people's lives[17]

The poet draws a simple vignette of urban life in China today, a life characterized by foreign imports (soccer and fashion) and consumerism (commercials). With humor the poet compares these foreign attractions to an inescapable pitfall: just as you can't help tripping over a piece of watermelon skin on a pitch-dark night, so you are not immune to the contagious frenzy with which China embraces foreign things and trends. Indeed, "feverish" or "crazed" (*re*) connotes that the situation is getting out of control. The "I" in the poem is no exception. He too puts on a World Cup T-shirt, because it is the fashionable thing to do, although he is aware at the same time that he is losing his individuality to market forces—he compares himself to a walking commercial. Further, the connection of the soccer game with eroticism in line 1 suggests that the poet is not unaware of the common strategy of selling a product by associating it with sexuality. Against the background of summer heat ("dripping glass" in line 4 may be a figure of speech for sweating spectators at a soccer game), the eroticism of sports is also intimated. Thus summer, sports, and fashion are all conflated into a ubiquitous consumerism.

As the poem progresses, a profound critique of the rising tide of commercialism is made by the repeated displacement of political phrases or images in a newly available commercial context. No reader can fail to note the political nature and origin of such images as "uniting the people" (*tuanjie renmin*), "propaganda phrases and slogans" (*biaoyu he kouhao*), and "guiding people's lives" (*zhidao renmin shenghuo*). The disjunction in tone between the laconic political rhetoric and the casual consumer lifestyle conjured up by soccer and summer fashion renders the critique both humorous and effective. Consumerism, the poet suggests, seems to have replaced communism as the most powerful, omnipresent force shaping people's lives these days. Like the "I," people blindly follow the latest consumer trend just as they blindly followed political trends in an earlier era. In the changing society of contemporary China, economic interests may prove to be more powerful than the political system, although—as implied in the displacement of politics with economics—they are similar in that both impose values on people and result in the loss of individuality. In view of the critique, we further detect irony in the title of the poem sequence: it supposedly depicts a moment from an "individual" life, which turns out to be markedly devoid of individuality.

It is not surprising that the three conditions of contemporary life that we have discussed so far: political, economic, and cultural, bring out an acute sense of alienation in the avant-garde poet. As poets face the political-cultural establishment, which is repressive and hostile, and society in general, where they find themselves increasingly pushed to the side, alienation creates a kind of heroism that lies at the center of the "cult of poetry." The other side of alienation and crisis, I submit, is heroism and martyrdom. For this we turn to the image of the poet as hero and martyr.

The Poet as Hero and Martyr

In the wake of the revival of aesthetic consciousness in the late 1970s and early 1980s, avant-garde poets have sought to redefine the role of the poet. Bei Dao's oft-quoted lines from "Xuangao" (Declaration): "In an age without heroes / I just want to be a human being," implicitly reject the official role of the poet. Instead of serving the proletariat and singing praises of the Party, he sees the poet as a human being who is alone and lonely, at odds with the system, seeking solace in nature or romantic love—the latter a taboo in the Maoist era—and blindly groping along the path of history, which is itself blind.[18]

If Bei Dao and others of the *Today* group were among the first to reassert the individuality of the poet in poetry, as the decade progressed avant-garde poets found themselves marginalized in an increasingly commercialized and materialistic society. The sense of crisis is clearly articulated in the preface to a 1985 mimeographed compilation entitled *Dangdai Zhongguo shige qishiwu shou* (Seventy-five contemporary Chinese poems). The editors, Bei Ling and Meng Lang, begin in the preface with this statement: "In a world full of formalities and temptations, it is difficult to be a poet," and proceed to pose these questions: "Is poetry still possible? Is art still possible?"

In the second (1994) issue of *Zhongguo qingnian yanjiu* (Studies of Chinese youth), a special report entitled "Dalu qingnian shiren zai liulang" (Young mainland poets are wandering) makes the following observation:

> At the end of the century, are there still wandering young poets? In the past, they refused to enter the mainstream political culture; today they refuse to enter the mainstream commercial culture. For the sake of guarding the last piece of pure land in the kingdom of poetry, they live away from home, beg for food, and borrow money, drifting in an amphibian life of "material beggars" and "spiritual aristocrats."[19]

The paradoxical image is also found in the essay "Yeying zai gechang" (Nightingale sings), where the young poet Lan Cun (literally, "blue village"), after giving a catalogue of great poets, describes them as "living in rich spirituality, poor in materiality and the flesh."[20] In the same vein, *Liuxuesheng xinwen* (Overseas students news), a Chinese-Japanese bilingual monthly gazette published in Japan, refers to a group of avant-garde poets in Shanghai as a "nomadic people" (*youmu minzu*): "In the margins of the city, they sigh from time to time, make their voices heard from time to time."[21]

The image of the poet as someone who chooses a life of wandering and poverty in order to follow the sacred calling of art, who courageously and defiantly rejects the dehumanizing system and vulgar society, finds vivid expression in the following description of the poet Hei Dachun. Nicknamed the "Drunkard of the Yuanmingyuan" (Yuanmingyuan jiugui), Hei is a central figure among a group of poets, artists, and rock singers in Beijing who, until it was closed down by the authorities, lived together in a commune next to the ruins of the leisure palace from China's last dynasty.

> Much of his food and clothes are gifts to art from his friends. Seeing his religious spirit of dedication, his friends feel that they should do something for art. The worship of art and the eternal need of humans for art makes him believe firmly in the art of poetry which he engages in. He will not waste his energy and life on things he dislikes just in order to lead a normal life; therefore, he does not work, does not bow to the leadership, does not sell his life which belongs to art. He'd rather drift about, embrace death.[22]

In the epilogue to Hei's collected poems, Hai Lei, a fellow poet, not only refers to him as a "wanderer of the soul" but also as an advocate of romanticism whose "devotion approaches insanity."[23] The motif of insanity, as we shall see, appears repeatedly in the discourse of the "cult of poetry."

Poetry is associated not only with "religious spirit" but also with the sacrifice of one's own life. In the essay "Yilu liulang" (Wandering all the way), the poet Wang Qiang connects aimless wandering with poetry and death: "The purpose of wandering is poetry, the purpose of poetry is death, the purpose of death is to receive life's existence, the mode of the existence is wandering."[24] Two other related images are those of the survivor and the madman. The Survivor is the name of a club founded in Beijing in 1988 by a group of poets led by Mang Ke and the poet-critic Tang Xiaodu. The name has at least two meanings. In the narrow sense, these poets, most of whom were born in the late 1940s through the mid-1950s, see themselves as survivors of the Cultural Revolution, the "ten-year turmoil" that deprived them of family life and education and set them adrift on the bitter tide of fate. However, they are also survivors in a broader, more philosophical sense, referring to the profound alienation that poets feel in contemporary society.

Shi Zhi (literally, "index finger," the pen name of Guo Lusheng) is probably the most revered forerunner of post-Mao avant-garde poetry. Like millions of youths, he was sent to live in the countryside during the Cultural Revolution. He wrote poetry in the late 1960s that was new and refreshing in that it veered away from the officially sanctified "political lyric" (*zhengzhi shuqing*) and focused on personal feelings and private aspirations. His poetry was widely circulated among rusticated youngsters and even attracted the disapproving attention of Jiang Qing. Political persecution possibly precipitated his schizophrenia in 1973, and he has since been institutionalized intermittently. In recent years he has been able to resume poetry writing and has become something of a cult figure. A group of poets held a poetry reading in his honor in Beijing and a collection of his poems was published in 1993. Despite a slim volume of work, he is one of the most respected figures in the unofficial poetry scene in China and has been compared to Ezra Pound, another "mad genius."[25]

Not only is the poet no longer the bugle boy of the Party, but according to the Shanghai poet Chen Dongdong, he has also lost his former glorious roles as "the prophet, the proclaimer, the legislator, the revolutionary, the central character, the soul of the people." He has become "a heathen to the people, a man to be punished, a victim of beauty, and a man who sets himself on fire for poetry." Echoing Wen Yiduo's poem "Hongzhu" (Red candle) from the 1920s, which compares the poet to a candle that brings light to the people by sacrificing its own life, Chen urges: "In order to light the fire of the soul in the realm of the divine, the poet has no choice but to set himself on fire."[26]

Central to the cult of poetry is the polarization of the mundane world versus the divine world of poetry, "material beggars" versus "spiritual aristocrats," marginalization versus mainstream status. The religious undertone is undeniable in Cai Hengping's poem "Hanyu—xian'gei Cai, yige Hanyu shougongyi ren" (The Chinese language—dedicated to Cai, a craftsman of Chinese), from which I quote the concluding lines:

Nowadays, Han people, this is our only surviving treasure
To guard the divine diamond in extreme poverty
who is like me, enjoying the kingdom and its glory?[27]

Although addressing the Han people as a whole, these lines end with a rhetorical question, the answer to which is that few are like the poet-speaker who alone enjoys "the kingdom and its glory."

It is against this background that we can better understand the suicides of several young poets in recent years, most notably Haizi and Ge Mai. On March

26, 1989, Haizi, the pen name of Zha Haisheng, lay on the railroad track between Shanhai Pass and Longjiaying in Hebei and ended his young life. He left behind a large corpus of writings: about three hundred lyric poems, one long narrative poem, three plays in verse, a chorale, a ritual play, a novel in verse, as well as some short stories and essays of literary criticism. Ge Mai, born Chu Fujun, drowned himself on the campus of Qinghua University in Beijing in September 1990; before he died, he disposed of all his writings in a book pack, which, fortunately, was later retrieved.

As I have discussed elsewhere, although Haizi's death can be attributed to varying personal circumstances (e.g., the love-guilt that haunted him immediately before his suicide, his illness), an important factor may be his self-perceived imminent failure as a poet.[28] To summarize, Haizi hoped to write his magnum opus, an epic entitled *Taiyang* (The sun), which was to encompass and supersede the greatest accomplishments of human civilization. Living in Changping, a small town in the outskirts of Beijing, he lived in impoverished circumstances, writing all night, sleeping a few hours in the morning, and reading (mostly Western poets) in the afternoon. The Spartan lifestyle probably contributed to his declining health, and signs of cerebral aneurysm reportedly appeared some time before his death. His deteriorating physical condition must have aggravated the fear that he would not live to complete his epic. Sadly, his articulated romantic notion that geniuses die young turned out to be a self-fulfilling prophecy.

After his suicide Haizi underwent apotheosis and became a cult hero in the unofficial poetry scene in China, as indicated by a plethora of memorial essays describing him as a "martyr of poetry."[29] The poet Han Gaoqi, for instance, refers to Haizi's suicide as a "saint-like blood-sacrifice."[30] The comparison to a saint may not sound out of place to Haizi after all, who once described himself as living "in holy purity."[31]

To a lesser extent, Ge Mai was also hailed as a hero after he died. Zang Di, a fellow poet, compares him to Jing Ke, the heroic swordsman of the Warring States period (403–221 B.C.), who undertook the mission to assassinate the ruthless king of Qin, knowing full well it would cost him his life regardless of the outcome. Speaking in the first person, the swordsman says:

> I am secretly in love with immortality and I know the mystery of choice
> only involves being and nonbeing—it has nothing to do with more and less.[32]

The most widely publicized suicide is that of Gu Cheng. In October 1993, after brutally murdering his wife Xie Ye, also a poet and prose writer, Gu hanged himself. Although the deaths were clearly related to the breakup of their marriage, many reminiscences and memorial essays that appeared after the tragedy held a rather understanding, if not forgiving, attitude toward Gu. Referring almost always to his precocious poetic talent and occasionally also to his previous attempts at suicide (according to Gu himself, he had tried to commit suicide many times since the age of seventeen), they tend to see in him a romantic genius beyond the laws of this world, who consequently perhaps should not be judged in accordance with the "normal" criteria of right and wrong.

One article, for example, describes the poet this way: "This famous *menglong* poet since adolescence has written astonishing poems with an imagination exceeding that of the average person. His extraordinary imagination places his mind in a region where fantasy and reality are blurred and causes him to go at last from different to abnormal, to insane."[33] Escalating mental aberration is suggested by the succession of three similar but subtly different adjectives in the last part of the second sentence: Gu, according to the author, started out as "different" (*yichang*), then became more and more "abnormal" (*fanchang*), until finally he was downright "insane" (*shichang*). The rhetorical sliding from one mental state to the next, however, downplays significant differences between them in terms of moral and social consequences. Such downplaying is justified only by Gu's poetic genius, as seen in the title and the conclusion of the essay: "Gu Cheng is a genius. He has an extraordinary imagination, and this extraordinariness results in his abnormality and insanity. *After all*, between the genius and the madman there is only a thin line."[34]

When poetry is upheld as a religion that promises immortality, only the poet who sacrifices his life for poetry's sake, whether in a literal or symbolic sense, is worthy of being its high priest or saint. The poet is, as the subtitle of Pan Yiuqiang's essay so aptly puts it, "Yongheng de shiren: xunzhao tiantang de shengtu" (The eternal poet: The saint in search of heaven).[35]

The "Genealogy" of Poets

In a poem entitled "Mei" (Beauty), Hai Long describes the consequences for the poet who pursues the supreme beauty of art:

> Beauty brings destruction, all kinds of impossibilities
> suffering, a genius's short life, a man's struggle
> against the infinite with the finite.[36]

Destruction, a short life, constant suffering and struggle—these are the defining characteristics of the poet as the hero and martyr. Alienated from official ideology on the one hand and the commercialized society on the other, Chinese avant-garde poets look elsewhere for sympathy and affinity.

Besides such martyrs of poetry as the above-mentioned Haizi, Ge Mai, and Shi Zhi, a few other contemporaries are regarded as role models. For instance, Luo Yihe, Haizi's best friend and former schoolmate at Beijing University, died of a stroke in Tiananmen Square on May 14, 1989. He was hailed as "the first victim of China's 1989 democracy movement" (Zhongguo bajiu minyun diyiwei xishengzhe). Zhu Xiang, a poet of the May Fourth period, committed suicide at the age of twenty-nine, possibly driven by the dismal prospect of a jobless, uncertain future. In the poem "Jinian Zhu Xiang" (In memoriam: Zhu Xiang), he is held up as a "martyr" by Bai Hua, an influential Sichuan poet:

> I noticed your form at a glance
> a figure raving in the autumn wind
> but so serene in a book
>
> A solitary seemingly unintelligent drinker
> a martyr of fathomless sensitivity
> before dying he drinks another large cup
> bows his body down and enters into that long, inevitable sleep
>
> I know, since you were a child you've practiced the martyr's bearing
> your green spring had its fill of roving through gossip
> but your songs can only belong to heaven
>
> Ach, why did this exemplar only come to light at death
> and then leave us busy memorializing
> busy talking, corresponding
> busy with all that, up until 1989?[37]

The poem portrays Zhu as "a figure raving in the autumn wind." "Autumn wind" symbolizes the cold, inhospitable environment in which the poet stands alone. Despite the inclement weather, however, he "raves"—*kuangdan*—suggesting fierce individuality and uncompromising dignity. The image of a sensitive lover of learning and solitary drinker invariably evokes such famous predecessors as Tao Yuanming and Li Bai, and Zhu's final act of drowning himself in a river cannot but remind us of Qu Yuan, the "father of Chinese poetry." The opposition between the petty, hostile world ("roving through gossip") and immortal literary creations ("songs can only belong to heaven") applies equally well to Qu and Zhu, although the causes of their suicides were vastly different.

The poem employs several devices to present a romanticized portrait of Zhu Xiang. First, by suggesting a parallel with Qu Yuan, it elevates Zhu's suicide to a higher moral and spiritual plane. Second, the poem romanticizes death by also linking the modern poet with Li Bai, who according to the popular legend, drowned while trying to catch the moon in the river. Finally, by tracing the nobility of the poet to his childhood ("since you were a child, you've practiced the martyr's bearing"), the poem further reinforces the image of Zhu as a modern exemplar who sacrifices his life for the sake of poetry. In each of these devices, the poem departs significantly from historical and personal facts in order to present an idealized, romantic image of the poet and of the genealogy of poets.

Michael Day, whose translation is cited above, offers a different interpretation of the poem, based mainly on his reading of the last stanza. Relating the poem to the Tiananmen Square massacre—the year 1989 appears as the very last word of the poem—Day finds instead a criticism of the glorification of Haizi's suicide, which occurred "*after* the massacre and continued on into 1990 and 1991." According to him, Bai Hua is in fact admonishing against the portrayal of the poet as a martyr of poetry: "China's poets devote their energies to the eulogies of a pointless suicide, ignoring the numerous, more meaningful deaths that now litter the landscape. Memorializing Haizi up until the massacre in 1989 would have been a human response, a relevant response. After the massacre it becomes something else entirely."[38]

My disagreement with Day's interpretation is based on the following considerations. In the context of the poem, which is an explicit eulogy of Zhu Xiang, such a complete turn-about in attitude—himself eulogizing Zhu but admonishing others against eulogizing Haizi—is implausible. The poem, after all, is about Zhu, not about Haizi, and the former is portrayed in extremely positive terms throughout the poem. The last stanza can thus be read as expressing sadness at how poets in general are marginalized in society: when they are alive, no one pays them much attention. As to the date 1989 at the end of the poem, I believe it *is* an evocation of Haizi's suicide by drawing a parallel between Zhu and Haizi and seeing a continuity between generations of modern Chinese poets, Haizi being the youngest in a long line of poet-martyrs. If Zhu's suicide is considered noble and exemplary, as it is in the poem, how could Haizi's be pointless? What the poem attempts to do, I would argue, is to find precedents for Haizi in Zhu Xiang and, through him, in Qu Yuan, Li Bai, and others. Such an attempt, romantic in nature as already pointed out, is part of the invention of a "genealogy" of poets as heroic martyrs in the discourse of the cult of poetry.

If the poets we have seen so far are all drawn from the Chinese tradition, more often the contemporary Chinese avant-garde identifies with non-Chinese poets as spiritual forebears. Although no exact statistics are possible, in skimming through the pages of hundreds of unofficial poetry publications, I find some of the frequently mentioned names in the poetry and prose discussions are Friedrich Hölderlin, Rainer Maria Rilke, Jorge Luis Borges, Marina Tsvetayeva, Osip Mandelstam, Arthur Rimbaud, Sylvia Plath, Boris Pasternak, Joseph Brodsky, Paul Celan, John Keats, Percy Bysshe Shelley, and Dante Alighieri.

What the majority of the poets in this list have in common is personal tragedy. Many ended their lives in suicide. Tsvetayeva, a major symbolist poet and generally considered one of the greatest Russian poets, hanged herself when her husband and her son were taken away from her and she was totally isolated from the literary community under the Stalin regime. A leading American confessional poet, Plath committed suicide, possibly torn between her family situation (a recent divorce, two children in her care) and her desire to write. The German-speaking Jewish poet Celan was obsessed by the memory of the Holocaust, which destroyed his family. In exile in Paris, he drowned himself in the Seine. Tsvetayeva's contemporary and dear friend, Mandelstam, also perished under the persecution of a totalitarian regime. Initially arrested for writing a satire on Stalin, he died in a transit camp, the exact cause and date of his death unknown to this day.

Some of the poets saw their writing careers cut short either by personal choice or by insanity. Rimbaud, the precocious poetic genius, had a meteoric career as a poet before he abruptly stopped writing and severed all ties with poetry. Hölderlin became insane at the age of thirty-two; after a brief period of improvement, he spent the last thirty-seven years of his life in insanity and complete seclusion. For different reasons, these two poets can be seen as suffering symbolic deaths. Still others were struck by blindness. Borges became blind in his old age; he is often mentioned together with Homer, the blind bard of the first Western epics, and occasionally, with John Milton, who also turned blind in mid-life. Inevitably, blindness is interpreted as a threshold between physical mortality and literary immortality. Two young poets think so. Cai Hengping says of Borges: "Because Beauty demanded a price, so he was blinded," and Huang Canran, writing on the same poet, compares him to Jesus Christ: "Jesus bends over and writes on the sand. Nobody knows what he writes, / but someone is enlightened, his conscience is saved."[39]

As for the others, Rilke spent much of his life in voluntary exile, wandering from one place to another in search of a sanctuary of solitude and freedom from the material world. Pasternak was ostracized in his own country and was forced to decline the Nobel Prize for Literature in 1958. Another Russian Nobel laureate, Brodsky was sentenced to internal exile on a state farm and was forced to leave Russia in 1972. Both Keats and Shelley died young (and are extolled by Haizi as poetic geniuses *par excellence*). Dante of *The Divine Comedy* is seen as a dedicated pilgrim attaining the divine under the guidance of Beatrice. All of these poets are often invoked for inspiration and emulation.[40]

Although far from complete, this list of foreign poets nevertheless reveals some of the central themes of the cult of poetry. Post-Mao avant-garde poets are particularly drawn to those who are acutely aware of their alienation from society, suffer from extraordinary hardships, or experience unrecoverable personal or creative crises in life. That they tend to be more familiar with Russian poets is understandable. After all, the two systems are much alike and for the most part are mutually accessible. It is interesting to note, however, that Sergey Yesenin and Vladimir Mayakofsky, both well-known poets who also committed suicide, are mentioned less often in the discourse of the cult, probably because of their close associations with the communist regime. In sum, foreign poets are held up as exemplars because of the shared sense of alienation and victimization. They are all, to quote from Rilke's *Duino Elegies*, "squanderers of pain." Commonality welds a spiritual bond and makes them literary kin.

The notion that great suffering is the price great poets have to pay clearly corresponds to the sense of crisis that we have discussed earlier. It finds articulation in "Shiren" (The poet) by the Sichuan poet Sun Wenbo, who warns his fellow poets about sacrifices to come:

> Please forget your dream
> your anxiety
> You should know that in the great storm
> all this is trivial
>
> You should know that the vogue of insanity
> awaits sacrifices[41]

And Hai Long's 1993 poem "Tiancai" (Genius) defines poetic genius almost entirely in terms of suffering:

> A man says to life: kill me
> or you are the killer

> Life makes a promise: I am the leader of the mediocre
> I forgive you, I forgive you, I declare you the king of the dead
>
> Rebel, escape, get free, be humiliated for humanity
> A man dies at the speed of poetry.⁴²

Underlying the cult of poetry is an unmistakably romantic strand. From romanticism to symbolism to high modernism, alienation of the individual is a major theme in poetry, while the concomitants to alienation, solitude and loneliness, are regarded, even celebrated, as requisites for the creation of great poetry. The sense of crisis as well as the image of the poet as a heroic martyr form the core of the cult of poetry, and the foreign poets whom they look up to as spiritual kin only further validate and reinforce this belief.

A Critical Analysis

Having examined the major features of the cult of poetry in contemporary China, we cannot help asking: Why? Why poetry? Why a religious poetics? Why does it appear when and where it does? In the following I would like to suggest a few angles from which to reflect on the questions without presuming to offer definitive answers. My intention is to understand the cult of poetry by analyzing the diverse historical and cultural forces behind it and, in the process, also to problematize it by pointing out the tensions and contradictions inherent in such a discourse.

Perhaps a ready-made explanation for the cult is this: it is a response of poets to the spiritual vacuum in the wake of the Cultural Revolution. In view of the destruction of traditional Chinese values and mores, coupled with the widespread disaffection among the intellectuals with the Communist Party in the post-Mao era, it is understandable that poets seek to redefine themselves beyond the pale of official ideology. The cult of poetry represents a search for an alternative value system, a new identity of the self in contradistinction from, and in defiance of, that dictated by the Party. As I noted earlier, the emergence in the 1980s and 1990s of a religious poetics is significant because religion, like many other topics of a private and individual nature, has been a taboo under the communist regime; its reemergence thus represents a veering away from the official ideology. As Brodsky observes: "If art teaches anything (to the artist, in the first place), it is the privateness of the human condition. Being the most ancient as well as the most literal form of private enterprise, it fosters in a man ... a sense of uniqueness, of individuality, of separateness—thus turning him from a social animal into a perceptible 'I.' "⁴³

From a positive point of view, then, I see the cult of poetry as another manifestation of the quest for self-identity, an assertion of creative freedom and artistic autonomy among writers and artists that first began on a full scale in the late 1970s and continued through the mid-1980s. The quest is not only observable in poetry—although it pioneers it to a great extent—but also in art (e.g., the Star Painting Society in the late 1970s), fiction (e.g., "scar literature" in the early 1980s and the root-seeking movement in the mid-1980s), film (e.g., the Fifth Generation), and the intellectual circles in general (e.g., "cultural reflections" or *wenhua fansi* in the mid-1980s).

In the more recent period which is the focus of this study, the emphasis on poetry as a religion and a way of life is a confirmation of the self alienated from a politically repressive system on the one hand and an increasingly materialistic, commercialized society on the other. According to the fiction writer Kong Jiesheng, since June 1989 a "collective unconscious that emphasizes the flesh over the soul has permeated every corner of the civilian society,"[44] as indicated by the renewed interest in traditional breathing exercises, sexual promiscuity, and a generally hedonistic attitude toward life. If Yi Chuan's poem on the World Cup represents the avant-garde poet's humorous yet critical response to consumerism, then Zhou Lunyou's essay "Jujue de zitai" (The gesture of refusal) is openly defiant toward the political-cultural establishment by urging his fellow poets to declare: "We shall never compromise with the false value system."

> Reject their publications and honoraria!
> Reject their evaluations and recognition!
> Reject their publishing houses and referee system!
> Reject their podium and non-scholarly conferences!
> Reject their "Writers' Association," "Artists' Association," "Poets' Association" etc., these pseudo-art yamens that corrupt art and suppress creativity![45]

However, even if we accept the background of the Cultural Revolution and the more recent socioeconomic and cultural changes as explanations of the poets' sense of victimization and disillusionment, the question still remains: Why poetry? This question is central when we note the uniqueness of the cult in the cultural sphere. Surely, poets are not the only ones who feel marginalized and alienated in contemporary society. In fact, according to Ying-shih Yü, the Chinese intelligentsia as a whole has undergone rapid marginalization in the modern period. Beginning in the late nineteenth century, it went through the transition from the traditional gentry in the May Fourth period and "reached the end of the marginalization process by 1949."⁴⁶ Thus the question is: If poets share the sense of alienation and the quest for a new identity among intellectuals on the one hand, and the celebration of the freedom and autonomy of art among writers and artists on the other, why has avant-garde poetry alone developed a religious discourse of such an extensive scope and significant influence?

To account for the uniqueness of the phenomenon, we should keep in mind the rather unique prestige that poetry has traditionally enjoyed in China as the loftiest, most refined and respectable form of art. Parallel to and enhancing the high status granted to poetry in the Chinese tradition are the modern Russian and Eastern European traditions, where the poet is extolled as a prophet and revolutionary hero. The influence of the latter is equally great, if not greater, because before the late 1970s they were among the few foreign cultures to which Chinese poets were allowed access and with which they were familiar. Thus both the East and the West place the poet in a special, privileged position, a contrast that must be immensely appealing to the marginalized avant-garde poets in post-Mao China.

Yet another, more recent source of influence may be that since the early 1980s Western—especially Anglo-American and European—literature in translation has become popular among Chinese writers, and modernism in particular has received much attention. The modernist theme of alienation strikes a sympathetic chord in the Chinese avant-garde. Further, the symbolist view of poetry as a substitute religion in the modern world and the proverbial bohemian lifestyle of some of the European symbolists are consonant with the ethos of the Chinese cult of poetry.

The cult of poetry is thus underlined by a convergence of positive and negative forces: the quest for self-identity and creative freedom, the marginalization of poetry and the poet in the modern period, the sense of dual alienation (from the political establishment and the fast-growing consumer culture) in post-Mao China, and the inspiration of the invented "genealogy" of poet-heroes drawn from traditions both indigenous and foreign. However, the relations between "the cult of poetry" and sociopolitical reality may be more complex than what has been described.

In his essay on post-Mao literature and art, the critic Wang Gan notes:

> The disaster and malaise born of the Cultural Revolution would not end with the end of the external form of the Cultural Revolution.... This means that Chinese avant-garde writers write under a shadow; in other words, they must eliminate the numerous latent or apparent forms of erosion by the Cultural Revolution mentality, yet in the process of elimination they also con-

sciously or unconsciously use the mentality and modes of operation of the Cultural Revolution.[47]

Has the cult of poetry escaped the "shadow" of the Cultural Revolution? How successful has it been in eliminating "the numerous latent or apparent forms of erosion" by Mao-speak as a whole?

An apt point of departure may be the image of Qu Yuan in the cult of poetry. Our earlier discussion of Bai Hua's "In Memoriam: Zhu Xiang" has already suggested that Qu Yuan is often invoked by avant-garde poets as an exemplar of the poet-martyr. The legend of Qu Yuan has a long history in China. As Laurence Schneider has pointed out, the legend has undergone extraordinary developments in post-1949 China. "The most obvious function of the lore since 1949 . . . has been to provide a means for the intellectuals, especially creative writers, to evaluate their place in the polity and society."[48] In contrast to the communist portrayal of Qu as a selfless, patriotic poet and a hero of the people, the poet-martyr in the contemporary discourse of the cult of poetry emphasizes the image of the individualist, the "madman of Chu." It distinguishes itself, in other words, from the official version by bringing back the "individualism," "willfulness," even the poet's role as "visionary and prophet" that the establishment has tried to mitigate.[49] This is an example of how the discourse of the cult draws upon an existing symbol of the system and reverses it to counter that system.

However, the emphasis on the poet as the heroic martyr of poetry also leads to ambivalence vis-à-vis the system. In his essay "Chenggong huozhe bu chenggong de" (The successful and the unsuccessful), the poet Lan Cun says:

> I am delighted to see the efforts made by many fine poets to uphold poetry's sublime position. At the same time that I fell in love with poetry I fell deeply in love with the creator-gods and guardian-gods of poetry. We don't have any reason to feel sorry for their violent actions (which, of course, include the torment they inflict on themselves). The whole of humankind should remember forever these singers who dedicate their body and soul to poetry in realizing the unity of poetry and personality.[50]

What is intriguing about this passage is the logical consequence of exalting the poet to the status of a hero, namely, the unquestioned equation between the poet's personality and his work. This tendency is amply seen in the earlier discussion of the images of the poet: Haizi the martyr, Shi Zhi the mad genius, Hei Dachun the bohemian, Yu Xinjiao the pilgrim, several "buried poets" (*bei maizang de shiren*)—besides Shi Zhi, also Mang Ke, Yan Li, and Huang Xiang.

When Ye Yunchao speaks of the price one has to pay for great poetry, he declares: "For me, having this realization is better than not having it. It is not only for the sake of poetry but above all for the poet's sake, because *the poet is more important than the poetry*."[51]

When the poet is held as more important than the poetry, death—especially self-inflicted death—becomes the ultimate poem, the poem to end all poems. Eulogizing Haizi's suicide, the critic Zhu Dake remarks: "Through the genius's careful design, he completed in his suicide the purest articulation of life and the final, great poem; in other words, he completed his *ballade* of death, his swan song."[52] Zhu compares Haizi's suicide to "action art" and repeatedly describes the poet and his work in terms of divinity (*shenxing*). It is no surprise that one of the illustrations accompanying Zhu's essay depicts the Crucifixion.

In contrast to Zhu, who is very much a part of the cult discourse in China, Maghiel van Crevel comments on the poet-worship from a critical point of view. He recounts an incident involving an obscure poet named Yue Bing, who was killed after a quarrel in a restaurant in Chuzhou, Anhui, in May 1992. Although his death had nothing to do with poetry (or being a poet, for that matter), he was honored by the local media with these lines:

> Certain it was his soul could never
> Endure the shame of men's disdain;
> He braved the world's harsh frown—as ever
> Alone!—and struggled—and was slain![53]

The poem quoted here was written by Mikhail Yurievich Lermontov to commemorate the death of Alexander Pushkin. The incongruity of the quotation in the context of Yue Bing's death only goes to show the extensive influence and extremity of the cult of poetry. It is paradoxical that although avant-garde poetry is politically repressed and economically disenfranchised, being an avant-garde poet nevertheless gives one a special status, abuses of which have been reported from time to time.[54]

The tendency of the cult of poetry to equate the poet's personality and personal life with his work is, first of all, no more than a romantic myth. It is demythologized by none other than Byron, the romantic poet *par excellence*. In his letter to Thomas Moore in 1821, Byron was both amused and annoyed by the fact that he could "never get people to understand that poetry is the expression of an excited passion, and that there is no such thing as a life of passion any more than a continuous earthquake or an eternal fever."[55]

The romantic myth of the poet is parodied in *Life Is Elsewhere* by Milan

Kundera, who has been widely read in China since the mid-1980s. The novel satirizes the romanticization of the poet as young and passionate, divinely inspired, different from and more special than the ordinary person. The protagonist of the novel, Jaromil, lives in such self-delusion, first encouraged by his mother (who worshiped Lermontov!) and later perpetuated through his love affair. Jaromil's first discovery of his artistic talent is described in the episode in which the young boy draws a human with a dog's face; for this he earns profuse, unexpected praise from his teacher, a local artist of some reputation:

> Until now . . . his differentness had been something empty, vague, an incomprehensible hope or an incomprehensible rejection; but now it had received a clear designation at last: original inner world. . . . Of course, Jaromil knew perfectly well that he owed his lauded discovery of dog-people to sheer accident, that it derived purely and simply from his inability to draw a human face; this gave him the impression that the uniqueness of his inner world did not emanate from any active endeavor but consisted of everything that passed willy-nilly through his head. . . . From that time on he began to pay careful attention to all his thoughts and ideas, and to admire them.[56]

Jaromil's delusion about his own artistic talent leads to a false sense of identity. For him the image of the artist is far more important than the art, which is only an excuse for rationalizing and perpetuating the empty self-importance in which he lives.

The romanticization of the poet is problematic in that it contradicts the credo of the independence of art, which is central to avant-garde poetics. Paradoxically, despite the Chinese avant-garde's claim to be contemporary and international, such emphasis echoes the traditional Chinese aesthetic view that one can understand and judge the character of the poet by reading his work—*ren ru qi wen*—a view that blurs the distinction between moral judgment and aesthetic evaluation.

Finally, what is probably most problematic about the overwhelming interest in the poet rather than the poetry is its ambivalent relation to the mentality underlying the cult of an earlier era—the personality cult of Mao. Is there any relationship between the cult that endows the poet with a special status and the fact that Mao was a poet? From the deification of poetry and the equation of the poet with his poetry it is but one step to the deification of the poet—the martyr, the tragic hero, the prophet *manqué*. To look to the poet, especially the "master poet" (*dashi*) as the ultimate embodiment of poetry comes close to the worshiping of a cult figure.

It is perhaps in this sense that the cult of poetry embodies a subtle form of complicity with communist ideology. The deification of poetry and the canonization of the poet reveal an absolutist, utopian frame of mind that at least implicitly excludes other approaches to poetry both in theory and in practice. Are alienation and the sense of crisis the necessary driving forces behind the creation of poetry? Why is the poetry that emphasizes suffering and sacrifice regarded as nobler or better than the poetry that does not? Why does the poet have to be perceived in heroic terms? However much the cult of poetry resists the establishment, is it merely substituting the object of worship but still functioning within the same framework of thinking and writing?

Viewed from this perspective, it is not surprising that while avant-garde poets are at odds with the political-cultural establishment, many make references to Mao in positive ways. What is noteworthy is not so much the presence of Mao in the poetry per se as the kind of language used in the "cult" that sounds strangely similar to Mao-speak, which has permeated every aspect of Chinese life for decades. The epigraph to Bai Hua's "Maizi—jinian Haizi" (Wheat, in memoriam: Haizi) quotes the following lines from Mao's poem "Arriving at Mount Shao" ("Dao Shao shan"):

> Only in sacrifice lies a lofty ambition
> That dares replace the sun and the moon with a new sky.

And Bai Hua's poem ends with:

> Please proclaim, wheat, the next step, next step.
> The next step is sacrifice,
> the next step is not a banquet.[57]

The last line echoes Mao's famous maxim that to engage in revolution is not like being treated to a banquet. It is highly ironic that these allusions to Mao are used to commemorate an avant-garde poet who is, at least in spirit, opposed to the Mao regime for its ironclad control of literature and the arts and the persecution of writers and artists.

The Mao heritage from which many avant-garde poets seem unable to escape is also seen in prose. In an essay in *Shanchahua* (Camellia) Lan Cun says:

> The pioneers' blood lights up the path we are to walk on, guiding us to move along without stopping. We mount the horse of life and set out at night, a cluster of brilliant stars over our heads till dawn. We become one of the stars burning eternally, lonely, singing, then breaking—they are Hölderlin, Yesenin, Mandelstam, Rimbaud, Haizi, . . . and many other great voices that I don't know of and we have not discovered, those pure and fragile souls going insane or committing suicide for art.[58]

Again, the images of pioneers and blood are typical of the revolutionary rhetoric of the Communist Party.

The poet Yu Jian was among the first to see the connection. He criticizes the cult of poetry as "a utopian and mythical mode of writing" and associates it with the Maoist way of thinking. He also criticizes the unreserved adulation of foreign poets, especially the Nobel laureates, as "a typical reflection of cultural colonialism" and "an essentialism that is the basis of a totalitarian society: on the one hand, they [such poets as Haizi] are subjected to Eurocentrism and the inferiority complex derived from cultural colonialism; on the other hand, they talk up culture under the names of Chinese holism and mysticism."[59] Yu's remark reveals a paradox underlying the cult of poetry. Looking to Western poets as forebears and emphasizing Chinese identity do not contradict each other but are in fact two sides of the same coin.

What Yu refers to here is the fervent hope of many avant-garde poets for a world-class master poet or *dashi*. In an early essay, "Guanyu xiandaishi de suixiang" (Reflections on modern poetry), the poet-critic Ouyang Jianghe calls poetry "a king's undertaking" and anticipates that "modern [Chinese] poetry [will] contribute a few world-class masters for China." He goes on to elaborate: "A master is a kind of cultural atmosphere and phenomenon of life; he is an abnormal transformation in the evolutionary process of the spirit of the race, the summation of one or several generations."[60] The combination of religious and secular symbolism is intriguing and harks back to the influence of Mao-speak discussed earlier. Besides Wang Gan and Yu Jian, Bei Ling is another poet-critic who decries the apparent complicity between Mao-speak and the cult of poetry: "Poetry in essence is very private ... but in China it is a movement, a banner, a bugle, an ism, a power, even an unmovable icon—it becomes 'Maoism.' "[61]

Can this connection to the personality cult of Mao explain the uniqueness of the cult of poetry in China, in sharp contrast to its absence in other cultures, including postwar Taiwan? The contrast between China and Taiwan is worth pursuing because on the surface there are significant similarities between postwar Taiwan and post-Mao China. Not unlike the Cultural Revolution, World War II and the civil war between the Nationalists and the Chinese communists left indelible scars and ruins in Taiwan. In the cultural sphere a vacuum was created by the ban of all pre-1949 literature written by Chinese writers who remained on the mainland and by a general paranoia about communist infiltration. As a result, foreign literature primarily from the West but also from Latin America, in particular symbolism and various forms of modernism, became a major influence on avant-garde poets in Taiwan. Under these similar circumstances, why is it that the Taiwanese avant-garde did not respond to the situation by turning poetry into a religion the way their mainland counterparts did some thirty years later? In addition to economic differences (e.g., accelerated commercialization in post-Mao China creates a far more dramatic and drastic impact on society), I would submit that the long, absolute domination of Maoist discourse on the mainland is a key factor.

In the case of Taiwan, the metaphor of the poet as Christ and the alienated hero also appears in avant-garde poetry of the 1950s and 1960s. A prime example is Ya Xian. In "Po" (Dissection), the prefatory poem in his collected work, he, too, sees the poet as a modern-day Christ figure:

> There is a man
> he is really as skinny as Jesus Christ
> He hopes someone will crucify him
> (maybe he'll become famous this way)
> and blood will splash on his robe
> a thorny crown—even if made with paper—
> will fall on his lowly forehead
> molested by city noise.[62]

However, the wish of the third-person protagonist is unlikely to be fulfilled. Because of the escalating price of lumber, the poem goes on to say, no one would waste it on the poet. Besides, modern people have lost interest in religious persecution; they don't even care to

> spit curses on his not-too-high nose,
> or carry for him
> a second ridiculous cross.

When we compare Ya Xian's poem from the late 1950s to China's cult of poetry of the 1980s–1990s, what seems to be missing in the latter is the element of irony and self-parody. The title of Ya Xian's poem not only implies a critique of a materialistic society, which is found in post-Mao avant-garde poetry, but also suggests self-reflection and self-critique. The poem refrains from placing the poet on the moral and spiritual pedestal that is inevitably implicit in the cult of poetry in contemporary China.

The last observation I would like to make is this. Throughout the discussion thus far I have used male personal pronouns whenever I refer to Chinese avant-garde poets as a group. This was not an oversight. Another significant aspect of the discourse of the cult, another aspect of its hidden tension and contradiction, is that not only are all of the poets (and critics, for that matter) of the cult whom I have quoted so far male, but few women poets can be found actively participating or closely involved in the discourse. It is true that a number of women poets have achieved a national, even international reputation in post-Mao China, most notably Shu Ting and Wang Xiaoni in the early 1980s and Zhai Yongming and Lu Yimin since the mid-1980s. However, none of them have played a significant role in the discourse of the cult. One major reason, I believe, is that all the unofficial poetry publications are founded, edited, and published by male poets; they are the initiators and organizers. This does not mean, of course, that the women poets are passive or silent; their work is primarily published in the same venues as the male poets, and a few have been invited to serve on editorial boards.

When women poets do talk about poetry, they seem far more interested in issues specifically related to women as writers than in the status of the poet or poetry. Zhai Yongming, for instance, published an influential preface to her poetic sequence entitled "Nüren" (Woman) in 1984, in which she compares the inner world of women to the night and advocates giving free expression to women's innermost, "darkest" consciousness. Other women poets have more or less followed the same direction. It is possible that for the women poets the primary concern is their identity as *women* vis-à-vis men, rather than as *poets* vis-à-vis society. This different concern on the women's part is understandable when we situate it in the context of post-1949 Chinese society, where the issue of gender has been dismissed as irrelevant or nonexistent, where during the Cultural Revolution "women were not allowed to wear long hair or skirts," where women "have existed only in order to complete the grand narrative of a certain ideology."[63] If this analysis is valid, then the conspicuous absence of women in the cult of poetry should be understood as carrying both positive and negative implications.

On the positive side, women poets are struggling to create a gender identity for themselves, to carve out a space where they can freely express themselves as gendered and sexual beings. On the negative side, their absence in the cult of poetry bespeaks exclusion from a male-centered, male-dominated discourse, which, ironically, is part of *why* they are struggling and *what* they are struggling against. Does the avant-garde poetry scene embody the same gender relationships as society as a whole? If so, then what does it say about the framework within which the former operates in comparison with the latter?

To put the sexual politics in another perspective, there is no doubt that the women poets are often influenced by the same poets that inspire their male counterparts. Lu Yimin, for instance, acknowledges writing under the influence of Sylvia Plath, who was recommended to her by her husband and fellow poet, Wang Yin. However, unlike their male fellow poets, they seldom engage in the discourse on poetry as a religion and the poet as the heroic martyr, and this is despite the fact that some of them, like Lu Yimin, are married to poets.

There are gray areas, of course. Shen Rui, until recently the wife of the poet Wang Jiaxin, reveals an ambivalent relation to the cult in her poem "Zhi An Saikesidun" (To Anne Sexton):

> That day I followed you on your way to the mental hospital
> Half-way there, you turned back with a lit cigarette and sat back down before the typewriter
> Left in the woods, I had to cook for myself
>
> From that day on I ate your poetry. I found a key
> in your pocket and hid it under a rock
> I danced round it, singing; it let me own you
>
> Why did you bite your heart in two so that I couldn't sew the pieces back together?
> I have a needle, thread, and a thumb tack. Day after day
> I try and try till my eyes can no longer see
> You watered the flowers, bathed your daughters, attended PTA meetings
> you drove your car, ignoring my hitch-hiking gesture
> you were alone in your room and, without my help, you did it
>
> I blame you, hate you, nail you to my cross
> Leaning our backs on each other, we comfort each other. Ha!
> we are of the same kind, so we tease each other, how we are of the same kind.[64]

There is a strong resonance between Shen Rui's poem and the cult of poetry. The rapt attention Shen focuses on Sexton bespeaks her empathy and identification with a Western poet who committed suicide. The image of the poet as struggling alone and the symbolism of the Crucifixion also tie the poem to the discourse of the cult as discussed earlier. On the other hand, I would argue that Shen's poem also departs in significant ways from the cult. In her poem the mundane details of daily life—cooking, gardening, caring for children, sewing—draw the picture of a typical mother and housewife who also happens to be a poet. There is little romanticization of the poet or glorification of poetry—the image of Sexton writing poetry on her typewriter is so casually mentioned along with the other activities that it is presented as just another part of her quotidian life. This deemphasis of poetry as something transcendental and supreme finds further support in the intimate and informal tone in which Shen addresses Sexton not only as a poet but also, maybe more importantly, as a woman. Sexton is not treated as someone larger than life, someone who is placed on a pedestal for being a poet. Instead, the poem suggests a process of how a deep bond develops between Shen and Sexton—how she first discovers Sexton's poetry (second stanza), gets to know her world intimately ("key" and "it let me own you" in the third stanza), and shares her pains (following Sexton to the mental hospital in the first stanza, trying to sew the poet's broken heart back together in the third, and the entire last stanza). It is a bond that exists between two women, not between a hero and a worshiper, or between a master and a disciple. Finally, even in her use of the cross, the central symbol of the cult of poetry, Shen expresses a touch of irony and self-satire that is absent in the male poets' tragic sublimity. Nailed to the cross, the women tease at the same time they comfort each other. In sum, the poem embodies a gendered perspective on the cult of poetry, and as such, it is an exception rather than the rule to the discourse.

In the final analysis, the cult of poetry in post-Mao China is a paradox. It advocates creative freedom and individuality; however, in elevating poetry to the status of a religion, it imposes arbitrary limits on poetry. It defies the official ideology, yet it is unable to escape entirely the absolutist, utopian mentality in its worship of the poet and deification of poetry. It resists and detests consumerism, yet it is by no means immune from becoming a commodity itself. When it is perceived by the outside world as "dissent literature" in a totalitarian regime, Chinese avant-garde poetry can easily be turned—or some may say, has already been turned—into a commodity in the international, primarily Western, cultural market.[65]

These contradictions and pitfalls—artistic, ideological, and economic—point to the intrinsic limitations of the cult of poetry, and "anti-cult" reactions have come from various angles since the mid-1980s. Besides the critiques from such poets and critics as Wang Gan, Yu Jian, and Bei Ling that have been mentioned earlier, the poetry in *Tamen* (They), with Han Dong and Yu Jian as the major representatives, and the poetry of "the stream of life" can be seen as the 1980s' reactions against the cultist tendency. In the early 1990s, the work of Yi Sha parodied the cult through a radical desecration of the romanticized poet. The rapid transformations that society and culture are undergoing in China in the late 1990s, however, make it hard to predict the development of the cult. But it is my belief that the contention between them will be a significant force in shaping the next phase of avant-garde poetry in China.

Chapter 11

Tianya, the Ends of the World or the Edge of Heaven: Comparative Literature at the Fin de Siècle

EUGENE CHEN EOYANG

> A thousand, ten thousand sorrows,
> Extreme sorrow at the end of the world;
> The mountain moon knows nothing of the heart's affairs,
> The drizzling rain falls in vain on the blooms before her eyes;
> Dark jasper clouds slip by.

This *ci* by Wen Tingyun typifies the many traditional uses of the phrase "tianya," which is defined as "frontier border," "the outer limits," and which has been variously rendered as "the ends of the world," "the world's end," or "the edge of the world." The image usually connotes pathos, an expression either of self-pity in being relegated to the outer reaches of the empire, or of longing for a beloved in distant exile. Here, it's "Extreme sorrow at the end of the world"—matching the extremity of sorrow with the antipodes of the world.

What follows is a deconstruction of this image, which will involve: displacement (physical misappropriation as well as deliberate mistranslation); linguistic imperialisms (subordinations, advertent or inadvertent); and the ambivalence of interstices, interludes, and transitions, involving a consideration of what Leo Spitzer characterizes as "the predicament of marginality." At the end, I should like to consider the concept of provinciality and the appreciation of limits as a new basis for knowledge. If I succeed, I hope to show that the other face of "the end of the world" may be, in a comparative perspective—and through the displacements of translation—appreciated as "the edge of heaven."

It is fashionable to think of exile as a modern phenomenon, but we need only recall the Book of Ruth in the Old Testament and the *Medea* of Aeschylus, to be reminded that the condition of being displaced, culturally, geographically, and linguistically, is nothing new. The traditional image of exile is one of sadness and lamentation, of alienation and of homesickness. Immigrants are labeled "displaced persons," the flotsam and jetsam of civilization, decentered, "out of it," "out of touch," "out of the loop." Yet I would like to propose that being displaced is exactly where, to continue the use of the vernacular, "the action is." Estrangement and *dépaysment* aside, one may claim that it is precisely the exile who sees with a binocular focus and a special clarity: "The more one is able to leave one's cultural home," Edward Said writes in *Orientalism*, "the more easily is one able to judge it, and the whole world as well, with the spiritual detachment and generosity necessary for true vision."[1] But the vision is not merely self-directed, for in the wider perspective, "The more easily, too, does one assess . . . alien cultures with the same combination of intimacy and distance."[2] The exile is one who, perforce, has left home. *Dépaysment* for an exile is both a calamity and an opportunity.

The time-honored siren call for exiles in China—*burugui* (Better go home!)—haunts the poetic imagination, yet one wonders how much poetry would have been written if everyone stayed at home. The decisive epics of Greek literature, the *Odyssey* and the *Iliad* are, after all, about an individual and an army far from home. The distresses of immigration are, of course, all too familiar: in a ritual performance at a public elevator in Los Angeles, titled "The Loneliness of the Immigrant," a text on the wall read: "Moving to another country hurts more than moving to another home. . . . In one way or another we all are or will be immigrants. Surely one day we will be able to crack this shell open, this unbearable loneliness, and develop a transcontinental identity."[3] What may not be as familiar are the deconstructive uses of immigration, the benefits that accrue despite, or because of, the pain of being "untimely ripped from the womb" of one's own country. Displacement can be identified in various processes. Colonialization, imperialism, the spread of civilization, are each in their more or less virulent ways, forms of displacement. The issue is not whether there is displacement but rather whether one is aware of it or not. Current studies into the theory of ethnography detect the possibility of an "intellectual displacement," which may be pernicious if not recognized, but which may be fruitful if exposed. As James Clifford puts it:

> A modern "ethnography" on conjunctures, constantly moving between cultures, does not, like its Western alter ego "anthropology," aspire to survey the full range of human diversity or development. It is perpetually displaced, both regionally focused and broadly comparative, a form both of dwelling and of travel in a world where the two experiences are less and less distinct.[4]

In the modern perspective, what is undoubtedly new is the unprecedented speed at which the migration of people and ideas can take place. Edward Said is not alone in observing that "electronic communications, the global extent of trade, of availability of resources, of travel, of information about weather patterns and ecological change have joined together even the most distant corners of the world."[5] The shibboleth of contemporary business—"Think global, act local"—reflects the schizophrenic, both near- and far-sighted optics of the modern weltanschauung. "The 'exotic' is nearby"; "The 'exotic' is uncannily close"; "the familiar turns up at the ends of the earth," James Clifford reminds us in *The Predicament of Culture*.[6] Indeed, Clifford's characterization of Victor Segalen and his attempts to exoticize China reveals a reflexive outcome: "A displacement occurs. By the end of his career, the self, not the other, has become exotic."[7]

The student of comparative literature may be guided by the words of Erich Auerbach, who said, as early as 1952: "In any event, our philological home is the earth: it can no longer be the nation. The most priceless and indispensable part of a philologist's heritage is still his own nation's culture and language. Only when he is first separated from this heritage, however, and then transcends it does it become truly effective."[8] The truly effective heritage is, then, polyglot, a multilingual, not to say multicultural, perspective. Auerbach was an old-fashioned philologist, but his advice was distinctly postmodern in thrust. He enjoined us to revert to the view of a "prenational medieval culture" before national boundaries were determined, and cited a text from the Latin of Hugh of St. Victor (*Didascalicon* 3.20), which Edward Said rendered in 1978 as follows:

> The man who finds his homeland sweet is still a tender beginner;
> he to whom every soil is as his native one is already strong;
> but he is perfect to whom the entire world is as a foreign land.

For Said as for Auerbach, what was of immediate relevance is "the humanistic tradition of involvement in a national culture not one's own."[9] In 1982, Tzvetan Todorov ended his *Conquest of America* with the same quotation, adding parenthetically: "I myself, a Bulgarian living in France, borrow this quotation from Edward Said, a Palestinian living in the United States, who himself found it in Erich Auerbach, a German exiled in Turkey."[10] Three years later, at the 1985 congress of the International Comparative Literature Association in Paris, I could not resist borrowing the quotation as well, this time, with Todorov's beautiful addendum (the paper ultimately appeared in the epilogue to my *Transparent Eye* in 1993).[11]

Subsequently, Said came back to the same text in his *Culture and Imperialism* (1994), this time using it as a coda to his book, but he expanded the scope of the citation and included both the sentence before and after in the original. In its enlarged context the quotation reads as follows:

> It is therefore, a source of great virtue for the practiced mind to learn, bit by bit, first to change about in visible and transitory things, so that afterwards it may be able to leave them behind altogether. The person who finds his homeland sweet is still a tender beginner; he to whom every soil is as his native one is already strong; but he is perfect to whom the entire world is as a foreign place. The tender soul has fixed his love on one spot in the world; the strong person has extended his love to all places; the perfect man has extinguished his.[12]

The emphasis in this instance is clear, and Said stresses that the truly liberated mind is one who "achieves independence and detachment by *working through* attachments, not by rejecting them." To overcome a passionate partisanship, a conscious chauvinism, one must proceed first to develop pluralistic patriotisms, an allegiance to multiple subjectivities, before one can aspire to perfect objectivity.

I cite this not merely for its anecdotal value, or to illustrate the myth of eternal return, but to illustrate the different ways in which the same quotation can be used. Hugh of St. Victor originally conceived of the quotation to inspire novices to abjure the world, to forgo the ties of personal affection, and to serve God by spreading His word. By his own admission, Auerbach converts this sentiment to more secular purposes: he sees it as an ideal point of reference—his word is *Ansatzpunkt*, "a handle, as it were"—for research in the humanities.[13] Said revisits the same text to argue for an intercultural perspective in literary studies;[14] whereas Todorov uses the quotation as a postmodernist allegory exemplifying the exile's "double exteriority," which characterizes "a being who has lost his country without thereby acquiring another."[15] I used the quotation as an example of the compositeness of the self, in which many "others" are implicated. Said returned to the quotation to emphasize the importance of national allegiances as a precondition to perfect exile. Todorov's fructifying parenthesis, which not only glosses on the quotation from Hugh of St. Victor, but also traces the cultural genealogy of each person who quoted the passage, reminds us that the context of a passage may be as important, if not more important, than the text itself. These contextual variations around the same textual theme are but further illustrations of the "displacements" that occur in interpretation as well as in translation.[16]

"I see to the dregs the bitterness of a parting at world's end / Don't speak about coming back," Wang Guowei writes in a *ci*, and adds in the next stanza: "One skein of new joys / Old sorrows by the thousands."[17] Into the thousand threads of old sorrows weaves in a single thread of new joy. The equation may be unbalanced, the numbers disproportionate, but new joys will always be outnumbered by old sorrows, just as new insights will always be sparse when compared to the teachings of traditional wisdom.

The most ironical discovery in history was, of course, the one Columbus made: in searching for the old he found the new. Yet for those who were discovered—misidentified as Arawaks or Caribs, but who were actually the Tainos, the event was more a calamity than a blessing, since it meant their eventual extinction. Columbus's "discovery" of the West Indies is celebrated, but of those who first populated these islands, history—with very few exceptions—takes little note.[18]

One man's discovery can result in another man's destruction. The indigenous population of the Americas—whether Aztec, Arawak, Taino, Mohican, or Cherokee—can hardly be blamed for finding little to celebrate in Columbus's misguided search for a route to China. Those who followed were the pilgrims, the visitors to the new continent, but in time, these marginal settlers became dominant. No illustration of hegemonic discourse can be more poignant than the futile protestations of the Cherokee nation when they objected to the Indian Removal Act of 1830, which entailed, in Arnold Krupat's words, " 'trans-lating' the Eastern Indians westward."[19] Before the vote, the Cherokees tried to demonstrate their civilization in a florid remonstrance, intended to belie the unjust characterization of them as murderous savages: their words resound in our conscience, not merely because of the justice of their cause, not merely by the simple grace of their rhetoric in a language not their own, but also because of the pathetic futility of their cause.

> We have already stated to your honourable bodies, that our forefathers were found in possession of this soil in full sovereignty, by the first European settlers; and as we have never ceded nor forfeited the occupancy of the soil, and the sovereignty over it, we do solemnly protest against being forced to leave it, either by direct or indirect measures. To the land, of which we are now in possession, we are attached. It is our fathers' gift; it contains their ashes; it is the land of our nativity, and the land of our intellectual birth.[20]

Their trust in their interlocutors, their faith in the justice of their cause, and their deference to their oppressors could not have been more misplaced, or more callously disregarded:

> Your memorialists humbly conceive, that such an act would be in the highest degree oppressive. From the people of these United States, who, perhaps, of all men under heaven, are the most religious and free, it cannot be

expected. ... You represent a virtuous, intelligent, and Christian nation. To you they willingly submit their cause for your righteous decision.[21]

Despite these pleas, the Indian Removal Act passed by a margin of 28 to 20 in the Senate, and of 103 to 97 in the House, providing ambivalent solace that there was a sizable minority in the Congress of the United States who recognized that this cruel displacement of an indigenous population had no basis in law, either man-made or natural. The Amerindian population became a displaced people in their own country, exiles at home.

Translation is yet another, perhaps less obvious, form of displacement. Replacing words in the native language with words in a non-native language or, to reverse the model, to replace foreign words with the homegrown vernacular, are forms of semantic and cultural displacement. It is telling that Columbus took aboard six Tainos on his first voyage, "intending to teach them Spanish,"[22] but no effort was made to learn the language the Tainos spoke. This one-sided exchange, which imposes a hegemonic language (so disastrous for the Cherokees), is typical of the equation that Eric Cheyfitz makes between translation and colonization in *The Poetics of Imperialism*, to which he has appended as an epigraph Roland Barthes's oracular observation: "To rob a man of his language in the very name of language: this is the first step in all legal murders." This linguistic deprivation takes several forms. It totalizes the other: "the homogenizing of these diverse peoples under the name of 'Indians' being the primal act of translation" and it denigrates the other: "translation means precisely not to understand others who are the original (inhabitants) or to understand those others all too easily . . . solely in terms of one's own language."[23]

In addition to physical displacements (exile), psychological displacements (alienation), and linguistic displacements (translation), one might also consider epistemological displacements. Modest versions of this can be found in the disarming of the "kin-related" systems of thought that stress intuitions and relatedness in favor of the categorical systems that stress distinctions, differences, and autonomies, imposing a Western *episteme* on cultures based on alternative premises and modes of meaning. An extreme version may be found in a critique of artificial intelligence by John Searle. Searle constructs a Chinese room argument "that showed that a system could instantiate a program so as to give a perfect simulation of some human cognitive capacity, such as the capacity to understand Chinese, even though that system had no understanding of Chinese whatever."[24] For the argument to work, one must assume a reader unfamiliar with Chinese, for only then can one entertain the distinctions that are being set out.

> Simply imagine that someone who understands no Chinese is locked in a room with a lot of Chinese symbols and a computer program for answering questions in Chinese. The input to the system consists in Chinese symbols in the form of questions; the output of the system consists in Chinese symbols in answer to the questions. We might suppose that the program is so good that the answers to the questions are indistinguishable from those of a native Chinese speaker. But all the same, neither the person inside nor any other part of the system literally understands Chinese; and because the programmed computer has nothing that this system does not have, the programmed computer, qua computer, does not understand Chinese either. Because the program is purely formal or syntactical and because minds have mental or semantic contents, any attempt to produce a mind purely with computer programs leaves out the essential features of the mind.[25]

The issue I want to take here does not involve artificial intelligence, an area in which, in any event, I have no competence. I merely want to point out that a Chinese coming upon this text must think of himself or herself as either wildly improbable or totally chimerical. What interests me here is whether this same argument has equivalent force if something more familiar were substituted for Chinese. If one were to say, for example, "Simply imagine that someone who understands no English is locked in a room," etc., would the distinctions being made between providing the right answers ("in no way distinguishable from a speaker of English") and understanding ("neither the person inside nor any part of the system literally understands English") make any sense? I hardly think so. What does literal understanding mean? Is there a real distinction between literally understanding English and merely being programmed to appear as if one understood so well that the responses were indistinguishable from a native speaker of English? The very parable of understanding here is skewed by a biased use of an exotic, as opposed to a familiar, language.

The postmodern condition, the recognition of the multiplicity of perspectives, whether embodied in Said's emphasis on "intimacy and distance," or exemplified by Todorov's notion of "double exteriority," poses an epistemological problem. If all ideologies are susceptible to essentialist vulnerabilities—the ideology that disclaims its own essentialism is, *ipso facto*, self-convicted of being the most essentialist—how then can one establish a universalist discourse? How can one pursue the truth? How can we, to use Heidegger's term, recognize *aletheia*, the disclosures, the "unconcealments," the "clearings" that constitute the postmodern version of knowledge? That is, in large part, the question that occupies Arnold Krupat in his book, *Ethnocriticism: Ethnography, History, Literature*.

"Ethnocritical discourse regards border and boundary crossings," Krupat writes, "with their openness to a recognition of the inevitability of interactive relations, as perhaps the best means to some broadly descriptive account of the way things 'really' work in the material and historical world."[26] "Central to ethnohistorical work is the concept of *frontier*," Krupat insists ("frontier" here is reminiscent of "tianya"); but it is a frontier now designating not so much the "furthest point to which *civilization* has advanced," but rather, "as that shifting space in which two *cultures* encounter each other."[27] The truth must be perceived from what Victor Turner would have called a "liminal" space. "Given its frontier condition of liminality or betweenness," Krupat tells us, "ethnocriticism by its very nature must test any appeals to 'reason,' 'science,' 'knowledge,' or 'truth' it would make in relation to Other or non-Western constructions of these categories...."[28] To avoid essentialist, totalizing visions of reality, one must recognize that "all discourse, like all cultural practice and all actual speech, is inevitably plural...."[29] My citation of Hugh of St. Victor is unusual only in the sense that the plurality of voices is made explicit rather than implicit. One can identify the "voices" of Auerbach, Said, and Todorov in its formulation. There is a homology between these ethnocritical notions and the "true cosmopolitanism" of some recent analysts of American intellectual history. David Hollinger, in his book, saliently titled, *In the American Province*, has given what appears to be not only a decisive, but ultimately a very functional definition.

> The "cosmopolitanism" to which I refer is the desire to transcend the limitations of any and all particularisms in order to achieve a more complete human experience and a more complete understanding of that experience. The ideal is decidedly counter to the eradication of cultural differences, but counter also to their preservation in parochial form. Rather, particular cultures and subcultures are viewed as repositories for insights and experiences that can be drawn upon in the interests of a more comprehensive outlook on the world. Insofar as a particular ethnic heritage or philosophical tradition is an inhibition to experience, it is to be disarmed; insofar as that heritage or tradition is an avenue toward the expansion of experience and understanding, access to it is to be preserved.[30]

In the process, Hollinger explodes the false polarity of what he calls the "booster-bigot" trap, in which indiscriminate approval of and unmitigated hatred for certain ethnic groups may be seen as two faces of the same essentialist coin of prejudice. Hollinger inveighs against simplistic cause-and-effect notions, implicit in such paradigms as "influence," "stimulus/response," or "impact," as if the processes involved discrete identifiable entities, rather than "reciprocal, dialectical interchanges."[31] Even time-honored and shopworn distinctions as "self-and-society," so easily manipulated, yet so neglectful both of the societies-in-the-self and of the different selves-in-society, purvey totalizing habits of mind that are, by now, so ingrained that one scarcely recognizes that they obscure rather than illuminate the object of study.

The problem is a fundamental one: it might be characterized as a "centrist" bias—not merely a biased placement of the center at a subjective locus, but a primary privileging of center as center. Yeats's famous, "The centre cannot hold / Mere anarchy is loosed upon the world," is only the most familiar expression emphasizing the importance of not only positing, but of holding the center. Yi-fu Tuan writes, "Metaphors of location appear to transcend culture: 'I am central' can only mean 'I am important—someone to be looked up to'; 'I am peripheral' is a humbling admission in any language."[32] The primacy of the image of the center confers upon it an epistemological weight, which gives rise, as Said reminds us, "to semi-official narratives with the capacity to authorize and embody certain sequences of cause and effect, while at the same time preventing the emergence of counter-narratives."[33] The "center" is a metaphor, a "black hole" which is both enormously dense, yet invisible. "There is no reason in principle," Hollinger argues, speaking of the American intellectuals of mid-century, "why an individual could not have Whitman's 'multitudes' within him or her," nor was the belief strange "that a subculture could be complex and variegated without losing its integrity."[34]

Things do not necessarily fall apart when the center cannot hold; indeed, it may be that the center needs to be shifted to the circumference. What one may need in the postmodern world is a reversion to the anonymous aphorism that St. Bonaventure popularized, but without the Christian mysticism: "The nature of God is a circle of which the centre is everywhere and the circumference is nowhere."

> Withered wicker vines, old trees, crows at dusk;
> A small bridge, flowing waters, some settlements;
> On an ancient road, a scrawny horse in the west wind.
> Twilight sets in the west,
> Heartbroken, he who lives at the end of the world.

This *ci* by Ma Zhiyuan uncannily evokes Spengler's *Decline of the West*, or *Der Untergang des Abendlandes*: the West wind and evening is mentioned, the vines are withered, the trees are old, the road is ancient, the horse scrawny, and the onset of night is presaged by crows at dusk. We are centered here, at the end of the world. We are living on the edge.

It is the symbolic space, of living on the edge, in the margins, that I should like to explore next. For the notion of edge, or the shore and the beach, the margin between land and sea—is what animates one of Li Qingzhao's *ci*. "This year at the edge of the sea, at the end of the world," she writes, providing us with a point of departure, an *Ansatzpunkt*, to speculate on the nature of our thoughts, and of our feelings. "Symbolic space," Yi-fu Tuan reminds us, "offers good examples of how the human imagination works.... Symbolic space is a mental artifact, necessary to the ordering of life."[35] Where, in traditional Chinese poetry, "the end of the world" almost always bespoke isolation and loneliness, the modern perspective conjures up a multitude of margins. The littorals of the world are dotted with major coastal cities, and dense populations inhabit, for the most part, not the inland centers but the ports on the edge of the sea. Nowhere is this truer than in the New World, where most of the metropolises are not in the center of the continent, but at its periphery (Chicago, significantly, lies in the center of the United States, but is known as "The Second City"—second, that is, to New York, a coastal city).[36] What this suggests is that we must deconstruct our traditional notions of center, as well as our ideas of margins.

It is currently fashionable to invoke, with particular piety, an interest in "non-Western" literature. As convenient and perhaps as inevitable as this term is, there is something faintly obnoxious about it. So is the more current locution that separates the world into "the West" and "the Rest." This posits a "leftover" world which fundamentally compromises the possibility of a clear perspective on the objects in view. The logical flaw in such formulations is that the object is seen in terms of what it *is not* rather than in terms of what it *is*. What all non-Western literatures share—whether they be Chinese, Japanese, African, Arabic—is that they are not the literatures of the West. But the producers and consumers of those literatures are scarcely aware that they are dealing with something non-Western, no more than a Western reader of Jane Austen is aware that she is reading something non-Chinese. Even so, the monolithic notion of dividing the world into the West and the Rest can hardly be sustained. The modern literatures of many cultures—including those of the "Far East"—have subsumed, to various degrees, elements that were previously identified with the West. And the West/Rest dichotomy fails to adequately reflect the composite nature of so-called Western culture, which crucially incorporated Arabic elements (in mathematics), Indian currents (in philosophy), African and Asian motifs (in art), and Babylonian concepts (in astronomy).

The peripheralization of subject matter conceived as marginalization poses yet another catachresis. For the concept of margins presumes a textual standard of discourse. The text-model of analysis has pervaded literary and cultural studies: everything is understood as a "text." Yet this approach undermines the nontextual form of many phenomena that constitute "art in words,"—which is what I mean by "literature." By defining "literature" in these terms, I make no distinction between the spoken and the written word, and I am therefore not as discommoded as the strict literalists of literature who insist that the written word must constitute the basis of artistic productions in language. This textual myopia has restricted our field of vision to only that which can be printed: it excludes the nonverbal as well as the nonliteral (the two are not synonymous, because "verbal"—contrary to the popular solecism—subsumes *both* the oral and the written). The hegemony of the text is evident in the relations of the West with the Rest.

"Margin" is a two-dimensional, print-oriented paradigm: it is spatial and it is static. What would "margins" be in oral cultures? How would the blank frame of a text page be conceived of in cultures that do not have script or print? Might the notion of "margin" itself, subsuming a hidden bias toward the text model, preclude conceiving of more dynamic, more diaological, less discrete, less categorical paradigms? Pauses, interludes, interruptions, silences would be the counterparts in oral discourse to "margins" in written discourse, yet they have about them a totally different semantic feel: far from being trivialized, diminished in importance, these pregnant moments—one thinks of "rests" in music, or Derrida's notion of "trace"—are crucial elements in conveying meaning. I am not interested here in rehearsing the distortions in literary history caused by the neglect of this disjunction between the oral and the written,[37] what concerns me is the sometimes mischievous effect of model-paradigms on our way of conceiving of space, time, and culture. In oral cultures, there are no meaningful counterparts to "margins": the cyclical nature of the thought in many indigenous cultures is well known. The Aristotelian emphasis on beginnings, middles, and ends, as if these were generic attributes of any discourse, has prevailed in Western concepts of unity, coherence, and meaning. They have been strengthened over the last five hundred years, since Gutenberg, with the advent of the printed book, which reinforced these notions with a chimerical cover-to-cover coherence.

The discussion of "canon" strikes me as text-biased as well. For the compilation of lists of authorized or recommended books is obnoxious only when the list remains static: the disagreement over canon should not be whether there should or should not be a canon. There is always a canon. The question is whether that canon is dynamic or static—whether it is constantly under revision or whether it remains fixed on the page. Oral traditions have no arguments over canons, which evolve in an evolutionary process that is far from arbitrary. But literary traditions, particularly those that do not see tradition as evolutionary, but as final and established, have difficulty with changes in the canon. In a fit of scholarly solipsism, they misconceive the evolutionary processes that led to the achievement of any received canon, and judge that the canon, now that perfection has been reached in one's own lifetime, must be preserved. Having determined what is Scripture—writing—they now arbitrarily label anything untoward as "false scripture", i.e., "pseudoepigraphal" or as "apocryphal," indicating works of unknown authorship or authenticity.

In intellectual terms, it is precisely the areas characterized as "marginal" which yield new insights, new knowledge. Cognitive science per se hardly existed more than a generation ago, its subject matter relegated to peripheral status by computer scientists, linguists, engineers, physiologists, psychologists, and animal behaviorists. Translation studies were ignored by the standard departments in national literatures, since no one bothered to examine the consequences of talking about Ibsen, Dostoyevsky, or Omar Khayyam in English, without any knowledge of Norwegian, Russian, or Persian. The study of modern Chinese literature, including the study of contemporary Chinese literature, was scorned by most universities and university presses as recently as twenty years ago. Chaos theory, fuzzy logic, Women's Studies, Ethnic Studies, African American studies, and Native American studies are conspicuous examples of areas of study that emerged in spite of and in the face of the hegemony of book-biased, document-based, script-oriented notions of knowledge.

"Remember the exile miles away at the world's end," Ouyang Xiu writes to a friend who sent him a poem consoling him in his exile, and he concludes with these lines:

Things in foreign lands appear strange to us:
Only the East Wind seems as familiar as before.

These depictions of exilic experience involving the strange and the familiar strike me as emblematic of imaginative thinking. For it is precisely the familiar that gives us a point of reference from which to grasp the unknown, and it is precisely the strange, which casts light on the familiar, "unconcealing" it from our tendency to take it for granted. In our encounter with strange objects, there are two impulses: the first more popular than the second. Most people look askance at foreigners, and are impatient with the strange: their question is: "Why aren't *they* more like *us*?" A very few look at foreigners, and are impatient with the familiar: their question is: "Why aren't *we* more like *them*?" In this category, we can number Marco Polo and Matteo Ricci; among the moderns, Ruth Benedict and Margaret Mead would also qualify. It is this second attitude, it seems to me, that embodies the seeds of new insights, for it involves not only the "self-fashioning," but also the "self-questioning" that is at the root of every important discovery.

Part of our self-fashioning and our self-questioning relates to how we see the world from our individual vantage points. There are no more graphic illustrations of this subjectivity, this assumption of self-as-center, than various "disproportionate" maps from particular points of view, where the detail is the more definitive the closer to the subject, and the more indistinct the further away. Here, for example, is a map of the United States viewed from the vantage point of a provincial Californian; here is another from the vantage point of a Texan; and here is a third from the vantage point of a Bostonian.[38] Saul Steinberg provided a "disproportionate" map for the cover of the *New Yorker*.[39] These are accurate descriptions of inaccurate, but familiar, perspectives. But we do not need to resort to distortions to be reminded how habituated we are to accustomed ways of thinking. Here's an objective map of the Western hemisphere, with the North at the bottom, the South at the top. It's an image few North Americans encounter. These maps remind us, with an uncanny plausibility, how provincial we all are. The only difference is that some of us are aware of it, and some of us are not.

If you will permit a personal anecdote, I'd like to share a story that I heard when I first arrived in Bloomington, Indiana, after growing up, attending school, and working in the East Coast. In the sixties, a Shakespearian scholar, who had taught at Amherst for many years, served as chairman of the English Department at Indiana University for a decade, then decided to move to one of the SUNY campuses, was asked at a reception how he would compare the Midwest and the East Coast. His reply was both tactful and astute. He said, "Oh, I don't know that there is an awful lot of difference between the Midwest and the East Coast." "The only difference that I notice," he continued, "is that, in the Midwest, they *know* they are provincial." Knowing that one is provincial is a hallmark of the most erudite minds, from Newton, who saw himself as a little boy throwing rocks at the vast ocean, to Einstein, who saw the self as a "delusion, a kind of prison for us, restricting us to our personal desires and to affection for a few persons nearest to us."[40]

Indeed, these "provincial" maps, risible and fanciful as they are, illustrate some important lessons of mapmaking. "The three attributes all maps share are scale, projection, and symbolization," a theorist of mapmaking advises us, "all advantages and limitations derive from the degree to which maps reduce and generalize reality, compress or expand shapes and distances, and portray selected phenomenon with signs that communicate, without necessarily resembling, visible or invisible characteristics of the landscape."[41] With very few modifications these criteria for mapmaking can be adapted for criteria with which to judge literary research. We may assess the value of our work in terms of scale: the significance of our work, and its ramifications; of projection: the largeness of spirit and the depth of the sympathy implied by the discourse; and of symbolization: the aptness and the accuracy of the words used to describe the phenomenon which words, in no visible or invisible way, resemble.

If we examine these three criteria—of scale, projection, and symbolization—and reflect on the research we encounter, how much would be found adequate in one, two, if not in all three respects? There are some efforts that reflect accuracy in symbolization and sympathy in projection, but are sadly wanting in a sense of scale. Arcaneness, a wasteful attention to minutiae, is the result. If something is truly fascinating, it can be, and should be, related to something broader. There are others, true to scale and apt in symbolization, that reflect no sympathy for the subject. Aridity, a jejueneness of thought, emerges to deadly effect. One wonders why an imaginative mind should be so preoccupied with anything so picayune. And finally, there are efforts which are just in scale, and zealous in their enthusiasm, that are so far from being apt in symbolization that they belie not only their own value, but the value of the object of study. Philistinism becomes rampant. Examples, I trust, need not be cited, for each one of us can identify instances of arcaneness, aridity, or philistinism.

The disproportionate maps resemble some of our research productions: aptly symbolized, vividly projected, but woefully lacking in scale. Yet they are heuristic revelations, since they indicate in graphic terms our tendency toward a subjective bias. Note how their outlandishness varies according to the standpoint of the viewer. New Yorkers, for example, would find the disproportionate Californian's map more absurd than their own. There is no way of looking at these subjective distortions of the world without wondering what our own distortions might be. We are, in other words, all provincials. Only some of us know it. Just so, we all are or will be immigrants, exiles. Only some of us know it. One who knew it was Matteo Ricci, whose map in Chinese places his own home at the periphery, and the Middle Kingdom in, well, the middle. It is a graphic example of a mapmaker whose self was not, for a change, the center of existence.

We may ask, along with Guan Yunshi, "Lord of the East, where is the world's end?" And we may answer, to paraphrase John Donne, "Ask not where the end of the world is, you are at the world's end." Our discoveries must be at the frontier, but every new cosmopolitanism has implicitly an as yet unsuspected parochialism. The discourse we promote is at once what undermines our own discourse, and its most reliable. "Do I contradict myself? Very well, I contradict myself," Walt Whitman proclaims, "I am large. I contain multitudes . . ." "Now I have just said something," Zhuangzi stated, in the *Qiwu lun* chapter, "But I don't know whether what I have said has really said something or whether it hasn't said something."[42] That is why James Clifford's comment on Edward Said's *Orientalism* is both apt and profound: "Said himself writes in ways that simultaneously assert and subvert his own authority."[43] They declare, in the interests of objectivity, what Clifford characterizes as "a blatantly partial perspective."

Said's insights are similar to those of the disproportionate maps: they do not profess to cast a neutral Mercator's projection on the world, nor do they view the object from an Olympian supraworldly perspective. His project is to detect distortion by the use of another inevitable distortion. What Clifford says about ethnographers resonates for comparatists: "In the last decades of the twentieth century, ethnography begins from the inescapable fact that Westerners are not the only ones going places in the modern world."[44] He is right: "Paradigms of experience and interpretation are yielding to discursive paradigms of dialogue and polyphony."[45] What we are collecting, in comparative literature, is an entire atlas of "disproportionate" maps, not for any frivolous purpose, but ironically to see the whole without false objectivity, without untenable disclaimers of one's own subjectivity. Our language, Clifford reminds us, quoting Bakhtin: "lies on the borderline between oneself and the other. The word in language is half someone else's." We should be looking toward our exile as a voyage of discovery, of journeys "Tomorrow, to fresh woods, and pastures new" (to borrow from Milton). As Qian Qianyi advises in one of his "Willow Songs,"

> Don't throw away the blooms of lamentable times:
> Flowers blossom and flowers fall;
> River borders are green as fragrant grasses,
> Following forever the vagrant exile—to the ends of the world.

As we approach not only the end of the decade, not only the end of the century, but also the end of the millennium, we should not forget the lines with which T. S. Eliot began and ended the "East Coker" section of *The Four Quartets*: "In my beginning is my end" and "In my end is my beginning."

Reference Matter

NOTES

Introduction

A shorter version of this introduction was presented at the University of Iowa in March 1996.

1. See John J. Deeney, ed., *Chinese-Western Comparative Literature:Theory and Strategy* (Hong Kong: Chinese University Press, 1980); William Tay, Ying-hsiung Chou, and Heh-hsiang Yuan, eds., *China and the West: Comparative Literature Studies* (Hong Kong: Chinese University Press, 1980). See also Ying-hsiung Chou, ed., *The Chinese Text: Studies in Comparative Literature* (Hong Kong: Chinese University Press, 1986), and Tak-wai Wong, ed., *East-West Comparative Literature: Cross-Cultural Discourse* (Hong Kong: Hong Kong University Press, 1993).

2. For a number of obvious paradigm shifts and institutional changes in comparative literature, see the 1993 report, "Comparative Literature at the Turn of the Century," issued by the American Comparative Literature Association, and the responses to the report collected in Charles Bernheimer, ed., *Comparative Literature in the Age of Multiculturalism* (Baltimore, Md.: Johns Hopkins University Press, 1994). For the argument in favor of a more fundamental change in the institution of literary studies, see Hans Ulrich Gumbrecht, "The Future of Literary Studies?" *New Literary History* 26, no. 3 (Summer 1995): 499–518. In particular, Gumbrecht foresees a necessary separation of "cultural research and epistemological discussions" in the humanities, something comparable to "the bifurcation that took place about 1900 in the field of the sciences between engineering and more theory-oriented forms of research and teaching" (p. 514).

3. For the difficulty in defining the current scholarship of comparative literature in conventional terms, see Clayton Koelb and Susan Noakes, eds., *The Comparative Perspective on Literature:Approaches to Theory and Practice* (Ithaca, N.Y.: Cornell University Press, 1988), pp. 4–6. The terms "French hour" and "American hour" are used by Claude Guillién, who contends: "Historically, there was no French 'school' (an inappropriate term for the twentieth century), and of course no American 'school' either"; see his *Challenge of Comparative Literature*, trans. Cola Franzen (Cambridge, Mass.: Harvard University Press, 1993), p. 47.

4. One such chart of taxonomies of the French and the American schools, in

comparison with the Chinese school, is found in Cao Shunqing's "Bijiao wenxue Zhongguo xuepai jiben lilun tezheng jiqi fangfalun tixi chutan" (The Chinese school of comparative literature: The essential features of its theory and a tentative study of its methodology), *Zhongguo bijiao wenxue*, 1995, no. 1: 40. Major publications on comparative literature in mainland China over the past decade include Lu Kanghua and Sun Jingyao, *Bijiao wenxue daolun* (Introduction to comparative literature) (Haerbing: Heilongjiang renmin chubanshe, 1984); Yue Daiyun, ed., *Zhongxi bijiao wenxue jiaocheng* (Textbook on Chinese-Western comparative literature) (Beijing: Gaodeng jiaoyu chubanshe, 1988); Chen Dun and Liu Xiangyu, *Bijiao wenxue gailun* (Introduction to comparative literature) (Beijing: Beijing shida chubanshe, 1988); Cao Shunqing, *Bijiao wenxue shi* (History of comparative literature) (Chengdu: Sichuan renmin chubanshe, 1991); and Liu Jiemin, *Bijiao wenxue fangfalun* (Methodology in comparative literature) (Tianjin: Tianjin renmin chubanshe, 1993).

5. See Cao, "Bijiao wenxue Zhongguo xuepai," pp. 20–22. A diametrically opposing view is articulated in David Palumbo-Liu, "The Utopias of Discourse: On the Impossibility of Chinese Comparative Literature," *CLEAR (Chinese Literature: Essays, Articles, Reviews)* 14 (1992): 165–76; reprinted in this volume as Chapter 3.

6. The term "mutual parochialism" is from Pauline Yu, "Alienation Effects: Comparative Literature and the Chinese Tradition," in Koelb and Noakes, *Comparative Perspective on Literature*, p. 162.

7. Rey Chow, *Woman and Chinese Modernity: The Politics of Reading Between West and East* (Minneapolis: University of Minnesota Press, 1991), p. xvi.

8. The phrase is used by John Deeney in his criticism of Ku Tim-hung (Gu Tianhong) and Chen Hui-hua (alias of Chen Pengxiang); see Deeney, "Modern Developments in Chinese-Western Comparative Literature Studies: A Golden Decade (1977–1987) for the 'Chinese School,'" *Tamkang Review* 18, nos. 1–4 (1987–88): 52. On an earlier occasion, Cecile Chu-Chin Sun uses the term "hypermetropic" to describe a type of comparative study whose "primary purpose is to apply Western theories and methodologies, particularly those of the structuralist and post-structuralist persuasions, to Chinese literature, often in a wholesale fashion"; see Sun, "Problems of Perspective in Chinese-Western Comparative Literature Studies," *Canadian Review of Comparative Literature* 13, no. 4 (December 1986): 533.

9. Perry Link, "Ideology and Theory in the Study of Modern Chinese Literature," *Modern China* 19, no. 1 (January 1993): 7.

10. Murray Krieger, *The Institution of Theory* (Baltimore, Md.: Johns Hopkins University Press, 1994), p. 3. Krieger's book is based on a set of three lectures he gave at the Academia Sinica in Taipei, Taiwan, in May 1991.

11. Jonathan Hart, "The Ever-changing Configurations of Comparative Literature," *Canadian Review of Comparative Literature* 19 (March/June 1992): 3.

12. Gu and Chen's collection was published by Dongda tushu gongsi. For a

recent clarification of the disputes, see Chen Pengxiang, "Jianli bijiao wenxue Zhongguo xuepai de lilun he buzhou" (Theory and strategies for building the Chinese school of comparative literature), *Zhongwai wenxue* 19, no. 1 (June 1990): 115–16. For Deeney's recent claim to being the originator of the Chinese school, see his "*Vale atque Ave*: Superlative Literature in the Next Millennium," *Chinese/International Comparative Literature Bulletin* 6–7 (March 1994): 4.

13. Quoted in Chen Pengxiang, "Jianli bijiao wenxue," p. 105.

14. Deeney's article is reprinted in his collection, *Bijiao wenxue yanjiu zhi xin fangxiang* (New orientations for comparative literature) (Taipei: Lianjing chubanshe, 1978), pp. 265–70.

15. For instance, Yang Zhouhan endorses the notion of the "Chinese School" in a short article for the inaugural issue of *Zhongguo bijiao wenxue* (Comparative literature in China), 1984, no. 1: 9. Other endorsements are made by Jia Zhifang and Ji Xianlin; see Sun Jingyao, "Wei 'Zhongguo xuepai' yibian" (An argument in favor of the "Chinese school"), *Wenxue pinglun*, 1991, no. 2: 42–43.

16. Deeney, "Modern Developments," p. 58.

17. Ibid., p. 61. More specifically, Deeney promoted the study of "traditional Chinese literary criticism" in order for China "to maintain its cultural identity" (p. 59). In recent years, he narrowed the scope of his endeavors by positing "terminology translation" (i.e., the English translation of key critical terms and concepts in the Chinese tradition) and "comparative poetics" as "two especially useful ways of demonstrating some of the distinctively 'Chinese School' contributions to world letters" ("*Vale atque Ave*," pp. 3–5).

18. Cao, "Bijiao wenxue Zhongguo xuepai," pp. 19–40. Obviously, Cao's understanding of the three schools is rather reductionist, even though his intention might be justified on pedagogical grounds in China. In his schematic depiction, the "French school" excels in studying common themes, genres, and literary movements shared by (mostly European) national literatures, while the "American school" excels in studying the interrelationships between literature and other arts (e.g., painting, music, opera). For China to offer an "unique" contribution to the world, it has to be a cultural one, but Cao does not elaborate how, theoretically speaking, one can cross "cultural borders" and what, more fundamentally, is the difference between the "cultural" and the "national" borders.

19. Lawrence Grossberg, Cary Nelson, and Paula A. Treichler, eds., *Cultural Studies* (New York: Routledge: 1992), p. 1.

20. See Bernheimer, *Comparative Literature*.

21. John Deeney, for instance, has been working hard to dissociate this implication from his notion of the "Chinese school" (see "Modern Developments," p. 58; "*Vale atque Ave*," p. 4).

22. Among the five elected presidents of the AACCL so far, Xiaomei Chen (1987–88), Sheldon Hsiao-peng Lu (1991–92), and Gloria Shen (1995–96) received their Ph.D.'s in comparative literature from Indiana University, and Yingjin Zhang (1993–94) holds a faculty appointment there. Henry Remak and Ulrich

Weisstein, two key figures of the American school, are on the Indiana faculty, and so are Horst Frenz and Eugene Eoyang. Horst Frenz founded Indiana's Comparative Literature Department in 1949 and promoted a series of Oriental Conferences triennially from 1954 to 1987. Eugene Eoyang was president of the ACLA (1995–97) and one of the all-time supporters of the AACCL.

23. Quoted from Eugene Eoyang's personal communication to me dated August 11, 1995.

24. Pauline Yu, "Critical Theory and the Rethinking of Chinese Literary Studies," *Chinese/International Comparative Literature Bulletin* 6–7 (March 1994): 16.

25. For instance, the theme of the second AACCL conference was "Rethinking Critical Theory and Chinese Literary Studies"; that of the fourth conference was "Literature, History, Culture: Re-envisioning Chinese and Comparative Literature." For examples of recent engagements in critical debates, see Liu Kang, "Politics, Critical Paradigms: Reflections on Modern Chinese Literature Studies," *Modern China* 19, no. 1 (January 1993): 13–40; Zhang Longxi, "Out of the Cultural Ghetto: Theory, Politics, and the Study of Chinese Literature," ibid., pp. 71–101; and Yingjin Zhang, "Re-envisioning the Institution of Modern Chinese Literature Studies: Strategies of Positionality and Self-Reflexivity," *Positions* 1, no. 3 (Winter 1993): 816–32.

26. Cf. Eugene Eoyang's cautionary note in this regard: "Binary oppositions between Western and non-Western exclude a significant population of people who are both Western and non-Western, or to put it another way, who are both Chinese and non-Chinese." See his "Thinking Comparatively: Orienting the West and Occidenting the East," *Chinese/International Comparative Literature Bulletin* 6–7 (March 1994): 32.

27. Yu, "Critical Theory," p. 15; Eoyang, "Thinking Comparatively," p. 32.

28. Guillién, *Challenge of Comparative Literature*, pp. 93–105. Guillién arrives at these five categories after an extended survey of the taxonomies provided by the earlier scholars of comparative literature, such as Renato Poggioli, Paul Van Tieghen, Ulrich Weisstein, A. Owen Aldridge, and François Jost.

29. Andrew Plaks, "Full-length *Hsiao-shuo* and the Western Novel: A Generic Reappraisal," in Tay, Chou, and Yuan, *China and the West*, pp. 163–76; C. H. Wang, "The Bird as Messenger in Allegorical Poetry," ibid., pp. 69–76; Han-liang Chang, "Towards a Structural Generic Theory of T'ang *Ch'uan-chi*," in Deeney, *Chinese-Western Comparative Literature*, pp. 25–49; Marián Gálik, "The Comparative Aspects of the Genesis of Modern Chinese Literary Criticism," in Chou, *Chinese Text*, pp. 177–90; Tak-wai Wong, "Period Style and Periodization: A Survey of Theory and Practice in the Histories of Chinese and European Literature," in Tay, Chou, and Yuan, *China and the West*, pp. 45–67.

30. Stuart McDougal, "Breaking Away: President's Address," *ACLA Bulletin* 25, no. 1 (Fall-Winter 1994): 13.

31. Gerald Graff, *Professing Literature: An Institutional History* (Chicago: University of Chicago Press, 1987), p. 14.

32. See, for instance, James Clifford and George E. Marcus, eds., *Writing Culture: The Poetics and Politics of Ethnography* (Berkeley: University of California Press, 1986), and James Clifford, *The Predicament of Culture* (Cambridge, Mass.: Harvard University Press, 1988).

33. Gumbrecht, "Future of Literary Studies?" p. 511.

34. Yu, "Alienation Effects," p. 162. For her illustration by way of anecdotes, see her "Critical Theory," p. 15.

35. One such example is Fredric Jameson, whose study of Lao She's *Camel Xiangzi* is generally ignored in the China field, and whose theory of "national allegory" has encountered a great deal of resistance. See his "Literary Innovation and Modes of Production: A Commentary," *Modern Chinese Literature* 1, no. 1 (Spring 1985): 67–77, and "Third-World Literature in the Era of Multinational Capitalism," *Social Text* 15 (Fall 1986): 65–88.

36. Yu, "Alienation Effects," p. 162. Admittedly, in Chinese-speaking cultural areas, the situation differs drastically from the one I describe here. At least in those prestigious Chinese departments on the mainland and in Taiwan and Hong Kong, philological work still commands respect and comparative literature is relatively new. To say the least, Western theory does not have much effect in the research of ancient or classical Chinese literature.

37. Chow, *Woman and Chinese Modernity*, p. xii. She further claims that her "use of 'Western theory' to understand the non-West is . . . a reversal of what happens historically" and would thus correct the unequal distribution of power and knowledge (p. xvi).

38. For instance, Rey Chow's recent book on contemporary Chinese cinema is packaged and distributed as "a rejoinder to some of the most urgent debates about cross-cultural studies, sexuality, ethnicity, identity, authenticity, and commodity fetishism" in the West; see the back cover of her *Primitive Passions: Visuality, Sexuality, Ethnography, and Contemporary Chinese Cinema* (New York: Columbia University Press, 1995).

39. James J. Y. Liu's works are the early examples of this influential method; see his *Art of Chinese Poetry* (Chicago: University of Chicago Press, 1962), and *Chinese Theories of Literature* (Chicago: University of Chicago Press, 1975). Pauline Yu further enhances this method with *The Reading of Imagery in Chinese Poetry* (Princeton, N.J.: Princeton University Press, 1987). Recent books on comparative poetics and aesthetics include Zhang Longxi, *The Tao and the Logos: Literary Hermeneutics, East and West* (Durham, N.C.: Duke University Press, 1992); Eugene Eoyang, *The Transparent Eye: Translation, Chinese Literature and Comparative Poetics* (Honolulu: University of Hawaii Press, 1993); and Haun Saussy, *The Problem of a Chinese Aesthetic* (Stanford, Calif.: Stanford University Press, 1993). Many essays on Chinese comparative literature that appeared in recent issues of *Comparative*

Literature Studies and *Canadian Review of Comparative Literature* fall in the category of comparative poetics.

40. The contestation with Western theory by way of a critical reading of Chinese texts is a characteristic of many essays collected in Liu Kang and Xiaobing Tang, eds., *Politics, Ideology, and Literary Discourse in Modern China: Theoretical Interventions and Cultural Critique*, foreword by Fredric Jameson (Durham, N.C.: Duke University Press, 1993).

41. As Perry Link assures us, "No one should doubt that the generation of the 1980s is a most welcome addition to the modern Chinese literature field" ("Ideology and Theory," p. 7). In a more enthusiastic way, Pauline Yu states: "Young [Chinese] scholars in particular in the United States who are bringing new theoretical perspectives and inquiry to their research on Chinese literature have attracted great attention to their work, are effecting a slow but discernible sea change in the field, and are changing the face of institutions who are increasingly eager to recruit them" ("Critical Theory," p. 9). The "sea change" Pauline Yu describes here is predicted to have a long-term effect, as Leo Ou-fan Lee assesses the essays based on the first AACCL conference held at Duke University in October 1990: "It is a volume with which the next generation of students of modern Chinese literature will have to come to terms" ("Postscript," in Liu and Tang, *Politics, Ideology, and Literary Discourse*, p. 301).

42. See Chen Pingyuan, "Jin bainian Zhongguo jingying wenhua de shiluo" (The downfall of the Chinese elite culture over the past century), *Ershiyi shiji* (The twenty-first century) 17 (June 1993): 11–22; see also a critical forum chaired by Wang Xiaoming, significantly titled "Kuangye shangde feixu" (Ruins in the barren land), *Shanghai wenxue*, 1993, no. 6: 63–71.

43. See, for instance, Chen Xiaoming's "Tianping honggou, huaqing jiexian—'jingying' yu 'dazhong' shutu tonggui de dangdai chaoliu" (Fill in the gap, draw up the dividing line: A contemporary trend whereby the "elite" and the "popular" converge and move in one direction), *Wenyi yanjiu*, 1994, no. 1: 42–55.

44. These fashionable "post's" are listed by Zhao Yiheng in a sarcastic way; see his "'Houxue' yu Zhongguo xin baoshou zhuyi" ("Post-ism" and Chinese neoconservatism), *Ershiyi shiji* 27 (February 1995): 4. Zhao's essay generated a heated debate in the subsequent issues of *Ershiyi shiji* up to the end of 1996. For an English version of Zhao's essay as well as other relevant issues, see "Cultural Studies: China and the West," *New Literary History* 28, no. 1 (Winter 1997).

45. Lydia H. Liu, *Translingual Practice: Literature, National Culture, and Translated Modernity—China, 1900–1937* (Stanford, Calif.: Stanford University Press, 1995), p. xviii. An early version of chapter 2 of Liu's book was presented at the Princeton conference on which our current volume is based.

46. I borrowed the term "polycentric world" from Aihwa Ong and Donald Nonini, eds., *Ungrounded Empires: The Cultural Politics of Modern Chinese Transnationalism* (London: Routledge, 1997), p. 15. For more elaboration on these issues in terms of transnational studies, see the concluding section in Yingjin Zhang,

"Chinese Cinema and Transnational Cultural Politics: Reflections on Film Festivals, Film Productions, and Film Studies," *Journal of Modern Literature in Chinese* 2, no. 1 (Spring 1998): 108–35.

1. East-West Comparative Literature

1. Susan Bassnett, *Comparative Literature: A Critical Introduction* (Oxford: Blackwell, 1993), p. 41.
2. Ibid., p. 47.
3. Ibid., p. 9.
4. Ibid., p. 48.
5. For a critique of postcolonial intellectuals and their theories, see Arif Dirlik, "The Postcolonial Aura: Third World Criticism in the Age of Global Capitalism," *Critical Inquiry* 20 (Winter 1994): 328–56. For a critical yet sympathetic consideration of the use of subaltern theory in the Chinese context, see Gail Hershatter, "The Subaltern Talks Back: Reflections on Subaltern Theory and Chinese History," *Positions* 1 (Spring 1993): 103–30, and Jing Wang, "The Mirage of 'Chinese Postmodernism': Ge Fei, Self-Positioning, and the Avant-Garde Showcase," *Positions* 1 (Fall 1993): 349–88.
6. Jonathan Hart, "The Ever-changing Configurations of Comparative Literature," *Canadian Review of Comparative Literature / Revue Canadienne de Littérature Comparée* 19 (March/June 1992): 2.
7. Ibid., p. 3.
8. Claudio Guillén, *The Challenge of Comparative Literature*, trans. Cola Franzen (Cambridge, Mass.: Harvard University Press, 1993), p. 16.
9. Ibid., p. 85.
10. David Palumbo-Liu, "The Utopias of Discourse: On the Impossibility of Chinese Comparative Literature," *CLEAR* 14 (1992): 165.
11. Dominic Baker-Smith, *More's Utopia* (London: HarperCollins, 1991), p. 75.
12. Quentin Skinner, "Sir Thomas More's *Utopia* and the Language of Renaissance Humanism," in Anthony Pagden, ed., *The Languages of Political Theory in Early-Modern Europe* (Cambridge: Cambridge University Press, 1987), p. 123.
13. For the "revival of the Utopian impulse" in Western Marxism, see Fredric Jameson, *Marxism and Form: Twentieth-Century Dialectical Theories of Literature* (Princeton, N.J.: Princeton University Press, 1971), pp. 110–14 (on Marcuse), and pp. 120–58 (on Bloch). For emphasis on the political and ideological significance of the utopian vision, see Vincent Geoghegan, *Utopianism and Marxism* (London: Methuen, 1987); for an argument for the continuing appeal of utopia in a humanistic Marxism, see Zhang Longxi, "Marxism: From Scientific to Utopian," in Bernd Magnus and Stephen Cullenberg, eds., *Whither Marxism? Global Crises in International Perspective* (New York: Routledge, 1995), pp. 65–77.
14. Krishan Kumar, "The End of Socialism? The End of Utopia? The End of

History?" in Krishan Kumar and Stephen Bann, eds., *Utopias and the Millennium* (London: Reaktion Books, 1993), pp. 63–80. For a comprehensive and commodious study of utopia, see Krishan Kumar, *Utopia and Anti-Utopia in Modern Times* (Oxford: Blackwell, 1987).

15. See Qian Zhongshu, *Tanyi lu* (Discourses on the literary art) (Beijing: Zhonghua shuju, 1984) and *Guanzhui bian* (The tube and awl chapters), 4 vols. (Beijing: Zhonghua shuju, 1979).

16. See John J. Deeney, "Modern Developments in Chinese-Western Comparative Literature Studies: A Golden Decade (1977–1987) for the 'Chinese School,'" *Tamkang Review* 18 (Autumn 1987–Summer 1988): 39–64; Yang Zhouhan, "Bufang xianyou chengli Zhongguo xuepai de shexiang" (Envisioning the Chinese school of comparative literature), *Zhongguo bijiao wenxue* 1984, no. 1: 8–10; and Chen Peng-hsiang, "Jianli bijiao wenxue Zhongguo xuepai de lilun he buzhou" (Theory and strategies for building the Chinese school of comparative literature), *Zhongwai wenxue* 19 (June 1990): 103–21.

17. Guillén, *Challenge of Comparative Literature*, p. 47.

18. Ibid., p. 61. 19. Ibid., p. 41.

20. Ibid., pp. 69, 70. 21. Ibid., p. 70.

22. Risking conspicuous oversight on my part of some important works that may support my claim, I want nevertheless to mention specifically two recent studies of Matteo Ricci as shining examples: Haun Saussy, *The Problem of a Chinese Aesthetic* (Stanford, Calif.: Stanford University Press, 1993), esp. pp. 13–46; and Lionel M. Jensen, "The Invention of 'Confucius' and His Chinese Other, 'Kong Fuzi,'" *Positions* 1 (Fall 1993): 414–49. In mainland China, interest has been recently revived in Ricci and the early contact between Jesuit missionaries and Chinese culture. Zhu Weizheng has some excellent discussion in *Zouchu zhongshiji* (Out of the middle ages) (Shanghai: Shanghai renmin chubanshe, 1987), esp. pp. 142–221; Zhu also edited an important collection of essays, *Jidujiao yu jindai wenhua* (Christianity and modern culture) (Shanghai: Shanghai renmin chubanshe, 1994). We have of course the classic example of a study of literary contacts and transformations between China and the West in an essay by Qian Zhongshu, "Hanyi diyishou Yingyu shi 'Rensheng song' ji youguan ersan shi" (*The Psalm of Life*: the first English poem rendered into Chinese), in *Qizhui ji* (Collection of seven essays) (Shanghai: Shanghai guji chubanshe, 1985), pp. 117–42.

23. Heh-hsiang Yuan, "East-West Comparative Literature: An Inquiry into Possibilities," in John J. Deeney, ed., *Chinese-Western Comparative Literature: Theory and Strategy* (Hong Kong: Chinese University Press, 1980), p. 21.

24. V. M. Zhirmunsky, "Syntaktischer Parallelismus und rhythmische Bindung im alttürkischen epischen Vers," in *Beiträge zur Sprachwissenschaft, Volkskunde und Literaturforschung, Wolfgang Steinitz zum 60. Geburtstag* (Berlin: Akademie-Verlag, 1965), p. 290; quoted in Guillén, *Challenge of Comparative Literature*, p. 79.

25. See Yu-kung Kao and Tsu-lin Mei, "Meaning, Metaphor, and Allusion in T'ang Poetry," *Harvard Journal of Asiatic Studies* 38 (December 1978): 281–356.

26. Andrew Plaks, "Where the Lines Meet: Parallelism in Chinese and Western Literatures," *CLEAR* 10 (July 1988): 47.

27. Ibid., pp. 48, 49.

28. Guillén, *Challenge of Comparative Literature*, p. 77.

29. Roland Barthes, "From Work to Text," in his *Image-Music-Text*, trans. Stephen Heath (New York: Hill & Wang, 1977), p. 155.

2. Utopias of Discourse

A shorter version of this essay was presented at the Second American Conference of the Association of Chinese Comparative Literature, "Chinese Literature and Critical Theory," held at UCLA in March 1992. It was first published in CLEAR 14 (1992): 165–76.

1. One such attempt is Stephen Owen, "Ruined Estates," *CLEAR* 10 (1988): 21–41.

2. All quotations in this paragraph are taken from the *Oxford English Dictionary*, 2d edition (Oxford: Clarendon Press, 1989), 4: 750–51.

3. Paul Kroll, review of Ronald C. Miao, ed., *Studies in Chinese Poetry and Poetics*, vol. 1, in *CLEAR* 2 (1980): 149.

4. Stephen Owen, "A Defense," *CLEAR* 1 (1979): 258.

5. From *L'Avenir de la science*, quoted in Edward Said, *Orientalism* (New York: Vintage Books, 1979), p. 132.

6. Kroll, review of Miao, p. 147.

7. Jonathan Chaves, "From the 1990 AAS Roundtable," *CLEAR* 13 (1991): 80.

8. Kroll, review of Miao, p. 148.

9. Chaves, "From the 1990 AAS," p. 77.

10. Paul De Man, *The Resistance to Theory* (Minneapolis: University of Minnesota Press, 1986), p. 21.

11. Chaves, "From the 1990 AAS," p. 80.

12. Ibid., p. 77.

13. James Woods, "Literature its own best theory?" *Times Literary Supplement*, June 7, 1991.

14. Chaves, "From the 1990 AAS," p. 80.

15. Jonathan Chaves, "Not the Way of Poetry," *CLEAR* (July 1982): 199–212.

16. Richard John Lynn, *Journal of Asian Studies* 36 (May 1977): 551–54; Jonathan Chaves, ibid., 37 (November 1977): 186–88; Edward Schafer, ibid., 37 (August 1978): 799–800.

17. Chaves, p. 187.

18. Gayatri Spivak, "Practical Politics of the Open End," in Sarah Harasym, ed., *The Post-colonial Critic* (New York: Routledge, 1990), p. 104.

19. Andre Lefevre, "Some Tactical Steps Toward a Common Poetics," in William Tay et al., eds., *China and the West: Comparative Literature Studies* (Hong Kong: Chinese University Press, 1980), p. 13.

20. Ibid., p. 20.

21. Heh-hsiang Yüan, "East-West Comparative Literature: An Inquiry into Possibilities," in John Deeney, ed., *Chinese-Western Comparative Literature: Theory and Strategy* (Hong Kong: Chinese University Press, 1980), p. 4.

22. Ibid., p. 5.

23. The literature on the subject is vast. Some easily accessible titles: Terry Eagleton, *The Ideology of the Aesthetic* (Cambridge: Basil Blackwell, 1990) and *The Function of Criticism* (London: Verso, 1984); Peter Uwe Hohendhal, *The Institution of Criticism* (Ithaca, N.Y.: Cornell University Press, 1982); and Barbara Herrnstein Smith, *Contingencies of Value* (Cambridge, Mass.: Harvard University Press, 1988).

24. Yüan, "East-West Comparative Literature," p. 8.

25. Ibid., p. 21.

26. Gayatri Spivak, *In Other Worlds* (New York: Routledge, 1988), p. 175.

27. Chaves, "From the 1990 AAS," p. 82.

28. Eagleton, *The Function of Criticism*, p. 124.

3. Chinese Canons, Sacred and Profane

1. Barbara Herrnstein Smith, "Contingencies of Value," in Robert van Hallberg, ed., *Canons* (Chicago: University of Chicago Press, 1984), p. 21.

2. The distinctions are implied by the respective etymologies. "Canon" derives from the Greek *kanon* for "reed" or "rod," meaning an instrument of "measure"; it subsequently developed the sense of "rule" or "law," and ultimately came to signify compliance with specifically ecclesiastical standards. "Classic" was first used to refer to select works of literature by Aulus Gellius in the second century; in its previous contexts, "the social application of the term which Aulus is adapting" pertained to the tax-paying class, i.e., it referred to what we would call the "aristocratic." See John Guillory, "Canon," in Frank Lentricchia and Thomas McLaughlin, eds., *Critical Terms for Literary Study* (Chicago: University of Chicago Press, 1990), p. 233, and Frank Kermode, *The Classic* (Cambridge, Mass.: Harvard University Press, 1983), p. 15.

3. For example, by James Legge, *The Chinese Classics* series (Oxford: Clarendon Press, 1895); John B. Henderson, *Scripture, Canon, and Commentary: A Comparison of Confucian and Western Exegesis* (Princeton, N.J.: Princeton University Press, 1991), p. 11; and Peter K. Bol, *"This Culture of Ours": Intellectual Transitions in T'ang and Sung China* (Stanford, Calif.: Stanford University Press, 1992), p. 112.

4. Pi Xirui, *Jingxue lishi* (History of classic studies) (Beijing: Zhonghua, 1959); Henderson, *Scripture*.

5. Thus, Herbert Fingarette's characterization: *Confucius—The Secular as Sacred* (New York: Harper & Row, 1972).

6. David McMullen's *State and Scholars in T'ang China* (Cambridge: Cambridge University Press, 1988) is a general study of the role of the Confucians within the Tang imperial system which examines the functions and interrelations

of canonical scholarship, the cult of Confucius, official education, and the civil service examination system. On the subject of state ritual, see Howard J. Wechsler, *Offerings of Jade and Silk: Ritual and Symbol in the Legitimation of the T'ang Dynasty* (New Haven, Conn.: Yale University Press, 1985).

7. The *Shijing* is believed to include materials that, like sections of the *Classic of Changes* (Yijing) and the *Classic of Documents* (Shujing), date from the Western Zhou (c. 1200–771 B.C.). Cf. H. G. Creel, *The Origins of Statecraft in China* (Chicago: University of Chicago Press, 1970), pp. 444–63.

8. The matter is, in fact, somewhat complicated. According to one view, as represented in the *Huainanzi, Shuoyuan,* and other texts, the *Shijing* and the other Zhou classics are all products of a Golden Age in its *decline,* although they remain "epitomes of learning," nonetheless. For a brief discussion of the associations traditional commentators have perceived between the political and moral order of the Zhou and the Confucian canon, see Henderson, *Scripture,* pp. 24–26.

9. For Xunzi's critical role in the formation of the Confucian *jing,* see Steven Van Zoeren, *Poetry and Personality: Reading, Exegesis, and Hermeneutics in Traditional China* (Stanford, Calif.: Stanford University Press, 1991), pp. 74–79; John Knoblock, *Xunzi: A Translation and Study of the Complete Works,* vol. 1, *Books 1–6* (Stanford, Calif.: Stanford University Press, 1988), pp. 41–49.

10. Van Zoeren, *Poetry and Personality,* pp. 25–48; Donald Holzman, "Confucius and Ancient Chinese Literary Criticism," in Adele Austin Rickett, ed., *Chinese Approaches to Literature* (Princeton, N.J.: Princeton University Press, 1978), pp. 33–35.

11. The Han historian Sima Qian is regarded as the source of the legend, in *Shiji* (Taibei: Dashen, 1982), 47: 1936.

12. Van Zoeren, *Poetry and Personality,* p. 219.

13. These poems have often been compared with "The Song of Songs," since their natures and the problems they have caused for orthodox interpreters seem similar.

14. Van Zoeren, *Poetry and Personality,* pp. 76–79, 169–71, 218–22, 228–29, 247.

15. Zhu Xi, *Zhu wengong wenji* (Collected works of Master Zhu), *Sibu congkan* edition, 76: 13a–14b. Cf. Richard John Lynn, "Chu Hsi as Literary Theorist and Critic," in Wing-tsit Chan, ed., *Chu Hsi and Neo-Confucianism* (Honolulu: University of Hawaii Press, 1986), pp. 343–46. The notion of *bian feng,* "changed Airs," and *bian ya,* "changed Odes," in the *Shijing* first appears in the Great Preface; also, Zheng Xuan of the Han dynasty, rather than Zhu Xi, is credited with the interpretation of *bian* as marking a decline. However, the meaning of *bian* in this context is debatable.

16. Cf. Van Zoeren, *Poetry and Personality,* pp. 116–253; Daniel K. Gardner, *Chu Hsi and the Ta-hsueh: Neo-Confucian Reflection on the Confucian Canon* (Cambridge, Mass.: Harvard University Press, 1986).

17. C. H. Wang's views are representative: "In Confucius' time the poetry of

ancient China ... was taking its final, definite shape; its prototypical form, of great diversity and unity, was becoming for the Chinese in the following millennia the form of *Shih Ching*. The form of *Shih Ching* was the only basic form of *shih*, or poetry; and the content, which the form defines, embodies some of the most trenchant and surging themes to recur and vary throughout the Chinese tradition." See his *Bell and the Drum: Shih Ching as Formulaic Poetry in an Oral Tradition* (Berkeley: University of California Press, 1974), p. ix.

18. Western literary histories of Chinese poetry typically adopt the traditional Chinese perspective in a wholesale manner, employing a vocabulary of "decline," "eclipse," "revival," and "development" to construct a "super"-generic genealogy that proceeds from the *Shijing* poems, culminates in the Tang, and runs on weakly but uninterrupted through the last dynasties of the empire. Ostensibly presenting their analyses in formal terms, the historians do not pause to doubt the basic validity and utility of the model of generic continuity, much less point out the ideological factors that may support or demand it. See esp. Burton Watson, *Chinese Lyricism: Shih Poetry from the Second to the Twelfth Century* (New York: Columbia University Press, 1971), and the essays by both modern Chinese and Western scholars in Shuen-fu Lin and Stephen Owen, eds., *The Vitality of the Lyric Voice: Shih Poetry from the Late Han to the T'ang* (Princeton, N.J.: Princeton University Press, 1986).

19. Foreword to Arthur Waley's translation, *The Book of Songs* (New York: Grove Press, 1987), p. xxiv.

20. Henderson, *Scripture*, pp. 24–26.

21. See Holzman, "Confucius," and Van Zoeren, *Poetry and Personality*, esp. pp. 80–115.

22. Owen, "Foreword," in Shuen-fu Lin and Owen, *Vitality*, p. xxxiv.

23. Confucius claimed that his task was to "transmit ... not innovate" (*Analects* VII.2); it is said that after he completed the compilation of the *Chunqiu* annals came news of a captured unicorn.

24. The standard edition of Li Bo's poetry is that of Wang Qi, which appears in the *Sibu congkan* and has been reprinted in China as *Li Taibai quanji* (The complete works of Li Taibai) (Beijing: Zhonghua, 1958). Therein, the "Ancient Airs" are preceded only by the "Ancient-Style Rhapsodies" series (*gufu*, another highly orthodox form with sanctioned themes). See discussion below on the metrical influence of the *Chuci* tradition and later comments on the *Wenxuan*.

25. On the practice of poetic composition during the Tang, see McMullen, *State and Scholars*, pp. 206–50; on the nature of Tang historical writing, see ibid., pp. 159–205.

26. I prefer to contrast respective social functions and styles, rather than draw a strict boundary between fiction and nonfiction. Recent scholars, notably Stephen Owen and Pauline Yu, have argued vigorously for the nonfictional reading of Chinese poetry.

27. The most respected work of traditional fiction by general acclaim, *Dream of the Red Chamber* (Hongloumeng), perhaps owes not a little of its prestige to the

salient way in which it appropriates the poetic tradition, by means of its own lyrical qualities, the direct use of classical poetic compositions within the text, and the lengthy and very serious conversations by the novel's characters about the reading and writing of traditional verse. See Yu-kung Kao, "Lyric Vision in Chinese Narrative: A Reading of *Hung-lou Meng* and *Ju-lin Wai-shih*," and Wong Kam-ming, "Point of View, Norms, and Structure: *Hung-lou Meng* and Lyrical Fiction," in Andrew H. Plaks, ed., *Chinese Narrative: Critical and Theoretical Essays* (Princeton, N.J.: Princeton University Press, 1977).

28. David Hawkes, trans., *The Songs of the South: An Anthology of Ancient Chinese Poems by Qu Yuan and Other Poets* (New York: Penguin, 1985), p. 15.

29. Ibid., p. 26. See also the first edition of this book, David Hawkes, trans., *Ch'u Tz'u: The Songs of the South, An Ancient Chinese Anthology* (Oxford: Oxford University Press, 1959), pp. 9–10.

30. Ibid.

31. Wang Yi, *Chuci zhangju* (The songs of the south annotated) (Taibei: Yiwen, 1967), pp. 69–72. Cf. Laurence A. Schneider, *A Madman of Ch'u: The Chinese Myth of Loyalty and Dissent* (Berkeley: University of California Press, 1980), pp. 18–31.

32. Schneider, *A Madman of Ch'u*, pp. 25–27.

33. Liu Xie, *Wenxin diaolong*, "Bian Sao"; translation from Vincent Shih, *The Literary Mind and the Carving of Dragons* (New York: Columbia University Press, 1959), chap. 5, p. 28.

34. Shih, *Literary Mind*, pp. 28–29.

35. Ibid., p. 29. The Three Dynasties are the Zhou together with the Xia and Shang which preceded it; the Warring States period is the era of political disunity that occurred between the Zhou and the Han reigns. *Feng* (airs), *ya* (elegentia), and *song* (hymns) are subgenres of the *Shijing*.

36. Zhu Xi, *Zhu Wengong wenji*, 76: 33Ab–34b; translation from Richard Lynn, "Chu Hsi," p. 346.

37. Hawkes, *Ch'u Tz'u*, pp. 3, 7.

38. It also is pertinent to earlier remarks about the collected poetry of Li Bo, in which his *gushi* (Ancient-style airs) are preceded by his *gufu* (Ancient-style rhapsodies).

39. Burton Watson, *Chinese Rhyme-Prose: Poems in the Fu Form from the Han and Six Dynasties Period* (New York: Columbia University Press, 1971), pp. 2–4.

40. See especially Pauline Yu, "Poems in Their Place: Collections and Canons in Early Chinese Literature," *Harvard Journal of Asiatic Studies* 50, no. 1 (June 1990): 163–96; Adele Austin Rickett, "The Anthologist as Literary Critic in China," *Literature East and West* 19, nos. 1–4 (January–December 1975): 145–65; and Wang Yao, *Guanyu Zhongguo gudian wenxue wenti* (On issues related to Chinese classical literature) (Shanghai: Gudian, 1956), p. 46.

41. Yu, "Poems in Their Place," pp. 168–71; Rickett, "Anthologist."

42. David R. Knechtges, *Wen xuan, or Selections of Refined Literature* (Princeton, N.J.: Princeton University Press, 1982), pp. 1–2, p. 486 nn. 1–2.

43. Ibid., pp. 24–27.
44. *Wen xuan*, ll. 122–23; Knechtges translation, p. 87.
45. Cf. James R. Hightower, "The Wen Hsüan and Genre Theory," *Harvard Journal of Asiatic Studies* 20 (1957): 512–33; reprinted in John L. Bishop, ed., *Studies in Chinese Literature* (Cambridge, Mass.: Harvard University Press, 1965), pp. 142–63.
46. *Wen xuan*, ll. 23–24; Knechtges translation, p. 75.
47. *Wen xuan*, ll. 37–40; Knechtges translation, p. 75.
48. *Wen xuan*, l. 54; Knechtges translation, p. 77.
49. Anne Birrell, trans., *New Songs from a Jade Terrace* (New York: Penguin, 1986), p. 6.
50. Ibid., p. 2.
51. Ibid., pp. 4–5.
52. James R. Hightower, *Topics in Chinese Literature* (Cambridge, Mass.: Harvard University Press, 1962), p. 46; Ronald C. Miao, "Palace-Style Poetry: The Courtly Treatment of Glamour and Love," in Miao, ed., *Studies in Chinese Poetry and Poetics* (San Francisco: Chinese Materials Center, 1978), 1: 8 n. 10. Cf. Emperor Jianwen (viz. Xiao Gang), "Yu Xiangdong Wang shu," in *Quan Liang wen* (The complete works of the Liang dynasty), 11: 3–4.
53. Miao, "Palace-Style Poetry," p. 8.
54. In Hightower's numbering, line 72; my translation. Cf. Hightower, "Some Characteristics of Parallel Prose," in Bishop, *Topics*, p. 132, and Birrell, *New Songs*, p. 340.
55. *Yutai xinyong*, preface, ll. 81–84; Hightower, *Topics*, p. 133; Birrell, *New Songs*.
56. Miao, "Palace-Style Poetry," pp. 1–42.
57. As demarcated by Lin Wen-yüeh, "The Decline and Revival of *Feng-ku* (Wind and Bone): On the Changing Poetic Styles from the Chien-an Era through the High T'ang Period," in Shuen-fu Lin and Owen, *Vitality*, p. 131.
58. See ibid., pp. 130–66.
59. The fourth line may be read, "Ornateness not enough to be worthy of treasuring," which suggests a more paradoxical judgment—and perhaps subtly communicates Li Bo's own problematical relation to the orthodox.
60. As collected in *Tangren xuan Tangshi* (Tang poetry collected by the men of the Tang) (Beijing: Zhonghua, 1960), these include the following titles (with names of original editors and probable dates of compilation): *Caidiao ji*, Wei Hu, 935; *Guoxiu ji*, Rui Tingzhang, mid-eighth cent.; *Heyue yingling ji*, Yin Fan, 753; *Jixuan ji*, Yao He, 830; *Qiezhong ji*, Yuan Jie, 760; *Souyu xiao ji*, anon., 725–50; *Tang xieben Tangren xuan Tang shi*, anon., 740–50; *Youxuan ji*, Wei Zhuang, 900; *Yulan shi*, Linghu Chu, 806–20; and *Zhongxing xianqi ji*, Gao Zhongwu, 780–90. Six of these anthologies—*Guoxiu ji*, *Heyue yingling ji*, *Jixuan ji*, *Qiezhong ji*, *Souyu xiao ji*, and *Zhongxing xianqi ji*—were published together in one volume by an unknown editor between 1522 and 1566. Between 1628 and 1643, these were edited and

again published (as *Tangren xuan Tangshi*) by Mao Jin (1599–1659) with two additions, *Caidiao ji* and *Yulan shi*. To the Zhonghua shuju edition, first published in 1958, two further anthologies were added: *Tang xieben xuan Tang shi* and *Youxuan ji* (the former from a manuscript found at Dunhuang).

61. Yu, "Poems in Their Place," p. 194.

62. Five of the ten "Tang" anthologies were compiled between 740 and 760, and a sixth in 780. Of the remaining four, two were put together in the early ninth century, one dates from the final years of the dynasty in the early tenth century, while the most recent is in actuality a product of the Five Dynasties period. None was compiled more than a decade prior to the An Lushan Rebellion of 755–63—a watershed event which was preceded by a series of imperial difficulties on the battlefield and in administration, and whose conclusion marked an irremediable downturn in the dynasty's fortunes. The political and social fragmentation that occurred during the two centuries in point, and the sense of crisis it must have aroused in the educated elite, which sought a variety of solutions to the situation, conceivably contributed to the perceived diversity of these anthologizing efforts—as well as to their strongly polemical aspects and other qualities (as discussed further below). Cf. David McMullen, "Historical and Literary Theory in the Mid-Eighth Century," in Arthur F. Wright and Denis Twitchett, eds., *Perspectives on the T'ang* (New Haven, Conn.: Yale University Press, 1973), pp. 307–42.

63. *Yulan shi* was compiled by imperial command in the Yuanhe reign. It consists of 289 poems by only thirty poets, mostly writers popular in the later eighth century.

64. Yu, "Poems in Their Place," pp. 182–83.

65. Ibid., p. 183.

66. Ibid., p. 182.

67. Stephen Owen, *The Poetry of Meng Chiao and Han Yü* (New Haven, Conn.: Yale University Press, 1975), esp. pp. 1–24; McMullen, "Historical and Literary Theory"; Bol, *"This Culture of Ours."*

68. Yu, "Poems in Their Place," pp. 194–95.

69. See Stephen Owen, "Ruined Estates: Literary History and the Poetry of Eden," *Chinese Literature: Essays, Articles, Reviews* 10 (1988): 21–41.

70. Rickett, "Anthologist," pp. 153–56.

71. Ibid., p. 153.

4. Xu Wei's 'Ci Mulan' and 'Nü zhuangyuan'

1. Taking terminology from James Watson and Denis Twitchett, Dorothy Ko argues that "Inner/outer is a relational category that describes a series of nested hierarchies whose boundary changes with context." See her *Teacher of the Inner Chambers: Women and Culture in Seventeenth-Century China* (Stanford, Calif.: Stanford University Press, 1994), pp. 144–45. By calling this ambiguity "sociological

ambivalence," Ambrose Y. C. King makes a similar argument: "There are tensions and conflicts between Confucian cultural aspirations and structural norms. . . . Actual role transactions are more or less the result of a stable working compromise between ideal prescription and a flexible role-making process." See his essay "The Individual and Group in Confucianism: A Relational Perspective," in Donald J. Munro, ed., *Individualism and Holism: Studies in Confucian and Taoist Values* (Ann Arbor: University of Michigan Press, 1985), pp. 60–61.

2. See Qian Mu, *Zhuzi xinxue an* (New study records of Zhuzi) (Taipei: Sanmin, 1971), p. 289.

3. Michael D. Bristol, "Subversion," in Irena R. Makaryk, ed., *Encyclopedia of Contemporary Literary Theory: Approaches, Scholars, Terms* (Toronto: University of Toronto Press, 1993), p. 636.

4. Ibid., p. 637. Bristol here rephrases Althusser's view that subversion is "always already" contained by dominant structure and is therefore self-defeating.

5. For an exploration of the notion of counterculture and heterodoxy, see Charlotte Furth, "The Patriarch's Legacy: Household Instructions and the Transmission of Orthodox Values," in Kwang-Ching Liu, ed., *Orthodoxy in Late Imperial China* (Berkeley: University of California Press, 1990), pp. 206–7.

6. This view can be found in a number of writings, such as Yu Weimin, "Mingdai xiqu chuangzuo qingxiang de bianqian" (The transmutation of dramatic creation in the Ming dynasty), *Zhonghua xiqu* 14 (August 1993): 398, and Zhang Xiaoyu, *Xu Wei yanjiu* (The study of Xu Wei) (Taipei: Xuehai, 1978), p. 147.

7. Liu Dajie, *Zhongguo wenxue fazhan shi* (The history of the development of Chinese literature) (Taipei: Huazheng, 1988), p. 1018.

8. Stephen Greenblatt, *Renaissance Self-Fashioning: From More to Shakespeare* (Chicago: University of Chicago Press, 1980), p. 4.

9. See Mary Beth Rose, ed., *Women in the Middle Ages and the Renaissance: Literary and Historical Perspectives* (Syracuse, N.Y.: Syracuse University Press, 1986), p. 147. See also Karen Newman, *Fashioning Femininity and English Renaissance Drama* (Chicago: University of Chicago Press, 1991), p. 48.

10. See Keith McMahon, *Misers, Shrews, and Polygamists: Sexuality and Male-Female Relations in Eighteenth-Century Chinese Fiction* (Durham, N.C.: Duke University Press, 1995), p. 124.

11. Confucius expressed his distaste of fixed principle in a number of lines such as in *Lunyü* 13: 20, 14: 24, and 15: 26; Mencius developed the notion of expediency (*quan*); see *Mengzi*, in *Xinyi sishu duben* (New interpretations of four books) (Taipei: Sanmin, 1987), p. 480.

12. *Ci Mulan* and *Nü zhuangyuan* are collected under "*Sisheng yuan* jiaozhu" (Notes and commentaries on *Four shrieks of a gibbon*), in Liang Yicheng, ed., *Xu Wei de wenxue yu yishu* (Xu Wei's literature and arts) (Taipei: Yiwen, 1976), pp. 317–69.

13. Ibid., pp. 318–19. The translation of these passages is adapted from Jeannette Louise Faurot, "Four Cries of a Gibbon: A Tsa-chu Cycle by the Ming

Dramatist Hsu Wei (1521–1593)" (Ph.D. diss., University of California, Berkeley, 1972), pp. 86–87.

14. Liang Yicheng, *Xu Wei*, pp. 334–35.

15. See *Nü jie* (Admonishment for women), in Xie Wuliang, *Zhongguo funü wenxueshi* (History of Chinese women's literature) (Taipei: Zhonghua, 1979), p. 62.

16. Liang Yicheng, *Xu Wei*, p. 322.

17. See Juliet Dusinberre, *Shakespeare and the Nature of Women* (New York: Harper & Row, 1975), pp. 233, 265.

18. See Gao Dapeng, "Lun *Si sheng yuan*" (Discussing *Four shrieks of a gibbon*), *Zhonghua wenhua fuxing yuekan* 9, no. 11 (1976): 62.

19. Based on her revision of Freud, Nancy Chodorow argues that gender ideology is created through family patterns of child rearing. Although Chodorow's reliance on Freud's Oedipus complex does not readily translate to the Chinese situation, her notion that mothers reproduce the current gender system in their different ways of teaching sons and daughters appears valid here. See Chodorow, *The Reproduction of Mothering: Psychoanalysis and the Sociology of Gender* (Berkeley: University of California Press, 1978), p. 199.

20. Liang Yicheng, *Xu Wei*, p. 350.

21. For detailed discussion about various views of women's talent and virtue, see Wing-chung Clara Lau, " 'Talent' vs. 'Virtue': A Study of the Traditional Chinese Attitudes, with Special Reference to the Discussions on Women (1644-1795)," *Journal of Oriental Studies* 25, no. 1 (1988): 95–115.

22. Kirsten Hastrup, "The Semantics of Biology: Virginity," in Shirley Ardener, ed., *Defining Females: The Nature of Women in Society* (New York: Halsted Press, 1978), p. 55.

23. Liang Yicheng, *Xu Wei*, p. 323.

24. Ibid., p. 353.

25. Ibid.

26. For a detailed discussion on this topic, see Wing-chung Clara Lau, " 'Talent' vs 'Virtue.' "

27. Dorothy Ko, "Pursuing Talent and Virtue: Education and Women's Culture in Seventeenth- and Eighteenth-Century China," *Late Imperial China* 13, no. 1 (June 1992): 17.

28. Liang Yicheng, *Xu Wei*, p. 92.

29. Ibid., p. 351.

30. Mary Jacobus, *Reading Women: Essays in Feminist Criticism* (New York: Columbia University Press, 1986), p. 3.

31. Teresa de Lauretis, *Technologies of Gender: Essays on Theory, Film, and Fiction* (Bloomington: Indiana University Press, 1987), p. 2.

32. Maureen Robertson, "Voicing the Feminine: Constructions of the Gendered Subject in Lyric Poetry by Women of Medieval and Late Imperial China," *Late Imperial China* 13, no. 1 (June 1992): 67.

33. Judith Butler, *Gender Trouble* (London: Routledge, 1990), p. xiii.

34. See Charlotte Furth, "Androgynous Males and Deficient Females: Biology and Gender Boundaries in Sixteenth- and Seventeenth-Century China," *Late Imperial China* 9, no. 2 (December 1988): 3.

35. The notion of androgyny here denotes a combination of masculine and feminine qualities and implies bisexuality rather than gender neutrality. See Roger T. Ames, "Chinese Sexism: A Propaedeutic," in David L. Hall and Roger T. Ames, *Thinking from the Han: Self, Truth, and Transcendence in China and the West* (Albany, N.Y.: SUNY Press, 1997). For further discussion of bisexuality and women, see Sarah Kofman, *The Enigma of Woman: Woman in Freud's Writings*, trans. Catherine Porter (Ithaca, N.Y.: Cornell University Press, 1985), pp. 122–27.

36. Newman, *Fashioning Femininity*, p. 50.

37. For extensive writing about the literati's autobiographical treatment of their works, see Martin W. Huang, *Literati and Self-Re/Presentation: Autobiographical Sensibility in the Eighteenth-Century Chinese Novel* (Stanford, Calif.: Stanford University Press, 1995). About the literati's presence in dramatic texts, or their " 'autobiographical' appropriation of drama," see ibid., pp. 22–23.

38. Liang Yicheng, *Xu Wei*, pp. 184–85.

39. For a discussion of this economic boom, expanded education, and the prospects for scholars' official careers, see Evelyn S. Rawski, "Economic and Social Foundations of Late Imperial Culture," in David Johnson, Andrew J. Nathan, and Evelyn S. Rawski, eds., *Popular Culture in Late Imperial China* (Berkeley: University of California Press, 1985), pp. 7–14. See also Ping-Ti Ho, *The Ladder of Success in Imperial China: Aspects of Social Mobility, 1368–1911* (New York: Da Capo Press, 1976), pp. 89–92.

40. Robertson, "Voicing the Feminine," p. 66.

41. In his heyday (1554–62), Hu Zongxian was assigned to be commander of seven southeastern provinces; his main duty was fighting the Japanese pirates along the coast. See Liang Yicheng, *Xu Wei*, p. 186, and Tseng Yu-ho, "A Study on Hsü Wei," *Ars Oriental* 5 (1963): 245.

42. Among fifteen biographical accounts of Xu Wei (by Xu's contemporaries or later historians) compiled by Liang, more than half of them include accounts of Xu Wei's gruesome suicide attempts. See Liang Yicheng, *Xu Wei*, pp. 149–62.

43. See *Xu Wei ji* (The Collection of Xu Wei), vol. 2 (Beijing: Zhonghua shuju, 1983), p. 555.

44. See Tseng Yu-ho, "A Study on Hsü Wei," p. 243; see also Zhang Xiaoyu, *Xu Wei yanjiu*, p. 146.

45. See Xu Wei's "Ziwei muzhiming" (My obituary), in Liang Yicheng, *Xu Wei*, pp. 50–52. The fact that Xu Wei lost his father during his infancy and was raised by his stepmother till the age of fourteen perhaps had some links to Xu Wei's self-consciousness and his eccentric personality. See Tseng Yu-ho, "A Study on Hsü Wei," p. 244, and Liang Yicheng, *Xu Wei*, pp. 2–3.

46. Although it may be not completely applicable to Chinese childhood, Chodorow's psychoanalysis is worth quoting here. She considers that a mother plays an overwhelmingly important role in one's psychological development regarding the sense of self; she also states, in *Reproduction of Mothering*, pp. 76, 165, that a boy's major goal is to achieve "personal masculine identification with his father... through superego formation."

47. Tseng Yu-ho, "A Study on Hsü Wei," p. 249.

48. See Xu Wei's "Ziwei muzhiming," p. 51. Tseng Yu-ho has translated a large portion of Xu Wei's self-obituary; see "A Study on Hsü Wei," pp. 248–49.

49. Xu Wei's "Ziwei muzhiming," p. 51.

50. Xu Wei studied Buddhist thought and Daoism extensively and even personally practiced alchemy. See his autobiography "Chipu," in *Xu Wenchang yigao* (The manuscripts of Xu Wenchang) (Taipei: Danjiang, 1956). See also Liang Yicheng, *Xu Wei*, p. 175.

51. See Daniel L. Overmyer, "Attitudes Toward the Ruler and State in Chinese Popular Religious Literature: Sixteenth- and Seventeenth-Century *Paochuan*," *Harvard Journal of Asiatic Studies* 44, no. 2 (1984): 353. See also Yu Songqing, "Ming Qing shiqi minjian zongjiao jiaopai zhong de nüxing" (Women in the Ming Qing periods' folk religions), *Nankai xuebao* 1982, no. 5: 29–31.

52. See Xu Lun, *Xu Wenchang* (Shanghai: Shanghai renmin chubanshe, 1962), p. 69; Liang Yicheng, *Xu Wei*, p. 325; and Li Yumei, "Xu Wei dui shehuiji zhengzhi gaigezhi guannian" (Xu Wei's concepts of social and political reform) (master's thesis, University of Hong Kong, 1984), pp. 1186–87.

53. See, for instance, Xu Wenchang, *Xu Wenchang quanji* (The collected works of Xu Wenchang) (Hong Kong: Guangzhi), p. 59. Li Yumei also quotes numerous writings by Xu Wei to support this; see Li Yumei, "Xu Wei," pp. 1162–79.

54. T'ien Ju-K'ang views scholars who were defeated by the civil examination as those who became violently misogynistic and often projected their anxiety onto women. See T'ien Ju-K'ang, *Male Anxiety and Female Chastity* (Leiden, The Netherlands: E. J. Brill, 1988), pp. 147–48.

55. Liang Yicheng, *Xu Wei*, p. 27.

56. For a discussion of Yuan Hongdao's powerful resistance to the deep-rooted literary trends about reviving and imitating the ancient models, see Yuan Zhenyu and Liu Mingjin, *Mingdai wenxue piping shi* (History of Ming literary criticism) (Shanghai: Guji, 1991), pp. 442–61.

57. Ibid., p. 426.

58. Yuan Hongdao, "Xu Wenchang zhuang" (The biography of Xu Wenchang), in *Xu Wenchang sanji* (The three collections of Xu Wenchang) (Taipei: National Central Library, 1968), pp. 21–28. See also Liang Yicheng, *Xu Wei*, p. 148. The English translation is largely taken from Ming-Shui Hung, "Yuan Hung-tao and the Late Ming Literary and Intellectual Movement" (Ph.D. diss., University of Wisconsin, Madison, 1974), p. 121.

59. See Lü Kun, *Guifan* (The precepts of the women's quarters) (1590; a photocopy of the Ming edition, 1929), 2: 31–32. For an elaborate study of Lü Kun's *Guifan* and his emphasis on expediency, see Joanna F. Handlin, "Lü K'un's New Audience: The Influence of Women's Literacy on Sixteenth-Century Thought," in Margery Wolf and Roxanne Witke, eds., *Women in Chinese Society* (Stanford, Calif.: Stanford University Press, 1975), pp. 13–38.

60. See Tian Yiheng, *Liuqing rizha zhaichao* (The diary of Liuqing) (Taipei: Yiwen, 1966), 1: 13–14, and Xie Zhaozhi, *Wu zazu* (Shanghai: Zhongyuan, 1935), 1: 301–2.

61. Li Zhi, *Fenshu* (Burning books) (Beijing: Zhonghua, 1961), p. 57.

62. See, for instance, Liang Yicheng, *Xu Wei*, p. 369.

63. Xu Wei's writings about his first wife include at least a poem and an affectionate epitaph. See *Xu Wenchang sanji*, vols. 11, 26, and *Xu Wenchang quanji*, pp. 141, 310. See also Liang Yicheng, *Xu Wei*, pp. 8, 43, 370.

64. See Huang, *Literati and Self-Re/Presentation*, pp. 22, 25.

65. Wang Jide, "Qulü" (Regulations for drama), in *Zhongguo gudian xiqu lunzhu jicheng* (The anthology of classical Chinese drama) (Beijing: Zhongguo xiju chubanshe, 1982), 4: 167.

66. Xu Lun, *Xu Wenchang*, p. 76.

67. See Huang Wenyang, *Quhai zongmu tiyao* (The compendium of drama) (Beijing: Renmin wenxue, 1959), 5: 237.

68. Liang Yicheng, *Xu Wei*, p. 350.

69. Ibid., p. 353.

70. Virginia Woolf, *Orlando* (New York: Harcourt, 1956), p. 133.

71. Both Huang Yuanjie and Wang Duanshu were women of talent and ability who assumed male roles in the public sphere to earn a living. They also appealed to expediency and claimed that they were acting as they were to fulfill familial obligations. For an extensive analysis of Huang Yuanjie and Wang Duanshu, see Dorothy Ko, *Teacher of the Inner Chambers*, pp. 117–37.

72. Ibid., p. 125.

73. The notion of flexible, tolerant *yin-yang* relations is most apparent in Daoism, but is also perceived in Confucian texts such as *Lunyü* (Analects) and *Zhongyong* (The doctrine of means). See my article "The Construction of Women in Traditional Chinese Culture: A Review of the Early Classics and Historical Conduct Books," *Journal of Chinese Language and Culture* 2, no. 1 (1997).

5. Wang Anyi's Four Tales

1. See Christina Gilmartin, "Gender, Politics, and Patriarchy in China: The Experiences of Early Women Communists, 1920–27," in Sonia Kruks, Rayna Rapp, and Marilyn B. Young, eds., *Promissory Notes: Women in the Transition to Socialism* (New York: Monthly Review Press, 1989), pp. 83–84. She argues that Liang Qichao and the political revolutionaries during the 1890s and at the turn of the

century advocated transforming the inferior condition of Chinese women (a symbol of national weakness) to fight against Western imperialists.

2. The Chinese constitution guarantees women the right to work and the right to vote. A 1950 family law provided for freedom of choice in marriage, abolished concubinage, and gave women the right to own property and sue for divorce. See "Holding Up Half the Sky—Women," in Fox Butterfield, *China: Alive in the Bitter Sea* (New York: Times Books, 1990), p. 165.

3. For a detailed discussion of the political overtones of *funü*, see Tani E. Barlow, "Introduction," in Tani Barlow and Gary J. Bjorge, eds., *I Myself Am a Woman—Selected Writings of Ding Ling* (Boston: Beacon Press, 1989), pp. 41–42, and Lydia H. Liu, "The Female Tradition in Modern Chinese Literature: Negotiating Feminisms across East/West Boundaries," *Genders* 12 (Winter 1991): 23–24. Under the umbrella slogan that women are equal to men, the Communist Party must deny the existence of gender differences and reject many forms of femininity as subversive to their puritanical ideology. For an interesting study of why female sexuality is considered dangerous and subversive and how, in particular, it affects Chinese women's dress codes, see "The Pleasures of Adornment and the Dangers of Sexuality," in Emily Honig and Gail Hershatter, *Personal Voices: Chinese Women in the 1980s* (Stanford, Calif.: Stanford University Press, 1988), pp. 41–80.

4. See Lydia Liu, "The Female Tradition," p. 24.

5. Marilyn Young, "Chicken Little in China: Women After the Cultural Revolution," in Kruks, Rapp, and Young, *Promissory Notes*, p. 237.

6. I choose to leave *yu* untranslated in order to retain the linguistic ambiguity and cultural complexity of its meanings.

7. Jianying Zha, *China Pop: How Soap Operas, Tabloids, and Bestsellers Are Transforming a Culture* (New York: New Press, 1995), p. 139.

8. Meng Yue and Dai Jinghua analyze the transformation of sexual mores under the Communist ideology through an examination of the elimination of sexuality in the woman character Xi'er in the play *Baimaonü* (White-haired girl). Written in the 1940s and popular in the ensuing decades, the play enjoyed great success in the Cultural Revolution when Mao's wife Jiang Qing made it one of the eight model plays. Over the years, Xi'er's sexuality was stripped away through rewriting. She turned from a girl raped by her landlord, and a battered single mother, to a virgin. Any implications of a romance between her and the revolutionary Dachun were removed from the text. Instead Dachun was "not just a male character in general fairy tales, he was one with a special identity—a symbolic 'Father' figure—the Communist Eighth Route Army." Meng and Dai argue that not just Xi'er's sexuality but her very identity was eliminated when she became no more than a subsidiary to the patriarchal Communist Father. See Meng Yue and Dai Jinghua, *Fuchu lishi dibiao* (Floating above historical horizon) (Zhengzhou: He'nan renmin chubanshe, 1989), pp. 263–369.

9. Rey Chow argues that romantic love in the early twentieth century is a social issue intertwined with the liberation of women from patriarchy and the liber-

ation of the nation from Western and Japanese imperialism. See her *Primitive Passions: Visuality, Sexuality, Ethnography, and Contemporary Chinese Cinema* (New York: Columbia University Press, 1995), pp. 67–68.

10. See Zeng Zhennan, "Ai de zhuiqiu weishenme xupiao?—ye tan 'Beijiguang'" (Why the pursuit of love is so superficial?—comments on "Northern Lights"), *Guangming ribao*, December 24, 1981.

11. Zhang Jie, "Ai, shi buneng wangjide" (Love cannot be forgotten), in *1980 nian duanpian xiaoshuo xuan* (Selected short stories of 1980) (Beijing: Renmin wenxue chubanshe, 1981), p. 16.

12. See Wang Anyi, *Yu, shashasha* (Rain, shashasha) (Taipei: Xindi chubanshe, 1988), pp. 1–18.

13. "'Xiaobaozhuang,' wenxue xugou, dushi fengge qignian zuojia Wang Anyi yu Fudan daxue zhongwenxi xuesheng duihua" ("Baotown," literary fabrication, and cosmopolitan style—a dialogue between young writer Wang Anyi and students from the Chinese department of Fudan University), *Zhongguo xiandai dangdai wenxue yanjiu*, 1987, no. 6: 175.

14. Wang Anyi wrote in her diary on October 29, 1983, "[*Women in Love*] is a film representative of Lawrence's philosophy. He thinks that man is part of nature, whatever man does is done with instincts. Things done out of instincts are all beautiful and should be respected and protected. He abhors modern industrialization and thinks that it will inevitably alienate human nature. He describes man as a son of nature. Since man is conditioned by society, tragedies happen one after another." See Ru Zhijuan and Wang Anyi, *Munü tong you Meilijian* (Mother and daughter travel together in America) (Hong Kong: Sanlian shudian, 1986), p. 248.

15. Wang Anyi, Sitefanya, and Qin Lide, "Cong xianshi rensheng de tiyan dao xushu celue de zhuanxing—yifen guanyu Wang Anyi shinian xiaoshuo chuangzuo de fangtanlu" (A transformation from real-life experience to narrative strategy—an interview on ten years of Wang Anyi's fiction writing), *Dangdai zhongguo wenxue pinglun*, 1991, no. 6: 34.

16. Wang Zheng, "Three Interviews: Wang Anyi, Zhu Ling, Dai Qing," *Modern Chinese Literature* 4 (1988): 115.

17. See "Liangge liujiu jie chuzhongsheng de jixing duihua" (An unrehearsed dialogue between two junior high graduates of class 1969), in Chen Sihe, ed., *Bizou longshe* (A collection of literary criticisms) (Taipei: Yeqiang chubanshe, 1991), p. 245.

18. See Zhang Xiaotian, "Gongkai de neican" (Inside information made public), *Xiaoshuo yuebao*, 1982, no. 4: 61–87.

19. Dai Fang, "Tiaozhan" (Challenge), in Chen Ziling and Shi Feng, eds., *1983–1984 duanpian xiaoshuo zhengmingji* (Selected controversial short stories of 1983–1984) (Ji'nan: Shandong wenyi chubanshe, 1985), pp. 103, 108.

20. Ibid., pp. 104–5.

21. See Wang Anyi, Sitefanya, and Qin Lide, "Cong xianshi," pp. 31–32.

22. Wang Anyi, *Yu, shashasha*, p. 260.

23. Ibid., p. 255.
24. Ibid., p. 260.
25. See Wang Zheng, "Three Interviews," pp. 100–111. To Wang Anyi, Western feminism seems to deny the distinction between men and women by insisting that gender differences are entirely socially constructed. She, however, thinks that gender differences are partly biological and men cannot do whatever women are able to do, such as having a baby, and vice versa. In another interview, she says that if our world is designed by male standards, and it has lasted for thousands of years, there must be some legitimate reasons behind it. She thinks it is impossible for feminists to subvert everything. See Wang Anyi, Sitefanya, and Qin Lide, "Cong xianshi," p. 33.
26. Wang Anyi, *Yu, shashasha*, pp. 191, 223.
27. Ibid., p. 292.
28. Cheng Depei argues that "His" passion is nothing other than a yearning for maternal love and contends that if his affair disrupts his illusion that his wife has turned him into a man, the affair itself, however, does not turn him into a man either, but only realizes his dream and love for a mother figure. Cheng points out that "He" has memories of senses except that of seeing when he is dying, because he cannot find appropriate and adequate language to express himself and has never developed an acumen for life. See Cheng Depei, "Miandui ziji de juezhu—Ping Wang Anyi de 'Sanlian' " (Competing with herself—a criticism of Wang Anyi's "romance trilogy"), *Dangdai zuojia pinglun*, 1987, no. 2: 67.
29. Wang Anyi, "Nanren yu nüren, nüren yu chengshi" (Man and woman, woman and city), in Lin Jianfa and Wang Jingtao, eds., *Zhongguo dangdai zuojia mianmianguan: sisui, sisui, shui le shi pinjie* (A survey of contemporary Chinese writers: Tear up, tear up, tear up, and patch up) (Changchun: Shidai wenyi chubanshe, 1991), p. 111.
30. Ibid., p. 113.
31. Ibid., p. 114. Both Wang Anyi's progressive views and the notion of *yinsheng yangshuai* (female on the rise, male in decline) in popular culture point to an intriguing paradox in a male-dominated society. On the one hand, even though the socialist society discriminates against women in many ways, with the little freedom they win and given similar opportunities women prove to be more competent and resilient than men, especially morally and spiritually. On the other, communist ideology, like repressive feudal patriarchy, suppresses creative and individual will, and the frequent political purges foster the timid and fainthearted, thus favoring men who are submissive and passive. It inadvertently perpetuates the deeply ingrained notion of a feminization of men as a form of the cultural collective unconscious. "Cream-puff" males in recent decades are not just offsprings of communist ideology, but can also claim roots in traditional Chinese politics, philosophy, and aesthetics. In this context, it is not surprising that a campaign against feminized men broke out in the post-Mao years. It started in the late 1970s when young female viewers, enamored by the tough and virile image of a

Japanese movie star Ken Takakura, questioned why Chinese films were saturated with "cream-puff" male actors and why Chinese men were physically effeminate and morally and spiritually spineless. It evolved into cultural debates on the feminization of men in newspapers and magazines and later in film and literature. Since the feminization of men is seen as a symbolic malady of the frail and weakening cultural body, the onging search for the *nanzihan* (real man) reflects the cultural consciousness to modernize and rejuvenate Chinese culture through reevaluating the sediments of traditional Chinese culture and absorbing the cultures of the industrial giants of the world. For an analysis of the feminization of Chinese language and culture, see Lin Yutang's "Nüxing xing" (Feminization), in his *Yutang suibi* (Essays by Lin Yutang) (Hong Kong: Xinsheng chubanshe), pp. 122–25. For a historical examination of the politics and aesthetics of the feminization of men, see Yuejin Wang, "Red Sorghum: Mixing Memory and Desire," in Chris Berry, ed., *Perspectives on Chinese Cinema* (London: British Film Institute, 1991), pp. 82–93.

32. Wang Anyi, *Yu, shashasha*, p. 254.

33. Ibid., p. 270. 34. Ibid., pp. 270–71.

35. Ibid., p. 200. 36. Ibid., p. 265.

37. Zhang Xian, "Bei aiqing yiwang de jiaoluo" (The corner forgotten by love), in *1980 nian duanpian xiaoshuo xuan*, p. 115.

38. Wang Anyi, *Xiaocheng zhilian* (Love in a small town) (Taipei: Linbai chubanshe, 1988), p. 125.

39. Ibid., pp. 165, 160.

40. Ibid., p. 185.

41. Ibid., pp. 171, 103, 184.

42. See, for example, Lao Gui, *Xuese huanghun* (Blood-red sunset) (Beijing: Gongren chubanshe, 1987).

43. Wang Anyi, "Gangshang de shiji" (A century on a small hillock), in Wang Anyi, Yu Hua, et al., *Jinguo nanchang* (Forbidden fruit hard to taste) (Taipei: Yeqiang chubanshe, 1990), pp. 208, 233.

44. Ibid., p. 159. 45. Ibid., pp. 156, 206.

46. Ibid., p. 157. 47. Ibid., pp. 155, 205.

48. Ibid., p. 167. 49. Ibid., p. 199.

50. Ibid., p. 208. 51. Ibid., p. 156.

52. Ibid., pp. 156–57. 53. Ibid., pp. 232–33.

54. Wang Anyi, "Jinxiugu zhi lian" (Love in Splendor Valley), in her *Xiaocheng zhilian*, p. 17.

55. Ibid., p. 27.

56. In her later work, "Shushu de gushi" (The story of the uncle, 1990), Wang Anyi openly questions the reliability of her previous narratives and consciously tackles the problem of fictionality.

57. See Wang Anyi, Sitefanya, and Qin Lide, "Cong xianshi," p. 32.

58. Wang Anyi, *Xiaocheng zhilian*, p. 18.

59. Ibid., pp. 17, 101, 47, 79.

60. Ibid., pp. 18, 34, 48.
61. Ibid., p. 48.
62. Lydia Liu, "The Female Tradition," p. 35.
63. Wang Anyi, *Xiaocheng zhilian*, p. 37.
64. Ibid., pp. 17, 101.
65. Wang Anyi, "Nanren yu nüren, nüren yu chengshi," pp. 114–17.
66. Xiaobing Tang argues that China, submerged in if not submissive to postmodern discourse, while redefining its cultural logic in an era when seemingly contradictory modes of production synchronically exist, has "easily" declared "the disappearance of all [Maoist] master narratives." See his "Residual Modernism: Narrative of the Self in Contemporary Chinese Fiction," *Modern Chinese Literature* 7, no. 1 (Spring 1993): 7–8.
67. While both Wang Anyi and Jia Pingwa have been criticized for useless depiction of sex, critics of Wang are usually prudish conservatives, yet those of Jia are liberal-minded and well-educated, especially female intellectuals. Among the factors that make *Ruins of the Capital* a best-seller that has sold over a million copies, two are extremely exploitative: the media's focus on themes of money and sex, and the author's "self-censorship," which is actually intended to titillate the reader's sexual appetite. Jia inserts blank blocks followed by a note in parentheses—"here the author deleted a number of words"—into the graphic descriptions of sex scenes. For an examination of the controversy surrounding *Ruins of the Capital* and an interview with Jia, see Jianying Zha, *China Pop*, pp. 129–39, 146–64.
68. For a discussion of the seriousness of Wang Anyi's novel *Jishi yu xugou* (Document and fictionalize, 1993) and the lightheartedness of other writers' works in recent years, see a dialogue between Wang Anyi and critics in Chen Sihe, Wang Anyi, Hu Yuanbao, Zhang Xinying, and Yan Feng, "Dangqian wenxue chuangzuo zhong de 'qing' yu 'zhong'—wenxue duihualu" (The "light" and "heavy" in recent literature—a literary dialogue), *Dangdai zuojia pinglun*, 1993, no. 5: 14–23. In *Document and Fictionalize*, Wang Anyi intends to formulate a historical heroism as an alternative to communist idealism. Using her mother's uncommon surname "Ru" as a clue, Wang Anyi traces her ancestors to the *rouran* minority in Mongolia two thousand years ago. The novel consists of two parallel parts, one chronicling the history of her ancestors on her mother's side, the other her personal history from child to writer; the novel draws its significance mostly from the former. Through descriptions of victory and defeat, migration and integration, Wang Anyi extols the tenacity of her people. However, she does not single out her mother, a Party veteran, as a heroic symbol. Instead she glorifies Ghenghis Khan, the great Mongolian emperor who conquered half of the world and the inspiration of fighters and dreamers for centuries, and her great-grandmother, the young widow who fought against adversity and bequeathed lasting spiritual hope to her granddaughter and later generations. Together these two embody courage, ambition, determination, resilience, and above all, the invincibility of the human spirit.

6. The Fluid Body of Josie Packard

Earlier versions of this essay were presented at conferences. I would like to thank the organizers and participants of "Console-ing Passions: Television, Video, and Feminism," held at the University of Southern California in April 1993, and "Literature, History, Culture: Re-envisioning Chinese and Comparative Literature," held at Princeton University in June 1994. My thanks to Amanda Berry, Jane Gaines, Terri Geller, John Hilgart, and Yingjin Zhang, and special thanks to Jennifer Doyle and Sabine Engel.

1. Joan Chen (Chen Chong, b. 1962) met early acclaim in the Shanghai film industry prior to acting as May-May in Dino de Laurentiis's television miniseries *Tai-Pan*. According to some reports, her work in Bernardo Bertolucci's film *The Last Emperor* as the last empress Wan Jung brought her to the attention of David Lynch.

2. Edward Said, *Orientalism* (New York: Vintage, 1978), p. 20.

3. For an excellent and intriguing analysis of the culture of consumption in the United States, see Mark Seltzer, *Bodies and Machines* (New York: Routledge, 1992). See especially pp. 121–45.

4. Lisa Lowe usefully argues for analyzing orientalism as specific to the situation and to the practitioner and examines several moments where orientalism works not only from the "occident" but with the participation of the "orient." See her *Critical Terrains: French and British Orientalisms* (Ithaca, N.Y.: Cornell University Press, 1991).

5. This perhaps paves the way for the success of a show such as CBS's *Northern Exposure*. Prime time soap operas and dramas in the vein of *Dallas, Dynasty, Falcon Crest* and *thirtysomething* are joined by or even replaced by series located in remote towns rather than major cities.

6. In a simplistic fashion, one could say that Dallas the city is represented by the Ewing family. The Carringtons and the Colbys form the dynastic families of Denver in *Dynasty*. The opening credit sequences of *Dallas, Falcon Crest*, and *Dynasty* include exterior bird's-eye view shots of the family home. The home (even if it is a mansion or huge ranch) is as important, if not more so, as the other regional landmarks.

7. For an excellent analysis of the political implications of Hong Kong's contemporary situation for postcolonial theory, see Rey Chow, "Between Colonizers: Hong Kong's Postcolonial Self-Writing in the 1990s," *Diaspora* 2, no. 2 (1992): 151–70.

8. The practice of using multiple plot lines was first recognized and celebrated in *Hill Street Blues*, though it was not the first series to use it. Critics celebrated the multiple plot lines of *Twin Peaks* as one of the prime attractions of the series.

9. Viewers familiar with David Lynch productions, notably the film which broadened his viewership, *Blue Velvet*, expected to recognize his mark on the tele-

vision series. Cultural critics note the almost instantaneous cult status of the series and continue to speculate on the spectacular popularity of *Twin Peaks* in the first season, only eight episodes long, and the dramatic decline in viewership in the second (and last) season. For discussions of the series as a cult phenomenon, see David Lavery, "Introduction: The Semiotics of Cobbler *Twin Peaks*' Interpretive Community," and Henry Jenkins, " 'Do You Enjoy Making the Rest of Us Feel Stupid?': alt.tv.twinpeaks, the Trickster Author, and Viewer Mastery," both in David Lavery, ed., *Full of Secrets: Critical Approaches to Twin Peaks* (Detroit, Mich.: Wayne State University Press, 1995), pp. 1–21, and 51–69.

10. According to the Nielsen rankings, the show was the highest-rated ABC Sunday program since the November 13, 1988, airing of *War and Remembrance*. ABC promoted *Twin Peaks* as the creation of auteur director David Lynch, who had already gained a reputation for his unconventional visions with several films: *Eraserhead, The Elephant Man, Dune,* and *Blue Velvet*. Of the many writers and directors who participated in Lynch-Frost Productions, David Lynch and Mark Frost were most frequently acknowledged by the press as the creators of the series. This practice ignores the collaborative aspects of a program where a number of writers and directors contributed. Reportedly (perhaps playing on the hype of film director David Lynch directing a program for television) the network considered airing the episode without commercials and decided to run 20 percent fewer network commercials than is usual for a Sunday movie program. See Rick Kogan, "*Twin Peaks* hits the heights for hype and hoopla," *Chicago Tribune*, April 1, 1990. Newspaper coverage of the series was augmented by full-page advertisements for the premiere. See Dylan Jones, "Nielsens: ABC claims rare Sunday win," *USA Today*, April 11, 1990, sec. D, p. 3. For a discussion of the multimedia selling of *Twin Peaks*, see Jim Collins, "Television and Postmodernism," in Robert Allen, ed., *Channels of Discourse, Reassembled: Television and Contemporary Criticism*, 2d ed. (Chapel Hill: University of North Carolina Press, 1992), pp. 327–49. The premiere was filmed in spring 1989 and scheduled for broadcast in May 1989, moved back to fall 1989, rescheduled for March 1990, and then for fall 1990. The series was a replacement made mid-season (April) and appeared regularly, after the Sunday night premiere, on Thursday nights. After only two episodes, its Nielsen ranking was 22. See Chuck Ross, "An upbeat end for TV season but the networks' share of overall TV audience takes another dive," *San Francisco Chronicle*, April 18, 1990, sec. E, p. 2.

11. Seltzer, *Bodies and Machines*, p. 122.

12. Homi K. Bhabha claims, "It is precisely these two forms of 'identification' that constitute the dominant strategy of colonial power exercised in relation to the stereotype which, as a form of multiple and contradictory belief, gives knowledge of difference and simultaneously disavows or masks it." See Bhabha, "The Other Question: Difference, Discrimination and the Discourse of Colonialism," in Russell Ferguson, Martha Gever, Trinh T. Minh-ha, and Cornel West, eds., *Out There: Theories of Marginalization and Culture* (Cambridge, Mass.: MIT Press, 1991),

p. 81. The series treats mirrors as revelatory devices that uncover differences in certain characters. The camera sets up the viewer so that to look at someone who is also looking at her/his reflection in a mirror is both voyeuristic and fetishistic.

13. On the "to-be-looked-atness" of female characters, see Laura Mulvey's seminal article, "Visual Pleasure and Narrative Cinema," *Screen* 16, no. 3 (1975): 6–18.

14. In an article about the program's use of substitutions of body parts, Alice Kuzniar argues that *Twin Peaks* offers viewers a fantasy that someone, notably, a male character, possesses the knowledge necessary for understanding the events. Kuzniar, "Double Talk in *Twin Peaks*," in Lavery, *Full of Secrets*, pp. 120–29.

15. Second season, eleventh episode, December 15, 1990. Written by Barry Pullman, directed by Duwayne Dunham.

16. Lynn Joyrich, "All That Television Allows: TV Melodrama, U.S. Postmodernism and Consumer Culture," *Camera Obscura* 16 (1988): 129–54.

17. See Darrell Y. Hamamoto, *Monitored Peril: Asian Americans and the Politics of Television Representation* (Minneapolis: University of Minnesota Press, 1994). For a discussion of the feminization of Asian men, see Richard Fung, "Looking for My Penis: The Asian Gay Male in Gay Video Porn," in Bad Object-Choices, eds., *How Do I Look? Queer Video and Film* (Seattle, Wash.: Bay Press, 1990), pp. 145–60.

18. Second season, first episode, September 30, 1990. Written by David Lynch and Mark Frost, directed by David Lynch.

19. First season, eighth episode, season finale, May 23, 1990. Written and directed by Mark Frost.

20. Second season, fourteenth episode, January 26, 1991. Written by Scott Frost, directed by Uli Edel.

21. Second season, fourth episode, October 20, 1990. Written by Jerry Stahl, Mark Frost, Harley Peyton, and Robert Engels, directed by Todd Holland.

22. The program shows that Catherine Martell's performance succeeds with some characters who are alert to the alleged visit of a renowned travel critic who works incognito. The viewer learns that no one knows whether this famous critic, M. T. Wentz, is a man or a woman. Thus, Catherine's disguise may be excused by several characters who assume she (Tajimura) is the critic incognito.

23. Second season, sixth episode, November 3, 1990. Written by Harley Peyton and Robert Engels, directed by Lesli Linka Glatter.

24. The history of passing in the United States refers specifically to African Americans performing and being viewed by white Americans as white and thereby gaining independence, mobility, access to livelihoods, and privileges otherwise denied to them.

25. Bhabha, "The Other Question," pp. 72.

26. Richard Dienst, *Still Life in Real Time: Theory After Television* (Durham, N.C.: Duke University Press, 1994).

27. I am invoking Eve Kosofsky Sedgwick's analysis of homosocial triangles in *Between Men: Homosocial Desire in the Nineteenth-Century British Novel* (New York: Columbia University Press, 1985).

28. Second season, fourteenth episode, January 26, 1991. Written by Scott Frost, directed by Uli Edel.

29. Second season, fifteenth episode, February 9, 1991. Written by Harley Peyton and Robert Engels, directed by Diane Keaton.

30. Second season, sixteenth episode, February 16, 1991. Written by Tricia Brock, directed by Lesli Linka Glatter.

31. Five weeks later on March 28, 1991, in part due to fan requests and critical laments, ABC began broadcasting the remaining six episodes, which had already been shot. The final episode that was broadcast ended with Cooper staring at his reflection in the mirror, where the reflection is that of BOB.

32. Martha Nochimson argues that the "Little Man" dressed in a red suit and most often appearing in the red curtained room is a phallic image. See Nochimson, "Desire Under the Firs: Entering the Body of Reality in *Twin Peaks*," *Film Quarterly* 46, no. 2 (Winter 1992–93): 22–34.

33. Second season, twenty-first episode, June 10, 1991. Written by Barry Pullman, directed by Pullman and Tim Hunter.

34. At the 1992 conference "Dangerous Liasons? Literature, Film and Video," held at the University of Southern California, Terri Geller suggested that Josie's death might be an AIDS allegory. I believe that visibility is the crucial element supporting my claim.

35. Cindy Patton points out a serious problem in diagnosing early cases of AIDS, such diagnoses partially dependent on evaluations of previous health. See Cindy Patton, *Inventing AIDS* (New York: Routledge, 1990).

36. Bhabha, "The Other Question," pp. 76–81.

37. Jenkins, "Do You Enjoy," pp. 51–69.

38. Said, *Orientalism*, p. 20.

39. Ibid., p. 67.

7. Travel and Translation

This essay is a substantial revision of two seminar papers for Frederic Wakeman and Lydia Liu. Paul Rabinow's seminar on the anthropology of science in spring 1995 provided the intellectual framework for an integrated discussion. Samuel Cheung kindly read and commented on an early draft of the portion on Lu Xun. The author also benefited from a discussion with Robert Holub on the Jewish question in Germany. Yingjin Zhang made important suggestions in terms of the essay's final presentation.

1. *Yangwu* was a term that became current in the 1860s that covered both diplomatic interactions with Western powers and the selective adoption of Western weaponry, technologies, and scientific knowledge.

2. Henry Louis Gates argues that African American literature tends to be double-voiced because of its susceptibility to influences of the white literary canon as well as the black cultural traditions. See his "Introduction," in *The Signi-*

fying Monkey (New York: Oxford University Press, 1988), pp. xix–xxviii. I think the concept is particularly useful in characterizing the contentious relationship between the Chinese and Western cultural legacies in the discourse on Chinese modernity.

3. For a comprehensive treatment of the period, see Mary Wright, *The Last Strand of Chinese Conservatism, The T'ung-Chih Restoration, 1862–1874* (Stanford, Calif.: Stanford University Press, 1957).

4. For a discussion of *Zongli Yamen*, see Masataka Banno, *China and the West, 1858–1861, The Origin of the Tsungli Yamen* (Cambridge, Mass.: Harvard University Press, 1964). For regional administrations, see Philip Kuhn, *Rebellion and Its Enemies in Late Imperial China, Militarization and Social Structure* (Cambridge, Mass.: Harvard University Press, 1970).

5. Among the earliest advocates of self-strengthening, Feng Guifeng called for the revision of school curricula to accommodate Western languages and sciences in 1860 and submitted his *Jiaobin lu kangyi* (Humble suggestions from the jiaobin hall) to Zeng Guofan in 1861. Later in the century, Zheng Guanying reiterated Feng's points in his popular *Shengshi weiyan* (Critical remarks in a prosperous age, 1892). The first school with an emphasis in these two areas opened in Beijing in 1862 as "Tongwen guan," or the Institute of Language Assimilation. Its Shanghai version was set up in the following year. After that, Canton and Fuzhou also established language schools. For a description of the student life in Tongwen guan, see Qi Rushan, *Qi Rushan huiyi lu* (Memoirs of Qi Rushan) (Taipei: Zhongyang wenwu gongyingshe, 1956).

6. The translation bureau at Jiangnan Arsenal was the predominant publisher of translated works in China until 1887, when the "Society of the Diffusion of Christian and General Knowledge among the Chinese" began to function under the auspices of the missionaries and prominent Western figures such as Robert Hart.

7. Bin Chun, a low-ranking Manchu official, headed the 1866 diplomatic team that visited France, Britain, Holland, Hamburg, Denmark, Sweden, Finland, Russia, Prussia, Hanover, and Belgium.

8. Yung Wing led the first group of Chinese students to the United States in 1872. See Thomas La Farge, *China's First Hundred, Educational Mission in the United States, 1872–1881* (Pullman: Washington State University Press, 1987).

9. Bin Chun completed his European tour in less than four months. But appointed the first minister to the West in 1876, Guo Songtao resided in London and Paris from January 21, 1877, to January 31, 1879.

10. Students of Tongwen guan furnished the nascent diplomatic service with a large portion of its staff. But clearly, they were not depended upon as a sole means of knowledge acquisition. Besides a distinctly hermeneutic approach directed toward understanding, the instrumentalist, third-party mode of observatory engagement was also very much at work.

11. For instance, Yung Wing went to Yale University and later married a New England woman. See Yung Wing, *My Life in China and America* (New York: H. Holt, 1909).

12. One sign of the popularity of knowledge about the West was that it began to invade the traditional genre of *biji* or collected notes/anecdotes. Wang Tao, who later became the doyen of Western scholarship in Shanghai while heading the Gezhi college, wrote in his *Wenyou yutan* (Remaining anecdotes at the dilapidated residence) during his exile in Hong Kong that the five continents on the earth identified by Western geographers in fact constituted only two of the four land masses indicated in the Buddhist scriptures, and that should the Western explorers go beyond the north and south poles, there might be another two continents hanging from the earth. See Wang Tao, *Wenyou yutan*, in *Biji qizhong* (Seven collected anecdotes of the Qing dynasty) (Shanghai: Shanghai wenyi chubanshe, 1992), pp. 49–50.

13. The lack of an accepted code for translation was evident even in the works of prominent translators such as Yan Fu and Lin Shu. For brief discussions of the publications, see He Lin, "Yan Fu de fanyi" (Yan Fu's translations), and Zheng Zhenduo, "Lin Qinnan xiansheng" (Mr. Lin Shu), in Luo Xinzhang, ed., *Fanyi lunji* (Discussions of translation) (Beijing: Shangwu yinshuguan, 1984), pp. 146–60, 184–92.

14. Because of the demand for translated texts, members of the literati without knowledge of Western languages sometimes cooperated with Western missionaries and their students in translation projects. The standard process was that the person capable of both Chinese and Western speech rendered the text orally for the literatus, while the latter transcribed the oral speech into polished classical Chinese. Such a process could result in inaccuracies such as those in Lin Shu's translations. See Zhang Juncai, *Lin Shu pingzhuan* (Biography of Lin Shu) (Tianjin: Nankai daxue chubanshe, 1992), pp. 63–84.

15. For a discussion of literary translations in early modern China, see Guo Yanli, *Zhongguo jindai wenxue fazhanshi* (History of early modern Chinese literature) (Ji'nan: Shandong jiaoyu chubanshe, 1993), 3: 2168–2248 (chap. 42).

16. A good comparison is made by Zhong Shuhe between "Helan zhuan" (The history of Holland) in the high-Qing official compilation of *Mingshi* (The history of the Ming dynasty), and the notes about Holland in Bin Chun's travelogue. In "The History of Holland," there is the following description, "Holland, whose other name was [the country of] red-bristled barbarians, is located near Portugal.... The residents there have deep-set eyes and long noses. Their hair, eyebrows, and beards are all of a red color. Their feet tend to have a length of one foot and two inches.... The people under their mastery are called black ghosts. They do not sink in water, and [have the ability to] walk on the surface of the sea as on level ground. In the rear of the rudder, they mount sea mirrors which have a diameter of several feet, and are capable of shining upon hundreds of miles." In

Bin Chun's account, however, things are much different, "The entire country borders on the Atlantic. Level and without mountains, its territory is divided by many a canal. The people are affected by the harm of water, and therefore are accustomed to irrigation, and are good at building dams. Furthermore, they are also good at sailing afar. They erected harbors in all the countries on the southern sea. The access to the [Chinese] Southeast by boat was begun by Holland." See Zhong Shuhe, "Dongtu xilai diyiren" (The first envoy from East to West), which is a preface to Bing Chun's travelogue *Chengcha biji* (Notes on the boat), in Zhong Shuhe, ed., *Zouxiang shijie* (To the world) (Changsha: Yuelu chubanshe, 1984), 2: 76–77; translation mine.

17. Lin Zexu's *Sizhou zhi* (Records of the four continents, 1839) and Wei Yuan's *Haiguo tuzhi* (Illustrated gazette of maritime countries, 1842, 1847, 1852) were two important sources on the West before the self-strengthening movement. But unlike Guo's personal reflections in his diary, these works focused on strategic matters of immediate relevance to national defense rather than on matters of intrinsic and therefore enduring value.

18. In Kang Youwei's visionary writings about the reforms in China in the 1895–98 period, the Meiji restoration and the French revolution served as the ultimate examples of success and failure.

19. James Clifford suggests that Western anthropological writings about the non-West invariably possess allegorical meanings in reference to the West. Likewise, I argue that the representation of the West also made consequential reference to China, only that because of the specific historical context in which projects such as the self-strengthening initiatives and the post-1895 reform were situated, such a reference carries a specific set of connotations about China's insufficiencies and needs. See James Clifford, "On Ethnographic Allegory," in James Clifford and George Marcus, eds., *Writing Culture* (Berkeley: University of California Press, 1986), pp. 98–121.

20. For instance, Guo Songtao specified the priority of political and educational reform over industrial and commercial modernization.

21. No doubt, the sense of want was predominant in the purchase of Western ships and weaponry as part of the self-strengthening measures. But with the presence of numerous translated texts and descriptive accounts about the West, other needs were also created, such as the effective political and educational institutions for Guo.

22. The first person to serve as the plenipotentiary representative of the court was Anson Burlingame, who was the American minister to China between 1861 and 1867. In 1868, on the request of the Qing government, he headed a team of Chinese officials to negotiate various treaties with the West. He died during his service in 1870 in Russia. For a discussion of Guo's mission in the West, see J. D. Frodsham, *The First Chinese Embassy to the West, The Journals of Kuo Sung-tao, Liu Hsi-hung, and Chang Te-yi* (New York: Oxford University Press, 1974).

23. A. R. Margary, interpreter for the British embassy, was killed in Yunnan Province in the spring of 1876.

24. Guo Songtao, *Lundun Bali riji* (Journals from London and Paris), in Zhong Shuhe, *Zuoxiang shijie*, 1: 20.

25. The following record of the conversation constituted virtually the first detailed review of events in the travelogue of Guo's entire journey.

26. Guo, *Lundun Bali riji*, pp. 28–29; translation mine.

27. As Zeng Guofan observed: "His lordship Guo is a man of sophisticated sentiments. But he is talented in composition and interpretation rather than in voluminous and intensive [administrative] work." See "Fu Li Shaoquan" (Response to Li Hongzhang), in *Zeng Wenzhenggong shuzha* (Correspondences by Zeng Guofan), cited in Zhong Shuhe, "Lun Guo Songtao" (On Guo Songtao), in Zhong Shuhe, *Zouxiang shijie*, 1: 8; translation mine.

28. Guo spoke no language other than Chinese and brought with him two Tongwen guan graduates.

29. One *li* equals half a kilometer. One *jin* corresponds to half a kilogram. One *zhang* approximates three and a third meters.

30. Guo, *Lundun Bali riji*, pp. 80–82; translation mine.

31. See Roland Barthes, "L'effect du réel," *Communications*, no. 11 (1968): 84–89.

32. The first job Wang held after arriving in Shanghai on his first trip from his native Haining in 1898 was at *Shiwu bao* (Journal of current affairs), which was the major mouthpiece for the reformers headed by Liang Qichao. Later, he became a protégé of Luo Zhenyu, the editor of the influential *Nongxue zazhi* (Journal of agricultural studies), which survived the coup of 1898 for its practical emphasis, and helped the latter edit a different journal on education. Many of his own essays appeared in this last-mentioned journal.

33. Wang Guowei, "Lun xinxueyu zhi shuru" (On the introduction of neologisms), in *Jing'an wenji* (Writings by Wang Guowei) (Beijing, 1927), 1: 97–101; translation mine.

34. This no doubt bears structural similarity to Guo's initial reaction toward the British warship anchored near Shanto University.

35. See, for instance, Wang Guowei, "Lun jinnian zhi xueshujie" (The academia in recent years), in *Jing'an Wenji*, 1: 94–97.

36. The one reason he cited for his abandonment of Western philosophy was that whereas speculative thinking held the most appeal for him, his rational mind only found empiricism convincing, and thus the remark, "I admire that which I do not trust, I trust that which I do not admire." See Wang Guowei, "Zixu II" (Autobiography II), in *Jing'an Wenji*, 2: 21–23. In relation to the question of translation, Wang obviously could not articulate his favorite modes of sameness without incurring moments of idiosyncrasy.

37. Lu Xun, "Xu" (Preface) to *Nahan* (Outcry), in *Lu Xun quanji* (Complete

works of Lu Xun) (Beijing: Renmin wenxue chubanshe, 1973), 1: 269–76; and "Tengye xiansheng" (Mr. Fujino), in *Zhaohua xishi* (Morning blossoms gleaned at dusk) (Beijing: Renmin wenxue chubanshe, 1973), pp. 61–67.

38. Lu Xun, "Tengye xiangsheng," p. 61.
39. Lu Xun, "Xu," p. 271; translation mine.
40. Ibid.; translation mine.

8. Baoyu in Wonderland

1. The "science fiction novel" is sometimes called the "reasoning novel" (*lixiang xiaoshuo*) or the "educational novel" (*jiaoyu xiaoshuo*).
2. A parallel view to this intellectual response to the West is a prevalent conviction that China's problems stemmed from a breach in cultural-intellectual coherence and could be solved only in immanent, holistic terms. See Yu-sheng Lin, *The Crisis of Chinese Consciousness: Radical Anti-traditionalism in the May Fourth Era* (Madison: University of Wisconsin Press, 1979), pp. 26–55.
3. For a book-length discussion of renovated literary form, see Marston Anderson, *The Limits of Realism: Chinese Fiction in the Revolutionary Period* (Berkeley and Los Angeles: University of California Press, 1990).
4. Liang Qichao, "Lun xiaoshuo yu qunzhi zhi guanxi" (On the relations between fiction and ruling the people), in A Ying, ed., *Wanqing wenxue congchao: xiaoshuo xiqu yanjiujuan* (Compendium of late Qing literature) (Beijing: Zhonghua shuju, 1960), pp. 12–15; Chen Duxiu, "Wenxue geming lun" (On literary revolution), in *Duxiu wencun* (Writings of Chen Duxiu) (Hefei: Anfei renmin chubanshe, 1987), 1: 135–40; Hu Shi, "Jianshe de wenxue geming lun" (On constructive revolution in Chinese literature), in *Hu Shi wencun* (Taipei: Yuanliu, 1986), 1: 289–306; Lu Xun, preface to *Nahan* (A call to arms), in *Lu Xun quanji* (The complete works of Lu Xun) (Beijing: Renmin wenxue chubanshe, 1982), 1: 417. See also Wen Rumin, *Xinwenxue xianshi zhuyi de liubian* (Changes in modern Chinese realist literature) (Beijing: Beijing daxue chubanshe, 1988), pp. 3–29.
5. This does not mean that Chinese society has always lagged behind the West in material culture. On the contrary, earlier use of printing, the compass, and gunpowder in medieval China had indicated her relative advancement over medieval Europe. See Su-yu Teng and John K. Fairbank, *China's Response to the West: A Documentary Survey, 1839–1923* (Cambridge, Mass.: Harvard University Press, 1954), pp. 15–17.
6. The term *yangwu* was first used in 1840 by a Chinese official. After 1860, it was used to refer to everything related to China's relationship with the West. From 1860 to 1880, debates about the yangwu issue were prevalent among Chinese intellectuals. See John K. Fairbank and Kwang-ching Liu, eds., *The Cambridge History of China*, vol. 10, *Late-Ch'ing, 1800–1911*, part 2 (Cambridge: Cambridge University Press, 1978), pp. 535–602.

7. I am indebted to Professor Theodore Huters's inspiration and generosity in sharing with me his manuscript of "Appropriations: Another Look at Yan Fu and Western Ideas," which has helped me to develop the main argument of this study. See note 17 below for details.

8. Wu Jianren, *Xin shitouji* (The new story of the stone) (Zhengzhou: Zhongzhou guji chubanshe, 1986). It was first published in *Nanfang bao* (Southern newspaper) in 1905, and later serialized in *Yueyue xiaoshuo* (Monthly novel) in 1907. All quotations are taken from the Zhengzhou guji edition.

9. In my dissertation, "The Writing Subject in Late Qing Polygeneric Novels: Romance, Detective Novel, and Science Fiction (1898–1911)" (Ph.D. diss., University of California, Los Angeles, 1998), I suggested that late Qing popular novels are neither a purely organic form nor a structured discourse; they are to be read as novels made of many encoded subforms which problematize form and cut across modes of discourse. I named this corpus of novels "Polygeneric Novels."

10. Lu Xun, *Yuejie lüxing* (Tokyo: Progressive Society, 1902). It is based on the Japanese translation of Jules Verne's work *From the Earth to the Moon* done by Inoue Isutomu (Jinshang Qin). Since the Japanese translation might have already included some rewriting, a comparative study of the Japanese influence on Lu Xun is an interesting project in its own right. *Didi shijie* is serialized in *Zhejiangchao* (Zhejiang tide) in 1903. Other literati-writers had also translated well-known works of Western science fiction; among them are Zeng Guangquan's *Changshengshu* (The trick of longevity), translated from Sir Henry Rider Haggard's *Allen Quartermain* (1887), and Xue Shaowei's *Bashiri huanyou ji* (Traveling around for eighty days), translated from Jules Verne's *Around the World in Eighty Days*(1873). Other late Qing science fictions include Liang Junchao's *Shijie mori ji* (A history of the end of the world, 1903), Wu Jianren's "Dianshu qitan" (The strange talks on electricity, 1903), Huangjiang Diaosou's "Yueqiu zhimindi xiaoshuo" (The moon colony, 1904), Donghai Juewo's "Xin Faluo xiansheng tan" (The new story of Mr. Faluo, 1905), Biheguan zhuren's "Xinjiyuan" (The new era, 1908), Dalu's "Jinnian weixin" (This year's reform, 1908), Wu Jianren's "Guangxu wannian" (Guangxu the millennium, 1908), and Nunu's "Dixia lüxing" (Traveling to the underground, 1908). For a synopsis of some of these novels, see David Der-wei Wang's "Jia Baoyu zuo qianshuiting: Wanqing kehuan xiaoshuo xinlun" (Jia Baoyu on submarines: A new approach to the late Qing science fiction novel), in his *Xiaoshuo Zhongguo: Wanqing dao dangdai de zhongwen xiaoshuo* (Seeing China from Chinese novels: The Chinese novel from the late Qing to the present) (Taipei: Maitian, 1993), pp. 229–36.

11. Lu Xun, " 'Yuejie liixing' bianyan" (Words on "Traveling to the Moon"), from *Lu Xun quanji*, 10: 151–52.

12. It is also said that Lu Xun translated two other science-fiction works, *Beiji tanxian ji* (Adventure at the north pole) and *Wuli xinlun* (New essays on physics), but they have not been located so far. See "Kexue wenyi shishang yongbu diaoxiede xianhua—Lun Lu Xun bianyide Rule Fanernade liangben kexue huanxiang xiaoshuo" (The everlasting blossoms in the literary history of science—

Reading on Lu Xun's translation of Jules Verne's two science fictions), in Huang Yi, ed., *Lun kexue huanxiang xiaoshuo* (On science fiction) (Beijing: Kexue puji chubanshe, 1981), pp. 2–7.

13. In Chinese mythology, the Goddess Nüwa is known for her act of "patching up the sky" with magic stones.

14. These two books are reprinted in Zhong Shuhe, ed., *Zouxiang shijie congshu* (Towards the world: An anthology) (Changsha: Yuelu shushe, 1985).

15. I am indebted to Marion Eggert's inspiring project on the Chinese travelogue. Her article, "The Genius of Native Soil: The *Lao Can youji* as Travelogue," is forthcoming in *Ming Qing yanjiu*.

16. For the history of the Foreign Affairs movement, see *Chouban yiwu shimo* (The complete record of the management of barbarian affairs), Tongzhi 46.45a (p. 4499). Reprinted Taipei: Wenhai chubanshe, 1966; also reprinted in Zhongguo shixue hui (Chinese historical association), ed., *Yangwu yundong* (The foreign affairs movement) (Shanghai: Shanghai renmin chubanshe, 1961), 2: 24. See also Mary Wright, *The Last Stand of Chinese Conservatism: The T'ung-chih Restoration (1862–1874)* (Stanford, Calif.: Stanford University Press, 1962), pp. 243–48; Ting-yu Kuo and Kwang-ching Liu, "Self-Strengthening: The Pursuit of Western Technology," in John K. Fairbank and Kwang-ching Liu, *The Cambridge History of China*, 10: 528–31.

17. For an insightful and penetrating analysis of the reception and resistance of the Western ideas in the late Qing, see Theodore Huters, "Appropriations: Another Look at Yan Fu and Western Ideas" (Nuoyong: zai lun Yan Fu yu xifang sixiang), *Xueren* (Scholars), no. 9 (1996): 296–348.

18. For Chinese utopian literature, see Chang Hui-chuan, "Literary Utopia and Utopian Literature: A Generic Appraisal" (Ph.D. diss., University of Massachusetts, 1986).

19. We find a considerable number of titles that refer to traveling as "youji" in Yang Jialuo's bibliography of late Qing fiction, *Mingguo yilai chuban xinshu zongmu* (Bibliography on new books published after the [establishment of] Republican China) (Taipei: Zhongguo cidian guan, 1972).

20. See Wu Jianren, *Xin shitouji*, p. 256.

21. Ibid., p. 285.

22. See *Xin xiaoshuo* (The new novel), nos. 1–5. Note that the author's name is marked as Lu Jiedong in no. 1 but as Hong Xisheng in nos. 2–5.

23. For the purposes of this chapter, I will not compare these two stories in great detail but read *Haidi lüxing* as it might have appealed to the Late Qing imagination in this specific moment of Chinese history.

24. Hong Xisheng, *Haidi lüxing* (Journey to the bottom of the sea), in *Xin xiaoshuo* (The new novel), no. 1 (1902): 78.

25. Ibid., pp. 36–37.

26. Ibid., p. 38.

27. Lu Xun, *Didi shijie*, in *Zhejiangchao* 1 (1902): 103; translation mine.
28. See *Shen bao*, September 2, 1897; translation mine.
29. Ibid.
30. Lu Xun, *Didi shijie*, p. 120; translation mine.
31. For detailed study on urban literature in the early Republican period, see Perry Link, *Mandarin Ducks and Butterflies: Popular Fiction in Early Twentieth-Century Chinese Cities* (Berkeley: University of California Press, 1981).
32. As C. T. Hsia has pointed out, the obsession with "China," a deep-rooted concern for the people and for the country, has "haunted" the Chinese literatus-writer and ultimately become a negative force blunting the development of more varied and multidimensional forms of literary expression. See Hsia, "Xiandai Zhongguo wenxue zhongde ganshi youguo jingshen" (The spirit of "obsession with China" in Chinese literature), in his *Xiandai Zhongguo xiaoshuo shi* (A history of modern Chinese fiction), trans. Ding Fuxiang (Taipei: Zhuanji wenxue chubanshe, 1982), pp. 533–52. See C. T. Hsia's *A History of Modern Chinese Fiction* (New Haven: Yale University Press, 1971).
33. In fact, the Commercial Press was not the first to publish the textbooks; two smaller companies—called "Civilization" (Wenming) and "Expanding wisdom" (Guangzhi)—had published a set of textbooks by four Wuxi school teachers before 1903. For the Commercial Press's other projects, see Leo Ou-fan Lee, "The Cultural Construction of Modernity in Early Republican China: Some Research Notes on Urban Shanghai" (paper delivered at the Workshop on Chinese Cultural Studies, Harvard University, October 12, 1995). For a comprehensive study of *Dongfang zazhi* and the Commercial Press, see Jean-Pierre Drege, *La Commercial Press de Shanghai, 1897–1949* (Paris: Institute des hautes etudes chinoises, College de France, 1978).
34. See *The Eastern Miscellany (Dongfang zazhi)*, November 1911.
35. By the late Qing period, the circulation of Western science and technology within China had a history several centuries old. At the turn of the sixteenth century, Matteo Ricci had brought a considerable portion of Renaissance science to China, and it received a good deal of attention and dissemination. From that time on, Jesuit scientists were in charge of maintaining the official calendar through the Qing era. According to contemporary Jesuit reports, the Kangxi emperor (1622–1722) had an intense interest in science and mathematics and studied them assiduously under Jesuit instructors. For a concise account of Kangxi's scientific career, see Lawrence D. Kessler, *K'ang-hsi and the Consolidation of Ch'ing Rule, 1661–1684* (Chicago: University of Chicago Press, 1976), pp. 146–54.

9. The Texture of the Metropolis

Earlier drafts of this essay were presented at Duke University in February 1995 and at Stanford University in May 1995. This is a slightly expanded version of my essay of the same title published in Modern Chinese Literature *9, no. 1 (Spring 1995): 11–30.*

1. See, for example, Yan Jiayan, *Zhongguo xiandai xiaoshuo liupai shi* (A history of the schools of modern Chinese fiction) (Beijing: Renmin wenxue chubanshe, 1989), pp. 125–248.

2. Yingjin Zhang, *The City in Modern Chinese Literature and Film: Configurations of Space, Time, and Gender* (Stanford, Calif.: Stanford University Press, 1996), pp. 3–27.

3. As noted below, the study of realist fiction constitutes a major achievement in the field of modern Chinese literature. Since this essay is not intended as a comparative study of modernist and realist fiction, nor as a historical study of representations of Shanghai, I will not address the issues of authenticity and history in Chinese narratives of the 1930s. To focus on the aesthetic vision of the city in early Chinese modernist writings, I have excluded many sociopolitical issues relevant to city literature and urban experience in modern China, such as colonialism and imperialism.

4. Klaus R. Scherpe, "The City as Narrator: The Modern Text in Alfred Döblin's *Berlin Alexanderplatz*," in Andreas Huyssen and David Bathrick, eds., *Modernity and the Text: Revisions of German Modernism* (New York: Columbia University Press, 1989), p. 165.

5. Ibid., pp. 165–66.

6. Ibid., p. 166.

7. Ibid., p. 167.

8. Shen Congwen's annoyance with politics is documented in his letter to Shi Zhicun, dated December 25, 1934; see *Shen Congwen wenji* (Collected works of Shen Congwen) (Hong Kong: Sanlian shudian, 1985), 12: 19. For Shen's condescending view of the jaded urban readers, see his *A Jin* (Hong Kong: Wenli chubanshe, 1960), p. 5.

9. So far I have been unable to find a clear example of Scherpe's fourth mode, the functional or structural, in modern Chinese literature. This apparent lack might be attributed to a generally hostile attitude toward modernist writings—and therefore their lack of development—in China from the 1930s to the 1980s, or to the insubstantial grounding of Scherpe's fourth category in literature (for he finds more examples in film). In either case, this lack does not pose any serious problem for modern Chinese literature.

10. C. T. Hsia, *A History of Modern Chinese Fiction* (New Haven, Conn.: Yale University Press, 1961); Marston Anderson, *The Limits of Realism: Chinese Fiction in the Revolutionary Period* (Berkeley: University of California Press, 1990); David Der-wei Wang, *Fictional Realism in Twentieth-Century China: Mao Dun, Lao She, Shen Congwen* (New York: Columbia University Press, 1992), esp. pp. 201–89.

11. See Li Ou-fan (Leo Ou-fan Lee), "Zhongguo xiandai xiaoshuo de xianquzhe" (Pioneers in Chinese modernist fiction), *Lianhe wenxue* 36 (October 1987): 8–14.

12. Lou Shiyi's review is reprinted in Ying Guojing, ed., *Shi Zhicun* (Selected works by Shi Zhicun) (Hong Kong: Sanlian shudian, 1988), pp. 305–7. The Japan-

ese new perceptionists include Hayashi Fusao, Kataoka Teppei, Kawabata Yasunari, Yokomitsu Riichi, and perhaps also Horiguchi Daigaku. See Randolph Trumbull, "The Shanghai Modernists" (Ph.D. diss., Stanford University, 1989), p. 51; Yan Jiayan, *Zhongguo xiandai xiaoshuo*, p. 126.

13. Su Xuelin was one of the early modern Chinese women writers who came to prominence during the May Fourth period. She has many fine scholarly publications in addition to literary works. However, because of her anti-leftist and anticommunist stance, she has long been neglected in mainland China. See Chen Jingzhi, *Xiandai wenxue zaoqi de nüzuojia* (Early women writers in modern Chinese literature) (Taibei: Chengwen chubanshe, 1980), pp. 103–48.

14. Su Xuelin, *Ersanshi niandai zuojia yu zuopin* (Authors and works in the twenties and thirties) (Taipei: Guangdong chubanshe, 1979), pp. 422–27.

15. See Shi Zhicun, "*Xiandai* zayi" (*Les Contemporains* in recollection), *Xinwenxue shiliao*, 1981, nos. 1–3, and Zhang Zhongliang, "*Xiandai* de fengdu" (The style of *Les Contemporains*), *Xinwenxue shiliao*, 1994, no. 3: 167–69.

16. Among the young writers closely associated with the new perceptionists are Dai Wangshu, Du Heng, Hei Ying, Xu Xiacun, and Ye Lingfeng. The new perceptionist influence had proved negative even in the 1930s. In a letter to Mu Shiying dated June 8, 1935, Ye Lingfeng mentioned some awful imitations of the new perceptionist writings in the market and jokingly held Mu Shiying and Liu Na'ou responsible. See Kong Lingjing, ed., *Xiandai Zhongguo zuojia shuxin* (Letters by modern Chinese writers) (Hong Kong: Yixin shudian, n.d.), p. 227.

17. When Hei Ying published "Wuyue de Zhina" (May in China, 1933) in the inaugural issue of *Wenxue* (Literature), critics like Mao Dun had already found his style similar to that of Mu Shiying. See Hei Ying, "Wo jiandao de Mu Shiying" (Mu Shiying as I knew him), *Xinwenxue shiliao*, 1989, no. 3: 142; the story is collected in Yan Jiayan, ed., *Xin ganjue pai xiaoshuo xuan* (An anthology of new perceptionist fiction) (Beijing: Renmin wenxue chubanshe, 1985), pp. 235–43. For a biographic note on Hei Ying, see Wu Fuhui, *Dushi xuanliu zhongde haipai xiaoshuo* (Fiction of Shanghai trends amid the urban swirls) (Changsha: Hunan jiaoyu chubanshe, 1995), pp. 329–30.

18. In a number of its 1934 issues, for instance, *The Young Companion* printed on its front cover this proud announcement in English: "The most attractive and popular magazine in China." For more information on the background of the pictorial, see Wu Fuhui, "Zuowei wenxue (shangpin) shengchang de haipai qikan" (Shanghai-style literary magazines as products of literature [commodity] production), *Zhongguo xiandai wenxue yanjiu congkan*, 1994, no. 1: 11–12.

19. Hei Ying, "Dang chuntian laidao de shihou" (When spring arrives), *Liangyou* 87 (April 1934): 26. See also May-lee Chai's English translation in *Modern Chinese Literature* 9, no. 1 (Spring 1995): 31–38.

20. As identified in the caption for a similar photograph of the twenty-two-story skyscraper in the February 1934 issue of *The Young Companion*, the skyscraper is the building of the "Sihang chuxuhui" (The four-bank savings incorpo-

rated); see *Liangyou* 85 (February 1934): 15. Completed in 1934, it was the newest skyscraper in East Asia in the 1930s, the highest building in old Shanghai, and the highest in mainland China before the 1960s; see Ma Xuexin, Cao Junwei, Xue Liyong, and Hu Xiaojing, eds., *Shanghai wenhua yuanliu cidian* (Dictionary of the sources and currents of Shanghai culture) (Shanghai: Shanghai shehui kexueyuan chubanshe, 1992), p. 217.

21. An English caption for a photograph on the page preceding Hei Ying's story thus refers to the Bailemen: "When Westerners call this dancing-hall Paramount, Chinese call it the "Door of Hundred Joys." See *Liangyou* 87 (April 1934): 25. The "Paramount" is the name of a first-rank dance hall established in 1932 and located inside the Bailemen Hotel; the dance hall had a reputation as the "number one pleasure-house in East Asia." See Ma Xuexin et al., *Shanghai wenhua*, p. 254.

22. Hei Ying, "Dang chuntian," p. 26.

23. Ibid., p. 27.

24. The longest and most famous street in the French Concession in Shanghai, Avenue de Joffre is now called Huaihai zhonglu. See Shanghaitong she (Society of Shanghai experts), ed., *Shanghai yanjiu ziliao* (Research materials on Shanghai) (Taipei: Zhongguo chubanshe, 1973), pp. 331–33.

25. As illustrated by two photographs, the chimney is clearly a phallic symbol of the industrial city which threatens to violate the natural, feminine qualities (e.g., beauty, peace, and tranquillity) embodied by the West Lake.

26. The closest English equivalent for the *huiliqiu* may be squash: both are played indoors but have different rules. Next to the horse and dog races, the *huiliqiu* games were an extremely popular form of gambling in Shanghai in the 1930s. As a joint venture established in 1929 by an American, two Frenchmen, and a Chinese, the *huiliqiu* sports facilities opened in 1932 on Ya'erpei lu (Avenue du Roi Albert, now Shanxi nanlu). See Ma Xuexin et al., *Shanghai wenhua*, pp. 262–63.

27. Hei Ying, "Dang chuntian," p. 27.

28. Michel de Certeau, "Practices of Space," in Marshall Blonsky, ed., *On Signs* (Baltimore, Md.: Johns Hopkins University Press, 1985), p. 124.

29. The two identical photographs (which differ only in size) of the skyscraper are placed at the beginning and the end of Hei Ying's story. In a striking manner, this framing technique appears in the opening and closing scenes of Yuan Muzhi's *Malu tianshi* (Street angel, produced by Mingxing, Shanghai, in 1937), where the identical low-angle shots of a skyscraper conveys the inaccessibility of the panoramic view to the majority of the city-dwellers who live, as announced in the film, on "the Shanghai subterrane." In spite of this visual resemblance, however, the question of modernist influence on a "leftist film" is nearly impossible to pursue here.

30. The "modernist" imprint in the story is illustrated both by a new way of perceiving the urban signs and by a strategic refusal to present the city "realistically."

31. Charles Baudelaire, *The Painter of Modern Life and Other Essays*, translated and edited by Jonathan Mayne (New York: Phaidon, 1965), p. 9.

32. Walter Benjamin, *Charles Baudelaire: A Lyric Poet in the Era of High Capitalism*, translated by Harry Zohn (London: NLB, 1973), p. 45.

33. See *Beiyang huabao*, July 7, 1928, 7.

34. "Intoxicated Shanghai," *Liangyou* 85 (February 1934): 14.

35. See Yan Jiayan, *Zhongguo xiandai geliupai xiaoshuo xuan* (Selections from various modern Chinese fiction schools) (Beijing: Beijing Daxue chubanshe, 1986), 2: 258–64.

36. Teresa de Lauretis, *Alice Doesn't: Feminism, Semiotics, Cinema* (Bloomington: Indiana University Press, 1984), p. 13.

37. Certeau, "Practices of Space," p. 139.

38. In addition to the young photographer in Edward Yang's (Yang Dechang) *Kongbu fenzi* (The terrorizer, produced by Central Motion Picture Corporation, Taiwan, in 1986), who aimlessly wanders on the streets and randomly takes snapshots of cars and pedestrians, the male protagonists in the following two recent films also exemplify the narrative strategy in question: a reckless, rootless wanderer in Wong Kar-wai's (Wang Jiawei) *A Fei zhengzhuan* (The days of being wild, produced in Hong Kong in 1990) and an abandoned, alienated ex-prisoner in Xie Fei's *Benming nian* (Black snow, produced by Beijing Qingnian in 1990). Respectively, these three films are set in three major metropolises—Taipei, Hong Kong, and Beijing.

39. Raymond Williams, *The Country and the City* (New York: Oxford University Press, 1973), p. 233. My discussion of the city as an object of the male gaze in new perceptionist writings does not exclude the possibility that a female character may adopt the same strategy of walking on the street and may thus create a female vision of the city. As I pointed out elsewhere, both Su Qing and Zhang Ailing (Eileen Chang) obtained such visions in their urban narratives of the 1940s. See Y. Zhang, *The City*, pp. 232–59.

40. Gongsun Lu, *Zhongguo dianying shihua* (A history of Chinese cinema) (Hong Kong: Nantian shuye gongsi, 1977), 2: 55–56.

41. Cf. Benjamin's speculation: "Modernism must be under the sign of suicide, an act which seals a heroic will that makes no concessions to a mentality inimical towards this will. This suicide is not a resignation but a heroic passion" (Benjamin, *Charles Baudelaire*, p. 75). It deserves mention that many twentieth-century writers committed suicide, not just in Europe and the United States, but also in China and Japan.

42. Shi Zhicun and Ying Guojing, eds., *Dai Wangshu* (Selected works of Dai Wangshu) (Hong Kong: Sanlian shudian, 1987), pp. 16–17.

43. See Yan Jiayan, *Xin ganjue pai*, pp. 127–46.

44. See Yan Jiayan, *Zhongguo xiandai geliupai*, 2: 258–64.

45. See Yan Jiayan, *Xin ganjue pai*, p. 204.

46. Li Ou-fan, "Zhongguo xiandai xiaoshuo de xianquzhe," p. 13; the passage is reprinted in Yan Jiayan, *Xin ganjue pai*, pp. 164–65.

47. For detailed discussion of the reversal in these two passages, see Trumbull, "Shanghai Modernists," pp. 162–65, and Y. Zhang, *The City*, pp. 154–81.

48. Hei Ying, "Chun" (Spring), *Qingqing dianying*, June 15, 1934.

49. In a truly narcissistic manner, Mu Shiying sometimes made his characters cite his own stories—not to mention other new perceptionist works—as objects of their admiration. See Wu Fuhui, *Dushi xuanliu*, pp. 73–74.

50. Matei Calinescu, *Five Faces of Modernity: Modernism, Avant-Garde, Decadence, Kitsch, Postmodernism* (Durham, N.C.: Duke University Press, 1987), pp. 41–42.

51. Ibid., p. 5.

52. There are, of course, exceptions, especially in Liu Na'ou's and Mu Shiying's early writings, which bear a visible leftist influence. But insofar as they relish the bourgeois taste in music (e.g., jazz and piano), painting (e.g., by Monet), and other forms of art and entertainment, the antibourgeois message in the new perceptionist writings is always outweighed by their fascination with the bourgeois lifestyles.

53. Yan Jiayan, *Zhongguo xiandai xiaoshuo*, pp. 141–55. For a more extensive study, see also Wu Fuhui, *Dushi xuanliu*, pp. 141–281.

10. Cult of Poetry

I would like to thank Maghiel van Creuel, Michael Day, Ouyang Jianghe, Meng Lang, Bei Ling, Mang Ke, and Mi Jiayan for providing invaluable material on which this chapter is based.

1. Michelle Yeh, "Light a Lamp in a Rock: Experimental Poetry in Contemporary China," *Modern China* 18, no. 4 (October 1992): 379–409.

2. Michelle Yeh, "Contemporary Chinese Poetry Scenes," *Chicago Review* 39, nos. 3–4 (1993): 279–83.

3. According to Mang Ke, an editor of *Xiandai Hanshi* (Contemporary Chinese poetry), the press run is 250 to 300 copies per issue. *Feifei* (Chengdu, Sichuan), however, is said to run 2,000 copies per issue.

4. Michael Groden and Martin Kreiswirth, eds., *The Johns Hopkins Guide to Literary Theory and Criticism* (Baltimore, Md.: Johns Hopkins University Press, 1994), p. 208.

5. *Qingxiang* (Tendency; Beijing), mimeograph, 1988.

6. Bei Ling and Meng Lang, eds., *Dangdai Zhongguo shige qishiwu shou* (Seventy-five contemporary Chinese poems) (Beijing & Shanghai: mimeograph, 1985), p. 27.

7. *Beihuiguixian* (The Tropic of Cancer; Hangzhou), no. 3 (1993).

8. *Guodu* (Transition; Beijing), mimeograph, 1988.

9. *Beihuiguixian*, no. 3 (1993): 95.

10. Unpublished essay provided by the poet.
11. Bei Ling and Meng Lang, *Dangdai Zhongguo shige*, p. 1.
12. *Beihuiguixian*, no. 3 (1993).
13. *Fengren* (Knife's edge; Hunan), 1993: 1.
14. Also, Meng Lang and Momo, two Shanghai poets, were taken into custody and detained for weeks without any charges after the Tiananmen crackdown. Their personal libraries, manuscripts, and correspondence were confiscated.
15. In recent years a large number of poets have "plunged into the sea" (*xiahai*) of commercialism. Some have gone into the publishing business, running bookstores or publishing popular literature. One successful example is the Feifei poets (Lan Ma, Yang Li, Jimu Langge, and He Xiaozhu), who run a "soft engineering" company in Chengdu, which specializes in product design, advertising, and promotion. A positive result of this is that with the profits they have made, they can now publish series of avant-garde poetry. The financial success, however, is not the norm; many avant-garde poets are in far less comfortable situations.
16. *Feifei*, 1993: 42.
17. *Babieta* (Tower of Babel; Beijing), mimeograph, 1991: 12.
18. See Michelle Yeh, "Light a Lamp."
19. Ye Mang, "Dalu qingnian shiren zai liulang" (Young mainland poets are wandering), *Zhongguo qingnian yanjiu* (Studies in Chinese youth), 1994: 2.
20. Lan Cun, "Yeying zai gechang" (Nightingale sings), *Shanchahua* (Camellia; Jiangxi), no. 16 (1993): 15.
21. Yi Ke, "A 'Nomadic People' in Great Shanghai," *Liuxuesheng xinwen* (Overseas students news; Japan), 1993: 12.
22. Yin Nan, "Chuntian de jiugui Hei Dachun" (Hei Dachun, a drunkard in spring), *Dasaodong* (Great turmoil; Guizhou), no. 1 (mimeograph, 1991): 68–69.
23. Hai Lei, Epilogue to Shi Zhi and Hei Dachun, *Xiandai shuqingshi heji* (A joint collection of contemporary lyrics) (Chengdu: Chengdu keji daxue chubanshe, 1993), p. 4.
24. Wang Qiang, "Yilu liulang" (Wandering all the way), *Heidong* (Black hole; Beijing), mimeograph, 1988: 10.
25. See Maghiel van Crevel, "Experimental Poetry in the 1960s-70s," *Modern Chinese Literature* 9, no. 2 (Fall 1996): 169–219, and Lin Mang, Preface to Shi Zhi and Hei Dachun, *Xiandai shuqingshi heji*, p. 4.
26. Chen Dongdong, "Yao haizhe xiwang" (We must have hope), *Epoch Poetry Quarterly* (Taiwan), no. 99 (Summer 1994): 64.
27. *Faxian* (Discover; Beijing), no. 1 (mimeograph, 1990): 27.
28. Michelle Yeh, "Death of the Poet: Poetry and Society in Contemporary China and Taiwan," *Literature East and West*, no. 28 (1995): 43–62.
29. Zhu Dake, "Zongjiao shiren: Haizi yu Luo Yihe" (Religious poets: Haizi and Luo Yihe), *Ershiyi shiji* (Twenty-first century; Hong Kong), no. 11 (June 1992): 119–23; Matei Mihalca, "Dead Poet's Fans: Ignored in Life, He Is Now a Hero," *Far Eastern Economic Review*, April 1993, 39.

30. Han Gaoqi, "Shige fangcheng" (Poetic formulae), *Yuanze* (Principle; Zhejiang), 1994: 23.

31. Zhou Jun and Zhang Wei, eds., *Haizi Luo Yihe zuopin ji* (Collected work of Haizi and Luo Yihe) (Nanjing: Nanjing chubanshe, 1991), p. 308.

32. Zang Di, "Yong Jing Ke" (Ode to Jing Ke), *Xiandai hanshi*, 1992, no. 1: 14.

33. Yu Congzhe, "Tiancai yu fengzi zhicha yixian—shiren Gu Cheng de duancu shengming" (Only a thin line between genius and insanity: The short life of Gu Cheng the poet," *Jiushi niandai* (The nineties; Hong Kong), no. 286 (November 1993): 78.

34. Ibid., p. 79, my emphasis.

35. *Tailao shibao* (Tailao poetry gazette; Fujian), 1993: 1.

36. *Women* (We; Shaanxi), mimeograph, 1993: 16.

37. Michael Day, "Chinese Poets and June Fourth 1989: A Human Response," pp. 4–5. I would like to thank the author for providing me with a copy of this paper, which he presented at the University of California, Davis, in the summer of 1995.

38. Ibid., p. 6.

39. Cai Hengping, "1990 xiatian zihua xiang" (A self-portrait in summer 1990), *Babieta*, 1991; Huang Canran, "Boerhesi de shiming" (Borges' blindness), *Mingbao yuekan* (Mingbao monthly; Hong Kong), 1996, no. 3: 88.

40. In addition to the poets discussed here, a number of Nobel laureates are mentioned with much frequency. Besides Brodsky, Czeslaw Milosz, Odysseas Elytis, and Derek Walcott are also familiar names. The intense attention that Chinese avant-garde poets have focused on the Nobel Prize is itself significant, although they are by no means alone in this. In recent years a large number of books on the Nobel Prize for Literature have been published in China. Such titles as *Appreciation of the Poetry of Nobel Prize Winners* and *In Pursuit of Twentieth-Century Literary Masters: Notes on the Nobel Prize for Literature* suggest how Chinese writers, both of the establishment and the avant-garde, covet the prize. For the avant-garde poet, the indifference of society and the hostility of the establishment probably make him particularly eager to be recognized by, and become part of, the international literary community.

41. Sun Wenbo, "Shiren" (The poet), *Hongqi* (Red flag; Sichuan), no. 2 (mimeograph, 1987): 8.

42. Hai Long, "Tianci" (Genius), *Women*, 1993: 16.

43. Joseph Brodsky, "Nobel Lecture, 1987," in Lev Loseff and Valentina Polukhina, eds., *Brodsky's Poetics and Aesthetics* (New York: St. Martin's Press, 1990), p. 3.

44. Kong Jiesheng, "Zhuyi guojia fang liangbian, jinqian xing'ai bai zhongjian—liusi shijian hou dalu shehui jiazhi guan de bianqian" (Out go isms and the nation, in come money and sex: Change in mainland China's social values after the June Fourth incident), *Xin xinwen* (The journalist; Taiwan), no. 327 (1993): 90.

45. Zhou Lunyou, "Jujue de zitai" (The gesture of refusal), *Xiandai hanshi*, 1992, no. 2: 116.

46. Yü Ying-shih, "Zhongguo zhishi fenzi de bianyuan hua" (The marginalization of the Chinese intelligentsia), *Ershiyi shiji*, no. 6 (August 1991): 20.

47. Wang Gan, "Yige youling: zishen yu pipan—xinchao wenyi zhongde wenge yinying" (A phantom: Introspection and critique?—the shadow of the Cultural Revolution in new-wave literature and art), *Wenyi zhengming* (Contending voices in literature and art), 1994, no. 1: 63.

48. Laurence A. Schneider, *A Madman of Ch'u: The Chinese Myth of Loyalty and Dissent* (Berkeley: University of California Press, 1980), pp. 159–60.

49. Ibid., p. 159.

50. Lan Cun, "Chenggong huozhe bu chenggong de" (The successful and the unsuccessful), *Shanchahua*, no. 16 (1993): 16.

51. Ye Yunchao, *Yuanze*, 1993: 7, my emphasis.

52. Zhu Dake, "Zongjiao shiren," p. 122.

53. Maghiel van Crevel, *Language Shattered: Contemporary Chinese Poetry and Duoduo* (Leiden, Netherlands: Research School CNWS, 1996), p. 235.

54. This author has been told by a number of poets about cases where imposters pretend to be well-known avant-garde poets (e.g., Chen Dongdong, Meng Lang, Bai Hua) in order to get free food, borrow money, or win women's hearts. Even *Shikan* (Poetry monthly), the largest state-run poetry magazine in China, published an article in the 1995 February issue to warn readers about a man named Peng Ming, who passes himself off as a famous poet by having pictures taken with established writers and Party officials. Using these pictures and other fraudulent means, he has lied his way all over China since 1992.

55. Quoted in James Fenton, "Some Mistakes People Make about Poetry," *New York Review of Books*, March 25, 1993, 19.

56. Milan Kundera, *Life Is Elsewhere*, trans. Peter Kussi (New York: Penguin, 1986), pp. 30–31.

57. Bai Hua, "Maiei—jinian Haizi" (Wheat, in memoriam: Haizi), *Jiushi niandai* (The nineteen-nineties; Sichuan), 1989: 58–59.

58. Lan Cun, "Chenggong huozhe bu chenggong de" (The successful or the unsuccessful), *Shanchahua*, no. 16 (1993).

59. Yu Jian, "Huida shiren Zhu Wen de ershiwu ge wenti" (Responses to the poet Zhu Wen's twenty-five questions), unpublished manuscript provided by the poet in 1993, p. 6.

60. Ouyang Jianghe, "Guanyu xiandaishi de suixiang" (Reflections on modern poetry), *Ririxin* (Make it new; Sichuan), mimeograph, 1985: 5.

61. Bei Ling, "Guanyu shi de yifen xin" (A letter reflecting on poetry), *Mingbao yuekan*, 1994, no. 3: 110.

62. Ya Xian, "Po" (Dissection), *Ya Xian shiji* (Collected poems of Ya Xian), 2d edition (Taipei: Hongfan, 1982), p. 2.

63. Cui Weiping, Preface to *Pingguo shangde bao: nüxing shijuan* (A panther on

an apple: An anthology of women poets) (Beijing: Beijing shifan daxue chubanshe, 1993), p. 2.

64. Ibid., pp. 41–42.

65. This is arguably seen in the large number of translations of *menglongshi* and more recent Chinese avant-garde poetry in North America, Europe, and Asia. Bei Dao, the most famous of the *menglong* poets, has been translated into more than twenty languages. In the wake of the Tiananmen Square Massacre, Chinese dissent literature has also received much attention from the international community, which can be seen, for instance, in the publications of *Today*, conceived as a forum for Chinese writers "in exile"—whether understood as voluntary exile or internal exile, and of *Tendency*, which emphasizes its dissident role. Both journals are published outside China and are revivals of those originally published in China (see *Jintian*, 1978–80, and *Qingxiang*, 1988, 1990–91).

11. Comparative Literature at the Fin de Siècle

This essay is based on my concluding address at the Fourth International Conference of the American Association of Chinese Comparative Literature, entitled "Literature, History, Culture: Re-envisioning Chinese and Comparative Literature," held at Princeton University in June 1994.

1. Edward Said, *Orientalism* (New York: Vintage Books, 1978), p. 259.

2. Ibid., p. 259.

3. Guillermo Gomez-Pena, *Warrior for Gringostroika* (St. Paul: Graywolf Press, 1993), p. 125.

4. James Clifford, *The Predicament of Culture: Twentieth-Century Ethnography, Literature, and Art* (Cambridge, Mass.: Harvard University Press, 1988), p. 9.

5. Edward Said, *Culture and Imperialism* (New York: Vintage Books, 1994), p. 6. It is ironic, particularly for someone who opposes the hegemonic excesses of imperialism, that Said should admit that "this set of patterns . . . was first established and made possible by the modern empires" (ibid.).

6. Clifford, *Predicament of Culture*, pp. 10, 13, 14.

7. Ibid., p. 161.

8. Erich Auerbach, "Philology and *Weltliteratur*," *Centennial Review* 13, no. 1 (Winter 1969): 17.

9. Said, *Orientalism*, p. 259.

10. Tzvetan Todorov, *The Conquest of America*, trans. Richard Howard (New York: Harper & Row, 1985), p. 250.

11. The passage, and the sequence, attracted Yvonne Hsieh as well. See her *Victor Segalen's Literary Encounter with China: Chinese Moulds, Western Thoughts* (Toronto: University of Toronto Press, 1988).

12. Said, *Culture and Imperialism*, p. 335. In *Culture and Imperialism*, Said credits

Jerome Taylor for the translation: there is no attribution for the translator in *Orientalism*.

13. Auerbach, "Philology and *Weltliteratur*," p. 14.

14. Said, *Orientalism*, p. 259.

15. Todorov, *Conquest of America*, p. 249.

16. One notes that the text cited survives in four versions: the original Latin; Said's translation into English; Todorov's translation into French; and Richard Howard's English version in his translation of Todorov, which differs from Said's—it is not clear whether Todorov translated from the original Latin or from Said's English translation, nor is it clear whether Richard Howard, Todorov's translator, rendered the text directly from the original Latin, or from Todorov's French version.

17. Quoted from Wu-chi Liu and Irving Yucheng Lo, eds., *Sunflower Splendor: Three Thousand Years of Chinese Poetry* (Bloomington: Indiana University Press, 1975), p. 227.

18. Cf. Irving Rouse, *The Tainos: Rise and Decline of the People Who Greeted Columbus* (New Haven: Yale University Press, 1992), p. 138. What is also ironical, as Rouse points out, is that "directly or indirectly, Columbus has supplied most of our ethnohistorical information about the Tainos" (p. 139). One could suggest that China was the "final cause" for Columbus's discovery of the Americas, since China was his ultimate destination: Irving Rouse tells us that "Columbus himself believed that he had reached Japan or a peninsula (perhaps Korea?) that would lead him westward to China (p. 143).

19. Arnold Krupat, *Ethnocriticism: Ethnography, History, Literature* (Berkeley: University of California Press, 1992), p. 133.

20. Reprinted in ibid., p. 173.

21. Ibid.

22. Rouse, *Tainos*, p. 142.

23. Eric Cheyfitz, *The Poetics of Imperialism: Translation and Colonization from The Tempest to Tarzan* (New York: Oxford University Press, 1991), p. 105.

24. John Searle, *The Rediscovery of the Mind* (Cambridge, Mass.: MIT Press, 1994), p. 45.

25. Ibid.

26. Krupat, *Ethnocriticism*, p. 26.

27. Ibid., p. 5.

28. Ibid., p. 27.

29. Ibid.

30. David Hollinger, *In the American Province: Studies in the History and the Historiography of Ideas* (Bloomington: Indiana University Press, 1985), p. 59.

31. Ibid., p. 55.

32. Yi-fu Tuan, *Passing Strange and Wonderful: Aesthetics, Nature, and Culture* (Washington, D.C.: Island Press, 1993), p. 171.

33. Said, *Orientalism*, p. 58.

34. Hollinger, *In the American Province*, p. 72.

35. Tuan, *Passing Strange and Wonderful*, p. 172.

36. All the major cities of the U.S. interior whose significance predates the automobile are ports. Indeed, St. Louis is on the edge of one of the largest rivers in the world and Chicago itself is, in a sense, on the edge of a sea, for the Great Lakes are between the United States and Canada, and via the St. Lawrence Chicago is connected to the Atlantic Ocean. In a sense then the periphery penetrates to the very center.

37. The consequences of this lacuna for the study of Native American literature have been discussed by Arnold Krupat in his *Ethnocriticism*, pp. 43–45.

38. J. B. Post, compiler, *The Atlas of Fantasy* (Baltimore: Mirage Press, 1973).

39. *The Complete Book of Covers from the New Yorker, 1925–1989* (New York: Knopf: 1989), p. 308 (the cover of the March 29, 1976 issue).

40. *New York Times*, March 29, 1972.

41. Mark Monmonier, *Maps, Distortion, and Meaning* (Washington, D.C.: Association of American Geographers, 1977), p. 1.

42. Burton Watson, trans., *Chuang Tzu: Basic Writings* (New York: Columbia University Press, 1964), p. 38.

43. Clifford, *Predicament of Culture*, p. 11.

44. Ibid., p. 17.

45. Ibid., p. 41.

CHARACTER LIST

This Character List includes primary authors and texts, selected secondary authors, books, journals, and newspapers, as well as some characters and special terms romanized in the chapters. Entries are alphabetized letter by letter, ignoring word and syllable breaks.

A Fei zhengzhuan	阿飛正傳
"Ai, shi buneng wangji de"	愛,是不能忘記的
Ai Xia (1912–34)	艾霞
A Jin	阿金
An Lushan	安祿山
A Xia	阿霞
A Ying (1900–77)	阿英
Babieta	巴別塔
Bai Hua (b. 1956)	柏樺
Bailemen	百樂門
"Baimaonü"	白毛女
Ban Gu (32–92)	班固
Ban Zhao (ca. A.D. 44–120)	班昭
Bashiri huanyou ji	八十日環遊記
Bashu xiandai shiqun	巴蜀現代詩群
"Bei aiqing yiwang de jiaoluo"	被愛情遺忘的角落
Bei Dao (b. 1949)	北島
Beihuiguixian	北回歸線
"Beijiguang"	北極光
Beiji tanxian ji	北極探險記
Bei Ling (b. 1959)	貝嶺
bei maizang de shiren	被埋葬的詩人
Beiyang huabao	北洋畫報
Benming nian	本命年
bense	本色
bian	變
Biancheng	邊城
bianfeng	變風

bianji	邊際
biansao	辨騷
bianya	變雅
"Bianyan"	辨言
biaoyu he kouhao	標語和口號
Biheguan zhuren	碧荷館主人
biji	筆記
Bijiao wenxue daolun	比較文學導論
Bijiao wenxue de kentuo zai Taiwan	比較文學的墾拓在台灣
Bijiao wenxue fangfalun	比較文學方法論
Bijiao wenxue gailun	比較文學概論
Bijiao wenxue shi	比較文學史
Bijiao wenxue yanjiu zhi xin fangxiang	比較文學研究之新方向
Biji qizhong	筆記七種
Bin Chun	斌椿
Bing Xin (b. 1900)	冰心
burugui	不如歸
buxiu	不朽
cai	才
Cai Chusheng (1906–68)	蔡楚生
Caidiao ji	才調集
Cai Hengping (b. 1966)	蔡恆平
caizi jiaren	才子佳人
Cao Shunqing	曹順慶
Cao Zhi (192–232)	曹植
chanfa fa	闡發法
Chang Han-liang	張漢良
Changhenge	長恨歌
Changshengshu	長生術
chaoyue	超越
Chen Dongdong (b. 1961)	陳東東
Chen Dun	陳惇
Chen Duxiu (1880–1942)	陳獨秀
Chengcha biji	乘槎筆記
"Chenggong huozhe bu chenggong de"	成功或者不成功的
Cheng Maochao (b. 1962)	成茂朝
Chen Jingzhi	陳敬之
Chen Pengxiang (Chen Huiha)	陳鵬翔 (陳慧樺)
Chen Pingyuan	陳平原
Chen Rong	諶容
Chen Xiaoming	陳曉明

Chen Zhongyi	陳仲義
chongbai	崇拜
chonggao	崇高
Chonggu	崇嘏
Chouban yiwu shimo	籌辦夷務始末
Chou Ying-hsiung	周英雄
Chow, Rey	周蕾
Chuangshiji	創世紀
chuanqi	傳奇
Chuci	楚辭
Chuci zhangju	楚辭章句
Chu Fujun	儲福軍
Chunqiu	春秋
Chuntao	春桃
"Chuntian"	春天
ci	詞
ci	雌
Ci Mulan	雌木蘭
Cishenglin	次生林
Daguanyuan	大觀園
Dai Fang	戴舫
Dai Jinhua	戴錦華
Dai Wangshu (1905–50)	戴望舒
Dalu	大陸
"Dalu qingnian shiren zai liulang"	大陸青年詩人在流浪
"Dang chuntian laidao de shihou"	當春天來到的時候
Dangdai Zhongguo shige qishiwu shou	當代中國詩歌七十五首
Dangdai Zhongguo wenxue pinglun	當代中國文學評論
Dangdai zuojia pinglun	當代作家評論
daoyi	道義
dao Zhongguo renqun yi jinxing	導中國人群以進行
Dasaodong	大騷動
dashi	大師
dazhong wenhua	大眾文化
de	德
"Dianshu qitan"	電術奇談
Didi shijie	地底世界
"Dixia lüxing"	地下旅行
"Dixiongmen"	弟兄們
Dongfang zazhi	東方雜誌
Donghai Juewo	東海覺我
Du Fu (712–70)	杜甫

Du Heng (1907–64)	杜衡
"Duhui de ciji"	都會的刺激
duihua yanjiu	對話研究
Dushi xuanliu zhongde haipai xiaoshuo	都市漩流中的海派小說
Duxiu wencun	獨秀文存
erhu	二胡
Ersanshi niandai zuojia yu zuopin	二三十年代作家與作品
Ershiyi shiji	二十一世紀
fanchang	反常
Fangzhou	方舟
Fanyi luncong	翻譯論叢
Faxian	發現
feiche	飛車
Feidu	廢都
Feifei	非非
feng	風
Feng Guifen	馮桂芬
Fengren	鋒刃
fu	賦
Fuchu lishi dibiao	浮出歷史地表
fugu	復古
fugu yundong	復古運動
fulian	婦聯
funü	婦女
funü jiefang	婦女解放
"Gangshang de shiji"	崗上的世紀
Gao Zhongwu	高中武
gediao	格調
Ge Mai (1965–91)	戈麥
"Geren shenghuo de shunjian"	個人生活的瞬間
"Gexing riben lai"	歌星日本來
Gezhi shudian	格致書店
gong'an pai	公安派
Gongheguo jiaokeshu	共和國教科書
"Gongkai de neican"	公開的內參
"Gongmu"	公墓
Gongsun Lu	公孫魯
gongtishi	宮體詩
guanfang	官方
Guangming ribao	光明日報

Guangxue hui	廣學會
"Guangxu wannian"	光緒萬年
Guangzhi	廣智
Guan Jinpeng (b. 1957)	關錦鵬
Guan Yushi	貫雲石
"Guanyu xiandai shi de suixiang"	關於現代詩的隨想
Guanyu Zhongguo gudian wenxue wenti	關於中國古典文學問題
Guanzhui pian	管錐篇
Gu Cheng (1956–93)	顧城
gufeng	古風
gufu	古賦
Guifan	閨範
Guodu	過渡
Guo Songtao (1818–81)	郭嵩燾
Guoxiu ji	國休集
guoxue	國學
Guo Yanli	郭延禮
gushi	古詩
Gu Tianhong	古添洪
Haidi lüxing	海底旅行
Haiguo tuzhi	海國圖志
Hai Lei	海雷
Hai Long	海龍
Hailu	海錄
haiwai huaren	海外華人
Haizi (1964–89)	海子
Haizi Luo Yihe zuopin ji	海子駱一禾作品集
Han Dong	韓東
Han Gaoqi	韓高琦
"Hanyu—xiangei Cai, yige Hanyu shougong yiren"	漢語——獻給蔡,一個漢語手工藝人
Hei Dachun (b. 1960)	黑大春
Heidong	黑洞
"Hei mudan"	黑牡丹
Hei Ying (Zhang Bingwen, b. 1915)	黑嬰(張炳文)
He Lin	賀麟
Hengtang tuishi	蘅塘退士
Heyue yingling ji	河嶽英靈集
hongchen	紅塵
Hongloumeng	紅樓夢
Hongloumeng yanjiu jikan	紅樓夢研究集刊
Hongqi	紅旗

Hong Xisheng	紅溪生
Hongzhu	紅燭
Huaguoshan	花果山
Hua Hu	花弧
Huaihai zhonglu	淮海中路
Huang Canran (b. 1963)	黃燦然
Huang Gu	黃姑
Huangjiang Diaosou	荒江釣叟
"Huangshan zhi lian"	荒山之戀
Huang Xiang (b. 1941)	黃翔
Huang Yi	黃伊
Huang Yuanjie	黃媛介
Hu Die (1907–89)	胡蝶
huiliqiu	回力球
Hu Qiuyuan (b. 1910)	胡秋原
Hu Shi (1891–1962)	胡適
Hu Shi wencun	胡適文存
"Jia Baoyu zuo qianshuiting"	賈寶玉坐潛水艇
Jian an	建安
Jiang He (b. 1949)	江河
"Jianshe de wenxue geming lun"	建設的文學革命論
Jianwendi	簡文帝
Jiaobinlu kangyi	校邠廬抗議
jiaoyu xiaoshuo	教育小說
Jia Pingwa (b. 1953)	賈平凹
Jia Zhifang	賈植芳
Jidujao yu jindai wenhua	基督教與近代文化
jing	經
Jing'an wenji	靜安文集
Jing Ke	荊軻
Jingpai xiaoshuo	京派小說
Jingxue lishi	經學歷史
jingying wenhua de shiluo	精英文化的失落
"Jinian Zhu Xiang"	紀念朱湘
Jin Kaicheng	金開誠
"Jinnian weixin"	今年維新
Jinshangqin	井上勤
Jintian	今天
"Jinxiugu zhi lian"	錦繡谷之戀
Jishi yu xugou	紀實与虛構
Jiushi niandai	九十年代
jixian	極限

Ji Xianlin	季羨林
Jixuan ji	極玄集
"Jujue de zitai"	拒絕的姿態
junzi	君子
Kang Youwei (1858–1927)	康有為
kexue	科學
kexue xiaoshuo	科學小說
Kongbu fenzi	恐怖分子
"Kongchao"	空巢
Kong Jiesheng	孔捷生
kua wenhua yanjiu	跨文化研究
Lan Niao	藍鳥
Lao Gui	老鬼
Lao She (1899–1966)	老舍
Li	理
"Liangge shijian de buganzheng zhe"	兩個時間的不感症者
Liang Qichao (1873–1929)	梁啓超
Liang Shiqiu (1902–88)	梁實秋
Liangyou	良友
Lianhe wenxue	聯合文學
Liao Yiwu (b. 1958)	廖亦武
Li Bai (Li Bo, 701–62)	李白
Li Dasan (John Deeney)	李達三
Lieman	列曼
Liji	禮記
Li Meng	李夢
Linghu Chu (ca. 766–837)	令狐楚
"Ling yu rou"	靈與肉
Lin Mang	林莽
Lin Shu (1852–1924)	林紓
Lin Shu pingzhuan	林紓評傳
Lin Yutang (1895–1976)	林語堂
Lin Zexu (1785–1850)	林則徐
Li Ou-fan	李歐梵
Li Qingzhao (1084–1155?)	李清照
Lisao	離騷
Li Shangyin (ca. 813–ca. 858)	李商隱
Li Taibai quanji	李太白全集
"Liu"	流
Liu Dajie	劉大杰
Liu Jiemin	劉介民

Liu Na'ou (1900–40)	劉吶鷗
Liu Xiangyu	劉象愚
Liu Xie (466?–539?)	劉勰
Liuxuesheng xinwen	留學生新聞
lixiang xiaoshuo	理想小說
Li Yawei (b. 1965)	李亞偉
Li Zhi (1527–1602)	李贄
Lou Shiyi (b. 1905)	樓適夷
Lu Jidong	盧藉東
Lu Kanghua	盧康華
Lü Kun (1536–1618)	呂坤
Lundun Bali riji	倫敦巴黎日記
Lun kexue huanxiang xiaoshuo	論科學幻想小說
"Lun xiaoshuo yu qunzhi zhi guanxi"	論小說與群治之關係
Lunyu	論語
Luotuo Xiangzi	駱駝祥子
Luo Xinzhang	羅新璋
Luo Yihe (1964–89)	駱一禾
lüshi	律詩
Lu Xun (1881–1936)	魯迅
Lu Xun quanji	魯迅全集
Lu Yimin (b. 1962)	陸憶敏
Maikenxi	麥懇西
"Maizi—Jinian Haizi"	麥子——紀念海子
Malu tianshi	馬路天使
Mang Ke (b. 1951)	芒克
Mao Dun (1896–1981)	茅盾
Mao Jin	毛縉
Maoshi zhengyi	毛詩正義
Ma Xuexin	馬學新
Ma Zhiyuan (ca. 1250–ca. 1324)	馬致遠
Mei	美
Meihua shuguan	美華書館
Mei Yaochen (1002–62)	梅堯臣
Meng Lang (b. 1961)	孟浪
Menglongshi	朦朧詩
Meng Yue	孟悅
Mengzi (372–289 B.C.)	孟子
minban kanwu	民辦刊物
Mingbao yuekan	明報月刊
Mingguo yilai chuban xinshu zongmu	民國以來出版新書綜目
Mingshi	明史

"Mini"	米尼
minzuxing	民族性
"Modao"	魔道
Momo (b. 1964)	默默
moshen feidao	魔繩飛刀
Mulan	木蘭
Mu Shiying (1912–40)	穆時英
Nahan	吶喊
nalai zhuyi	拿來主義
nan'er han	男兒漢
Nanfang bao	南方報
"Nanren de yiban shi nüren"	男人的一半是女人
nanzihan	男子漢
neibu jiaoliu	內部交流
nigu	擬古
Nongxue zazhi	農學雜志
nü	女
nüduojiao	女多嬌
Nüjie	女誡
Nünu	女奴
"Nüren"	女人
Nüwa	女媧
nüzhiqing	女知青
Nüzhuanyuan	女狀元
Ouyang Jianghe (b. 1956)	歐陽江河
Ouyang Xiu (1007–72)	歐陽修
panlong	攀龍
Pan Youqiang	潘友強
Peiming	培茗
pianwen	駢文
Pingguo shangde bao: nüxing shijuan	蘋果上的豹：女性詩卷
Pi Xirui	皮錫瑞
"Po"	剖
qi	奇
Qian Qianyi (1582–1664)	錢謙益
Qian Zhongshu (b. 1910)	錢鍾書
Qiezhong ji	篋中集
qimeng	啓蒙
qimeng jiaoyu	啓蒙教育

qing	情
qingbai zhicao	清白之操
Qingqing dianying	青青電影
Qingxiang	傾向
Qi Rushan	齊如山
Qi Rushan huiyi lu	齊如山回憶錄
qishu	奇書
Qiwu lun	齊物論
qizhong zhiqi	奇中之奇
Qizhui ji	七綴集
quan	權
Quan Liang wen	全梁文
Quhai zongmu	曲海總目
Qu Yuan (338–278 B.C.)	屈原
re	熱
Rendao zhongnian	人到中年
ren jie	人界
ren ru qi wen	人如其文
renwen jingshen de weiji	人文精神的危機
"Ren xin buzu, de long wangshu"	人心不足,得隴望蜀
Ririxin	日日新
rouran	柔然
ru	儒
Ruan Lingyu (1910–35)	阮玲玉
Rui Tingzhang	芮挺章
Rulin waishi	儒林外史
Ru Zhijuan (b. 1925)	茹志鵑
sancong side	三從四德
sanlian	三戀
sao	騷
Shanchahua	山茶花
shandong fangeming	煽動反革命
"Shanghai de hubuwu"	上海的狐步舞
Shanghai wenhua yuanliu cidian	上海文化源流辭典
Shanghai wenxue	上海文學
Shanghai yanjiu ziliao	上海研究資料
shangpin	商品
shangpinhua	商品化
shangpin jingji	商品經濟
Shanxi nanlu	陝西南路
shaoshu minzu	少數民族

Shen bao	申報
Shen Congwen (1902–88)	沈從文
Shen Congwen wenji	沈從文文集
Shen Deqian (1673–1769)	沉德潛
Shengshi weiyan	盛世危言
shengxue	聲學
Shen Rui (b. 1957)	沈睿
"Shensheng jitan"	神聖祭壇
shenxing	神性
shi	詩
shichang	失常
Shigong lizi	石工力子
Shiji	史記
shijiehua	世界化
Shijie mori ji	世界末日記
Shijing	詩經
Shikan	詩刊
Shipin	詩品
"Shiren"	詩人
Shiwu bao	時務報
Shiyin huaxue zhinan	石印化學指南
Shi Zhi (Guo Lusheng, b. 1948)	食指 (郭路生)
Shi Zhicun (b. 1905)	施蜇存
Shujing	書經
"Shushu de gushi"	叔叔的故事
Shu Ting (b. 1952)	舒婷
shuyuan saoni	叔援嫂溺
Sibu congkan	四部叢刊
Sihang chuxuhui	四行儲蓄會
Sima Qian (ca. 135–87? B.C.)	司馬遷
Sisheng yuan	四聲猿
Sizhou zhi	四洲志
song	頌
Souyu xiao ji	搜玉小集
Sun Jingyao	孫景堯
Sun Wenbo (b. 1957)	孫文波
Sun Wukong	孫悟空
Sun Zhu (1711–78)	孫洙
Su Qing (1917–82)	蘇青
Su Xuelin (b. 1899)	蘇雪林
Tailao shibao	太姥詩報
Taixi xinshi	泰西新史

Taixi xinzhi	泰西新知
Taixi yitan	泰西異譚
Taixu huanjing	太虛幻境
Taiyang	太陽
Tamen	他們
Tangren xuan Tangshi	唐人選唐詩
Tangshi sanbaishou	唐詩三百首
Tang Xiaodu (b. 1955)	唐曉渡
Tang xieben Tangren xuan Tang shi	唐寫本唐人選唐詩
Tanyi lu	談藝錄
Taohuayuan	桃花源
Tao Yuanming (365–427)	陶淵明
Tengye xiansheng	籐野先生
tengyun jiawu	騰雲駕霧
"Tiancai"	天才
tianya	天涯
Tian Yiheng	田藝蘅
"Tiaozhan"	挑戰
Tongwen guan	同文館
tuanjie renmin	團結人民
"Tulao qinghua"	土牢情話
"Tuwei"	突圍
Wang Anyi (b. 1954)	王安憶
Wang, David Der-wei	王德威
Wang Duanshu	王端淑
Wang Gan	王干
Wang Guowei (1877–1927)	王國維
Wang Jiawei (b. 1958)	王家衛
Wang Jiaxin (b. 1955)	王家新
Wang Jide	王驥德
Wang Qi (d. 158 A.D.)	王琦
Wang Tao (1828–97)	王韜
Wanguo gongbao	萬國公報
Wang Xiaoming	王曉明
Wang Xiaoni (b. 1955)	王小妮
Wang Yangming	王陽明
Wang Yao (1914–89)	王瑤
Wang Yi	王逸
Wang Yin (b. 1962)	王寅
Wanqing wenxue congchao: xiaoshuo xiqu yanjiujuan	晚清文學叢鈔：小說戲曲研究卷
weida	偉大

Wei Hu	韋縠
Wei Yuan	魏源
Wei Zhuang (ca. 836–910)	韋莊
wen	文
wenhua fansi	文化反思
wenhua mozi xungen fa	文化模子尋根法
wenhuashan	文化衫
Wenming jingjie	文明境界
Wen Tingyun (812?–66)	溫庭筠
Wenxin diaolong	文心雕龍
Wenxuan	文選
Wenxue	文學
"Wenxue geming lun"	文學革命論
Wenxue pinglun	文學評論
Wen Yiduo (1899–1946)	聞一多
Wenyi yanjiu	文藝研究
Wenyi zhengming	文藝爭鳴
Wenyou yutan	瓮牖余談
wokou	倭寇
Women	我們
Wu Fuhui	吳福輝
Wujing	五經
Wuli xinlun	物理新論
wusheng laomu	無生老母
wutishi	無題詩
Wutuobang youji	烏托邦游記
Wu Woyao (Wu Jianren, 1866–1910)	吳沃堯 (吳趼人)
"Wuyue de Zhina"	五月的支那
Xiafei lu	霞飛路
xiahai	下海
Xiandai	現代
Xiandai hanshi	現代漢詩
Xiandai shuqingshi heji	現代抒情詩合集
Xiandai wenxue zaoqi de nüzuojia	現代文學早期的女作家
"Xiandai Zhongguo wenxue zhongde ganshi youguo jingshen"	現代中國文學中的感時憂國精神
Xiandai Zhongguo xiaoshuo shi	現代中國小說史
Xiandai Zhongguo zuojia shuxin	現代中國作家書信
xianfu	賢婦
"Xianggang de qing yu ai"	香港的情與愛
xianqi liangmu	賢妻良母
xianshen weixueshu de xisheng zhi zhi	獻身為學術的犧牲之志

"Xiaocheng zhi lian" 小城之戀
Xiaofanghuzhai yudi congchao 小房戶齋寓地叢鈔
Xiao Gang (503–51) 蕭綱
xiaonü 孝女
xiaoshuo 小說
Xiaoshuo yuebao 小說月報
Xiaoshuo Zhongguo: Wanqing dao dangdai de zhongwen xiaoshuo 小說中國：晚清到當代的中文小說
Xiao Tong (501–31) 蕭統
Xie Fei (b. 1942) 謝飛
Xie Ye (1956–93) 謝燁
Xie Zhaozhe 謝肇淛
Xihai jiyou cao 西海記遊草
xinman yizu 心滿意足
"Xin Faluo xiansheng tan" 新法螺先生譚
xin ganjue pai 新感覺派
Xin ganjue pai xiaoshuo xuan 新感覺派小說選
xinger shangxue 形而上學
"Xinjiyuan" 新紀元
Xinmingci shiyi 新名詞釋譯
Xin nüxing 新女性
Xinqingnian 新青年
Xin shitouji 新石頭記
Xinwenxue shiliao 新文學史料
Xinwenxue xianshi zhuyi de liubian 新文學現實主義的流變
"Xin xiang" 心香
xin xiaoshuo 新小說
Xin xinwen 新新聞
xinxue 新學
Xiyouji 西游記
"Xu" 序
"Xuangao" 宣告
Xue Pan 薛潘
Xueren 學人
Xuese huanghun 血色黃昏
Xue Shaowei 薛紹微
Xueshu 學術
Xu Ling (507–83) 徐陵
Xu Lun 徐崙
Xunzi 荀子
Xu Wei (1521–93) 徐渭
Xu Xiacun (1907–86) 徐霞村
Xu Zhimo (1897–1931) 徐志摩

ya	雅
Ya'erpei lu	亞爾培路
Yalishi	亞離士
Yan Fu (1853–1921)	嚴復
Yan Fu de fanyi	嚴复的翻譯
yang	陽
Yang Dechang (b. 1947)	楊德昌
Yang Jialuo	楊家駱
Yang Lian (b. 1955)	楊煉
yangwu (yundong)	洋務 (運動)
Yang Xiong (53 B.C.–A.D. 18)	揚雄
Yang Xuguo	楊緒國
Yang Zhouhan	楊周翰
Yan Jiayan	嚴家炎
Yan Li (b. 1954)	嚴力
Yao He (ca. 779–ca. 846)	姚合
Ya Xian (b. 1932)	亞弦
Ya Xian shiji	亞弦詩集
Yecao	野草
Ye Lingfeng (1904–75)	葉靈鳳
Ye Wenling	葉文玲
"Yeying zai gechang"	夜鶯在歌唱
Ye Yunchao	葉運超
yichang	異常
Yi Chuan (b. 1968)	伊川
"Yidali zhi xia"	意大利之夏
Yijing	易經
yili	義理
"Yilu liulang"	一路流浪
yin	陰
Yin Fan	殷璠
yingxionghan	英雄漢
"Yingxiong zhuyi he Zhongguo wenyi fuxing"	英雄主義和中國文藝復興
yinsheng yangshuai	陰盛陽衰
yinshi	淫詩
Yi Sha	伊沙
"Yongheng de shiren: xunzhao tiantang de shengtu"	永恆的詩人: 尋找天堂的聖徒
Youji huibian	遊記彙編
youmu minzu	遊牧民族
Youxuan ji	又玄集
yu	欲

yuan	願
Yuanhe	元和
Yuan Hongdao (1568–1610)	袁宏道
Yuan Jie (719–72)	元結
Yuanmingyuan jiugui	圓明園酒鬼
Yuan Muzhi (1909–78)	袁牧之
Yuanze	原則
Yu Dafu (1896–1945)	郁達夫
Yue Daiyun	樂黛雲
Yuejie lüxing	月界旅行
"Yueqiu zhimindi xiaoshuo"	月球殖民地小說
Yueyue xiaoshuo	月月小說
Yu Jian (b. 1954)	于堅
"Yujie yuan"	玉階怨
Yulan shi	御覽詩
yunduan dazhan	雲端大戰
"Yu, shashasha"	雨,沙沙沙
Yutai xinyong	玉臺新詠
"Yu Xiang"	雨巷
"Yu Xiangdong Wang shu"	與湘東王書
Yu Xinjiao	俞心焦
"Zai Bali daxiyuan"	在巴黎大戲院
Zang Li (b. 1964)	臧力
zati xiaoshuo	雜體小說
Zeng Guangquan	曾廣銓
Zeng Guofan (1811–72)	曾國藩
Zhai Yongming (b. 1955)	翟永明
Zhang Ailing (Eileen Chang, 1920–96)	張愛玲
Zhang Jie (b. 1937)	張潔
Zhang Juncai	張俊才
Zhang Kangkang (b. 1950)	張抗抗
Zhang Manyu (b. 1964)	張曼玉
Zhang Xian (b. 1934)	張弦
Zhang Xianliang (b. 1936)	張賢亮
Zhang Xiaotian	張笑天
Zhang Zhongliang	張中良
Zhaohua xishi	朝花夕拾
Zhao Yiheng	趙毅衡
Zhejiangchao	浙江潮
Zheng Guanying	鄭觀應
Zheng Xuan	鄭玄
Zheng Zhenduo (1898–1958)	鄭振鐸

zhengzhi shuqing	政治抒情
"Zhi An Saikesidun"	致安塞克斯頓
zhidao renmin shenghuo	指導人民生活
zhiguai	志怪
zhi liangzhi	至良知
zhiqing	知青
Zhongguo bajiu minyun diyiwei xishengzhe	中國八九民運第一位犧牲者
Zhongguo bijiao wenxue	中國比較文學
Zhongguo dianying shihua	中國電影史話
Zhongguo jindai wenxue fazhan shi	中國近代文學發展史
Zhongguo qingnian yanjiu	中國青年研究
Zhongguo shixue hui	中國史學會
Zhongguo wenxue fazhanshi	中國文學發展史
Zhongguo xiandai wenxue yanjiu congkan	中國現代文學研究叢刊
Zhongguo xiandai xiaoshuo liupai shi	中國現代小說流派史
Zhongguo xuepai	中國學派
Zhong Hong (ca. 468–ca. 518)	鐘嶸
Zhong Shuhe	鍾叔河
Zhongwai wenxue	中外文學
Zhongxi bijiao wenxue jiaocheng	中西比較文學教程
Zhongxing xianqi ji	中興閒氣集
Zhongyong	中庸
Zhou Lunyou (b. 1952)	周倫佑
zhuangyuan	狀元
Zhuangzi (ca. 369–286 B.C.)	莊子
Zhu Dake	朱大可
zhunyin zheng	准印證
Zhu Weizheng	朱維政
Zhu Wengong wenji	朱文公文集
Zhu Xi (1130–1200)	朱熹
Zhu Xiang (1904–33)	朱湘
"Zixu"	自序
Ziye	子夜
"Zong xu"	總序
Zouchu zhongshiji	走出中世紀
Zouxiang shijie (congshu)	走向世界(叢書)
Zuozhuan	左傳

INDEX

With the exceptions of films and TV series, individual texts appear under their authors' names. Titles are listed in English translation, except in cases where *pinyin* terms have become standard (e.g., *Shijing* and *Wenxuan*). Only those critics mentioned explicitly in the book are listed here.

In this index an "f" after a number indicates a separate reference on the next page, and an "ff" indicates separate references on the next two pages. A continuous discussion over two or more pages is indicated by a span of page numbers, e.g., "21–22." *Passim* is used for a cluster of references in close but not consecutive sequence.

Adultery, 94, 96f
Aeschylus, 218; *Medea*, 218
Aesthetics, 9, 13, 18, 42, 49, 140–44, 197, 211
AIDS, 126f
Alienation, 15, 219, 223
Amazon, 75
American Association of Chinese Comparative Literature (AACCL), 6, 237n22
American Comparative Literature Association (ACLA), 5, 21, 24
Analects, see Lunyu
Anderson, Marston, 175
Androgyny, 82, 252n35. *See also* Gender
Anthology, 51, 58, 63f, 69
Anthropology, 147, 266n19
Asian studies, 35
Auerbach, Erich, 220f
A Xia, 191; "Eternity," 191; "Prayer," 191; "Prophet," 191; "Religion," 191

Bacon, Lloyd, 178
Bai Hua, 202f, 209, 212; "In Memoriam: Zhu Xiang," 202f; "Wheat, in Memoriam: Haizi," 212

Baker-Smith, Dominic, 26
Ban Gu, 60
Ban Zhao, 77; *Admonitions for Women*, 77
Barthes, Roland, 23f, 34f, 49, 143f, 223
Bassnett, Susan, 21f, 29
Bei Dao, 188, 197; "Declaration," 197
Bei Ling, 213; *Seventy-five Contemporary Chinese Poems*, 213
Bernheimer, Charles, 5, 24
Bertolucci, Bernardo, 127
Bhabha, Homi, 24, 114, 120, 128, 261n12
Bing Xin, 92; "Empty Nest," 92
Birrel, Anne, 65
Body, 90–129 *passim*, 173–87 *passim*
Borges, Jorge Luis, 204
Boundary, 4, 7, 13, 82, 88f, 108, 110, 123, 136, 225; linguistic, 23, 146; national, 100
Bristol, Michael D., 74
Brodsky, Joseph, 204ff
Butler, Judith, 82
Byron, George Gordon, 210

Cai Chusheng, 183
Cai Hengping, 199, 204; "The Chinese

301

Language—Dedicated to Cai, a Craftsman of Chinese," 199
Calinescu, Matei, 186
Canon, 50–70 *passim*, 85, 228f, 244n2
Canonization, 12, 69, 137
Cao Shunqing, 4, 237n18
Carre, Jean-Mairie, 25
Celan, Paul, 204
Center, 6, 12, 226f, 231; decentering, 15f, 219. *See also* Margin
Certeau, Michel de, 179, 181
Chang Han-liang, 7
Chaplin, Charles, 178
Chaves, Jonathan, 11, 39–44 *passim*, 49
Chen Dongdong, 199
Chen, Joan (Chen Chong), 13, 110–29 *passim*, 260n1
Chen Pengxiang (Chen Huihua), 3, 28
Chen Rong, 92; "Middle-Aged People," 92
Chen Zhongyi, 192
Cheng Maochao, 191
Cheyfitz, Eric, 223
Chin-chin Screen (Qing-qing dianying), 185
Chinese Tide (Zhejiangchao), 167
Chuci, 12, 51, 59–65 *passim*
Classic of Odes, see Shijing
Clifford, James, 219f, 232
Collected Travelogue, 158
Colonialism, 120, 124
Communism, 13, 26, 90ff, 193
Comparative literature, 1–17 *passim*, 21–49 *passim*, 218–32 *passim*, 237n17; the American school of, 2, 4, 22, 28f; the French school of, 2, 4, 28; the Chinese school of, 3ff, 28f. *See also* Poetics
Confucianism, 14, 62, 73–89 *passim*, 156, 161f
Confucius, 52–58 *passim*, 246n23
Consumerism, 15, 196
Consumption, 13, 110–29 *passim*, 194f
Les Contemporains, (Xiandai), 176
Cooper, Merian, 181
Cosmology, 73, 82
Cosmopolitanism, 30, 225
Criticism, 32, 38, 45, 47. *See also* Discourse; Ideology; Theory

Cubism, 152
Cult, 15, 188–217 *passim*
Cultural Revolution, the, 91, 100–101, 103, 193, 208f, 215
Cultural studies, 1–17 *passim*
Cultural trafficking, 14, 138f, 148

Dai Fang, 96; "Challenge," 96
Dai Wangshu, 177, 184; "The Alley in the Rain," 184
Dante Alighieri, 204f
Daoism (Taoism), 14, 51, 62, 84, 162
Day, Michael, 203
Death, 123, 190–217 *passim*
Deconstruction, 39–44 *passim*
Deeney, John (Li Dasan), 3f, 28, 236n8, 237n17
de Lauretis, Teresa, 81, 181
De Man, Paul, 40
Derrida, Jacques, 24, 39, 44
Desire, 76, 119f, 124f, 179, 181; sexual desire (*yu*), 13, 93–109 *passim*
Dienst, Richard, 121
Discourse, 37f, 42, 87, 137, 140, 153, 190. *See also* Ideology
Displacement, 15f, 127, 218–23 *passim*
Domesticity, 111, 124
Donne, John, 231
Dream of the Red Chamber, see Hongloumeng
Du Fu, 42, 70
Du Mu, 49; "Golden Valley Garden," 49
Duras, Margerite, 94; *The Lover*, 94

Eagleton, Terry, 49
Eastern Miscellany (Dongfang zazhi), 170
Eliot, T. S., 232; *The Four Quartets*, 232
Enlightenment, 146, 161, 170
Eoyang, Eugene Chen, 6f, 10, 67, 238n26
Ethnography, 232
Eurocentrism, 6, 22, 29
Exile, 15f, 164, 218–32 *passim*. *See also* Displacement
Experience, 3, 8f, 12, 14, 134–41 *passim*, 147–51 *passim*
Exoticism, 116, 158

Index

Fantasy, 13f, 26, 92, 106, 123, 129, 161, 171
Fascism, 44
Feifei, 194
Femininity, 76f, 81f, 88, 90f, 107–11 *passim*, 128. *See also* Gender; Masculinity
Femininization, 117, 257n31
Feminism, 13, 22, 82, 87, 90f, 94, 98, 106f
Femme fatale, 181
Flâneur, 174, 179
Fluidity, 13, 82, 89, 107, 110, 120–29 *passim*
Foot-light Parade, 178
Foreign Affairs Movement (*yangwu yundong*), 153, 159, 171
Formalism, 22
Frye, Northrop, 39
Futurism, 176

Gálik, Marián, 7
Gaze, 101, 113, 115, 128
Ge Mai (Chu Fujun), 200
Gender, 13, 73–109 *passim*, 110–29 *passim*, 215. *See also* Femininity; Masculinity; Sexuality
Genealogy, poetic, 62; of poets, 191, 201, 203, 208
Genre, 30, 57f, 64, 112, 155, 158, 269n9
Graff, Gerald, 8
Gu Cheng, 200f
Gu Tianhong (Ku Tim-hung), 3
Guan Yunshi, 231
Guide to Chemistry in Lithography, 168
Guillién, Claudio, 7, 21, 25, 28–33 *passim*
Guo Songtao, 10, 14, 140–50 *passim*

Hai Lei, 198
Hai Long, 201, 205; "Beauty," 201; "Genius," 205
Haizi (Zha Haisheng), 200, 203, 210
Han Dong, 217
Han Gaoqi, 200
Hart, Jonathan, 23f
Hastrup, Kirsten, 79
Hawkes, David, 61f
Hei Dachun, 198
Hei Ying (Zhang Bingwen), 10, 15, 176–79, 185ff; "When Spring Arrives," 176–79, 185ff; "Spring," 185

Heidegger, Martin, 224
Heroism, 15, 197–201 *passim*
Hölderlin, Friedrich, 204, 212
Hollinger, David, 225
Hong Xisheng (Lu Jiedong), 163, 170; *Journey to the Bottom of the Sea*, 163, 166
Hongloumeng (Dream of the red chamber), 154–57 *passim*, 246n27
Hsia, C. T., 175, 271n32
Huang Canran, 204
Hugh of St. Victor, 220f
Hybridity, 133, 153, 155

Identification, 114, 129
Identity, 75–82 *passim*, 90, 92, 110, 120, 215
Ideology, 12f, 26, 40f, 47f, 78f, 87f, 162, 206. *See also* Discourse
Imperialism, 135, 153
Interdisciplinarity, 30, 35
Interpretation, 43, 63
Intertextuality, 183ff

Jacobson, Roman, 24, 32f
Jia Pingwa, 108; *Ruins of the Capital*, 108, 259n67
Journey to Utopia, 160
Joyrich, Lynn, 117f

Kang Youwei, 140, 147
Kao Yu-kung, 33
Keats, John, 204f
King Kong, 181
Kipling, Rudyard, 27
Knechtges, David, 64
Knife's Edge (Fengren), 192
Knowledge, 136, 153, 166, 218, 224, 229
Ko, Dorothy, 73, 80
Kong Jiesheng, 207
Kroll, Paul, 39f
Krupat, Arnold, 222, 224f
Kumar, Krishan, 26
Kundera, Milan, 211; *Life Is Elsewhere*, 211
Kwan, Stanley (Guan Jinpeng), 184

Lan Cun, 197, 209, 212; "Nightingale Sings," 197; "The Successful and the Unsuccessful," 209

Language, 33, 39, 133f, 141
Lao She, 173, 176; *Camel Xiangzi*, 173
The Last Emperor, 127
Lawrence, D. H., 94; *Lady Chatterley's Lover*, 94; *Women in Love*, 94
Lee, Leo Ou-fan, 185, 240n41
Lefevre, André, 45f
Lermontov, Mikhail Yurievida, 210
Lewis, C. S., 40f
Li Bai (Li Bo), 57, 67, 203, 246n24; "Ancient Airs: No. 1," 67; "The Plaint of the Jade Stairs," 57, 67
Li Qingzhao, 227
Li Shangyin, 70
Li Zhi, 86
Liang Qichao, 153, 155
Little Studio Collected Travelogue, 158
Liu Dajie, 74
Liu, Lydia, 16
Liu Na'ou, 175, 181–86 *passim*; "Two Men Who Were Impervious to Time," 181–86 *passim*
Liu Xie, 60, 64
Lou Shiyi, 176
Lü Kun, 85; *Precept of Women's Quarter*, 85
Lu Xun, 14, 140, 148–51, 155, 166–71 *passim*, 176; *The World Underneath the Ground*, 14, 155; "Mr. Fujino," 140, 148f; "Preface to *Outcry*," 140, 148; *Morning Blossoms Gleaned at Dusk*, 149; "Defending Words," 155; *Traveling to the Moon*, 155; *Wild Grass*, 171;
Lu Yimin, 215f
Lunyu (Analects), 54f, 254n73
Luo Yihe, 202
Lynch, David, 13, 129, 260n9

Ma Zhiyuan, 226
McMahon, Keith, 75
Mandelstam, Osip, 204
Mang Ke, 188, 209
Mao Dun, 170–76 *passim*, 186; *Midnight*, 173–76 *passim*, 186
Mao Zedong, 103, 211ff
Map, 230ff
Margin, 12, 16, 227f. *See also* Center

Marriage, 78, 80, 93, 97, 128
Marxism, 26
Masculinity, 77, 81f, 88, 121, 257n31. *See also* Femininity; Gender
May Fourth literature, 133, 139f, 148, 156, 170f
Meaning, 25, 39, 43f. *See also* Interpretation
Mei Tsu-lin, 33
Mei Yaochen, 42
Mencius, 55, 75
Menglong(shi), see Poetry
Milton, John, 204
Misogyny, 116
Modernist Poetry Group of Sichuan (Bashu xiandai shiqun), 191
Modernism, 173–87 *passim*, 206, 208, 213
Modernity, 13ff, 133–40 *passim*, 151, 159, 172–87 *passim*
Morand, Paul, 176
More, Thomas, 26; *Utopia*, 26
Mu Shiying, 176, 184ff; "Black Peony," 184; "The Cemetery," 184; "Shanghai Foxtrot," 185f
Multiculturalism, 5, 49, 220

Narrative, 82, 86, 138, 153, 155, 174ff
Nation, 13, 25, 30, 32, 90, 153, 220, 222f
Nationalism, 23, 28, 30, 102, 111
Neo-Confucianism, 51, 53f, 83, 86, 90f, 93
New Criticism, 48
New History of the West, 167f
New Perceptionism, 176, 273n12, 273n16
New Songs from a Jade Terrace, 65f
New Women, 183
The New Yorker, 230
Novel, 152–72 *passim*

Orientalism, 13, 22, 39, 110–29 *passim*, 219, 232, 260n4
Orthodoxy, 60, 69f, 74, 86, 94, 105, 147
Ouyang Jianghe, 213; "Reflections on Modern Poetry," 213
Ouyang Xiu, 229

Overseas Student News (Liuxuesheng xinwen), 198
Owen, Stephen, 11, 39, 42f, 49, 56

Pacific Rim, the, 110, 112, 118, 122, 126
Palumbo-Liu, David, 10, 26f
Pan Youqiang, 201
Parallelism, 11, 32ff
Passing, 13, 119ff, 149, 262n24
Pasternak, Boris, 204f
Patriarchy, 12, 73–88 *passim*. *See also* Confucianism
Pei-yang Pictoral News (Beiyang huabao), 180
Perception, 179, 183
Philology, 9, 25, 36
Philosophy, 73, 82, 89, 227
Pilgrimage to the West (Xiyouji), 97
Plaks, Andrew, 7, 33
Plath, Sylvia, 204, 215
Poetics, 9, 25. *See also* Comparative literature
Poetry, 10, 15, 188–232 *passim*, 280n65; *menglong* poetry, 10, 15, 280n65
Poetry Monthly (Shikan), 189
Postcolonialism/postcoloniality, 22f
Postmodernism/postmodernity, 22, 108, 221, 224
Power, 13, 89, 97, 134–51 *passim*
Psychoanalysis, 152, 251n19, 253n46

Qian Qianyi, 232; "Willow Songs," 232
Qian Zhongshu, 28, 242n22
Qu Yuan, 60ff, 65, 202f, 209

Race, 118, 120
Radical alterity, 25f, 37
Realism, 106, 159, 175
Record of the Sea, 158
Renan, Ernest, 39
Ricci, Matteo, 231, 242n22, 271n35
Rilke, Rainer Maria, 193, 205; *Duino Elegies*, 205
Rimbaud, Arthur, 204
Robertson, Maureen, 81, 83
Romanticism, 108

Ruan Lingyu, 184
Ruth, Book of, 218
Ru Zhijuan, 94, 256n14

Said, Edward, 24, 111–17 *passim*, 219ff, 226, 290n5
St. Bonaventure, 226
Sartre, Jean-Paul, 194
Schafer, Edward, 42, 49
Scherpe, Klaus, 174, 272n9
Schneider, Laurence, 209
Schoedsack, Ernest, 181
Science, 139, 152–72 *passim*
Searle, John, 223
Second-Growth Forest (Cishenglin), 191
Seltzer, Mark, 114, 260n3
Sexuality, 13, 81, 84, 91–104 *passim*, 111, 124, 126, 255n3. *See also* Gender
Shelley, Percy Bysshe, 204f
Shen Congwen, 175; *Border Town*, 175
Shen Deqian, 70
Shen Rui, 216f; "To Anne Sexton," 216f
Shen bao, 158
Shi Zhi (Guo Lusheng), 199, 209
Shi Zhicun, 175f, 186; "At the Paris Theater," 176, 186; "Sorcery," 176
Shijing (Classic of odes), 12, 32, 51–60 *passim*
Short Story Monthly (Xiaoshuo yuebao), 176
Shu Ting, 188, 215
Sima Qian, 58, 245n11
Sinology, 9, 11, 25, 36, 38, 43, 145f
Skinner, Quentin, 26
Smith, Barbara Herrnstein, 51, 62
Socialism, 26, 90f, 108
Space, 25, 27, 36, 174, 187
Spengler, Oswald, 226
Spitzer, Leo, 218
Spivak, Gayatri, 24, 44
Spring and Summer Annals (Chunqiu), 54
Steinberg, Saul, 230
Structuralism, 24
Studies of Chinese Youth (Zhongguo qingnian yanjiu), 197
Su Xuelin, 176, 273n13

Subjectivity, 92–100 passim, 105, 134, 230, 232
Subversion, 74, 78ff, 87ff, 105
Suicide, 15, 101, 177, 184, 199–204 passim
Sun Wenbo, 205; "The Poet," 205
Sun Zhu, 69f
Supernationality, 25, 30ff
Symbolism, 191, 206

Talent (cai), 60, 80, 86, 251n21
Tang Xiaodu, 198
Tao Yuanming, 160, 202; "Peach Blossom Spring," 160
Taoism, see Daoism
Technology, 152f, 169
Television, 110–29 passim
Tendency (Qingxiang), 191ff
The Textbooks of the Republic, 170
Theory, 9, 16, 21, 24, 30f, 36, 43ff
They (Tamen), 217
Three Hundred Poems of the Tang (Tangshi sanbai shou), 51, 69f
Tian Yiheng, 86
Time, 174, 181, 186
Times Literary Supplement, 41f
Today (Jintian), 188f, 197
Todorov, Tzvetan, 220
Totalitarianism, 44, 49, 204
Tower of Babel (Babieta), 192
Transition (Guodu), 192
Translation, 14f, 133–51 passim, 161, 218–32 passim
Travel, 14, 133–51 passim
Travel of the Western Sea, 1847–49, 158
Tropic of Cancer (Beihuiguixian), 192f
Tsvetayeva, Marina, 188, 204; "The Poet," 188
Tuan Yi-fu, 226
Twin Peaks, 13, 110–29 passim

Utopia, 11, 14, 25f, 36ff, 47, 93, 152–72 passim, 217

Value, 22, 58f, 63, 170
van Crevel, Maghiel, 210
Van Zoeren, Steven, 54

Verne, Jules, 14, 152, 155, 163, 166; *From Earth to the Moon*, 155; *A Journey to the Center of the Earth*, 155, 163, 166
Virginity, 79f, 84, 100
Virtue (de), 60, 80, 86, 251n21
Voyeurism, 114, 181

Wang Anyi, 13, 93–109 passim, 256n14, 259n67; "A Century On a Small Hillock," 94f, 102–5 passim; "Love in a Small Town," 94f, 100ff; "Love in a Wild Mountain," 94–100 passim; "Love in Splendor Valley," 94f, 105–8 passim; "Rain, shashasha," 94; "Man and Woman, Woman and City," 99, 107; "Song of Everlasting Sorrow," 109
Wang, C. H., 7
Wang, David Der-wei, 175
Wang Gan, 208
Wang Guowei, 14, 140, 145–50 passim, 221
Wang Jide, 87
Wang Qiang, 198; "Wandering All the Way," 198
Wang Xiaoni, 215
Wang Yangming, 83, 85f
Wang Yi, 59f
Wang Zheng, 95
Wen Tingyun, 218
Wen Yiduo, 199; "Red Candle," 199
Wenxuan (Selections of refined literature), 51, 64–68 passim
Whitman, Walt, 32, 232
Williams, Raymond, 183
Woman, 12f, 73–129 passim, 180f, 215, 217
Women in Love (film), 256n14
Wong Tak-wai, 7
Woolf, Virginia, 88
Wu Woyao (Wu Jianren), 14, 154–62 passim, 171; *The New Story of the Stone*, 14, 154–62 passim, 171

Xiao Gang, 65f
Xiao Tong, 64f; "Preface to *Wenxuan*," 64f
Xie Ye, 200
Xie Zhaozhe, 86

Xu Ling, 65f
Xu Wei, 10, 12, 73–89 passim, 252n45; *Ci Mulan*, 73–89 passim; *Nü zhuangyuan*, 73–89 passim; *Sisheng yuan*, 82
Xu Zhimo, 177, 184
Xunzi, 53f

Ya Xian, 214; "Dissection," 214
Yan Fu, 140, 145–8 passim
Yan Jiayan, 186
Yang Xiong, 60
Yang Yuanhong, 193
Yangwu, *see* Foreign Affairs Movement
Ye Wenling, 92; "Xinxiang," 92
Ye Yunchao, 210
Yeats, John Butler, 226
Yeh, Michelle, 10
Yi Chuan, 195; "Italian Summer," 195; "Moments from an Individual Life," 195
Yi Sha, 217
Yin-Yang, 33, 73, 82, 89
The Young Companion (Liangyou), 15, 176, 180, 273n18
Yu Dafu, 170
Yu Jian, 213, 217
Yu, Pauline, 6f, 67ff
Yu Xinjiao, 192, 209

Yu Ying-shih, 207
Yuan Heh-hsiang, 31f, 46f
Yuan Hongdao, 85
Yue Bing, 210

Zha Jianying, 91
Zhai Yongming, 215; "Woman," 215
Zhang Jie, 92, 96; "The Ark," 92; "Love Cannot Be Forgotten," 92f
Zhang Kangkang, 92
Zhang Longxi, 10
Zhang Xian, 100; "The Corner Forgotten By Love," 100
Zhang Xianliang, 93; "Half of Man is Woman," 93; "Romance in Prison," 93; "Soul and Flesh," 93
Zhang Xiaotian, 96; "Inside Information Made Public," 96
Zhirmunsky, V. M., 32f
Zhong Hong, 50; "Preface to *Shijing*," 50
Zhou Lunyou, 194, 207; "The Gesture of Refusal," 207
Zhu Dake, 210
Zhu Xi, 54, 56, 61, 73
Zhu Xiang, 202f
Zhuangzi, 232

Library of Congress Cataloging-in-Publication Data
China in a polycentric world : essays in Chinese comparative
   literature / edited by Yingjin Zhang.
      p.   cm.
Papers delivered at the International Conference on Literature,
History, Culture: Reenvisioning Chinese and Comparative
Literature, held at Princeton University on June 24–26, 1994.
   Includes index.
   ISBN 0-8047-3186-1 (cloth). — ISBN 0-8047-3509-3 (pbk.).
      1. Literature, Comparative—Chinese and European.   2. Literature, Comparative—European and Chinese.   3. East and West.   I. Zhang, Yingjin.   II. International Conference on Literature, History, Culture: Reenvisioning Chinese and Comparative Literature d(1994 : Princeton University)   III. Title: Essays in Chinese comparative literature
PL2274.C453   1999
895.1'09—dc21   98-20766

This book is printed on acid-free paper.
Original printing 1998
Last figure below indicates year of this printing:
07 06 05 04 03 02 01 00 99 98

The authorized representative in the EU for product safety and compliance is:
Mare Nostrum Group
B.V Doelen 72
4831 GR Breda
The Netherlands

www.ingramcontent.com/pod-product-compliance
Lightning Source LLC
Chambersburg PA
CBHW021345300426
44114CB00012B/1081